ENVIRONMENTAL NOISE POLLUTION

Causes, Evils, Legislation and Controls

DR. VIJENDRA MAHANDIYAN

B.Sc., D.I.T., D.M.E., LL.M., Ph.D. (Law)

Advocate, Supreme Court of India

DEEP & DEEP PUBLICATIONS PVT. LTD.
F-159, Rajouri Garden, New Delhi-110027

ENVIRONMENTAL NOISE POLLUTION
Causes, Evils, Legislation and Controls

ISBN 81-7629-830-1

@ 2006 VIJENDRA MAHANDIYAN

Typeset by THE LASER PRINTERS, 8/15, 3rd Floor, Subhash Nagar, New Delhi-I 10064.

Printed in India at MAYUR ENTERPRISES, WZ Plot No. 3, Gujjar Market, Tihar Village, New Delhi - 110 018.

Published by DEEP & DEEP PUBLICATIONS PVT. LTD., F-159, Rajouri Garden, New Delhi-110027. Phones: 25435369, 25440916. E-mail: deep98@del3.vsnl.net.in Sales Showroom: 2/13, Ansari Road, Daryaganj, New Delhi-I 10002 Phone/Fax:23245122

ओ३म् भूर्भव: स्व: तत्सवितुर्वरेण्यं भर्गो
देवस्य धीमहि, धियो, योन: प्रचोदयात:

*The Book is Devoted
to my Reverred Parents
who abode in Heaven*

Contents

Contents

Preface

"Nature has for every man's need, but for no one's greed."

—*M.K Gandhi*

Nature is the common heritage of human mankind, irrespective of land water or space, and it is the nature, which constitutes the environment or the ecology for the man. Man's survival on this earth depends on his harmony with the nature but the pollution being caused for overnight developments or in the name of technological advancements, weakens the same. Society is shocked when a single kidnapping, rape or murder takes place, but the environmental pollution merely becomes news, whereas it kills in crores and destructs in billions. Ignorance of the day is that wealth and power are no substitute for good health and happiness of a man.

Although, a sweat music and soneral voice brings joy, cordiality, relaxations, mental peace, and makes life worth living but undesired noise brings disturbances to peace mental disorders and hence makes the life miserable. The health hazards of noise pollution are definite leading to deafness, poor concentration irritation, loss of sleep, nervousness, aggressive social behaviour, anxiety, depression, gastrointestinal problems, allergy, distraction, heart diseases, high blood pressure and lack of efficiency. The researches of this year 2005, reveal that the environmental pollutants from domestic and industrial waste and pesticides could be changing the ratio of sex chromosomes in sperm. It does not spare the foetus, animals, birds, plants wildlife and properties too. Consequently, it further leads elimination of the workforce and as consequence; the nation suffers a great economic loss. This book is an attempt to bring out all the possible causes of the noise alongwith its multifarious evils.

Of trio, water, air and noise, very heartening and surprising is that neither the term 'environmental pollution' nor 'environmental pollutant' includes "noise" as a pollutant, under any original Indian code. It is also of strange that in a long series of Indian Industrial Laws, no provision is there to check noise pollution, whereas in fact it is the industrial world, which has polluted the environment most, and it is the industrialists who are to pay for its up-gradation too. Law in action sensitizes the citizen to obey but in our country no specific law was enacted to curb noise pollution, a dire enemy of human brain. Indian law recognized it only in 1987 through an amendment in Air (Prevention and Control of Pollution) Act, 1987. Indian legal history bears separate code on Air and Water pollution but still no comprehensive code is there to control noise an 'omnipotent pollutant' whereas, the cry against is being heard from all the nooks and corners of the glob.

The Apex Court of India, which was often accused of being obstructive to social reforms and insensitive to environmental issues, has shown its dynamism in refreshing contrast to such allegations in the past. Casting its archaic rules of procedure, the Supreme Court of India became the supreme court for Indians and held that the citizen's right to life includes right to leisure, right to sleep, right to remain silent, right not to hear, right to read, right to speak with others, right to worship, right to meditation, right to live alone in peace and silence and right to think any matter. But the existence of noise certainly squeezes and steals away these rights of citizens and hence, the judiciary some time came out heavily on the executives and has bridged the gaps or lacunas by directing the authorities to enforce the environmental laws. Now, no one has a right to commit trespass on the mind or ear of another and commit an auricular or visual aggression. Recently in July 2005, our Apex Court has protected the public health by laying down some guidelines with a view to mitigate noise pollution.

Evil effects of noise on human brain, unawareness and ignorance among citizens to it, non-availability of comprehensive code and noise against the noise are the main causes that inspired the author to write this book, which contains, causes, evil effects/ dangers and legal controls of the noise pollution in detail, touching upon the issues of sustainable development, quality of environment, Role of PIL/NGOs and Duties of Citizens. It is an appeal to all that this planet earth which is polluted beyond limits is our home our only home in this life, we have no other home, we will have to suffocate till death, if increasing decibels of noise is left unchecked. It is a true compilation of all the scattered provisions in Indian Statutes having impact upon noise pollution provided with analytical commentary and possible amendments thereto.

In nature, neither there are neither rewards nor punishments, but only the consequences; Violence begets violence; Nature obeys this principle.

Additionally the book explains in lucid language as under:

- The mechanism, how a sound enters the brain through ears and becomes noise;
- The existing noise levels in India and abroad with recommended safe limits;
- The Environmental Management in India;
- Constitutions on Environment;
- Scattered Law in Indian Statutes on Noise;
- Noise, when Amounts to an Actionable Nuisance;
- Theory of Substantial Damage;
- Evolution of Environmental Law in India;
- Judicial Activism and Environmental Education;
- Fundamental Rights and the Environment;
- Right to Clean Environment;
- Noise Pollution *versus* Right to Religion;
- The Role of Public Interest Litigations;
- Asian Country's Constitution on Environment;
- Clean Environment: A neglected Human Right and Citizen's Ignored Duty.

For any error or omission, I respect the indulgence of readers and request that the same may kindly be brought to my notice so that it is taken care of in next edition. For each demerit of my exposition, I take the blame squarely on my own shoulders. I hope that this book will be of immense utility to all concerns viz. environmentalists, the green Bench, the Bar, the green authorities and public at large who are interested in ecology.

I have no words to express my heartfelt gratitude to my revered teacher, gifted Guru and Philosopher Dr. Sampat Raj Jain, Professor, Faculty of Law, University of Jodhpur for allowing me to be at privilege of working under his kind supervision and guidance.

I shall be failing in my duty, if I do not express high gratitude to Prof. S.C. Shrivastava and my best colleague Mr. Dalip Singh, a renowned Advocate in Delhi, who has not only kept me energetic but also boosted my morale at each walk of this journey.

Thanks are due to the Deep and Deep Publications Pvt. Ltd., New Delhi for giving good print, design and finish to this book.

DR. VIJENDRA MAHANDIYAN

Prelude

For the first time in his entire cultural history, man is facing one of the most horrible ecological-crisis, and that is, the problem of environmental pollution, which sometime in the past, was pure, virgin, undisturbed, uncontaminated, and basically quite hospitable. Thickly polluted and noisy environment reflects failure of mankind to design social and political institutions, which are capable of properly assessing and controlling technological innovations. Probably, the scientists, economists and the planners have forgotten the law of Newton that, "to every action, there is an equal and opposite reaction." What we give to the environment in the name of development and technological advancements, it re-bounces in multiple, in the form of natural calamities and poisonous environment, which is nothing but a slow agent of death. For instance, in 1963, the hand pumps of some area in Rajasthan started pumping-out coloured water, which was the result of filthy, discharges from 1500 small scale printing industries.[1] According to the projections made by Stockholm Environmental Institute, by the year 2025, the quantum of emission in Asia will multiply nearly three times of the emission in 1990. By the year 2050, the situation would become too worse to bear with, and would become difficult for human survival on the earth. The projections are based on sulphur emission factor, linked with fossil fuel and industrial output estimates. If the current rates of economic development and the consumption of two-third energy by one-third population continue, then the world will reach to its own death invited by itself.

Of trio, water, air and noise, very heartening and surprising is, that neither the term 'environmental pollution' nor 'environmental pollutant' includes "noise" as a pollutant, under any Indian Act, originally. Noise pollution is a dire enemy of human brain. It is not a new phenomenon, but is as old as the civilization itself is, and was conceived on the very day, when Adam dawned on this planet earth. But it was only in 1987, when the noise was recognized as a pollutant in India, by way of bringing an amendment in Air (Prevention and Control of Pollution) Act, 1987. Today, the cry is being heard from all the nooks and corners of the globe against noise, hence, it has become an 'omnipotent pollutant' in emerging industrialized societies and has challenged the fundamentals of human survival. It is also surprising, that noise pollution, which is in no way lesser hazard to health, there is no comprehensive law on noise, like that of water[2] and air[3] and the subject remained almost untouched at all levels, national and international.

To control "Noise Pollution" is a cause, perhaps the great 'cause' before the whole humanity, for its survival. This 'cause' becomes the subject matter of this treatise. This serious challenge constitutes the main theme of my analysis. Responsible is the curiosity, aroused in within of author on account of his bitter experiences with this horrible pollutant, when he was working and residing near airport, where noise-intensity reaches at its crescendo. Further, cause is the fact that this kind of pollutant incapacitates human brain, animals and birds, plants and wild life, hence deteriorates the property, and hence I choose this subject, against my better judgment. Inspiration was drawn at the time of selection of this subject when I found in myself a great love for natural peace and meditative environment. Persistent thirst of a humble student of law ever haunted my in-link to explore the possibility, whether the law can be helpful in keeping environment free from noise pollution. It is thus, that I have chosen this subject for my search and research.

The first chapter of this book is Introduction filled with, definitions of noise, its properties, constituents, and other related nexuses. Sound how turns into noise. Measuring unit is decibels (dB), the quantum of noise, which an average human can bear with.

One may be astonished to know the fact, that only 0.1% of

the total voice or the sound relayed in the air enters into the ear's liquid medium, whereas 99.9% unheard sound is reflected away from its surface itself. It is horrible to imagine, as to what would have happened had the total sound emitted from various sources entered into the ear, the plight would have miserable for the mankind, unimaginable by a man of ordinary prudence. This technical fact in the making of the ear by nature is wonderful to note. In spite of this scientific fact, the world is harping with the problem of noise pollution.[4]

In Chapter 2, various sources and activities, causing noise are made forth under three broad heads, viz. industrial, non-industrial and natural. Traffic noise has been explored in its trio dimensions, i.e. road, air and railway.

Chapter 3 is an attempt to bring out the health hazards of noise pollution. It has been observed that, though, a soft rhythmic sound, in the form of music and dance stimulates the brain in positive directions, removes boredom and fatigue.[5] But the excess of the same proves detrimental to human health in audio, bio, physio and psycho.

An impediment to assess the disturbing or annoying impacts of noise pollution is, that different people are affected differently by it. For example, a sweat melody of morning may be irritating to those who still want to be in the bed. On the other hand, a loud noise of music may be joyful to those who are the part of a dancing party in a club. Characteristically, a physicist, a founder of the Acoustical Society of America and a former Chancellor of California University[6] has called the noise a 'slow agent of death'. Dr. Colin Herridge, a British Psychiatrist, found in a two years study that persons living alongside of London's Heathrow airport have a significantly higher rate of admission to mental hospitals, than persons living in socially similar but quieter areas,[7] infant mortality near the airport found to be was 50% greater, heart diseases 57% greater, and cancer 37% greater than the place far from the airports.[8] As per the Ministry of Environment and Forest, the estimated cost of treating the effects of environmental pollution on health in India, is 240 billion rupees per year. Long back in 1961, the 'Time' Magazine estimated that the cost against noise pollution, which American industry pays is, 2 million dollars[9] a day in the form of compensation, for loss of working hours and diminished

xxvi   *Environmental Noise Pollution*

efficiency. A UN report reveals that natural calamities caused by change in climate, costs, world-over 300 billion dollars per year.[10] It is pointed out that noise pollution is leading to serious nervous disorders, emotional tensions leading to high blood pressure, cardiovascular diseases, increase in cholesterol level resulting in heart attacks and strokes and even damage to the foetus. During pregnancy, noise pollution adversely affects the development of foetus. Constant exposure to noise, between 110-120 dB can produce narrowing of vision and vertigo, which causes disruption of equilibrium in the unborn baby.[11]

1. Right to Sustainable Development

The concept of 'sustainable development' in itself is a remedy to resort 'right to healthy environment'. Sustainable development, if adopted, is the solution of many problems in this world, and to improve the quality of environment is no bar to it. To take cognizance and study this concept, a separate Chapter on 'Sustainable Development and Quality of Environment' has been ambitiously planned in this treatise, so as to discuss it, at length and dilate its every possible nook, to inspire the otherwise dormant public to think about and adopt. The UN General Assembly[12] has declared the right to sustainable development an inalienable human right. The 1992 Rio Conference declared that human beings are at the centre of concerns for sustainable development. The Earth Summits, 1992 and 2002, on sustainable development, show the world's seriousness towards making all the developments sustainable. The European Court of Justice, in *Portugal* Vs. *F.C. Council*,[13] has emphasized the need to promote sustainable development.

2. Role of NGOs and Citizens' Duties to Environment

Even the impossible solutions like awareness among the citizens and societies world over, which even the powerful Governments, neither like nor attempt to do so, NGOs have made them possible by their persistent efforts to make environment livable, through judicial actions like PIL, and even otherwise. In this new wake, a chapter 'Role of NGOs and Duties of Citizens' is there in this book. International NGOs have also played critical roles in translating international agreements and norms into domestic realities, to promote required societal changes, to free the glob from environmental pollutions. But, unfortunately, they are exceptionally few in number, who are honest and sincere for the cause.

3. Inadequacy of Law: The Great Handicap

In Chapter 5, it is proposed to probe whether there are provisions to control noise pollution, in particular, under the existing law? If so, to determine as to what extent these insufficient laws are catering to? The chapter is a sincere attempt, to compile available legal provisions on noise pollution at national as well as international levels. The author has tried to analyze and to comment upon each provision, for its oughtability or suitability, in curbing noise pollution. However, a separate head is chosen under which all the suggestions have been compiled at the last of this work.

It is surprising that the 'noise' has been the most ignored pollutant in India so far. Despite the fact that noise pollution incapacitates the psycho-power of mankind, our legislators remained psychomachy by not enacting comprehensive code on noise. The law relating to noise is scattered in Constitution and different legal statutes viz. I.P.C., Cr.P.C., C.P.C., Factories Act, Law of Torts, Police Acts, Municipal laws or the state laws, etc. Being the scattered law, it remained dead letter of the statutes or rather say the 'paper tiger'. Only available central legislation on noise pollution, is the Noise Regulation Rules, 2000, recently issued by the Ministry of Environment and Forest with consultation to Central Pollution Control Board.

4. Constitutional Amendments of 1976

The original Constitution of India was silent in this regard. The decisions taken at Stockholm Conference, 1972, compelled the Indian Government to think it necessary to amend the Constitution, so as to bring constitutional mandate for the protection and improvement of environment. In 1976, India became one of the first countries in the world by introducing two-fold provisions in its constitution under Articles 48A and 51A(g). Firstly, it gives directive[14] to the state for the protection and improvement of environment; and secondly, it casts a duty[15] upon every citizen to help preservation of natural environment. An important subtlety in the directive's language is the provision, that the Article "shall not be enforceable by any court," but "it shall be the duty of the state to apply these principles in making laws". This allows the directive to be an instrument of guidance for the government.

5. 'Right to Healthy Environment' (i.e. Pollution-free-Environment): An Attribute of 'Right to Life'

In today's emerging environmental jurisprudence, the rights which encompass a group of collective rights, are described as 'third-generation' rights. The 'first-generation' rights are generally political rights such as those found in International Convention on Civil and Political Rights while 'second-generation' rights are social and economic rights as found in the International Covenant on Economic, Social and Cultural Rights. Our Supreme Court is one of the first Courts in the world to evolve and develop the concept of right to "healthy environment" as a fundamental right, as an attribute of 'right to life' under Article 21.[16] It is no one but judicial activism which held that right to healthy environment is an obligation on states under Arts. 21 and 47 both.[17] This principle is now enured in various countries. The Supreme Court of South Africa, in a recent case in *Wildlife Society of Southern Africa* Vs. *Minister of Environmental Affairs and Tourism of the Republic of South Africa*,[18] has acted upon the right to healthy environment so as to make it an essential human right. About 60 nations, since 1990, have recognized, in their Constitutions, a right to healthy environment as a corollary duty to defend the environment.

6. Noise Pollution Vs. Right to Religion U/A 25

In fact, the freedom of speech and expression under Art. 19(1)(a) and freedom of religion under Art. 25 of the Constitution are inseparable, as one cannot be enjoyed without the exercise of other. For example, one, who wishes to propagate his religious ideas, as guaranteed by Art. 25, can make it possible only by exercising his right to speech and expression under Art. 19.

India being a secular country, the architects of its Constitution, perhaps drafted the Art. 25, intending to make India really secular in its true sense by way of giving equal opportunity to each religion to practice and propagate its own religion. But, indiscriminate use of loudspeakers in this behalf, has made this country so noisy, that being victimized by the religious noise, Himachal Pradesh High Court itself had to comment and admit in *Yoginderlal* Vs. *Municipal Corporation, Shimla* as under:[19]

"Though the conditions imposed on the use of loudspeakers are laudable indeed, they are mostly being observed in their breach. We may also record that in our court room many times, we have to stand the noise of the loudspeaker used by religious institutions, it appears that some religious institutions are bent upon insisting, the fear of God in the society by using loudspeakers, in such a way that these can be heard over by the maximum people of the town. It seems that in their zeal, the religious institutions are following the principles of home delivery services."

In yet another case *Masud Alam* Vs. *Commissioner of Police,*[20] it was held that the use of loudspeakers, causing disturbance in the area, could not be justified for the religious purposes and the ban on its use was upheld.

It was Indian Acoustic Institute which prepared a detailed Report in 1985 and expressed the felt need for comprehensive Noise Pollution Law in India, to prevent and control such pollution in urban and industrial areas and as a result thereof, Ministry of Environment and Forest had to appoint an expert committee, to study the levels of noise in the country and to submit its report to pave way for legislation. Environment (Protection) Act was passed in 1986 and noise was added as an environmental pollutant in its definition section.[21]

Keeping in view the seriousness of health hazards of noise, the Government thought it fit to enact a special law in regulation to control Noise Pollution. Consequently, in exercise of the powers conferred by clause (i) of sub-section (2) of section 3, sub-section (i) and clause (b) of sub-section (2) of section 6 and section 25 of the EPA, 1986 read with rule 5 of the EPR, 1986, the central government notified[22] the Noise Pollution (Control and Regulation) Rules in February 2000. These rules restrict the use of loudspeakers/public address system, and also laid down the ambient air quality standard in respect of noise.[23] The rules have prescribed different levels of noise for different zones, i.e. commercial, residence, industrial, and silence zones. These rules have entrusted the DC of the district to be the regulatory authority for its strict implementation.

A very brief account of the available legislation on noise pollution at international level has also been gathered into this work, such as US Noise Control Act of 1972, a major breakthrough in the Federal attempt to eliminate the excess noise of every level, New York City Noise Control Code, 1972, Chicago Noise Control Regulations, 1971, Connecticut Highway Noise Control Act, 1971, The Japanese Noise Regulation,[24] The Noise Abatement Act, 1960 of the UK, The Kanowitz Law (1961).

7. Judicial Trends

There is 'cause' perhaps—'a great cause', 'a challenge'—perhaps 'a serious challenge'. The cause and challenge before judiciary is to provide the masses with an environment into which they can breathe, eat, sleep and live peacefully without facing the fangs of noise pollution. To meet this challenge of providing noise-free environment in this industrial and luxurious world is not as easy as to 'Grow Roses in December'. The judges are called upon to prove the legitimacy of the existence of environmental courts.

It is apparent that law, justice and public authority had compromised with the technological advancements, unplanned urbanization and rapid industrialization, that are the main causes of noise pollution. The attitude of Judiciary towards noise nuisance was lukewarm. Courts, usually, take it very lightly and even did not regard noise as a public nuisance, unless it affects the whole locality or individual in specific damages.[25] Judicial approach to deal with the problem of environmental pollution was influenced to a very great extent by the Common Law Doctrine of 'Strict Liability' as laid down in *Rylands* Vs. *Fletcher*. However, there appears to be a marked difference in the judicial trend adopted in this context from time to time. While under the rule of strict liability a person is held liable as soon as a thing escapes from the premises of the person and causes injury to others. Noise is such a pollutant, which definitely escapes, i.e. transmitted out of the campus, if the volume is strictly not controlled. The court has generally preferred to maintain the *status quo*, possibly influenced by the freedoms guaranteed under Article 19 of the Constitution.

Therefore, the tenth Planning Commission Steering Committee on Environment for the Tenth Plan has suggested, revamp of environmental laws to ensure effective implementation, training of judicial officers in environmental laws, and strengthening of the enforcement mechanism. But, in the post-emergency era of PIL, judicial activism, and the liberal view of concept of *'locus standi'* could sow new seeds, so as to protect and improve environment in India, worth for peaceful living. Justice Holmes observed that law must be interpreted in terms of felt necessities of the society. It is appreciable that our activist judges of dynamic judiciary interpreted the environmental laws into the felt necessities, i.e. in favour of nature and public good, except few ones such as *D. Anant Prabhu* Vs. *The District Collector, Ernakulam and Others*[26] is the glaring case, in which it was observed that: "The right, which guaranteed by Art. 19(1)(a) is not merely a right to express and propagate one's views, but also includes in it the right to circulate one's views to others", by all such means as are available to the citizens to make known those views. Under the circumstances, in our judgment, any legislation or order, which puts a ban on the use of a loudspeaker, which helps the citizens in circulating his views to, as large audience as he can, will be *prima-facie* and infringement of his fundamental right of freedom of speech and expression unless the infringement is justified by clause (2) Art. 19. This judgment, plainly gives green signals to the persons, who are fond of playing loudspeakers or music at their pitch irrespective of inconveniences in the vicinity due to noise pollution in behalf of their right of speech and expression. Though, the court himself has been the captive audience of noise pollution and in *M.S. App Rao* Vs. *The Government of Tamilnadu and Others*[27] observed:

"In fact, this court has often been the victim of noise pollution. If we can put it mildly, it would be practically impossible to hear the arguments of the counsels. For example, on the 30th ultimo, which supposed to be a 'Sarvodaya Day' or 'Martyrs' Day', when the whole nation is supposed to pay homage to its Father, the authorities concerned had permitted public agitation by Bank employees on the public road abutting the High Court

xxxii *Environmental Noise Pollution*

compound, who were using loud speakers and sound amplifiers without any restriction for over five hours continuously, during the court working hours. We were somewhat surprised, if not shocked, that the concerned authorities were not aware of a notification issued under sections 6 and 25 of EPA, 1986, by the Ministry of Environment and Forest, New Delhi in 1989,[28] prescribing ambient air quality standards in respect of noise with regard to different categories of areas, classified as industrial area, commercial area, residential area and the silence zone.

In another case *Jacob* Vs. *The Supdt. of Police*,[29] it was observed that no one has a right to trespass on the mind or ears of another and commit auricular or visual aggression. Hence, limits must be drawn for liberties, lest they turn into licence and the antithesis of liberty in its true sense. In US case *Frisby* Vs. *Schultz*,[30] the court emphasized on the importance of right of privacy and said that individuals are not required to welcome unwanted speech into their own homes and the government may protect the said freedom.

In a recent case, *Church of God* Vs. *KRK Majestic Welfare Association*, the apex court has clearly ruled, that to pray with loudspeakers is not a fundamental right under Article 25 of the Constitution.[31]

However, taking cue on request made by Supreme Court in December 2000, the Law Commission of India is reviewing the whole range of environmental legislation in the country for the purpose of consolidation and codification.[32]

In RE: Noise Pollution reported in 2005 (5) SCALE, the Supreme Court observed that undoubtedly, the freedom of speech and right to expression are fundamental rights but the rights are not absolute. Nobody can claim a fundamental right to create nose by amplifying the sound of his speech with the help of loudspeakers. While one has right to speech, others have a right to listen or decline to listen. In this the apex court has issued various directions touching upon the causes of noise pollution.

8. Environment Management in India

To protect and improve the environment is the duty of both,

central as well as state governments. Simultaneously, we all must understand that the atmosphere cannot be used as a garbage neither by individual nor by the state.[33]

Pollution monitoring and standards enforcement agencies in India, Central Pollution Control Board (CPCB) and State Pollution Control Boards (SPCBs) were created under the Water Act, in 1974. These boards were entrusted additionally to deal with the matters of air pollution in 1981 and now made responsible to monitor the noise levels in the country. Department of environment was created in 1980 for environmental management, which later became the part of Ministry of Environment and Forestry, established in 1985. The Environment Ministry is contributing enough substantial to protect and improve environmental quality. Some states have also shown their love for the environment, by way of creating departments of environment in their states on the pattern of centre. No doubt, formation of separate ministry of environments and forests is a good step, towards environment management in India.

Until the enactment of Environment Protection Act, 1986, prosecution under Indian environmental laws, could be initiated only by the Government. Public interest groups and citizens had no statutory remedy against a polluter, who discharged effluents or emitted the pollutants beyond the permissible limit. But under section 19 of the Environment Protection Act, 1986, a citizen can prosecute the polluter, provided a 60-day notice is given of her/his intention to prosecute. Other provisions allowing citizens to participate in the enforcement of pollution laws are now found in section 43 of the Air Act, as amended in 1987, and also in section 49 of the Water Act as amended in 1988. Both these Amendments require the Pollution Control Board to disclose internal reports to citizens seeking to prosecute a polluter.

9. Enforcement of Pollution Laws

Pollution laws have achieved little success. The courts have been slow to respond to enforcement actions sought by State Pollution Boards. The boards themselves have been poorly funded and charges of corruption have been regular and widespread. Large industries have achieved pollution compliance more easily than small industries.[34] The reason is that they are afraid of taking risks. On identifying the driving force for better environmental performance, it was revealed that the implied current efforts in environmental management is driven largely by a fear of the penalty, that can be imposed by the government in case environmental laws are violated.[35]

In early days, before the development of environmental jurisprudence, the Common law remedy of Nuisance was the only means to provide remedy against noise pollution, and the same was wholly based on the discretion of the Judges. The movement against noise pollution could not find force with the people, because most of the people in India, did not consider noise as a pollutant but take it as a part of routine, and of modern life. In order to curb noise pollution, it is essential that citizens should first realize the dangerous consequences of noise and then to take some remedial measures. About 500 years before Christ; a Chinese philosopher, Kuan Tzu very rightly declared: "If you plan for a year, plant a .seed, if for ten years, plant a tree, if for two hundred years, teach the people."[36] Thus, when you sow a seed once, you will reap a single harvests, when you teach people, you will reap hundreds of harvests. Available scant rules, regulations and few state laws have started addressing the issues of noise pollution in part, confined to certain activities of noise. The Indian Constitution under Art. 19 grants to every citizen a fundamental right to freedom of speech and expression, with reasonable restrictions on the grounds of decency, morality, security of State, defamation, incitement of offence, etc. The use of loudspeaker as a means of expression is regulated by reasonable restrictions, so as to meet public order and peaceful living. The Judiciary, on its part, has come up with some interesting observations, as to the freedom of expression and right to religious practices, with that of noise-free environment.[36A] The Judiciary has thus, trying to maintain a balance between the needs of development and the health of peace loving citizens. The scientists have been by and large conscious about noise pollution. National physical laboratory has surveyed the noise pollution caused country over and revealed that noise level in Delhi, Mumbai, Kolkata and Chennai was very high in dense populated areas. By publishing such survey reports, awareness has been aroused among the public, who have started thinking that noise is also a pollutant to be taken seriously. To invite official attention of the authorities, government and others, towards this malady, a Conference was held, with the joint efforts of National Physical Laboratory and Indian Acoustic Institution. This Conference was attended by large number of scientists, engineers, Construction architects, Grafters, industrialists, transport officers, medical experts, advocates and Defence officers. Many facets of noise pollution were discussed at length seriously and they expressed their deep and great concern. Thus, the noise was raised against the noise pollution, collectively and individually.[37]

10. Stockholm Conference on Human Environment

In 1968, UN established a scientific advisory committee to consider the question of holding a conference on Human Environment, which was later, held in Stockholm from 5 to 16 June in 1972. This historic conference was attended by the delegates' world-wide, including the then Indian Prime Minister Late Smt. Indira Gandhi. The conference adopted '26 point declaration' of principles including controversial reference to nuclear weaponry besides providing certain recommendations as guidelines for the further conduct of states in environmental matters.

11. International Labour Organization

General Conference of ILO adopted a convention to protect workers against health hazards resulting from noise and vibrations.[38] Under this convention, each member has been directed after consultation with the representative organization of employers and workers to accept the obligation of this convention separately in respect of air, noise and vibration. The term 'noise' used in the convention includes all sounds, which result in hearing loss and harms the health.

12. World Health Organization (WHO)

This organization is to raise the standards of health for the people. WHO is not an authority to prescribe the limits of noise, yet it recommends some permissible limits of noise, which are just advisory for its member-states. The documents prepared by WHO on noise, recommends that in case of working environments, there is no risk of hearing damage as noise level of less than 75 dB(A) Leq (8 hrs).[39] For higher level, there is an increasing predicable risk and this must be taken into account when setting occupational noise standards.

For the first time, India and the US have signed a memorandum of understanding in the field of environment.[40]

NOTES AND REFERENCES

1. N.N. Mathur, N.S. Rathore and V.K. Vijay, *Environmental Pollution* (Hindi), p. 46.
2. Water (Prevention and Control of Pollution) Act, 1974.
3. Air (Prevention and Control of Pollution) Act, 1981.
4. The Industrial Environment—its Evaluation and Control, U.S. Deptt. of Health and Welfare Public Health Service Centre for Diseases, p. 312.
5. For example, Cardiovascular constriction. High blood pressure, heart attacks, heart beat increase, Gastro-intestinal modification (ulcers), Intestinal spasm, Endocrine stimulation, Respiratory modification, Skin resistance alteration, Headache, Muscular tension, Neurological disorder, Dilation of pupil, Paling of skin, Blinking, Dryness of mucous, and Adrenal secretion.
6. Dr. Mahesh Mathur, *Legal Control of Environmental Pollution*, p. 183.
7. Pramod Singh, Smt. Chughy, *Environment Pollution and Management*, pp. 120-21.
8. *Times of India*, January 25, 2001.
9. Dr. Mahesh Mathur, *Legal Control of Environmental Pollution*, p. 182.
10. *Times of India*, February 6, 2001.
11. R.K. Sapru, *Environmental Management in India*, Vol. I, p. 127.
12. Declaration on the Right to Development (1986).
13. [3 C.M.L.R. 331 (1997)].
14. Art. 48 A of the Constitution of India.
15. Article 51A(g) of Indian Constitution.
16. See *Bandhua Mukti Morcha* Vs. *Union of India* ((1984) 3 SCC 161: 1984 SCC (L&S) 389.
17. See *State of Punjab* Vs. *Ramlubhaya Bagga*, (1998) 4 SCC.
18. Dated 27-6-1996.
19. AIR 1984, NOC 137 HP.
20. AIR 1999 Cal 15.
21. Section 2 of EPA, 1986.
22. See Notification S.O. 123(E), dated 14th February, 2000 and further amended by S.O. 1046(E), dated 22nd November, 2000.

23. For details see Appendix "A", the Noise Rules, 2000.

24. AIR 1968 Cal. 91.

25. *Health* Vs. *Mayor of Brighton*, (1998) 98 LT 718 : 24 TLR 414.

26. AIR 1975 Kerala 117.

27. 1995 AIHC 4168.

28. See G.S.R. 1063 (E), dated 26 December, 1989.

29. AIR 1993 Kerala 1.

30. 447 US 447.

31. Reported in *Rajasthan Patrika*, August 31, 2000; see 2003 (3) KLT 651.

32. *Times of India*, 23 March, 2002.

33. R.K. Sapru, *Environment Management in India-I*; p. 64.

34. United States-Asia Environmental Partnership (1996). Industry and Environment in Asia: US-Asia Environmental Partnership. Retrieved from the World Wide Web: http://vvwvv.usaep.org/

35. Lau, R. and Srinivasan, R. (1997), *Strategic Issues of Environmental Management*, South Dakota Business View; 56(2), 1, 4.

36. *Employment News*, Weekly, 19-25 January, 2002.

36A. RE: Noise Pollution 2005(5) SCALE.

37. D.D. Ojha, *Noise Pollution*, p. 82 (Hindi).

38. N.S. Kamboj, *Control of Noise Pollution*, p. 32.

39. *Ibid.*

40. *Times of India*, January 18, 2002.

Abbreviations/Acronyms

Air Act	:	Air (Prevention and Control of Pollution) Act, 1981
Art.	:	Article
CPCB	:	Central Pollution Control Board
Cr.P.C.	:	Criminal Procedure Code
CSD	:	Commission on Sustainable Development
DOE	:	Department of Environment
EIA	:	Environmental Impact Assessment
EPA or Umbrella Act	:	Environmental Protection Act, 1986
Govt.	:	Government
ILO	:	International Labour Organisation
MoEF	:	Ministry of Environment and Forest
NGOs	:	Non-Governmental Organisations
OECD	:	Organisation for Economic Cooperation and Development
PPP	:	Polluter Pays Principle
Sec.	:	Section
SPCBs	:	States Pollution Control Boards
UNCED	:	Universal Conference on Environment and Development

UNDHR	: Universal Declaration of Human Rights
USAEP	: United States Asia Environmental Partnership, 1996
Water Act	: Water (Prevention and Control of Pollution) Act, 1974
WCED	: World Commission on Environment and Development
WHO	: World Health Organisation

Introduction

Environmental Noise Pollution, Its Constituents and Properties

"Nature has for every man's need, but for no one's greed."

—*M.K. Gandhi*

Over the years, there have been demographic explosion and technological advancement, which has led to the degradation of environment to such an extent that survival of the living being itself, has become very difficult. The poet Gilbraith has rightly said:

"In the world, into which economics was born, the four most urgent requirements were food, clothing, shelter and an orderly environment, in which the first three might be provided."

No doubt, the above observation of an eminent professor explains the stark reality for the survival of the existence, but the human craving and blind race for material gain has inflicted heavy damage on the nature's balance. Nature's balance is being disturbed today in various ways, from almost all directions. It is shocking to note that about 99% of India's original frontier forests have been lost, while 57% of the present frontier forests are being threatened. Each year a million people die of water pollution.[1] The recent unprecedented climatic changes leading to famines, droughts and floods, earthquake like that of Latur in Maharashtra (1998), Bhuj in Gujarat (2001), oceanquake of December 2004, poor agricultural production, malnutrition and human miseries and earthquake of 2005 in Pakistan, deaths have set in. Several varieties of fish are missing in North Bengal. According to fisheries department, 40 species of endangered varieties are at the verge of extinction. A large number of plants and animals species, become extinct each year. Every year we hear of such floods not seen or heard before. Hundreds of villages are submerged and thousands of people die. As per the findings of IUCN (International Union for Conservation of Nature—a subsidy of UNESCO), one species of bird is getting extinct everyday on account of environmental pollution. It has been estimated that about one quarter of our population consumes three quarter of world's primary resources. According to experts, one variety of fish—the nilsa toli (Mukhporailish) is now an extinct species because of an alarming rise in Pollution.[1A] Depletion of ozone layer is another environmental problem causing ultraviolet radiation, resulting into the increase of skin cancers and other related diseases like cataracts of eyes, damage to immunological system, etc.

Man's unprecedented excessive interference with environment in the name of development without proper planning and foresight has resulted into many serious miseries and more insidious consequences for human health by way of disturbing the delicate ecological balance, which in turn is disrupting life on this planet. Current population explosion has reached to 7 billion peoples, ever-increasing industrialization, unplanned urbanization, technological advancements and indiscriminate exploitation of nature has caused cancer to the environment. Probably, the scientists, economists and the planners have forgotten the law of Newton, that to every action, there is an equal and opposite reaction. What we give to the others, the same returns in multiple to us. The entire humanity is receiving the malady of cancer in return to causing cancer to the environment.

The noise pollution has added fuel to the fire and come out with greater consequences on human mind, animals and the properties. This newly recognized pollutant, i.e. 'noise' is adversely affecting all the walks of life, accelerating thereby, the degradation of environment.

1. What is Environmental Pollution?

Environmental pollution may be divided into two distinct terms, first, the 'environment' itself, and second, is the 'pollution' caused to it. Each has its own meaning. It is, therefore, most relevant here to know, what actually environment constitutes? And what pollution really means?

2. Environment

'Environment' is a term, which is widely used in so many disciplines. It would be indeed surprising, if every one agrees on the exact meaning of term or even the concept, it implies. When we think of environment, the things that instantly come to our mind are, air, water, land, wild life, birds, fish and forests. Also, the word environment means many different things to different people. To some, the word conjures up the thoughts of woodland scenes with fresh clean air and pristine waters. To others, it means their man-modified neighbourhoods or immediate surroundings. Still other related environment to ecology and think of plant, animal inter-relationship, food chains, threatened species and so forth.[2]

Environment literally means 'surrounding', and has wide connotation including physical, biotic and human aspects of the earth within its purview. It includes the earth surface with all its physical features and natural resources, the distribution of land and water, mountains, planes, minerals, plants, animals, the climates and all cosmic forces that play upon the earth and affect the life of man. Thus it also can be said that 'all that surround a designated ecosystem, is called environment'.[3]

3. Definitions Attempted

Encyclopedia of Environmental Science (1975) defines environment as the 'sum total of all conditions and influences that affect the development and life of organism'. This is quite a comprehensive definition as it stresses its totality. Since, every living organism from the lowest to the highest, has its own environment that is why, we find people talking about environment from all walks of life and all types, manner of vacations, may he be a politician, a civil servant, a common man or a scientist who finds environmentalism, a fertile field.[4]

Webster also rightly observes the environment as 'an aggregate of all the external conditions and influences, which affect the life and development of an organism'. These external conditions can be social, physical or the setting, which can be rural or urban. Since, man is an integral part of the environmental system, any change in the system will certainly affect the life of the man as well as other living organism.[5]

Environment is an 'inseparable whole' and is constituted by the interacting system of physical, biological and cultural elements, which are inter-linked individually as well as collectively, in myriad ways. Physical elements (space, landforms, water, bodies, climate, soils, rocks and minerals) determine the variable character of the human habitat, its opportunities as well as limitations. Biological elements (plants, animals, micro-organism and man) constitute the bio-sphere cultural elements (economic, social and political) are essential man-made features which go into the making of cultural milieu.[6]

Environment can also be defined as that congeries of forces and influences acting upon an organism and in relation to which the organism is capable of reacting and in return, influencing in relation to man. However, the environment is not confined to first one only, but is of several kinds.

According to L.V. Urban and G.S. Stacey, the environment is a combination of all these concepts, plus many more. It includes not only the areas of air, water, plants and animals, but also other natural and man-modified features, which constitute the totality of our surroundings. Thus transportation systems, land-use characteristics, community structure, and economic stability, all have one thing in common with carbon monoxide levels, dissolved solids in water, and natural land vegetation—they are all characteristics of the environment. In other words, the environment is made up of a combination of our natural and physical surroundings and the relationship of people with that environment, which includes aesthetic, historic, cultural, economic, and social aspects. Thus, in environmental impact analysis, all these elements are bound to be taken into account, and be considered.[7]

4. Pollution

There are different views regarding the origin of 'pollution crisis' on the planet earth. Many authors like Lynn White and Ian McHarg had blamed Judeo-Christian ethic for pollution. According to them this ethic taught man to believe that the earth was made for man to do with as he wished, and thereby encouraged exploitation. However, this view was contradicted by Wright, who pointed out that the Judeo-Christian religion teaches stewardship and he postulated that it is not religious belief but human greed and ignorance, which have permitted our culture to develop an ecological crisis like pollution.

There is no single but are many factors responsible for the pollution on this earth and they are such as population explosion, unplanned urbanization, fast deforestation, technological advancements, rapid industrialization, profit-oriented capitalism, increasing transportation and blind use of various comfort-appliances.

Pollution is an addition in any form to the environment, i.e. of any substance or energy-form (e.g. noise, heat, wastes), at a rate faster than the environment itself and the environment accommodates such unwanted additions by dispersion, breakdown, recycling, or storage in some harmless form. Pollution of the natural environment is a largely unintended and unwanted consequence of human activities in manufacturing, transportation, agriculture, and waste disposal. High levels of pollution are largely a consequence of industrialization, urbanization, and the rapid increase of human population, in modern times.

The word 'pollution' has been derived from the Latin word 'pollutus', which means, defiled, to make dirty or to pollute. An accurate definition of the term is not easy to attempt, as the known pollutants differ so much in nature, effect and origin that no common feature is discernible. What does rising noise do around airports, rising mercury levels in ocean, higher carbon dioxide level in the atmosphere or higher temperature in streams have in common? Perhaps the simplest answer is that each represents a substance, which in terms of man's environment, is in the wrong place, at wrong time, in the wrong extents and in the wrong physical and chemical form. It is a change in physical, chemical or biological conditions in the environment, which harmfully affect the quality of human life, causing effects on animals, plants, industries and the aesthetic assets.

Environmental Protection and Enhancement Act, 1974 of Iran, defined the term pollution, as the diffusion of foreign matter or the addition thereof, to water, air, soil or land to such an extent that their biological, chemical or physical composition or quality are changed or modified adversely so as to be harmful to man, other living animals, plants, monuments and structures.[8]

Another interesting definition is that given in the Malaysian Environmental Quality Act, 1974, viz. 'any direct or indirect alteration of the physical, thermal, chemical, biological or radioactive properties of any part of the environment by discharge, emitting or depositing wastes, so as to affect adversely its any part against beneficial use, to cause condition, which is hazardous or potentially hazardous to public health, safety, or welfare, or to animals, birds, wild life, fish or aquatic life or to plants, or to cause a contravention of any condition, limitation, or restricting to which a license under the act is subject.'

From the foregoing definitions or implied concepts of both, environment and pollution, it can be well inferred that these terms have been defined with reference to the so far known pollutants, like air, water, soil, etc. But, it is very interesting that these definitions do not include "noise" as a pollutant, which is rising pollutant of modern times and disturbs the peaceful living of the organism. Even, our so-called, Umbrella Act[9] has also omitted to include noise as a pollutant and defines environment as under:

"Environment includes water, air and land and the inter-relationship which exists among and between water, air and land, and property."

And defines pollutant as 'any solid, liquid or gaseous substance present in such concentration, as may be or tend to be, injurious to environment'.

It shows that the noise pollution has been neglected, in-spite of the fact that it is in no way lesser health hazardous than the other pollutants. This kind of pollutant is of recent origin in modern time. But it is only after passing of 'The Air (Prevention and Control of Pollution) Amendment Act of 1987',[10] that noise pollutant is included as a damaging pollutant. For this reason, the definition of air pollutant had to be amended and added with the word noise in section 2 of the Act.

5. Major Forms of Pollution

Major forms of pollution, which cause degradation to our environment, apart from the noise pollution, are of following kinds:

    (a) Water pollution;
    (b) Air pollution;
    (c) Soil pollution;
    (d) Radioactive pollution;
    (e) Thermal pollution;
    (f) Computer pollution;
    (g) Maritime pollution;
    (h) Light pollution;
    (i) Oil pollution; and
    (j) Many others increasing day-by-day such as light pollution.

6. Noise Pollution

The noise pollution, a dire enemy of human brain, is not a new phenomenon, but it is as old as civilization itself is. Today, its cry is being heard very loudly from all the nooks and corners of the glob. It was conceived on the very day, when Adam dawned on this planet earth, but now the same has become a major threat to the peaceful life of today's mankind and to the very existence of wild-life and properties. On one hand, the advancements of science and technology have added to the human comforts by providing us automobiles, electric appliances, supersonic jets, spacecrafts, inventions for medicines, sound amplifiers, musical enjoyment parties, better chemicals to control harmful insects and other pests. On other hand, this process of progress has generated various environmental problems to be faced and noise pollution is one of such major problems.

7. Meaning of Noise Pollution

Noise pollution, as a major contributor to the environmental pollution, is the creation of man himself. It is no less hazardous than the toxic chemicals. It is a shadowy public enemy whose growing menace has increased in modern age of industrialization, scientific and technological progress of the society. As soon as a person is born he or she comes in contact with noise pollution, may it be due to alarming bells, radio, television, loudspeakers, school bells, motor vehicles, aeroplanes, trains, industrial machineries, artillery practices by armed forces, and a lot of other objects which produce sounds of varying magnitude. Although, a soft rhythmic sound in the form of music and dance stimulates brain activities, removes boredom and fatigue, but the excessive of the same sound may prove detrimental to living things. Researches have proved that a loud noise during peak marketing hours creates tiredness, irritation and impairs brain activities so as to reduce thinking and working abilities.

Earlier, the noise pollution was confined to a few special areas like factory or mill, but today it engulfs every nook and corner of the glob, reaching its peak in urban areas. However, the noise pollution's most apparent victims of today are the residents in the neighbourhood of airports.[11] The introduction of Jet Planes have considerably increased their misery. A study carried out near Heathrow airport in UK reveals that the number of patients admitted into the mental hospitals are more, in comparison to others. According to a report by 'Suniye', an institute for deaf, on an average, four persons are turning to total deafness daily in Delhi including a child in womb itself.[11A] The extent, to which noise contributes to the deterioration of our environment, cannot be so easily determined, as is that of pollutions created by other sources. It has been possible to assess impurities in the air quantitatively, or to decide, which waters have been polluted as of biological oxygen demand. But not so in case of noise pollution, different people are affected differently when they are at home, and when they are outside or at work.[12] For example, a sweat melody of morning may be irritating to those who still want to be in the bed. Whereas, a loud noise of music may be joyful to those who are the part of a dancing party in a club. The definition of noise itself is highly subjective. To some people the roar of an engine is satisfying or thrilling, to others it is an annoyance. Broadly speaking, any form of unwelcome sound is noise pollution, whether it is the roar of a jet plane overhead or the sound of a barking dog, a block away. Thus, it is observed that there are differences of opinion as to what constitutes the noise pollution.

The word noise has been derived from a Latin word 'nausea' and is defined as 'sound without value; or any noise that is undesired by the recipient.

8. Noise: Some Definitions Attempted[13]

The definition of the 'noise pollution' is highly subjective and hence, cannot be easily defined. Part of this difficulty lies in the fact that in some ways, it is different from other forms of pollution. Noise is transient; once the source of pollution stops, the environment is free of it, which is not the case for chemicals, sewage, and other pollutants emitted into the air, soil, or water. Other forms of pollution can be measured, and scientists can estimate, what quantity of pollutants can be discharged into the environment before it harms the nature. Though, we can measure individual sounds that may actually damage human hearing, but it is difficult to monitor the cumulative exposure to noise or to determine, just how much is too much.

The noise may be defined as unwanted sound, which gets dumped in the atmosphere in regard to the adverse effect, it may have. In an electronic communication system, the term noise pollution may refer to perturbations that get interfered with communications. Such noise tends to increase with complexity and information contents of systems of all kinds. Thus, man is facing an increasing problem with electronic pollution as radio communication gets intensified. Therefore, in the widest sense, the noise pollution can be considered to be 'unexpected backlash' in concerned use of power.

A large number of psychologists have defined the term noise and Harrel is one of them according to whom 'noise is unwanted sound which increases fatigue and under some industrial conditions it causes deafness'.

According to *Encyclopaedia Britannica*, acoustics noise is defined as any undesired sound and according to this definition; a sound of church bell may be the part of prayer to some one but is the noise to another.

Encyclopedia Americana defines noise as: "Noise by definition is unwanted sound. What is pleasant to some ears may be extremely unpleasant to others and it depends upon a series of psychological factors. Even a sweetest music, which disturbs a person trying to concentrate or to sleep, is a noise to him, just as the sound of pneumatic riveting hammer. In other words, "any sound may be noise, if circumstances cause it to be disturbing."

J. Tiffin defined noise as a sound which is disagreeable to the individual and which disturbs the normal way of an individual.

In electronic communication system, the term noise may refer to perturbations that get interfered with communication.

According to *ILO*, the term noise covers all sound, which can result in hearing impairment or be harmful to health or otherwise dangerous. Noise has been a form of air pollution and affects the quality of life.[14]

Noise also has been defined as one or group of loud, harsh, non-harmonious sounds, or vibrations that are unpleasant and irritating to the ears. In determining whether a sound is a noise, mental attitude and environment are of major importance and it is interesting to note that groups of people with different backgrounds, or work experience, have differing annoyance thresholds. It is also said that what makes the sound a noise, is a matter of psychology, rather than acoustic.

Thus, it can be said that the noise is a subjective term for any unwanted or unpleasant sound beyond the levels required for a particular activity. It differs from man to man, place to place and time to time. Further, a vast variation occurs in the individual sensitivity relating to noise and the people get affected differently when they are at home and at outsight. Perhaps, a better definition of noise is 'wrong sound, in the wrong place, at the wrong time'.

A survey conducted by the US, Federal Council of Scientific and Technology has revealed that noise is a technology generated problem, every ten years in pace without social and industrial progress. This geometric progression-wise growth of noise could be mind-boggling in view of the ever-increasing, pace of technological growth. According to Robert Koch, a Noble Prizewinner, German bacteriologist, "A day will come when man

will have to fight merciless noise as the worst enemy of health."
According to him "noise like smog, has been a slow agent of
death."[15]

9. The Nature of Environmental Noise

Like India, even in Europe also environmental noise is one
of the main problems of local environments and it has become
the source of an increasing number of complaints from the public.
However, general action to reduce environmental noise has been
at a lower priority than other pollutions like air and water.

Road and rail traffic are considered as line sources within
the area of noise impact, parallel to the routes. The radiated noise
may be related to traffic parameters and to acoustically relevant
properties of the surface or superstructure. The assessment of air
traffic noise is more complicated, as the impact depends on the
altitude of aircraft, the noise emission characteristics of the
engines and its track. It is generally presented in the form of
noise exposure contours around airports.

Road noise, especially at some distance from the road can
be described as a steady state noise that does not fluctuate much.
In contrast to road noise, rail and aircraft noise are acoustically
characterized by high noise levels of relative short duration.

Noise from industrial installations, construction sites and
fixed recreation facilities radiates from a point source and the
shape of the exposure area is generally a circle. The radiated
noise is generally related to the installed power of the installation
and other acoustically relevant parameters. Depending on the
nature of the installation, noise from these sources may be steady
for long periods or fluctuate considerably and then rise for a
certain time.

The noise, caused by outdoor equipments such as those
used on construction sites, is not related to a fixed piece of
infrastructure like road or industrial noise. The equipment may
be used in different places and at different times by different
people, all of which makes regulation of the noise caused by
these products more difficult.

The basic level of road traffic noise emissions is determined
by engine noise and the exhaust system. The noise produced in
the contact between tyres and the road surface increases rapidly,
at higher speeds and with light vehicles. Tyres and the surface

are the dominant source at speeds above 60 km/h. This threshold is likely to fall to 50 km/h and even lower, when more stringent vehicle emission limits are enforced. In future, therefore, tyre-surface noise will become an important issue to be addressed in noise abatement strategies. In urban areas behaviour behind the wheel is an important factor, influencing noise emissions. Fast acceleration and reviving the engine in traffic, may result in emissions up to 15 dB(A) higher than the normal levels of emission resulting from smooth driving. Passenger and carrier use road infrastructure equally transport, although the percentage of heavy goods vehicles tends to vary considerably: It can represent up to 45% of traffic at night on a national motorway and less than 10% of traffic during the day in urban areas. Whereas assessing the shares of lorries and cars as far as their physical noise impact is concerned poses no problem, it is difficult to apportion the effects between both sources. However, studies have shown that people perceive the noise emitted by one heavy lorry to be as loud as that of seven light goods vehicles and in urban areas, where speeds are not constant to that of at least 10 cars.

At low speed, the main source of railway noise is the engine, while at traveling speed the noise produced by the interaction of the track and the wheels exceeds that of the engine. The level of this noise is dependent on factors such as the condition of the wheel, its characteristics, the construction of the rolling stock, speed plus the condition of the track. The emissions of freight trains at traveling speeds of 100 km/h are about 4-5 dB(A) higher than that of passenger trains at speeds of 200 km/h. At very high speeds aerodynamic noise will be the most important problem and will require particular measures.

Aviation noise, whose main source is aircraft engines, has the most impact during take-off and landing, and is generally recognised to be a significant source of annoyance at relatively low operating heights. Therefore, aviation noise is generally related to movements around airports.

10. Classification of Noise

Depending upon the sources, the noise may be classified as under:[16]

(a) Continuous wide band;
(b) Continuous narrow band;
(c) Impact/impulsive;
(d) Repetitive impact; and
(e) Intermittent.

Continuous noise is uninterrupted sound level, that varies less than 5 dB during the entire period of observation, e.g. fan. Intermittent noise is the noise, which continues for more than 1 second and is then interrupted for more than 1 second, e.g. drill machine. Impulsive noise is characterized as a change of sound pressure of at least 40 dB within 0.5 second within duration of less than 1 second, e.g. blasting.

11. Sound

The sound is only the constituent of noise and the excessiveness of the same entitles it to be called as noise pollution. Therefore, it becomes imperative to know the characteristics of sound.

Sound is a term of energy giving sensation of hearing (auditory sensation) and is produced by longitudinal, mechanical waves in matter including solid, liquid and gas and transmitted by oscillation of atoms and molecules of matter. It is produced when an object vibrates alternately compressing and expanding the air. It is characterized by its pitch, loudness and tone quality. However, these characteristics cannot be objectively measured because they have been psychological sensations and depend on the ear and judgment of individual observer. In physical terms, sound is defined as a fluctuation in pressure in an elastic medium. This definition gives rise to the objective characteristics of sound frequency, intensity and waveform. Sound travels at a different speed, which depends on the density and elasticity of the medium. The denser and less elastic is the substance, the slower is the speed of the sound waves. Sound travels in air with a velocity of 340 m/s at 20°C and normal to atmospheric pressure. Sound waves do not travel in a vacuum. Decibel is the basic unit of sound. The most important characteristics of sound wave are amplitude frequency.[17]

12. Amplitude

When an object vibrates, it disturbs air molecules near the object and sets them in vibration. These molecular vibrations produce small variations of definite frequency and amplitude in the normal atmospheric air pressure. Amplitude is regarded as a measure of the magnitude of these pressure variations. The greater the energy that goes into producing the sound, the greater is the amplitude of the sound produced. This is related to the intensity of sound.[18] The amplitude may also be described in terms of either the quantity of sound produced at a given location away from the source or the overall ability of the source to emit sound.

13. Pitch

Pitch is used as a measure of auditory sensation that depends primarily upon frequency but also upon pressure and wave of the sound stimulus.[19]

14. Frequency

The frequency of sound describes the rate at which complete cycles of high and low pressure regions are produced by the sound source. The unit of frequency is the cycle per second (cps), which is also called the hertz (Hz). The frequency range of the human ear is highly dependent upon the individual and the sound level, but a normal hearing young ear will have a range of approximately 20 to 20,000 cps at moderate sound levels. The frequency of a propagated sound wave heard by a listener will be the same as the frequency of the vibrating source if the distance between the source and the listener remains constant; however, the frequency detected by a listener will increase or decrease as the distance from the source is decreasing or increasing (Doppler Effect).[20]

15. Loudness

It is defined as the observer's auditory impression of the strength of a sound. It depends on the amplitude of the sound wave and pitch. It is directly proportional to the square of the amplitude and inversely proportional to the distance between the receiver and the source. The unit of loudness is phone or sone. The sone and phone values are related by the equation:[21]

Log_{10} S = 0.03 P – 1.2

where, S = loudness in sones, and
P = loudness in phons.

16. Phones

It is equited with the number of dBs produced at a frequency of 1000 Hzs has a loudness of 60 phones.

17. Sones

One sone is the loudness of sound measured to 40 dB sound pressure at 1000 Hzs. Therefore, 40 dB at 5000 Hzs means twice as loud and assigned the value of two sones and so on.

18. Intensity

Intensity of a traveling wave is the time average rate at which, energy is transmitted through a unit area, normal to the direction propagation, i.e. energy-flow per unit time, per unit area, perpendicular to the direction of flow. It is also defined as power (W) transmitted per unit area, normal to the direction.

$I = W/A; n/m^2$

Because of very large range of intensities over which, the human ear responds, the use of linear scale for expressing acoustic intensities, would be very difficult. That is why, a logarithmic rather than a linear scale is used, the unit is decibel (dB) and intensity level upon sound level is given by 10 times the logarithmic of the ratio of the sound intensity to the intensity at the threshold of audible sound, i.e. .... 10^{-16} w/cm^2.

$IL = 10 \ Log \ 1/10^{-16} = 10 \ Log \ 1+160$

where I = Intensity, and
IL = Intensity Level, dB.

The threshold of hearing is 10^{-16} w/cm^2, is given a value of zero dB. Because of logarithmic nature, a sound of 10^{-15} w/cm^2 intensity is 10 times as intense as this threshold is, and its intensity level in 10 dB and so on.

It is further related to P_{rms} (sound pressure) by the equation

$$I = P^2_{rms}/DV$$

where, P = sound pressure, pa
D = density of air or medium, kg/m^3
V = velocity of sound wave, m/s

19. Sound Intensity Level

It is given by:

$$L_1 = 10 \ Log_{10} \ I/I_0, \ dB$$

where, I = measured intensity, w/m^2
I_0 = reference intensity, $10^{-12} \ w/m^2$

Sound intensity is directly proportional to the square of the sound pressure level. If the intensity of the sound source is doubled, there is an increase of 3 dB in sound pressure level.[22]

20. Sound Power (P)

The sound power of source is the total sound energy radiated by the source per unit time. Sound power is normally expressed in terms of watts. Sound power is also expressed in terms of a level (Sound power level LP) in decibels referenced to 10^{-12} watts.

21. Sound Pressure

The fluctuating part of the air pressure is called sound pressure. It can be plus or minus, depending upon, whether the total pressure is above or below the average atmospheric pressure. The range of human hearing is: 0.00002–20Pa.

Sound Pressure (rms) = total atmospheric pressure; barometric pressure.

22. Sound Pressure Level

$$SPL = 20 \ Log_{10} P/P_{rms} \ dB$$

where P = measured sound pressure, n/m^2
P_{rms} = reference sound pressure level = $2 \times 10^{-5} \ N/m^2$

Relationship between sound pressure, sound intensity and intensity level (dB) are given below:[23]

Sound Pressure N/m²	Intensity W/m²	Intensity level dB
2×10^{-5}	10^{-12}	0
2×10^{-4}	10^{-10}	20
2×10^{-1}	10^{-4}	80
$2\ (2\times10^{0})$	10^{-2}	100
$20\ (2\times10^{1})$	$10\ (10^{0})$	120
$200\ (2\times10^{2})$	$100\ (10^{2})$	140

23. The Decibel (dB)

The decibel is the basic unit of sound and is designed to fulfil the scientific requirement of giving information about the physical amplitude of sound. The term Decibel (dB) is often used to indicate one-tenth bel. It can be applied to noise assessment, but its principal purpose is scientific rather than social, we must use it with care.

A sound of often 0 and 1 dB is the weakest, that the average human can hear. For testing purposes, '0' dB is considered to be the threshold of hearing. Dropping of a pin on the floor produces about 2 dB of sound. A marriage procession on an average produces about 80 dB of noise. Diwali crackers are much louder, producing as much as 120 dB. A public meeting causes, anywhere, between 85 and 90 dB. Market noises range between 72-80 dB as shown by the various studies.[24] A whisper is about 20-30 dB and average speaking voice is about 60 dB. Note that according to logarithmic relationship, 20 dB is 100 times as intense as the threshold and 60 dB is 10 lakh times as intense. The loudest sound that a person can stand without discomfort is 80 dB. Automobile horn may cause the sound of 90 dB, whereas a jet aeroplane, at a distance of 100 ft, may have an intensity of about 140 dB.[25]

In air, sound consists of pressure fluctuations about the atmospheric pressure. To be audible these fluctuations must have frequency (or frequency component) between 20 Hz and 20,000 Hzs. If the amplitude of pressure fluctuations has been P then the sound level in decibels has been given below:

$$L = Log_{10}\ [P/P_0]^2 dB$$

Where $P_0 = 2 \times 10^{-5} \, N/m^2$ (a reference pressure).

The dB has been thus, based on a ratio of pressure and so is dimensions.

The reason for the logarithmic nature of the decibel is that, the amplitude of audible pressure waves varies from $2 \times 10^{-5} \, N/m^2$ to above $10^6 \, N/m^2$, which is vast range. The range of more than $10^6 \, N/m^2$ cannot be scaled linearly with a practical instrument, because such a scale might be many miles in length. In order to obtain desired accuracy at various pressure levels, to cover very wide range of sound pressures with a reasonable number of scale divisions and to provide a means to obtain the required measurement accuracy at extreme pressure levels, the logarithmic decibel (dB) scale was selected. It has been found that, by and large, people judge that a sound, which has increased in level by 10 dB, is roughly doubled in subjective loudness. It is however, a mistake to take this too literally and then assume that an increase of 40 dB represents a loudness increase of 16 times. The decibel is useful for handling the large variations in pressure amplitude that cause small variations in subjective response. Note that we measure sound level in dB, the word 'level' whenever you see, it should remind you that you are dealing with a logarithmic measurement.

24. Sound Levels and Human Response[26]

Sound in dB	Human Response
0	Threshold of hearing
10	Just audible
30	Very quiet
50	Quiet
70	Telephone use difficult intrusive
80	Annoying, intolerable for phone use
90	Hearing damage (8 hours)
100	Very annoying
105	Maximum vocal efforts
130	Limit amplified speech
140	Painfully loud

25. Addition of Decibels

The logarithmic nature of the dB unit creates a lot of difficulty, when variation in sound level are considered, the correct use and understanding of the decibel is essential for any person endeavoring to control noise.

An important aspect of the scale has been that whenever sound power is doubled, for example, by adding two identical sources together, the resulting sound level is not doubled. The fact that a single motorcycle will create 100 dB at a curbside does not mean that two motorcycles will create 200 dB at the same point. The result of adding two identical sound levels together means an increase of only 3 dB in the sound level from one source. So, if one motorcycle produces 100 dB, two together will produce 103 dB, four will produce 106 dB and so on. Therefore, it is seen that an increase of 10 dB represents a tremendous increase in sound power or pressure. But subjectively a 3 dB change is needed to achieve substantial appreciation of noise level.

26. A-Weighted Decibels: dB(A)

The human ear can detect sound within a particular frequency range from approximately 20 to 20,000 Hzs. However, within this range, the ears particularly, are sensitive to sound at the frequencies between 1000 to 6000 Hz. These frequency characteristics are incorporated into how we measure and estimate noise levels by using a frequency weighting (the A-weighting) which weights the sound pressure level in such a manner, that it approximates, how we hear sound, i.e. it emphasizes frequencies between 1000 to 6000 Hz and de-emphasizes the rest of the audible range. Such a measured sound in A-Weighted decibels is called the noise level and expressed as dB (A).

27. Equivalent Sound Level (L$_{eq}$)

The equivalent sound level is a term that has been used primarily in industrial environment, when used to determine total sound of every exposure, it has been found to correlate well with noise induced hearing loss. The term designates that continuous, steady, and band noise, without impulses or pure tone components, is equivalent in sound energy over the period of interest to the actual varying noise level. In other words, it is intended to represent that level of a steady noise, which conveys the same amount of energy in a given time interval, as the actual noise. It should be noted that L_{eq} must always be referred to the total time interval that is under consideration. Recent studies of correlation between L_{eq} and noise annoyance caused by traffic noise have shown that L_{eq} is almost as good for the description of results as L_{10} (some times called the 10% level) which is the level exceeding for 10% of the averaging time. This is true that a comparison between L_{eq}, over a suitable time interval and aircraft noise, induces bearing in mind that noise data can predict only a limited percentage of individual's subjective reactions and considers the high correlation between all proposed noise measures. Furthermore, the United States Environmental Protection Agency (USEPA) has recommended a unit L_{eq} (the day-night level) based upon the L_{eq}, measured over a 24 hours period with a 10 dB penalty, applied to the interval between 2200 and 0700 hours. In the UK, the Noise Advisory Council has also recommended the adoption of 'A' weighted L_{eq} for new standards. Consequently much recently published legislation and codes of practice have adopted the L_{eq} measure of dB(A) in order to specify maximum levels. Many of newly introduced instrumentation packages are revised to measure L_{eq}.

28. Noise Measurements

There are probably the greater varieties of instruments available to measure noise. Almost every measurement-need can be satisfied with instrumentation available commercially today. However, there was felt need of such sound level meters, which could easily be kept, transported and used for all ranges of noise. The researcher, while interviewing the concerns in Ministry of Environment and Forestry, New Delhi, came to know that the Ministry has a plan to provide suitable sound level meter to each concerned departments at center and state level both. Even pocket size sound level meters have been invented and serving the purpose by the mobile units such as to measure the noise produced by the single cause such as individual type of vehicle, loudspeaker, horn, etc.

For measuring the ambient noise levels and percentile for various areas at Jodhpur, the sound level meter type CRL 2.37 B was used. The microphone fitted with windscreen was kept at a height of 1.5 meters above the ground at all the monitoring sites. This height is the average, taken for the position of the human ears. Monitoring was for a different period at different times of the day at each of sites, for an aggregate period, ranging from one to two days. Within the monitoring time period of 10 minutes, measurements were recorded at intervals of 10 seconds, totaling to 60 seconds readings for each monitoring period.

Inter-city Comparison of the Ambient Noise Levels in Rajasthan

Cities	Average L_{eq}							
	Residential		Commercial		Industrial		Sensitivity	
	Day	Night	Day	Night	Day	Night	Day	Night
Jaipur	75 (+20)	67 (+22)	78 (+13)	76 (+21)	78 (+3)	66 (-4)	77 (+27)	67 (+27)
Alwar	56 (+1)	33 (-12)	80 (+15)	36 (-19)	62 (-13)	42 (-28)	55 (+5)	51 (+11)
Jodhpur	68 (+13)	53 (+8)	76 (+11)	71 (+16)	67 (-3)	62 (-8)	71 (+21)	53 (+13)
Kota	54 (-1)	43 (-2)	68 (+2)	59 (+4)	53 (-22)	46(-24)	63 (+13)	55 (+15)
Pali	54 (-1)	—	72 (+7)	—	63 (-12)	62 (-8)	58 (+8)	—

Source: Ambient Noise Levels in Rajasthan; a report prepared by Rajasthan Divisional Pollution Control Board, Jodhpur.

Noise Data of Different Cities of India

Cities	Average L_{eq}							
	Residential		Commercial		Industrial		Sensitivity	
	Day	Night	Day	Night	Day	Night	Day	Night
Bombay	70	62	75	66	76	65	66	—
Bangalore	67	50	76	57	78	78	67	—
Calcutta	79	65	82	75	78	78	79	65
Hyderabad	65	46	76	65	70	70	70	56
Madras	66	48	78	71	71	71	63	49

Source: Ambient Noise Levels in Rajasthan; a report prepared by Rajasthan Divisional Pollution Control Board, Jodhpur.

It is clearly observed that the noise levels are the highest in Calcutta for all the zones.

Noise Levels of Different Cities in the World

Cities	Noise Levels in dB
New York	100-120
Washington	90-110
Paris	80-160
London	100-160
Brussels	100-150
Amsterdam	90-170
Bonn	80-115
Austria	90-120
Copenhagen	120-160
Frankfurt	110-170
Athens	80-120
New Delhi	100-160

Source: Ambient Noise Levels in Rajasthan; a report prepared by Rajasthan Divisional Pollution Control Board, Jodhpur.

The noise level is found maximum at Nai Sarak Choraha seconded by Jalorigate. Since traffic intensity generally remains at its pitch, hence it is revealed that Traffic noise is more at Jodhpur City.

Noise Levels Monitored During in Shillong City of Meghalaya State

Sampling Locations	Classifications	Noise Levels dB(A)		Permitted limits of noise in dB(A)	
		Day	Night	Day	Night
Jowai Govt. College	Silence Zone	48(-2)	43(+3)	50	40
Circuit House, New Hill	Residential	55	44(-1)	55	45
Lew Musiang Bazar	Commercial	63(-2)	53(-2)	65	55

The Level of Noise at Shillong on Deepawali and Normal Day

Place	Year	Deepawali Day		Normal Day	
		Day	Night	Day	Night
Shillong	2001	51.1 (8.43 p.m.) to 102.7 (7.52 p.m.)	41.4 (1.10 a.m.) to 90.0 (12.15 a.m.)	48.9 (2.15 p.m.) to 78.8 (5.00 p.m.)	38.9 (12.31 p.m.) to 60.3 (11.15 p.m.)

Source: International Status of Jowai, a report prepared by Meghalaya State Pollution Control Board, 'Arden' Lumpyngngad, Shillong in November 2001; p. 33.

First Hand Data Recorded in Jodhpur City

Date	Duration	Name of the Places at Jodhpur	L_{eq} in dB
25 and 26 September, 2000	07.00 Hrs to 08.00 a.m.	Sojati Gate	60.1 & 60.1
		Jalori Gate	62.2 & 59.0
		Akhaliya Choraha	58.7 & 60.2
		Mhamandir	— & 67.5
		Paota Choraha	— & 77.2
			68.3 & 60.2
25 and 26 September, 2000	1200 Hrs 1300 Hrs	Sojati Gate	65.9 & 70.3
		Jalori Gate	63.7 & 70.2
		Akhaliya Choraha	71.3 & 72.6
		Mhamandir	69.7 & 70.2
		Paota Choraha	
			78.2 & 86.8
-do-	1900h to 2000h	Sojati Gate	75.4 & 88.2
		Jalori Gate	76.9 & 84.8
		Akhaliya Choraha	71.9 & 67.8
		Mhamandir	71.3 & 80.3
		Paota Choraha	
			78.4 & 85.2
	2200h to 2300h	Sojati Gate	84.0 & 87.4
		Jalori Gate	74.3 & 65.0
		Akhaliya Choraha	63.2 & 74.0
		Mhamandir	68.2 &75.1
		Paota Choraha	
			78.3 & 74.1
April 11, 2001	08.00-1200h & 1600-2000h	Nai Sarak Choraha	76.0 & 77.7
		Jalori Gate	74.4 & 76.9
		Shanishture ji ka Than	74.2 & 73.5
		12th Road Choraha	
			101.9 & 98.2
May 23, 2001	0800-1200h & 1600-2000h	Nai Sarak Choraha	103.7 & 99.2
		Jalori Gate	96.1 & 90.1
		Shanishture ji ka Than	75.4 & 71.0
		12th Road Choraha	
			89.5 & 86.0
June 4, 2001	0800-1200h & 1600-2000h	Nai Sarak Choraha	89.8 & 88.4
		Jalori Gate	85.2 & 83.5
		Shanishture ji ka Than	74.8 & 73.2
		12th Road Choraha	
			78.8 & 79.8
September 22, 2001	0800-1200h & 1600-2000h	Nai Sarak Choraha	79.5 & 81.6
		Jalori Gate	75.8 & 65.6
		Shanishture ji ka Than	71.0 & 74.6
		12th Road Choraha	
			80.4 & 77.3
October 15, 2001	0800-1200h & 1600-2000h	Nai Sarak Choraha	78.8 & 80.6
		Jalori Gate	65.6 & 72.4
		Shanishture ji ka Than	78.0 & 76.6
		12th Road Choraha	

Source: Divisional Pollution Control Board, Jodhpur, Rajasthan.

It is observed that noise levels at shilling, which is hilly area full of greenery forests, are even lower than the prescribed standards except noise in a silence zone, which is 3 dB higher the prescribed ones. It proves that trees are diffusing the noise pollution to a good extent.

Ambient Noise Level at Different Places in Delhi during Deepawali Festival in the Year 1999-2002

Sl. No.	Locations	Average Noise Level in L$_{eq}$. dB(A)				
		1999	2000	2001	2002	Limit
1.	All India Institute of Medical Sciences	72	76	66	74	55
2.	Lajpat Nagar	—	81	85	82	55
3.	New Friends Colony	79	87	80	81	55
4.	East Arjun Nagar	80	83	85	76	55
5.	Connaught Place	79	72	73	66	65
6.	India Gate	69	68	70	67	50
7.	Mayur Vihar-II	81	84	80	80	55
8.	Patel Nagar	74	74	74	67	55
9.	Kamla Nagar	75	81	79	78	55

Exceedence of Percentage (%) Violation with Respect to Day Time Standard at Different Places in Delhi during Deepawali Festival 1999-2002

Sl. No	Locations	1999	2000	2001	2002
1.	All India Institute of Medical Sciences	31	38	20	35
2.	Lajpat Nagar	—	47	55	49
3.	New Friends Colony	44	58	45	47
4.	East Arjun Nagar	45	51	55	38
5.	Connaught Place	22	11	12	02
6.	India Gate	38	36	40	34
7.	Mayur Vihar-II	47	53	45	45
8.	Patel Nagar	35	35	35	22
9.	Kamla Nagar	36	47	44	42

Source: Central Pollution Control Board, New Delhi.

Ambient Noise Level at Different Places in Delhi during Deepawali days in the year 2003-04 Measured on 5th November, 2004 from 1800 hrs to 2300 hrs.

Sl. No.	Location	Average Noise Level in L_{eq}. dB(A)			
		Deepawali Day		Normal Day 2004	Stamdard Limit
		2003	2004		
1.	All India Institute of ʾedical Sciences (AIIMS)	78	64↓	80	55
2.	Lajpat Nagar	89	74↓	66	55
3.	New Friends Colony	90	75↓	57	55
4.	East Arjun Nagar	81	↑83	71	55
5.	Connaught Place	74	73↓	54	65
6.	India Gate	69	67↓	54	50
7.	Mayur Vihar Phase-II	81	↑87	67	55
8.	Raja Garden	—	80	52	55
9.	Pitam Pura	—	82	59	55
10.	Model Town	—	88	52	55
11.	Patel Nagar	73	↑79	78	65
12.	Kamla Nagar	78	↑79	69	55
13.	Dilshad Garden	80	80	56	55
14.	I.T.O.	77	74↓	72	65

Source: Central Pollution Control Board, New Delhi.

From the analysis of above table, it is revealed that the ambient noise level has increased on Deepawali day as compared to normal day at all locations. Also, the average noise values on Deepawali day were ranging from 64 to 87 L_{eq}. dB(A) against lost years average values of 69 to 90 L_{eq}. dB(A).

29. L_{eq} Meters

It is possible to calculate L_{eq} directly from statistical analysis of a large number of registrations of level at equal time intervals. However, this method is long and tedious. Because of the recent need to stabilize L_{eq} levels accurately and quickly, automatic instruments have been developed to measure this quantity directly. These instruments are much more complicated than the conventional ones, consequently they are typically more expensive. The most desirable characteristics of a L$_{eq}$ meter are as under:

(a) Large dynamic range;

(b) Continuous Sampling (integration) technique or spot sampling at less than 125 ms intervals in order to avoid errors due to omission of high-level impulsive peak; and

(c) Facility for taking short period L$_{eq}$ values in addition to longer term cumulative values in order to identify significant noise events during the monitoring period.

In recent years, there has been availability of digital real time analyzers, designed to obtain some of the statistical noise measures, including L$_{eq}$ and based upon integrating procedure. With appropriate and output interfaces, general-purpose micro-computers can be programmed to obtain L$_{eq}$. This has made it possible to apply the benefits of large-scale integration devices, to noise measuring instruments. These include increased performance and ability to handle large amount of data as well as increased reliability and reduction of size and cost. It is very likely that all future noise measuring instruments with the possible exception of minimum performance sound level meters will be microprocessor-based.

30. Mechanism of Hearing[26A]

Sound reaches the ear by three routes. Firstly, air conduction through the ossicular chain to the oval window; secondly, bone conduction directly to the inner ear; and thirdly, conduction through the round window. Under ordinary conditions, bone conduction and the transmission of sound through the round window are less significant than air conduction in the hearing process. An example of bone occurs, when one taps his jaw. The sound perceived, does not come through one's ears, but through the skull. Sound perception, through air conduction, is the most efficient route and it encompasses the external and middle ear conducting system.

Sound first, enters the ear through the outer canal, which is a small tube, about 25 mm long and varying in diameter. Little physical damage can be done to this tube except that it does tend to collect low-grade bacteria and a colony of these is established. It is very hard to shift. The sound waves then strikes the eardrum, which is not flat, but is a cone with an included angle of about 120°, having the apex on inside of the eardrum. The eardrum vibrates under the influence of incident sound wave. This vibration then gets connected through a bone, which reduce the amplitude, but increases the force upon inner window, and in turn, transmit the waves to liquid borne pressure waves within the circular canal called the Cochlea. The pressure fluctuations within the liquid in the Cochlea then excite small 'nerve-cells', which are also known as hair cells. Each of these hair cells has its own individual nerve and these nerves are connected together into the auditory nerves, which then go off to the appropriate brain center.

It is notable that the human brain has been a component of this audio system. The brain works as an on-line computer interpreting the signals, which it receives from the hair cells in Cochlea. There may be a lot of parallel information coming in, along the various nerves, and it is not that an individual nerve cell corresponds to a particular frequency. In fact group of nerve cells together tend to be responsible for human aural response at particular frequencies.

(a) Human Ear

It is most remarkable transducer, sensitive to a range of frequencies from 20 Hz to 20 KHz for a normal healthy adolescent. The sensitivity of human ear is greatest in childhood, but as we get older, our perception of high tones worsens, a condition labeled "presbycusis", the range of pressure fluctuations, with which ear can cope, is well over 100000 : 1, the lowest audible sound being fluctuated around the ambient pressure of ± .0002 micro bar and threshold of pain occurring at about 1 micro bar. The range of sound intensities, the human ear detect is vast. The intensity of threshold of pain is 10^{13} times that at the threshold of hearing, i.e. '0' dB, which represents the threshold of hearing and 130 dB, is the threshold of pain. The human ear is most sensitive to frequencies in the range 1 KHz to 4 KHz and progressively less sensitive to the lower and higher frequencies.

(b) Parts of Human Ear

From the point of view of hearing mechanism, the human ear can be divided into the following three parts:[27]

    (i) Outer ear (External portion);
    (ii) An air filled Middle ear; and
    (iii) A fluid filled inner ear.

The outer ear consists of the auricle and the external auditory meatus, or canal. The auricle is an ornamental structure in man. The two ears give us 'auditory localization' or 'stereophonic hearing', namely, the ability to judge the direction of sound. The middle ear, which is the special air filled space, houses three of the tinniest bones in the body: the Malleus (hammer); the Incus (anvil); and the Stapes (stirrup). The vibratory motion is transmitted through these three tiny bones to the Cochlea, which functions as a transducer. The fundamental problem that a middle ear must resolve is that of 'impedance matching', in other words, the ear must devise a mechanism of converting the sound pressure waves from an air to a fluid medium without a significant loss of energy. This is note worthy accomplishment, that only 0.1% of the airborne sound enters a liquid medium whereas, 99.9% is reflected away from its surface.[28]

The labyrinth or inner ear is a complex system of ducts and sacs, which houses the end-organs for hearing and balance. It consists of an outer bony and an inner membranous labyrinth. The center of the labyrinth, the vestibule, connects three semicircular canals and the cochlea. A watery fluid, perilymph, separates the bony from the membranous labyrinth, while inside the membranous labyrinth are fluids called endolymph and cortilymph. The cilia are the specific organs, which consists hair like processes, reacting the cilia produce nerve impulses: different frequencies are sensed at different locations along the length of the cochlea. The nerve impulses then reach the brain through the auditory nerve. Cochlea is the site of damage, where hearing impairment occurs. Damage to the cilia, a part of the organ of Corti, causes loss of hearing-usually permanent.[29]

31. Recommended Decibels of Sound for a Normal Person[30]

Sl. No.	Place of Activity	Decibels of Sound
1.	Bed Room	25
2.	Drawing Room	40
3.	Industrial Area	30-35
4.	Hotel or Restaurants	40-45
5.	Factory Workshop	40-60
6.	Educational Institutes	30-40
7.	Libraries	20-25
8.	Hospitals	20-35

32. Scientific Impacts of Mantra's Sound on Body

The power of words requires no mention. The words of a call, given to a person who is in sound sleep, enters into his ears and sensitize his audible nerve-cells of his brain, and conscious mind gets activated and in turns awakes him. Science researches reveal that sound contains energy and a special power like that of electromagnet and light. The capacity of sound waves is more penetrative than the others. The vastness of this power was known to our ancient 'Trikaldarshi' sages to see beyond time and space. Thousands of years ago, they had shown the tremendous power of the Mantras and virtually proved that they were based on scientific concepts. After deep researches, it has also been observed, that there are sounds in Mantra, chanting of which with deep meditation, emits the sound wave at the rate of approximately 10 lakh vibrations per second,[31] which results into the generation of heat energy. According to Dr. L.N. Follar, the constant chanting of the pious word 'OM' has definite impacts upon every mind, which meditates upon it. 'OM' is the master key to all spiritual meditations. The vibrations, produced by the chanting of OM, are very powerful and activate all passive powers of a man. The science also has recognized this fact.

From the above analysis, it can be inferred that the sound waves and their vibrations affect the body in many ways. If noise has adverse effects on body, the sound of sweat music and Mantras positive effects and definitely has spiritual benefits upon the same body.

33. Music Vs. Noise

The man is tied up with the music from his birth to his last journey, i.e. from cradle to the grave. If Music is the way to celebrate the birth of a child, the collective sound of 'Ram Nam Satya' is the form of music to extend deep sympathies and condolences to the persons left behind and a way to pray almighty to give departed soul the eternal peace.

Listening to music activates brain cells that releases endrophines which produce a feeling of happiness or peace. Therefore, music is used to treat ailments like Asthma, hypertension, arthrites, etc. New research in music therapy suggest that some Indian classical ragas, like Raag Yaman, induce a feeling of sadness in a mentally healthy person and of happiness in a depressed person.[31A]

There are some good effects of soft and rhythmic sound, which relieves the tension, form mind and stimulate it in positive direction. According to a recent study conducted by Hong Kong University, the memory power was found increased among the students who were getting music education in comparison to those who were not involved in music education. Not only this, music therapy, according to famous psychiatrist, Dr. Sanjay Chugh, music is a good line of treatment for blood pressure, leprosy, migraine, or other brain diseases. Pt. Shashank Katti of Mumbai is of the view that to sing "lorry" by a mother to get her child asleep, is the example of music therapy. He goes on to say, though Human heart has no provision to listen, but, because of being connected to ears through mind, it reacts to the sounds. For instance, a person starts tearing on listening a sad story and laughs on funny jokes. This is nothing but the result of hormones, produced in the body on listening.[32] But, it is well known fact that one's music may be disturbing noise to another. There are many noise hazards on health of human being, animals, birds, wild life. It deteriorates even the buildings and properties.

It is the music therapy by which Dr. Harchisan of America could successfully cure number of incurable diseases.[33] It is scientific that sweat music has its positive effects on humans, animals, birds and crops, etc. Sweat and melodious sound has direct effects upon the cows, which produced more milk than earlier. The growth becomes rapid and fruits become better in quantity and quality, if sweat music is played near the crop fields or gardens.

From the foregoing facts, the good effects of music can not be denied, but the high pitch of unwanted music has become a major source of today's noise pollution. Today, no ceremony is accepted as complete without the use of music irrespective of its disturbance caused in vicinity. Therefore, there is a great need to curb this unwanted noise, in the name of music, by suitable legislation and by creating public awareness against it. Simultaneously, it becomes the duty of we all citizens, to curb this unnecessary noise. If some one creates unnecessary noise, every one of the localities, should object, complaint, and if necessary, even should take the recourse to judicial actions against it. The executive and judiciary, in the interest of peaceful living, should come heavily on the noisemakers.

NOTES AND REFERENCES

1.   Masroo M. Gilani, *Green News*—Issue No. 60/98, masroor@greenpress.sdnpk.undp.org, Sat, 11 July 1998 11:38:30 +0500.

1A. *Times of India*, Delhi Ed., January 22, 2005.

2.   R.K. Jain, L.V. Urban and G.S. Stacey, *Environmental Impacts Analysis*, Ed. II, p. 2.

3.   V.S. Katiyar, *Environmental Concerns, Depleting Resources and Sustainable Development*, p. 5.

4.   *Ibid.*, p. 4.

5.   *Ibid.*

6.   *Ibid.*, p. 6.

7.   R.K. Jain, L.V. Urban and G.S. Stacey, *Environmental Impacts Analysis*, Ed. II, p. 2.

8.   Dr. Mahesh Mathut, *Legal Control of Pollution*, p. 62.

9.   *EPA*, 1986.

10. Ins. by Act 47 of 1987 (w.e.f. 1st April, 1988).

11. R.K. Sapru, *Environment Management in India*, p. 124.

11A. *Navbharat Times* of August 25, 2003.

12. Timmy Katiyar, M. Starke, *Environmental Pollution*, p. 220.

13. G.S. Nagi, M.K. Dhillon, *Noise Pollution*, p. 3.

14. ILO Convention No. 148, See Debi Prasad Tripathi, *Noise Pollution*, p. 5.

15. *Supra* 13.

16. *Supra* 14, p. 13.

17. *Ibid.*, p. 2.

18. *Ibid.*, p. 4.

19.   *The Industrial Environment—Its Evaluation and Control,* p. 299.

20.   *Ibid.*

21.   *Supra* 14, p. 5.

22.   *Supra* 12, p. 10.

23.   *Ibid.,* p. 7.

24.   *Himayala's Encylopaedic Dictionary of Environmental Pollution,* p. 37.

25.   *Ibid.*

26.   *Encyclopaedic Dictionary of Environmental Pollution,* p. 38.

26A. D.D. Ojha, *Noise Pollution* (Hindi).

27.   *The Industrial Environment—Its Evaluation and Control,* p. 309.

28.   *Ibid.,* p. 312.

29.   *Ibid.,* p. 29.

30.   N.N. Mathur, N.S. Rathore and V.K. Vijay, *Environmental Pollution,* p. 122.

31.   D.D. Ojha, *Noise Pollution,* p. 35 (Hindi).

31A. J.M. Khanzode, Biwandi, See Open Space in *Sunday Times of India,* New Delhi, August 17, 2003.

32.   *Dainik Bhaskar,* 24 Feb., 2002.

33.   *Supra* 31, p. 36 (Hindi).

Causes of Noise Pollution

In this technological age, the sources of noise are almost infinite. Noise pollution, which was previously, limited to a few special areas, like factory or mill, but today it engulfs every nook and corner, and every street, reading its peak in urban areas. The noise, most of the people complain about, comes from many sources. These can be grouped into many-fold categories. First, the 'Transport Noise' that comes from road, air, and rail traffics. Second is 'Industrial Noise', the main facets of which are manufacturing processes, air handling, water coolers, transformers, etc. Third, 'Construction Noise', which comes from large machineries, like trucks, cranes, general clatter, driving piles into the ground, concrete crusher, cement mixer, pulverizes and the like. Fourth, 'Domestic Noise', caused by neighbours, stereos, loudspeakers, gramophones, microphones, dogs, cockerels, parrots, and other more many noisy domestic activities. Fifth kind is the 'Natural Noise', which is the outcome of various natural activities, such as rain and lightening of clouds. Sixth, is the 'Background Noise', a general hum of noise, that keep on going all the time. It may come from anything, may be, low, high or too quiet, from far away, which stands to be particularly loud. Most background noise is from distant traffic.

In addition to above, the other various sources of noise pollution may also be termed as commercial, social, religious and political, etc. These are created through racing-buses, trucks, cars, deafening silencer-less motorbikes, a myriad of horns, automatic foundation diggers, blaring loudspeakers, chaotic shrieks of tyres, mill sirens, deafening marriage bands, religious sermons, religious and political processions, electioneering, various advertisements, machinery used in building construction, railway tracks, aeroplanes while take-off or landing, quarrel of partners, increasing use of fire crackers and similar devices causing high intensity of sound, are the different causes of noise pollution.[1] Among cultural factors which cause noise pollution with special reference to vehicular noise, the most important is in the religious fares. Even special vehicles are being plied on the occasions of such religious ceremonies. Kumbh Mela (at Haridwar, Allahabad and Nasik), Surya Grahan (at Kurukshetra), Guruparb (at Anandpur Sahib), Famous Rath Yatra (At Puri), Huge gathering to celebrate Ids, Moharrams, Christmus are only some examples of such religious fares. These religious events and rallies/ Processions, require heavy deployment of vehicles to convey the devotees to and fro, which in turn become the cause of noise pollution.[2] The noise caused by the hotels/restaurants/clubs/ dancing parties/musical nights till late night, has also proved the most disturbing pollution in the vicinity. Being victimised of noise pollution, the former Lt. Governor, Delhi complains that Farm House Parties which blatantly violate traffic, air and noise pollution have become as traditional as some wedding rituals and there seems no stoppage to this menace.[2A] In England, a Night Club, which was accused of producing too much noise, was fined, 3,000 pounds.[3] In the wake of above, the numerous sources, of noise, may broadly be classified into three viz. Industrial, Non-industrial, and Natural.

1. INDUSTRIAL

With the rapid development of the modern industry, industrial noise has become an international hazard. Mechanical noise is the major part of industrial noise. High noise levels are common in industries such as petrochemicals, steel, thermal power stations. Some industrial installations produce such a high intensity of sound that an ordinary human being cannot bear it, even for a few moments, without the help of ear protecting device. Inside thermal power station, there is very high noise. Everyone can feel numbness in his ears when he enters the power station generator rooms, which can be lasted for 5 minutes after emerging. None of the workers is equipped with protective ear. High noise level is due to faulty design of the plant, its defective functioning, out-dated machines and lack of anti-noise measures. About these extremely high noise levels, nothing at all seems to have been done. The Daily News of Los Angeles reports that several local associations of gardeners and one of the country's largest makers of leaf blowers, Echo Inc., have sued the city of Los Angeles over its ban on gas-powered blowers. A suit was filed in Los Angeles Superior Court, and argued that, if a ban is set on leaf blowers because of their noise, the ban also should apply to lawn movers and weed trimmers also.[3A] Many countries have laws against excessive noise levels, at power stations, but not in India. It is a matter of concern that in a long series of industrial laws in India, no provision lies to prevent and control industrial noise. However, protection to eyes has been provided in Factories Act of 1948, but protection to ear is missing there also. The disturbing qualities of noise emitted by industrial premises are because of loudness, distinguishing features like tonal or impulsive components, intermittency and duration. Wood working saw machines mostly used in wooden industry make great noise, reading maximum idling noise above 100 dB(A). Friction noise, vibration noise and aerodynamic noise are some other forms of noise, which we often come across in industrial areas. Another cause of industrial noise is impact vibration or reciprocation movements, friction, and turbulence in air or gas streams. Overall sound level in industries generally falls between 78 and 135 dB(A).[4]

Impact of vibrations and noises can considerably be reduced, if machines have been mounted on flexible supports. In addition, vibration and noises could be reduced by the mass, careful design of shape, and arrangement of parts of machines, so that resonance is avoided. Nevertheless, certain machines will remain inherently noisy, and demand to be surrounded with absorbent or insulating screens. Noise caused by gas streams can be attenuated or even eliminated by the use of suitable ducts and by correct design and positioning of inlets and outlets.

In order that a factory will not interfere unduly with the amenities of the surrounding area, attention is to be paid while towards noise emission and transmission. The noisiest parts of the factory should be kept as far as possible from the boundary of the site and from parts of the works. The intensity of noise diminishes, in proportion to the square of the distance between the origin of the sound and the observer. Sound screens, such as buildings, high walls and trees, perform valuable service in keeping noise down. These natural and artificial 'sound-screening devices' have been most effective, when placed close, to the origin of the noise or close to the people, who are to be protected.[5]

Presently, industrialists are not serious towards particular efforts to cut down pollution, mainly because, the laws and their application is stringent.

2. NON-INDUSTRIAL

Among the non-industrial sources, important ones are, street noise caused by hawkers, loudspeakers, construction work, radio, microphones, religious ceremonies/festivals, crackers, social-gatherings, election campaigns, strikes. However, this list is not exhaustive, as the number is on increase with industrial and technological advancement.

Even the hospitals are not free from noise. Too many patients and visitors add to the din. Most of the hospitals are situated along roadside, where heavy traffic passes on. 'No horn' rule has no meaning and is seen threat. The hospital generators, air conditioners, flooding toilets and diagnostic machines make their own contribution to raise the noise level high. Silence zone exists either only on paper or on the signboards. The London Free Press in Ontario, Canada reports that researchers at the University of Western Ontario undertaken a study to reduce noise from Magnetic Resonance Imaging (MRI) machines. MRI is extreme effective in detecting many diseases by using radio waves and magnetic fields. However, the machine contains a magnet, whose gradient coil generates significant amounts of vibration and noise. The noise is bothersome, and possibly damaging, to both patients and technicians. If MRI noise is reduced, it can be used to diagnose problems of the inner ear. Currently, MRI machines are unable to take images of the inner ear, because the noise from the MRI machines cause the inner ear to vibrate and move.[6]

3. NATURAL

Some natural activities also produce noise, which disturbs the human existence in many ways. Though, this source of environmental noise is unavoidable and inevitable, yet its health hazards may be reduced by way of protection. It is also proven true that man's infinite greed and blind exploitation of natural resources is offending the nature to retaliate and the day has come when its anger started bursting. A few of some activities of nature, responsible to cause noises such as lightening of the clouds, cyclones, earth quakes, storms in sea, volcanoes, heavy water falls.[7]

4. SOUND PRESSURE LEVELS OF SOME FAMILIAR SOUNDS[8]

Even dropping of a pin on the floor produces about 2 decibels of sound. Therefore, before discussing major and particular sources of noise in details, it would be relevant to have a general idea about the intensity of noises, caused by various sources/causes.

Nature of Sound	Sound Pressure Level in dB
Rustle of leaves in quite country side	10-15
Soft whisper	15-20
Broadcasting Studios	20
Library	30-35
Low volume Radio in a country residence	35-40
Light traffic noise	35-50
Normal conversation	35-60
Telephone conversation (normal)	60
Telephone conversation (Excited)	79
Noisy Restaurants	60-70
Noisy Bus	80
Noisy office/Alarm clock	70-80

Nature of Sound	Sound Pressure Level in dB
Heavy Truck/Garbage Truck	90
Motorcycle (25 ft away)	90
Newspaper press	100
Lion's roar (at 12 ft)	105-100
Silencer-less Motorcycle	110
Jet fly over 1000 ft	100-110
Train whistle at 50 ft	110
Stereos in discotheques	110-117
Propeller-driven aircraft (at 100 ft)	110-120
Pneumatic drills	120
Commercial jet aircraft (at 100 ft)	120-140
Sirens and loud horns	150
Jet plane at take-off	150
Space rockets (launching)	170-180

5. POLLUTION BY LOUDSPEAKERS

In India, one of the most common sources of noise pollution is the frequent and indiscriminate use of loudspeakers, which has all the characteristics of a public nuisance and indeed is a specie of public nuisance. Creator of such Pollution is no one else, but the human himself. The purpose, for which the loudspeaker was invented by H. Short of Britain in 1900,[9] was to provide relief to the speakers so that they need not cry at the pitch of their voice to be audible to the audience or the gathering. Their risk against the damage of their vocal cord is covered and protected by its use.[10] But now-a-days, no function or ceremony, religious or non-religious, public or private is complete without the use of loudspeakers at high pitch of the voice, continuously for hours together. It creates public annoyance, disturbs the peaceful living, aggravates the agony of ailing patients, and infringes the right to read. The improper use of this device came to have deafening effects on others, impairing their audition power, in addition to other inconveniences and health hazards.

Residential areas are victimized of this device, be it used for Night Kirtans, Jagrans, Jagaratas, Akhand paths, Kawalis, Musical Nights, Rama Lilas, Electioneering, or gaudy music in marriages. Even, the lottery sellers advertise on microphones and loudspeakers day in and day out.

The recent spate in "Jagarans" and other religious ceremonies, whether in temples or at private places, during the day and whole night completing in weeks and even in months, marks unabated use of loudspeakers, without a pause even for a moment. One is forced to hear the discourses, whether one likes or not. The author himself has been often victim of such maladies, while residing near Shiv Mandir, because of chanting mantras and shlokas, on almost all religious occasions, e.g. Shivratri, Krishna Janmashtmi, every year. Though, every one is forced to suffer and bear with the consequences of this man-made noise, but no one dares to invite the wrath of these fanatics by complaining against, be he the most victim, e.g. student preparing for the examinations, patient in agony, person going in meditation, or an employee, who has to sleep to go for duty early in the next morning. It is a matter of concern that this nuisance caused by the loudspeaker is adversely affecting national economy also, as a person disturbed in night, can not perform well in day.

There are statutory restrictions on the use of loudspeakers and prior permission is mandatory from the competent authority before its use. But, who bothers to obey the law, or to waste time and energy in this behalf, because of nil objections to such nuisances. Concerned authorities are also reluctant to enforce the statutory provisions and therefore, these laws are being proved only the paper tigers. Indiscriminate use of loudspeakers in India is being claimed as the fundamental right, under Articles 19 and 25 of the Constitution. There is a long series of court cases for right to freedom of speech and expression and right to religion, which has been discussed at length in a separate chapter under the provisions of Constitution. A recent case, *Ashok* Vs. *Chowgulay*, of West Bengal, against the use of loudspeaker for religious purposes, is worth mentioning here. In this case, the reluctance of Government and adamant attitude of the people using loudspeakers was exposed, before the court. The defendant contended that the use of loudspeakers while offering prayers and conducting puja, were matters of personal faith and belief. In *Mufti Md. Syed case*,[11] the contention was that a devout Muslim, according to Quran, must offer prayer five times a day.

But the question before the court was whether it is at all necessary to give 'azzan' (prayer) on loudspeakers or microphones, within a radius of five kms, disturbing the amicability of the people of different faiths, living in that area? The court was of the view that the earlier past practice of giving azaan five times a day from mosques was without microphones and the devoted Muslims never had such problem. Referring to the escalating pollution, the court said that our temples, gurdwaras, churches and mosques should help educate the religious people about the adverse effects of noise pollution because of which the very existence and essential peace is at stake. The court prescribed minimum permissible limits, for which the use of loudspeakers is permitted. But unfortunately, the government pedaled soft the crucial question of banning loudspeakers.[12]

In a recent case, *Church of God* Vs. *KRK Majestic Welfare Association*,[13] the apex court has clearly ruled, that to pray with loudspeakers is not a fundamental right under Article 25 of the Constitution. Also in RE: Noise Pollution[13A] the Supreme Court has reaffirmed its stand to ban the use of loudspeakers.

6. NOISE FROM CONSTRUCTION AND CIVIL ENGINEERING WORKS

Demolition and construction for urban renewal and expansions, always makes the urban man a victim of noise pollution. During demolition of old sites and construction of new buildings, huge machines, which produce a lot of noise, are being commissioned and it has become a common scene in every city, where construction work is in progress. Though, it might be created for 'social needs' but is hazardous to the mankind.[14] Noise from construction sites has been generally far worse than noise originating from factories. There are two main reasons for this. One is that construction is carried out anywhere, where the erection of roads, bridges and buildings becomes necessary. The other has been that civil engineering equipment is inherently noisy. The following are the decibels of noises, caused by some of the various equipments, used for construction work:[15]

Equipments	Noise Levels in dB
Tractor-scrapper	93
Rock drill	87
Unmuffled concrete breaker	85
Hand-held tree saw	82
Large rotary diesel compressor	80
1.5 Tonne dumper truck	75
Diesel concrete mixer	75

The effect of having or doubling the distance between the machine and the observer has been to add or subtract 6 dB from the above figures. For example, the noise level 7.5 m from a tractor-scrapper is 99 dB, while the noise level at 30 m from the same machine is only 87 dB. The noise given off by an individual piece of equipment gets increased, if it surrounds by building instead of an open site.

As can be observed, it is practically possible to reduce noise considerably on construction and demolition sites by expending a relatively small amount of extra money. There have been a number of methods by which the noise generated at construction sites can be reduced. First of all, the equipment, which can be used with mufflers, should not be used without the same. For instance, pneumatic drills fitted with fabric mufflers, are shown to produce up to 12 dB less noise than the same equipment without mufflers. It is also possible to reduce noise from construction equipment by erecting sheds around sites, with or without absorbent linings. Using a plain open-sided shed without lining and a screen in front, the noise level can be reduced by about 4 dB all round. If a similar shed with a screen lined with an absorbent layer of formed polyurethane or similar material is used, the reduction in noise level becomes as much as 10 dB all round. In places, where it has been absolutely necessary to maintain silence-zone close to hospitals for example—alternative equipment to pneumatic concrete drills and breakers can be employed. There have been diamond-tipped rotating drills, hydraulic drills powered by diesel, electric or gas generators, and flame-burning methods, all of which are more silent than conventional pneumatic rock drills.

Piling has been another civil engineering operation, producing loud noises. The pile-driver makes its own noisy impact. Vibratory pile-driver have many advantages over impact drivers—not least of which is the fact that they operate at a noise level of 70 dB at a distance of 15 m. Quieter-running electric motors can be used for providing power for many building operations instead of diesels.

The builders, public or private, the housing boards, and the societies should be dictated by law to keep the noise, at the construction site, within the prescribed limits. If they do not meet the requirement, penal action should be initiated against them, along with the cease order of construction work, at the pattern of police action at Cleveland against the constructors. The Plain Dealer reports that the Cleveland (Ohio) police fined two employees of the construction company, building the Jennings Freeway, for making too much noise till late night. The police came into action, only when the residents, living nearby the construction project, complained about this late-night construction noise. It is also pertinent to mention that most of the workers, employed in construction sector, are generally illiterates, uneducated, and unaware of noise hazards and hence, they need more protection from this kind of noise pollution.[16]

However, a possibility of restrictions on personal constructions for residential purposes or otherwise, cannot be ruled out. The criteria may be according to the size of the family and numbers of heads going to reside therein. Two-fold purposes, it shall serve. First, in addition to bringing construction noise levels down, it would be limitation for them, who are fond of living in huge buildings, whereas a very few are to reside therein. Second, the unnecessary acquisition of land for the residential areas could be avoided and the same may be utilized for national and social welfare purposes and hence national wealth can be saved.

By way of Amendment in EPA, the legislators made it mandatory for all construction projects over Rs. 50 crores, to have an environmental clearance. This could mean noise, hospitals, new townships, industrial estates, anything planned for 1000 peoples or anything that discharges 50,000 litres of sewage daily will have to get a clearance from the Delhi Government.[16A]

7. AGRICULTURAL NOISE

A detailed study, to measure the extent of noise pollution, which the machinery employed on farms and like places create, has been conducted by Punjab Agricultural University. According to Grewal and Bansal of this university, the main agricultural sources of noise are—tractor, threshers, combine harvesters, powered knap-sack sprayers, etc.[17]

(a) Noise by Tractor

These are most extensively used throughout the year and are correctly termed as the backbone of the mechanized farming. During the last two decades, tractors of varying capacities have been developed in India. Studies on the noise levels of various tractors were conducted while performing different operations and also with the tractor engine at idling. The noise levels were recorded while tractors were operated in 2nd/3rd low gear with cultivator attached. Noise levels were higher by 2-3 dB with disc plough, which requires maximum draft and hence power was used. The noise levels of other tractors were also found to be quite high and they lie between 90 to 98 dB. Frequency analysis of the noise levels of the tractors indicates that the high noise levels in all the tractors are mainly due to the engine combustion and the cooling fan or blower.[18]

(b) Threshers

The prime-mover noise level, especially the engine or tractor, when installed at a distance (less than 3 m), influenced significantly the overall noise level. Noise levels were recorded up to 95 dB, when the threshers were run with diesel engines or tractors. These were around 90 dB when run by an electric motor. Frequency analysis of the noise of threshers run by tractor indicated that major sources of noise in a thresher are the fan and the threshing drum, which needs to be reduced by legal or other measures on manufacturers.

(c) Combine Harvesters

Noise levels of different combine harvesters were studied while harvesting wheat as well as paddy. These noises included the self of the tractor. Overall noise level of both the machines was also measured, close to the ear of the operator, who occupied the seat on the tractor. The noise levels for various combines while performing the operations were recorded above 90 dB[19] and in some cases these were observed even above 95 dB. The noise levels are mainly due to the engine and the threshing unit.

(d) Powered Knap-sack Sprayers

These appliances are used to spray pesticides for plant protection. These rest at the back of the operator and are mounted on the shoulders with the help of straps. The blower and also its small engine, that runs it, are quite noisy and are very near to the ear of the operator. Noise levels of the sprayers were observed to be 93 dB.

Here, it is heartening that operators are exposed to agricultural noise levels varying from 90-98 dB, for hours together. It has been found that maximum of the operators/farmers are not aware that they are working in noisy environment. If asked, they say that the particular equipment emits slight more sound but do not deem it as noise pollution. Therefore, there is a great need to educate them about the long term harmful effects of this high noise and be encouraged to use the personal protective devices, when convenient. Noisy machines should not be allowed to operate for more than 4 hours by the same operator. Changeover of the engines, which are acoustically better ones, cannot be thought of as an immediate measure, but the use of better silencers and provisions of shields/screens should not be delayed. Diesel engines or the tractors should be placed at a maximum possible distance from the threshers.

8. WEAPON NOISE

Weapons' noise comes generally from muzzle blast. It is produced by propellant gas, bursting out of muzzle with bullet. According to its spectral characteristics and high sound pressure level, muzzle noise causes more severe injury to human body than steady noise. It is, therefore, imperative to effectively control the noise, right at the firing ranges, so as to protect the firing personnel from noise hazards, caused by weapons. The typical sound pressure levels recorded from one of the armored fighting vehicle, are found to vary from 88 to 112.5 dB,[20] whereas these levels measured from several work places in any military workshop, varies from 88 to 107 dB. Neither the Army Act, 1959, nor Air Force Act, 1950 makes any provision for the control of noise caused by the weapons, vehicles, aircrafts or any other means.

9. COMMUNITY NOISE

Of all sorts of noise, neighborhood noise is the greatest source of noise nuisance, which is often complained of. A survey carried out in the UK has estimated that 14% of the adult population was bothered by neighborhood noise, compared with 11% from road traffic noise, and 7% bothered by aircraft noise. The sources of neighborhood noise, in order of number of complaints, was Amplified music; barking of dogs; domestic activities; voices; car repairs; and 10% complaining about other noises.

Society not only 'imports' resources from the environment; but also 'exports' wastes and pollution back to it. Over-consumption and attendant resource depletion by the human economy have been paralleled by greater pollution. Pollution is not simply as a sign of bad management: its roots lie in the very laws of energy and matter.[21] The major source of noise is the population explosion and consequently the community noise. There are many sources of community noise such as market places in the open air, play grounds, public squares and so on. They often have noise effects on surrounding localities. It includes noise, generated by activities like organized sporting events, fairs and religious festivals. Amplified music, both live and recorded, is being emitted in an increasing number of public houses and clubs, over the last twenty years. The Milwaukee Journal Sentinel reports a special Planning Commission hearing was held in Mequon, Wisconsin, to address the issue of noise from a residence where swimming lessons were given.[22]

There has also been a steady growth in noises caused by the increasing number of disco-dances. The problem arises because of the high levels of amplification, which in such cases, often continuous up to the early hours of the morning. There is also the perennial problem of the use of portable radios and cassette players on beaches or other places where people go in search of peace and quietness. Noisiest of all sporting activities is probably motor sport, whether in rallies, scrambling, grass task racing or stock carrying on roads, on serial circuits or on privately owned land. However, in persuasion of Jodhpur High Court's directive issued in a PIL, activation has been recorded on the part of enforcement machinery, for restricting the indiscriminate use of loudspeakers in the city till late night. The case was filed under the Rajasthan Noises Act, 1963.

10. OCEAN NOISE

The ocean was flat and the winter darkness over Cape Cod Bay was unbroken by ship lights. But as per Christopher Clark, the times below the bay's surface were not as seen as they seemed. Noise in the sea though is not a big problem, but there are people, who are worried about it, and so engineers are trying to reduce it. It all comes back to whales, and lots of fish. But, people really worry about the whales, for whom, the ocean has always been a noisy place to live. Breaking waves cause lots of noise, shrimps click their claws, surf on the beach and various fishy noises all contribute to the general hubbub.

Some scientist believe the spreading of acoustic smog is essentially blinding marine life, affecting feeding, breeding and other crucial activities.[22A]

However, the greater amount of shipping has dramatically increased the noise in the ocean, suppressing all the natural noises. Huge engines, which drive the ships across the ocean, radiate sound from their propellers and through their hulls. Through such clamor, there is one creature, which really relies on hearing quiet-noises, across the vast distances, and that creature is the whale. Whale song has been popular for several years, but the whale fishes have been using it since its existence. It is widely believed that, the whales use their song as a means to communicate with each other, across hundreds of miles of ocean. With the increase of noise in the ocean, people have started worrying that the whales won't be able to hear each other, and so will be less likely to find each other. This could affect their migration patterns, and may so affect their generation leading to extinction of the specie. The responsibility, therefore, comes upon the legislator and the engineer to improve upon such a situation. The legislator should control the noise in the ocean through law, where as the engineer must develop such technology, which generate minimum noise. But the selfish ship owners, at the cost of their huge fortune, do not want to make their ships noiseless. So the government through legislation can compel the engineers and owners, to invent and use such technology that, the ships are cheaper, faster, and more efficient, but least noisy so as to allow the whales to sing in peace. The legislative bodies throughout the world must make provisions in the marine and mercantile laws.

11. TRANSPORT NOISE

Transport is a necessity, which is unavoidable. There may be few exceptional places on the globe, where transport noise may not be heard. An industrial society depends on mechanical transport for the efficient distribution of people and goods between dwellings, schools, shops, offices, factories, leisure centers, and many other places. Nonetheless, it is a major source of noise created day in and day out and poses a serious hazard to man, material and animals.

(a) What makes up Transport Noise?

There is a huge list, which can be split up into various different categories. But broadly, the transport noise can be discussed under the three heads. First is 'Road Traffic'; Second 'Air Traffic'; and 'Railway' is the third one.

(b) Road Traffic

An average citizen gets disturbed into his sleep every day by the grinding of wheels, may be of trucks, trolleys, buses, autorikshaws, motorcycles, scooters, and many others. He has to travel to work in old, outdated, and obsolete 'nagar-seva buses', in the roar of other road traffic.[23] Survey shows that 23% of the population are bothered by noise pollution caused by the road traffic.[24] Noise levels at traffic intersections in Delhi has become three-fold. Subways in highly industrialized countries are violators of urban peace. During the survey visit, in the North-Eastern part of India, the author has noted that the major noise is due to traffic. The increase in the level of noise pollution in the capital of India may be known from the fact that annual per capita oil consumption for personal mobility in Delhi is higher than any other city in the country. Without any aggressive abatement policies, oil demand in the transport sector is likely to almost double by the year 2015, as compared to the 1995/96 consumption levels, and noise pollution will intensify severely in the coming years.[25]

It has also been observed that some miscreants remove the silencer from their motorbikes and scooters, which produce undesirable noise commotion and this sort of nuisance annoys people. Road traffic noise, affects to a great extent, the people who live adjacent to the road sides.[26] It is also observed that people are fond of honking at road intersections, where the traffic signals turn red and the vehicles are expected to stop and wait till the signal returns into green. Inspite of written instructions, on the signboards near such intersections, that 'no horn within 100 meters from this point', people are seen honking while waiting for the light to turn green. The honking reaches a crescendo, when the lights turn green and people behind become impatient to cross-intersection before it turns into red again or try to overtake to reach fast. In other countries, it is considered rude to honk, while driving in lane.[27]

As a result of population growth and changes in travel pattern, in India too, transportation demand is continuing to increase. In 21st century, the urban areas in the country, confront a historic transportation. In the absence of good, convenient and efficient transport system in urban areas, there has been an increased trend towards more and more ownership and utilization of personalized motor vehicles. To conclude, it is not only more energy intensive and pollution causing, but also, more expensive to the national economy.

(c) Types of Traffic Noise

Traffic noises have been of two types. Firstly, the noises generated by individual vehicles; and secondly, the noises generated by a continuous flow of vehicles that create a channel causing continuous noise.

I. Individual Vehicles

Noises from individual vehicles can be categorized as follows:

(i) Noise from Engine, and Transmission System

Such noise markedly, depends upon the design of engine and particularly, upon the method of support, used for its moving parts. Expensive cars employ a more elaborate damping system so that noises are not transmitted to the body shell and thence to the outside world. Considerable improvements are now being made to improve the engine mounting systems, even in cheaper cars.

(ii) Exhaust Noise

The reduction of exhaust noise has been an acoustic problem and is being solved up to a great extent. Unfortunately, the more effective and elaborate exhaust system of a motorcar is heavier, bulkier, and more expensive. An efficient silencing system is capable of reducing the power output to any engine, and in consequence, the design of the exhaust system is a matter of compromise. Systems have been usually designed to keep within the law without significantly affecting cost and performance. On the contrary, the 'sport cars' deliberately attempt to retain maximum possible exhaust noise. The selfish purpose behind this deliberate attempt may be to constitute a powerful sale appeal.

(iii) Slamming of Car Doors

'Slamming' is the noise advertently caused by negligently and forcefully, closing and opening of the doors of the vehicles. This aspect of noise from motor vehicles causes irritation and annoyance to the listeners. At late light, it becomes an intense and intermittent noise that is most likely to disturb sleep. There is, of course, no law to control it. Though some of the good firms, manufacturing the cars have effectively solved the problem of this kind of noise, but most of the manufacturers still manufacture the vehicles, which make plenty of noise when doors are closed. Such a problem can only be solved at the design stage of a new car. For this, some legislation to force and control manufacturers is imperative, to produce noiseless door-shutting devices and this is technologically possible in this fast developing scientific era.[28]

(iv) Brake Squeal

'Brake squeal' is the noise, most irritating and unpalatable to ears, which has been particularly noticeable, because of the modern disc brakes. Drum brakes, too exhibits this phenomenon. The cause is, that the vibrations, produced during the application of brakes, resonates within the brake structure, and is then further magnified by the body of the car. It appears that, practically very little could be done about brake squeal, except by introducing some damping devices into the vehicle.

(v) Use of Horns

The fitment of horn system in the vehicle is very important for road safety. But indiscriminate use of unauthorized types of horn, have become the cause for many road accidents. Nowadays, there are many types of unauthorized horns in practice, producing funny sounds, like that of child weeping, laughing, singing, sirens, and many others. However, there is a provision to control such nonsensical noise, caused by the horns. Motor Vehicles Act, 1939 and Motor Vehicles Rules, framed by the states, deal with the vehicular noise caused by the horns. For example, Tamilnadu Motor Vehicle Rules, 1989 states that 'No driver of motor vehicle shall sound the horn or other device for giving audible warning, with which the motor vehicle is equipped, or shall cause or allow any other person to do so, to an extent beyond that, which is reasonably necessary to ensure safety'.[29] The Commissioner of police in the City of Madras and elsewhere the Superintendent of Police may, by notification in the official Gazette and by the erection in suitable places of traffic sign No. 7 as set forth in Part A of the Schedule to the Act, prohibit the use of any horn, or other device on a motor vehicle for giving suitable warning within such locality and during such hours as may be specified in the notification. In an important case, *M.S. Appa Rao*,[30] the court has issued appropriate and elaborate directions to enforce the same.

Bengal Motor Vehicles Rules, 1940 contains a provision that no transport vehicle can be fitted with a horn of any other form except a bulb horn. The transport authorities were held responsible, who owe a statutory obligation and a duty u/s 112 of the Motor Vehicles Act, 1939, to punish the person who contravened the Provision of/Bengal Motor Vehicles Rules.[31] Similarly, Central Motor Vehicles Rules, 1988, provides that, every motor vehicle shall be fitted with an electric horn or other device, conforming to the specifications prescribed by the Bureau of Indian Standards to be used by the drivers, for audible and sufficient warnings of approach or position of the vehicle.[32] No motor vehicle shall be fitted with any multitioned horn giving a succession of different notes or with any other sound-producing device, giving an unduly harsh shrill, loud or alarming noise.[33]

From the above elaborate discussion, it can be well observed that, there is attention paid on traffic noise pollution, but only on papers, and not in practice. As seen, there are some miscreants who use the horn for malafide and naughty purposes. Despite the fact, that there is a statutory provision, banning every driver of a motor vehicle, not to sound the horn for any purpose other than that ensuring road safety and not to sound it continuously.[34] Therefore, there is a dire need to check the use of unauthorized type of horns and their wrongful use in the interest of public health and road safety. It is pertinent to note, that a 'visual stimulus' like the flashing of headlights, is more effective than an audible one in attracting attention. Although, Delhi Traffic Police claims to have checks being put to prohibit unauthorised horns on two-wheelers but in fact nothing seems so.[34A]

(vi) Relative Noise of Vehicles

The tests have been carried out by using a test procedure which gave the following results:[35]

Luxury Bus	:	77 dB
Small Passenger Car	:	79 dB
Miniature Passenger Car	:	84 dB
Sports Car	:	91 dB
Motor Cycle (2-cylinder, 4-stroke)	:	94 dB
Motor Cycle (2-cylinder, 2-stroke)	:	80 dB

It is evident from the above results that, the difference between noise levels of a standard small passenger car and a sports car is not less than 12 dB, which means, the sports car is roughly 15 times more noisy than the saloon car. Motor cycles, with their exposed engines and inadequate silencing systems, are notorious noise producers, with a sound level roughly 30 times higher than that of a saloon car. Scooters produce noise of same level that a motorcar produces. The noisy vehicles not only contribute excessive noise to the environment, but also figure prominently in road accidents. Therefore, there is a need to enforce 'noise rules, 2000' issued by Ministry of Environment and Forestry, in its strict sense and it also can be argued with objective justification that the sports vehicles should be used only on enclosed race tracks, and not on the congested public highways.

II. Noise from a Vehicle of Continuous Stream

Noise, from a continuous stream of vehicle is perceived at the place where a series of vehicles are plied continuously. Busy highways, bus stops, red/green light stops are such places, where continuous stream of vehicles is seen. Overall noise level at such places remains higher than the noise caused by individual vehicle, as number of vehicles with their running engines, raise the level of back-ground noise. To reduce traffic noises as a whole, steps should first be taken to reduce the noise from each individual vehicle. Road re-planning can be of immense help. It has been found that vehicles produce the maximum noise when accelerate in low gear. For that the reduction of number of stops and starts shall lower down overall traffic noise. Byroads, ring roads, and urban motorways, all make a useful contribution in the direction of reducing urban noise. However, it is necessary to plan in such a way, that they do not themselves constitute a threat to the environment. Cutting, shading by artificial hills and planting bushes and trees near busy roads all play their part in cutting down traffic noise.[36]

III. Noise by Large Earthmoving Vehicles[37]

The large earthmoving vehicle, used primarily as a coal scrapper within the Central Electricity Generating Board (CEGB), is 14 meter long, and uses two propulsion units, each of nearly 300 hp, either of which, would normally be adequate for the heaviest commercial vehicles. The two units are called the tractor and scrapper, operate as pull and push partners and are made up from identical engine and transmission units. There are two kinds of noise problems created by this type of machine, which may be classified as internal and external.

(i) Noise by the Cooling Fans in Vehicles

The sources of noise in cooling fans are mainly 'boundary layer noise' and 'rotational noise'. The noise radiated by the cooling fan, installed in a vehicle has presented the designer with a number of problems. Firstly, the contribution of fan to the overall noise field radiating from the vehicle to an external observer is often very significant. The exhaust noise problem has received much attention, particularly in the last few years, and has yielded a considerable success in reduction. Secondly, the fan noise intrudes into the interior of the vehicle. The fan noise, being produced in the engine bay is carried as compressed waves by the air. Thirdly, the present inadequate knowledge of the mechanism of production of fan noise, prevents the designer from choosing the most efficient way of alleviating the attendant noise problem. It needs to increase the speed of the engine to produce more power output. Finally, why should the designer plan reduction of noise in the vehicle, once it does not bring any return or monitory gain? Reduction in noise on the contrary, can be obtained without sacrificing engine performance.

(ii) By Tyre-Road Interface

Though, it is essential that a tyre incorporates a tread pattern to provide grip under poor ground surface conditions such as in rain, mud, snow. Even 35-40 years ago, car tyres had their tread segments at variable pitches to break up any dominant noise frequencies. But in present times, noise work is mainly concerned with internal vehicle noise. With increasing traffic density and the advent of urban motorways, concern about excessive external vehicle noise has been growing. The three mechanism, which are responsible to tyre-road noise are:

    (i) Impacting between the tread and road;
    (ii) Micro-movements of rubber on the road; and
    (iii) Air pumping by the tread pattern.

Reducing Vehicle Noise: Some Suggestions

Though, high noise levels inside vehicles rarely seen to result into complaints from the traveling public. The possible reasons for this may be:

   (a) Passengers are accustomed to it;
   (b) On account of other pre-dominant considerations, such
       as thrill created by vehicle ride over the road attracting
       fellow travelers and comforts of soothing air by fast
       riding;
   (c) Unawareness of the passengers towards health hazards
       of the noise.

But this is not an excuse, for not attempting to produce a system, which shall generate acceptably low noise levels. It is quite possible to produce such a vehicle which is as quiet as we desire as per our requirement, but for that, all the conflicting considerations of design, such as low mass, capital cost are voluntarily ignored, which the vested interests do not permit. The all electric and hybrid assist indigenously-designed vehicle at IITD is an answer to tackle the vehicular pollution in our cities. It is worth mentioning that an eco-friendly transportation group of Instrument Design Development Centre in Indian Institute of Technology, Delhi has developed an electric vehicle which is free of vebrations, noise, heat and other pollutions.[37A] The essence of noise control, therefore, is to obtain the desired result with minimum additional mass, cost, and to ensure that all the efforts spent on obtaining it, are not nullified by some relatively minor details.

Through technology, the traffic noise can be controlled in several ways. One of the solutions is to place major thoroughfares in "ditches"—that is, constructing the in-troughs, which are normally 15 to 20 feet below the ordinary land surface. This is particularly necessary where the high-speed roads are extended into the heart of major cities. Some architects who look into the future, have predicted the use of covered tunnels for all vehicular traffic of cities. Even lining the streets and highways with trees, fences, earth banks, etc. help to insulate and to protect the surrounding area from noise.

There is another remedy available, which recommends a shift from individual automobile transportation to mass transportation. Perhaps, this should end the long romance with the automobile, but there should be a viable alternative in the form of fat, efficient and quiet mass transportation. The conversion to swift, silent and exhaust-free mass transport system will not be an easy task. It requires not only a tremendous capital investment in sophisticated new equipment but also the sacrifice of the already existing investment in conventional methods of transportation. Construction of peripheral express way for metro city like that of Delhi may also be an effort to curb pollution emerging out of heavy vehicles. As Delhi government planned to Rs. 500 crores to construct Eastern and Western peripheral express way project.[37B]

The author is of the view that, in-spite of the measures suggested above, the traffic quietness cannot be achieved without statutory compulsion. It is now-a-days popularly said that nothing comes out without pressure. So is the case here. Curbing of traffic noise without statutory provisions and their strict enforcement, hardly there is anyone who will like to bear the cost on this behalf. The example of Delhi is of great relevancy here. In Delhi, the level of pollutions has started to come down; it is none but judicial activism and decisional compulsions on environmental issues. The Supreme Court's decision to shift from diesel engine vehicles to CNG vehicles, as had been supported by Central Research Institute (CRRI) has immensely helped in curbing pollutions in Delhi. CRRI, in a study has declared CNG as a clean fuel from the point of environmental pollution. It can be observed by any body that CNG vehicles emit less noise in comparison to other vehicles whether run by diesel or petrol. A number of states in the western countries have introduced motor vehicle statutes prescribing mufflers on automobiles, trucks and buses to prevent excessive or unusual noise. New York and Connecticut and in several foreign countries, positive measures have been taken to restrict the noise of traffic through comprehensive anti-noise legislation, stipulating maximum decibel noise-levels for motor vehicles. For instance, in New York states, vehicles on toll ways, and on public high-ways, are put into limitations by law, to a decibel count of 88. The police of New York city, has been provided with the portable decibel meters at toll-booths, so as to enforce the law. It is reported there that the automobile noise level has been substantially lowered.[38] However, pollution checks are to go high tech in Delhi as per Transport Commissioner, Delhi.[38] The state of California has adopted a comprehensive anti-highway-noise legislation, which prohibits noise levels exceeding 82 dB for passenger car and 92 dB for trucks and buses at posted highway speeds.

As an additional measure, California is restricting the sale of new motor vehicles, which exceed the prescribed noise level. A new electronic system is being employed by the State Police of Connecticut, to record the noise level of passing vehicles and to photograph each car or truck exceeding the prescribed decibel level. If the noise emitted from the passing vehicle reaches a certain level, the system trips a Camera, which photographs a noise-level gauge, in a corner of the photograph of the offending vehicle. In the process, a signal is automatically relayed to the State Police patrol, so that an immediate warning or arrest could be effected.[39]

13. RAIL NOISE

Despite the fact that the railway noise touches high peak levels, as high as 120-130 dB(A), in this country, only a few public complaints are there in comparison to motor vehicles noise and the noise of aircraft in the nearing areas. One of the reasons for this may be, that almost all railway lines are long established and the majority of affected residents were aware of and accepted the situation.[40] If compared, two people exposed to the same amount of noise, one from airport and the other from trains, the airport person is far more likely to complain. No one is quite sure why it is so? It could be because the trains are accepted as more useful in common agreement between all people, or that the train noise is accepted as unavoidable in India. Whatever may be the reason, there is far less pressure on the railways to reduce its noise, than for road and air vehicles.

The impact of the noise pollution caused by trains in India has been reported to be the maximum in those areas, where railway tracks pass through residential areas or railway workshops are situated. The author interviewed the locality near railway tracks at Jodhpur and the railway employees at Kanpur, where high speed trains pass frequently. They complained about the excessive noise and told that it disturbs their daily life, causing hearing impairment. But they frankly told that they are habituated with that much of noise and it has become a way of their life. Even sometimes, they say that they are not able to sleep in the night, when the trains stop moving because of strikes or for any other reasons. Although, the children, migrated from lesser noisy areas, complained that their concentration is disturbed and hence train noise hampers their study. During the interview, one heartening fact came to the light, regarding awareness about the noise hazards and its control. Most of them replied that train noise is unavoidable, uncontrollable, and hence they have no option other than getting habituated to it. This does not however mean that the question can be completely ignored. The future expectation of increase in number and extent of rail rapid transit system, will lead to construction of new train tracks. Indian Railway Budget, each year, has a unique feature of increasing number of trains, route extensions, and the cycles of trains on the same limited tracks, with almost no effort to quieting of the trains and the tracks, on which they run with high speed. The Metro Rail plan in Delhi, has to be planned noise resistive, otherwise it would add another fuel to the fire and shall cause high number of decibels. Delhi is already one of the noisiest cities of the world.

Unfortunately, Indian Railways Act, 1890 is also silent on this crucial issue of noise pollution. This Act, which deals exclusively with railway matters, does not provide the protection to the ears of its employees, such as drivers of the engines, who run the risk of driving high-speed trains and the persons, who work in the railway workshops and acquire 'sensory-neural deafness'. The incidence of deafness among the employee of railway workshop is observed on increase. The railway mobile generators are being proved major contributors to the rail noise. Though, Indian Government, under Environmental (Protection) Act, 1986, notifies[41] that the noise limits for new generator sets, which run with petrol or kerosene, shall be maximum 90 dB after September 1, 2001 and 86 dB(A) after September 1, 2002. It was also notified that every manufacturer or importer of generator sets to which these rules apply, must have a valid certificate of type and make approval, for all the product models being manufactured or imported, after the specified dates.[42] The sale of such generator sets model, not having valid type approval certificate, or not complying with the noise limits, as determined by the verification for conformity of production, shall be prohibited.[43] But, still train generator sets emit highly uncomfortable intensity of noise. The major sources of railway noise are, railway engines, sirens, hawkers, venders, and rail-wheel contacts. As far as rail-wheel contact noise is concern, author came to know that railway engineers join the rail track gaps by welding, up to certain length, which was formerly left for thermal expansion of the track metal. It is pertinent that, these open joints, when come into the contact of running train wheel, cause two-fold noise. Firstly, impact between rail and wheel, while pressing the first end of open joint and secondly, due to the strike between rail wheel and next end of the same open joint.[44]

However, it is only over the past few years that concerns have been expressed about the ill-effects of rail noise, running through residential areas, particularly in view of the adverse reaction by the residents against high-speed trains in Japan. The same public reaction was recorded in South-Eastern England, when the route for the channel of tunnel rail link was proposed and the noise became a major environmental issue.[45]

Neither at national nor at international level any specification has been drafted to lay down the noise levels, which should not exceed inside rail vehicles. Indeed, this would not be a simple matter. A preliminary move in this direction, however, commenced in 1969 with the first drafting of an ISO specification 'acoustic measurement of noise inside rail bound vehicle'. Whilst this document also does not attempt to specify actual levels, it establishes a method of measurement aimed at obtaining repeatable and comparable measurement, a necessary pre-requisite to the specifications of actual noise levels.

It is the time for railway engineers/management to devise methods/devices, so as to bring the rail noise levels as down as they can, in the interest of public as well as their own health. However, railway workshop noise may be avoided by adopting ear protective devices. But due to unawareness, neither the employees are using such devices, nor management is pressing for the same. Regarding the noise caused by the rail siren, the report of Southbend Tribune is worth mentioning here, which states that the city of Elkhart, Indiana has received permission from the Indiana Department of Transportation (InDOT) to ban train whistles at 11 different railroad crossings throughout the city. According to the report, DOT studied safety levels at each of the eleven crossings. The crossings chosen have lights and gates that will still allow for safe vehicle crossing, even without a whistle. The city now, will begin posting signs warning, for drivers about the whistle. Also, the Vancouver Sun has reported that, citizens of Maple Ridge, Vancouver, Canada want train whistles silenced. An 800-name petition asked that city councilors do something about high-volume air horns. According to the report, the train whistles have made life miserable for persons living near the railroad tracks. Several dozen residents appeared at a municipal council meeting with 800 names of petitioners, demanding the ban on the trains' noisy air-horns.

13. AIRPORT NOISE

Many people regularly hear the sound of aircrafts. The sound may be attractive when heard from far, but is noise if exposed at sight. Those living near civil and military airports are severely affected by aircraft's take-off and landing noise. The impact is greatest near the perimeter of the airport and below the flight paths. This source of pollution is increasing steadily during recent years and, especially close to international airports, which have already constituted a very serious problem. Higher the speed of the aircraft, greater is the level of noise pollution. This problem has mainly arisen because of the widespread use of heavy long-range supersonic jet aircrafts. Noise made by jet planes has been intrinsically more disturbing than that of propeller-driven aircraft, because it is of higher pitch. Jet noise caused by the violent mixing of the jet of gases from the engine with the surrounding air. It is maximum during take-off, when the engine has to produce maximum thrust, and falls down rapidly when the aircraft climbed up. During landing, the main source of high-frequency noise has been the whine of the air compressor and turbine blades, as the engine is throttled back. Aircraft pass close to the ground for quite a distance during the landing operation and this noise often constitutes a more sustained environmental nuisance than the intense noise of shorter duration produced during take-off.[46]

Military aircrafts' noise also often causes annoyance to the residents even in distant areas, away from airfields, because they are to be flown at low altitudes as part of their normal daily training procedures. But little can be done about this, national defence, which even in peacetime will always take priority. There is no doubt that the phenomenal growth in the field of civil aviation has proved to be a boon. But at the same time, as is the case with all modern developments, it has given rise to new problems associated with environment. The increased operations of aircrafts contribute to environmental pollution in many ways. Firstly, air pollution due to engine emissions, secondly, noise pollution by its high intensity of sound, thirdly, radio wave pollution and fourthly, vibration by audio frequencies produced by engine tests. Among these environmental pollutions, the noise pollution has had the more serious impact on the human beings, animals and the properties. The take-off and landing of an aircraft produce unbearable noise to a normal human being. Animals are also frightened by the aircraft noise. It has been observed that supersonic jet planes are one of the biggest irritants in today's noisy world. The noise of these planes may sometimes break window's panes, crack brick's plaster and shake buildings. It is known from a study in UK, at Heathrow airport, that there are more number of mental patients in comparison to other quiet places. However, currently the Government of UK has taken direct responsibility for aircraft noise management at Heathrow, Gatwick and Stansted. Measures have been introduced to reduce aircraft induced noise on preferential routes and restrictions on night flights. Maximum noise limits for departing aircraft are set and monitored and noise insulation schemes operate. Noise from aircraft on the ground is the responsibility of the airport management company. Also the Heathrow, Gatwick and Stansted are made responsible for complaints about aircraft noise, including ground noise and have their own 24 hours lines.[47]

14. AIRCRAFT NOISE AND SONIC BOOM

Whenever a solid body travels at a speed, above the speed of the sound, a sonic boom gets produced, which can be heard up to 80 Km from the point of origin. The actual pressure exerted has been found to vary with the distance above the ground. A super sonic passenger aircraft flying at a height of 12,000 meters can produce a pressure-jump at ground level up to 100 N/M^2

(127 dB), which may not bring about actual damage to buildings, but can still be an unpleasant experience for the people who hear it. Supersonic passenger aircrafts bring about some other effects, including the destruction of ozone layer in the outer atmosphere, with consequent increase of harmful radiations. The construction and sale of supersonic aircraft has been at present a matter of national prestige and economics; but from the environmental standpoint these aircrafts are undesirable.

The expert committee of U.K. has said that the super sonic transport aircraft will raise the problem of sonic boom in a much more acute form and has further said:

> An aircraft flying at super sonic speed produces a complex system of shock waves. At a large distance from the aircraft, however, this wave system degenerates into a pair of shock waves, the so-called bow and tail waves. These two waves produce the sharp rise in pressure, separated by a region of gradual fall in pressure, which the ear receives as the characteristic "sonic boom."[48]

In United States, the attempts have been made to protect public from unnecessary aircraft noise and sonic boom. In this regard, the federal Government passed the Federal Aviation Act, 1958 and the Aircraft Noise Abatement Law in 1963 and other regulations which specifically provide for the control and abatement of aircraft noise and sonic boom which includes prescribing of standards for measurement of aircraft noise and sonic boom.

Another source of noise pollution connected with aeroplanes has been the source of scaring away of birds and the noise caused by the aircraft ground support systems, i.e. the servicing activities, ground equipments, aggregates used for servicing/ starting the aircraft on ground and pre-flight operations. One method of moving birds away from airfields has been to scare them with strong noise stimuli. Various types of devices for making noise have been used for this purpose. One of these has been, automatic gas cannon, which produces loud bangs at regular intervals by exploding propane or acetylene gas. These devices are also responsible for the increase of noise pollution at the air bases.

15. SATELLITE IN SPACE—A NEW SOURCE OF AVIONICS NOISE

A new source of noise pollution has been satellite programme by various countries. The satellites are projected into the space with the aid of high explosive rockets. Application and use of these rockets produce deafening noise at the time of "lifting off" a satellite. Tonnes of explosives are used in these operations, which cause noise pollution as well as other air emissions.[49] However, no serious consideration has yet been given to this kind of noise pollution.

Although, our standard of living is being made more and more descent, by these new inventions, but very few are aware that it is at the cost of our own health such as noise hazards.

16. CONTROL OF AVIONICS NOISE

Noise, due to aircraft operations would assume serious proportion, was first declared by the world aviation community in 1968 at the 16th assembly session of the International Civil Aviation Organization (ICAO) at Buenos Aires. It was recognized that the problem of aircraft noise was so serious in the vicinity of many of the world's airports, that public reaction was mounting to such a degree, which gave course for concern and hence requires urgent solution. It was also recognized that the introduction of future aircraft types could increase and aggravate the noise problem, unless immediate action is taken to alleviate the situation. Accordingly, a resolution was passed and adopted, under which, ICAO carried out a detailed study of the noise problem and developed laws in the form of International Standards and recommended practices for aircraft noise. These standards were finally adopted by ICAO in the form of annexure 16 to the convention on International Civil Aviation. According to these standards, all aircrafts are required to be 'noise certified' by the authorities of the state of registry of aircraft, on the basis of satisfactory evidence, that the aircraft complies with necessary requirements, which are at least equal to the applicable standards, specified in annexure 16.[50]

The law in US regarding noise control programme has eight basic features. They are aircraft noise research, aircraft operations, sonic boom research, airport and land use, natural environment, legal structures and human response.[51] The Airport and Airway Development Act of 1970 declares a national policy that airport development projects shall provide for the protection of the environment.

In Great Britain, the Airport Act, 1965 empowers the Department of Trade and Industry to give instructions to the British Airport Authority for the noise abatement and sound proofing schemes.[52] Bigham opined that the most effective means to control aircraft noise must lie in an international code, designed to specify requirements in the construction of new aircraft and, possibly, in a right of individual countries to ground offending machines where a positive breach of noise regulations can be effectively proved. It should be appreciated that no aircraft can be certain of being physically able to take a precise-pre-arrangement course on take-off, or for that matter or any other time, since it will always be at the mercy of cross-winds, head and tail-winds, thermal currents and other factors. Thus, flight paths must, of necessity, be relatively broad.[53]

The *Chicago Daily Herald* reports that a new computerized system, that will help in keeping planes on a quiet take-off path may be implemented at O'Hare International Airport. According to Robert Mccoppin, a pilot using the system would monitor a special screen in the plane's cockpit that would show the quietest route to take-off. This would generally mean using a route, that avoids flying over residential areas, opting for industrial areas, forest preserves, or highways instead. These are called "Fly Quiet" flight paths. Currently, air traffic controllers communicate the pilots on RT, which routes to use, but the pilots sometimes miss a 20-degree turning point, or planes may get blown-off the course by winds. Aviation department assistant commissioner Christopher Arman has said that computerized system shall help the pilots in keeping the planes on course and away from homes. In the late 1999, planes at O'Hare, were off the course by an average of a mile between 10:00 PM and 11:00 PM, and between 6:00 AM and 7:00 AM. These are generally the times when people are trying to sleep and are most sensitive to jet noise overhead. The equipment was recently tested on a jet simulator in Denver with the cooperation of United Airlines. O'Hare would be the first airport to use the system. Many planes already have the technology on board to enable them to use the system. The plane would focus on take-offs, which are noisier on ground than that of landings.[54] Florida's *Miami Herald* reports that Miami-Dade County's Aviation Department and the Federal Aviation Administration (FAA) have reached an agreement that will allow nighttime flights out of Miami International Airport to use a different flight path that will lessen noise over residential areas such as Brickell and Key Biscayne. The agreement was announced in March 2000.[55]

India is a member-state of ICAO and has accordingly accepted the noise specifications of said annexure 16 for implementation in India. India has issued an aeronautical information circular, a legal directive, which lays down that aircraft, which is not noise certified in accordance with the said annexure 16, will not be permitted to operate in India after 31st December, 1987.

However, to reduce noise from jet aircraft during take-off, noise suppressors can be fitted, but simultaneously these reduce take-off thrust and increase fuel consumption, drag and weight. The additional operating cost caused by fitting noise suppressors to an aircraft of the size of a Boeing is too high. Here, it is very pertinent to illustrate that a proposal to quiet the jet aircraft flown by commercial air carriers, corporations and individuals has been submitted to the Federal Aviation Administration of America by its Environmental Protection Agency. To meet the proposed standard, U.S. commercial air carriers would need to spend up to $880 million over a four-year period. The carriers would be required to retrofit about 1,800 airplanes with new jet engine housings (nacelles) lined with sound absorbing material. The cost to similarly back-fit, the businessmen's jet fleet of 650 airplanes was estimated by EPA at $300 million over a four-year period.

There has been increased commercial pressure to extend night operations so as to improve the profitability of aircraft and airports. Although there is mounting public resistance against this trend, the number of night flights from most airports continues to show a steady increase.

It appears that many airlines and most civil aviation authorities have been doing much to reduce the noise nuisance from aircraft; further major improvements can only come from the re-siting of airports away from the centers of population, preferably that both, take-off and landing flight-paths have no residential locality underneath. Presently, the way to avoid the detrimental effect of noise originating at large airports is to provide, sound proofing of houses, hospitals and schools in their vicinity. Open-able double-glazed windows complete with a mechanical ventilator and equipped with a noise attenuator, can reduce aircraft noise by about 40 dB, as against a figure of 20 dB with normal single windows. Also, the residents of airport area, needs to be made aware about the health hazards of such airport noise and be educated how to avoid the noise. If no ear protecting device is with them at the time of aircraft take-off or landing, they should block their ears by hands till the noise diminishes. Also, such victimized citizens should complain the matter to appropriate authority or to the court, if they are subjected to unbearable aircraft noise. As a group of residents in Suffield, Connecticut is threatening to sue the state, if noise from planes using the Bradley International Airport is not reduced. Residents insist that the noise has grown worse this year, and have submitted a petition with 195 signatures asking that the noise be controlled.[56]

However, there are the instances, where the authorities are indifferent and do not accept the aircraft noise as unreasonable. In such cases, one should go to the courts and get enforced their right to peaceful life and sleep.

17. TACKLING ANNOYING NOISE

The Government has a policy to reduce all annoying noise. It is trying to achieve this by gradually reducing the amount of noise that any new vehicle, building work, or factory can make, and also by reducing the hours during which an annoying noise can be made. The problem is, that it is still very difficult to predict what sort of noise, and how much noise will cause someone to complain. There are various ways of measuring noise scientifically. All come out with numbers, that rarely relate to complaint levels. Without a tool that allows the prediction of complaints, it is difficult to pass laws about what is acceptable, without upsetting people whose businesses will be damaged by limiting their noise. Another problem is that of weighing people's annoyance against the cost of reducing the noise. In an ideal world, there would be no noise complaints, but while there are limited resources to spend on reducing noise, a balance needs to be found between keeping people happy, and spending the money on something more useful.

NOTES AND REFERENCES

1.   R.K. Sapru, *Environment Management in India-I*, p. 27.
2.   Pramod Singh, *Environment Pollution and Management*, p. 112.
2A. *TOI*, 29.3.2005.
3.   *Coventry Evening Telegraph*, April 6, 2000.
3A. *The Daily News* of Los Angels, October 4, 1997.
4.   G.C. Nagi, M.K. Dhillon and G.S. Dhillon, *Noise Pollution*, p. 76.
5.   Timmy·Katiyar, M. Starke, *Environmental Pollution*, p. 235.
6.   *London Free Press*, April 4, 2000.
7.   *Paryavaran Bodh*, pp. 86-87.
8.   *Supra* 2, p. 114.
9.   Parivesh Batori, *Newletter*, SPCB, Assam, January to June, 2001.
10. *Encyclopaedic Dictionary of Environmental Pollution*, p. 72.
11. *Moulana Mufti Syed Md Noorur Rehman Barkati* Vs. *State of Bengal* (AIR 1999 Cal 15).
12. Posted By *Ashok* Vs. *Chowgule*, 7 March, 1999. (ashokvc@giasbm01.vsnl.net.in).
13. 2000(3) KLT 651 = 2000 JT (9) 575 1.
13A. 2005(5) SCALE.
14   R.K. Sapru, *Environment Management in India-II*, p. 88.
15. *Supra* 5, p. 233.
16   *The Plain Dealer*, September 28, 1997, BYLINE: Olivera Perkins.
16A. 'Environmental Clearance must for Public Buildings,' *TOI*, March 14, 2005.
17   G.S. Nagi, M.K. Dhillon and G.S. Dhaliwal, *Noise Pollution*, p. 80.
18   *Ibid*.
19. *Supra* 17, p. 81.
20. *Ibid*., p. 82.
21. Real World Resources Guide,1.4.iii. Pollution-General.
22. *The Milwaukee Journal Sentinel*, October 8, 1998.
22A. 'Is Rising Ocean Noise Harming Marine Life?,' *Times of India*, April 19, 2005.
23. *Supra* 2, p. 116.
24. *Transport Noise*, leaflet 12-5, *NSCA Information*, November 2000.
25. *Problem of Urban Transportation Pollution in Delhi: Reasons and Mitigation Strategies*, a Publication of TERI, Delhi.
26. G.C. Nagi, M.K. Dhillon, G.S. Dhaliwal, *Noise Pollution*, p. 77.

27. *Ibid.*, p. 77.
28. *Supra* 5, p. 229.
29. Rule 402 of Tamilnadu Motor Vehicles Rules, 1989.
30. *M.S. Appa Rao* Vs. *Govt. of TN*, 1995 AIHC 4168.
31. Rules 114(d) of Bengal Motor Vehicles Rules, 1940.
32. Rule 119(i) of Central Motor Vehicles Rules, 1988.
33. Rule 119(ii) of Central Motor Vehicles Rules, 1988.
34. Rule 21, Bihar and Orissa Motor Vehicle Rules, 1930.
34A. Now face the music with Bike Horns, *TOI*, 7-4-2005.
35. *Supra* 5, p. 230.
36. *Ibid.*
37. H.G. Gibbs and T.H. Richards, *Stress, Vibration and Noise Analysis in Vehicles*, p. 218.
37A. *TOI*, Delhi, dated 18-4-2005 (IIT Team Designs Noiseless Bus).
37B. *TOI*, January 30, 2005.
38. Dr. Mahesh Mathur, *Legal Control of Environmental Pollution*, p. 178.
39. *Ibid.*, p. 179.
40. *Supra* 37, p. 12.
41. Government Notification G.S.R. 742 (E) dated 25th September, 1986.
42. Clause 3 of *ibid.* notification.
43. Clause 5 of *ibid.* notification.
44. Information received by the author from an engineer of railway during the interview.
45. G.K. Nagi, M.K. Dhillon, G.S. Dhaliwal, *Noise Pollution*, p. 78.
46. *Supra* 5, p. 231.
47. *Ibid.*, pp. 232-33.
48. Dr. Mahesh Mathur, *Legal Control of Environmental Pollution*, p. 207.
49. R.K. Sapru, *Environment Management in India-II*, p. 88.
50   R.P. Anand Rahamutulla Khan and S. Bhatt, *Law, Science and Environment*, pp. 89-90.
51. *Supra* 48, p. 208.
52. *Ibid.*, 35.
53. *Supra* 5.
54. *Chicago Daily Herald*, April 8, 2000.
55. *Miami Herald*, April 4, 2000.
56. *The Hart Ford Courant*, October 2, 1997.

Evil Effects of Noise Pollution

The state of the health of people does not depend upon the number of doctors and hospitals, a city or a village has; but depends upon clean environment because if it is conducive to spread diseases, the state of health of the people has to be poor. Nonetheless, the system has to be preventive as well as curative and both are important. Nearly 80% of diseases, and more so in this developing world, can be linked with environmental pollution.[1]

> "When the lamp is scattered
>   The light in the dust lies dead
> When the light is scattered
>   The rainbow's glory is shed
> When the environment is slapped
>   The ecology is imbalanced
> When the pollution is caused
>   The poisoned inheritance is handed over
>   (to the next generation)."

The environmental degradation may be caused by single or

interaction of several sources of environmental pollution like noise, air or water. It is very difficult to discuss the effects of pollution that, it is merely on account of any one particular pollutant. In many cases, the combined effects of two or more pollutants are more severe or even qualitatively different from the individual effects of the isolated pollutant, a phenomenon that is known as 'synergism'. But sometimes, the combined effects of two pollutants are less rather than more severe, and this situation is referred to as 'antagonism'. Yet, these various sources of pollution are bound to have damaging effects on the behaviour of living as well as of non-living beings and some of the effects are so serious that they create risk even for their very survival. Frightened by these consequences, psychologists, scientists, administrators and legal experts have started studying the effects of these pollutants on different and various manners.[2]

In Unites States, one of the healthiest countries in the world, infants born in parts of Mississippi Delta region or the inner cities of Washington, D.C., or Baltimore, Maryland, have life expectancies similar to those in such developing countries as Namibia, Lesotho, or India.[3] According to a news released from Washington by Wilfried Karmaus-from—"a change in the proportion of boys to girls indicates that contaminants may play a role in human reproduction, he said that PCBs, the endocrine disruptors which are also known as dioxins, are reported to caused cancer, birth defects, and sexual organs in fish alligators which may be true in case of human too. Studies by the WHO suggest that pollution causes health hazards even at its levels much lower than those considered safe."[4]

Before 1972, environment was the exclusive preserve of sanitary engineers and health officers. But from 1972 onwards, the thinking got changed and it was realized that to cater the perpetuation of living systems (including human kind) on this planet, conservation of life support system becomes more essential.[5]

Important conclusions drawn by the citizen's Report of 1982,[6] released by the Centre for Science and Environment, regarding the state of environmental health of India shows that India faces two-fold burden of disastrous diseases. Because, most of the old diseases continue to be in rampant, while new ones are making rapid strides and hence the Indian death rate is no longer coming down. For instance:

(a) Diarrhoea's attack upon children in particular.
(b) Three dies every minute, above 1.5 million every year. This constitutes a permanent epidemic in our country.
(c) Most of the time, the water pipes remains empty and sewerage water gets mixed with the drinking water and the Hepatitis disease is increasing by leaps and bounds. This disease is not yet much noticeable.
(d) Increasing use of cigarettes and bidis, and greater use of chemicals because of the industrialization already results in half a million deaths from cancer every year.

The Citizens' Fifth Report[7] on the current state of India's environment, analyses and highlights two important themes, relevant to India's environmental future. First, if India learns from the outstanding work, undertaken in 1980s and 1990s, it will ensure that these efforts are replicated on a large scale in ecological regions, to which they are applicable; a large part of India's rural poverty can be wiped out in next 10-20 years. Second, India's urban areas, if continued reeling under increasing pollution, traffic-congestion and wastes, it shall make urban life almost unbearable. Thus, despite the rural situation gets improving, India would need innovative strategies, to address the environmental problems in the urban sector.

At least 11 million children of the world die every year, on account of poisons in their homes, in the form of contaminated drinking water, polluted air and noisy environment, which could be avoided. According to the recent research of this year, 2005, the Environmental Pollutants from domestic and industrial waste and pesticides could be changing the ratio of sex chromosomes in sperm. The author found that Swedish fishermen exposed to high levels of organochlorine pollutants have a higher proportion of the male 'Y' chromosomes in their sperm.[7A] Noise pollution damages their brain itself. According to an international study, released in July 1998, New Delhi is one of the world's most polluted 15 cities and of Asia's 13 such cities. Inside houses, 4 million people, mostly children under 5 years of age, die of acute respiratory infections caused due to the environmental pollution. One out of five residents of Delhi, suffers from breathing problems and according to doctors it is 5% at the national level. Respiratory diseases are one of the biggest killers in the state of Rajasthan. According to a National Family Health Survey, 1993 this state represents 3% of total cases and 7% of the deaths, due to acute respiratory diseases (ARI), amongst children under the age of five years. The National Family Health Survey (NFHS-I) Report, 2002 reveals that tuberculosis and disease of the respiratory tract cause the highest number of deaths and a good percentage of it is definitely due to the environmental pollution.[8] There has been a 50 percent increase in asthma cases in the last 10 years, and the respiratory disorder caused partially through environment pollution has risen dramatically throughout developed countries. Infact, one-fourth of the children in Delhi of pre-school age are recurrent wheezers, says Dr. Sanjiv Bagai of Batra Hospital. Post Diwali and upto February, it can be a particularly bad time for these children as in the mourn of November 2004, about 40-50% of cases in OPD have been related to respiratory orders, added Dr. Bajai.[8A]

Suresh Prabhakar Prabhu, when he was minister for environment and forests, estimated for treating the effects of environmental pollution on health in India, costs 240 billion rupees annually. Long back in 1961, the 'Time' Magazine estimated that the cost against noise pollution, which American industry pays is 2 million dollars,[9] a day in the form of compensation, lost hours and diminished efficiency. Not only the modern world is harping with noise pollution, but even the primitive world was also not untouched to this kind of malady. Though, the vehicular pollution was less in ancient times, yet the noise pollution was the cause due to which Julius Caesar banned the movement of chariots in Rome after sunset.

Not only India, the noise pollution engulfs all parts of each country, appearing on map of the world. For example, noise pollution, in different industrial locations in Kathmandu, is posing health hazards to the workers. In-door noise caused by machines and processes in industries, causes impact vibration or reciprocation movements, friction and turbulence in air or gas streams.

In a research paper, presented by 4 Nepalese scientists two years back has shown some glaring facts about noise pollution caused by 30 industries of Kathmandu Valley. The study carried out with the support of the Royal Nepal Academy of Science and Technology focused on different industries, i.e. textile, plastic, iron, steel and other noise producing industries. Scientists used an integrating sound level meter, NL-05, to monitor the noise levels in these industries. It was found that the textile industries produced the highest level of noise, exceeding the permissible noise limit of 90 decibel (dB) for 8 hours exposure. The highest recorded noise level was 120 decibels (dB) in Balaju Textile Area.

According to Occupational Safety and Health Act (OSHA), a federal legislation, noise level beyond 90 decibels becomes a health hazard. The same is the standard, set by International Labour Organisation (ILO) Convention No. 148, concerning the protection to workers against occupational hazards of pollution. 631 industrial workers were found suffering from physical diseases due to noise pollution. The effects of noise pollution may not be immediately visible but the deafness, poor concentration, irritation, nervousness, aggressive social behaviour, anxiety, heart diseases and high blood pressure were recorded at the later stage. The ultimate effect of noise pollution is the temporary or permanent elimination of the workforce through sick leave or early retirement, and as a consequence, the nation suffers a great economic loss.[10]

1. SPECIFIC IMPACTS OF NOISE

No one on earth can escape from the noise, an unwanted and disturbing sound, which causes a nuisance, in the eye of the beholder. Noise is a disturbance to the human environment, which is escalating with such a high rate, that it has proved to be a major threat to the quality of human lives. The noise in all areas, especially in urban, has been increasing rapidly, the adverse effects of which, are numerous on human environment.

As said, almost everyone has had one experience of being victim of temporary "deafness" on account of loud noise, often accompanied by ringing in the ears, though not permanent. For the normal hearing to return back takes few hours. The loss of partial hearing is called Temporary Threshold Shift (TTS). A TTS may be experienced at a gun firing point or after a long drive in the car, with the windows open. This type of exposure to noise does not have to be as loud as a gun being fired; it can be as simple as a person shouting in the room. The loss is caused by the destruction of the delicate hair cells and their auditory nerve connections, in the Organ of Corti, which is contained in the cochlea. Every exposure to loud noise destroys some cells, but prolonged exposure damages a larger amount of cells, and ultimately collapses the Organ of Corti, which causes deafness

In *Moulana Mufti Syed Md. Noorur Rehman Barkati* Vs. *State of Bengal*,[11] it has been accepted by the court that, there can not be any dispute to the fact that sound is known source of pollution. The adverse and ill-effects of sound has tremendous impact on the nervous system of human being.

Also, in Church of God's case, court observed as under:

"In these days, the problem of noise pollution has become more serious with the increasing trend towards industrialization, urbanization and modernization and is having many evil effects including danger to health. It may cause interruption of sleep, affect communication, loss of efficiency, hearing loss or deafness, high blood pressure, depression, irritability, fatigue, a gastrointestinal problems, allergy, distraction, mental stress and annoyance, etc. This also affects animals alike. The extent of damage depends upon the duration and the intensity of noise. Sometimes it leads to serious law and order problem. Further, in an organized society, rights are related with duties towards others including neighbours.

According to an article, which appeared in August 1982 issue of *Science Today* and *ICMR Bulletin* of July 1979 containing a Study on noise pollution in South India, wherein it was pointed out that it will lead to serious nervous disorders, emotional tension leading to high blood pressure, cardiovascular diseases, increase in cholesterol level resulting in heart attacks and strokes and even damage to the foetus.

Be it the Pollution of any kind, it may cause serious damage to man, animals, birds, aquatic life, crops, and vegetation, etc. Generation of unreasonable noise of any kind in the environment is regarded as a form of pollution and is very dangerous for human life, which lowers the quality of life. Although, it can not be ruled out that rhythmic musical/dancing sound stimulates the brain activities, removes boredom and fatigue. But excess of the same shall also prove detrimental. Characteristically, the noise has been called as a 'slow agent of death' by a physicist, founder of the Acoustical Society of America and a former Chancellor of California University.[12] Further, the research has proved that a loud noise, during peak marketing hours creates tiredness and irritation, which impairs activities of the brain, so as to reduce thinking power and working abilities. Noise levels in excess of 90 dB can cause loss of hearing. Single exposure of the 150 dB is known to cause permanent injury to the ear's internal mechanism.[13] A prolonged exposure to noise may contract the blood vessels, which may result into hypertension. Loud sound can cause an increased secretion of many hormones of the pituitary gland, e.g. adrenal-corticotrophin hormone (ACTH). ACTH, in turn, stimulates the adrenal gland, which secretes several other hormones and triggers various effects:

(a) Enhancement of the sensitivity of the body to adrenalin;
(b) Increase of blood-sugar levels;
(c) Suppression of immune system; and
(d) Decreasing the efficiency of liver and to detoxified blood.[14]

During pregnancy, noise pollution adversely affects the development of fetus. Constant exposure to noise, between 110-120 dB can produce narrowing of vision and vertigo, which shall cause disruption of equilibrium in the unborn baby.[15] A study of noise pollution, undertaken in a mechanical workshop, located at Roorkee, where the sound level was observed to vary from 75 dB(A) to 140 dB(A), is quite relevant to mention here. In this study, 13 workers were exposed to different levels of noise, as a sample survey. The subjective study was conducted through questionnaire. It was found that adverse effects were related to the intensity of noise levels, as well as the duration of exposure. Headache was reported to occur 'below normal' to 35.7% of workers, memory loss to 23.2% and annoyance to 60.7%. High blood pressure caused to 51.8% of workers. The time taken to recoup was 8 seconds by 20.5% of the workers, after exposure to noise.[16]

In a recent judgment, the court of Japan has observed that the ailments like stomach-ulcers, sleeplessness and hearing difficulties are caused due to the noise of jet flights. The court, while awarding the compensation to the people of Fukuto city, based its judgment on the aforesaid finding.

In another case, Hachioji Division of Tokyo district, awarded compensation to the inhabitants, living near the U.S. Air Force base, on the ground of noise pollution, which prevented them from sleep.

It is also a fact that the effects of noise are difficult to quantify, as peoples' tolerance to noise levels is different and varies considerably. However, there is scientific literature available at large which analyzes and assesses the effects of noise on human beings. The most recent and most comprehensive is, the WHO report, 'Community Noise—Environmental Health Criteria', which points out that the environmental noise may have a number of direct adverse effects, on people exposed, including disturbance of sleep, auditory and non-auditory physiological—basically cardiovascular—effects, interference with communication and general annoyance. Exposure to environmental noise causes noise induced hearing loss, where exposure is high over a long period.

The noise interferes with our activities at three levels:

Firstly, 'audio-logical level', i.e. interfering with the satisfactory performance of the hearing mechanism;
Secondly, 'biological level', i.e. interfering with the biological functioning of the body; and
Thirdly, 'behavioral level', i.e. affecting the sociological behaviour of the subjects.

To sum up, the effects upon human performance, physiology and psychology,[17] are given table on next page, which shows the effects of high intensity noise.[18]

Sl. No.	Noise Intensity (in decibels)	Effects
1.	0	Threshold of hearing
2.	0-25	Not significant difficulty with faint speech[19]
3.	25-40	Difficulty with faint speech
4.	40-55	Frequent difficulty with normal speech
5.	55-70	Frequent difficulty with loud speech
6.	80	Irritation
7.	90	Loss of hearing power
8.	100	Significant change in pulse rate
9.	110	Stimulations of reception in skin
10.	120	Threshold of pain
11.	130	Nausea, vomiting, dizziness
12.	150	Prolonged exposure causing burning skin
13.	160-190	Major permanent damage in a short time

And, in the next table given below, the impacts of noise stresses upon human responses are shown:[20]

Sl. No.	Impacts	Responses
1.	Hearing impairment	Hearing impairment: Temporary Hearing Impairment: Permanent Tinnitus
2.	Physiological impacts	Cardiovascular constriction (High blood pressure, heart attacks, heart beat increase, Gastro-intestinal modification (ulcers) Intestinal spasm Endocrine stimulation Respiratory modification Skin resistance alteration Headache Muscular tension Neurological disorder Dilation of pupil Paling of skin Blinking Dryness of mucous Adrenal secretion
3.	Communication Interference	Interruption in face to face talking Interruption in telephonic conversation

Sl. No.	Impacts	Responses
4.	Task Interference	Reduced work efficiency Increased proneness to accidents
5.	Sleep Interference	Awakening Medication Sleep stage alteration
6.	Personal Behaviour	Annoyance Fear Anxiety Nervousness Misfeasance Fatigue Startled response.

2. NATURE OF ILL-EFFECTS

(a) Psychological Effects

No doubt, the noise has many disastrous psychological effects on human beings. The question is how these effects can be assessed? And whether they lead to any damage? No clear case has been pointed out so far, in which, exclusive psychological damage is caused by high levels of noise. The levels that would cause hearing damage, only a small fraction of the people are exposed to it. Indeed, fears have been expressed that ". . . over emphasis on damage may backfire, when people come to realize that the truth of the matter seems to be simply, that people can express violently their dislike about being disturbed by noises. In Italy, a 44-year-old man, took an overdose of drugs because his eleven children made too much noise while he was watching the Olympic Games on television.[21]

What turns a sound into noise and becomes unpleasant or irritating to the ear, is a matter of psychology. So whether a sound is regarded as a noise and how noisy, depends upon the fact that who causes the noise and his relationship with person who hears it.[22] To a large extent, noise reaction varies with attitude of the individual to the noise cause and its source.

Number of behavioural changes, in human beings as well in animals are noticed and recorded, as a result of exposure to high-level noise. Certain symptoms have been observed clearly. The undesired sound does cause annoyance. Intolerable agony may also result when the source of the sound is not known. Interruptions in speech communications may impair performance, leads to errors, lower the output, and decreases efficiency. Noise causes tension in muscles, nervousness, irritability and strain.[23]

(b) Physiological Effects

The adverse effects of noise pollution on the human beings are manifested through physiological indications, such as loss of hearing, occupational deafness and noise induced diseases. Empirical researches conducted on pregnant female mice, have revealed that aircraft's taking-off which brings in 120-150 dB of noise levels, has caused miscarriages in them. Several birds have been observed to stop laying eggs. Apart from this the animals change their places of residence, if noise source existed there. It is also observed that, there is a decrease of number in migratory birds to their usual place, if it is subjected to noise. The rule of generalisability, if applied, high noise is capable to create these disturbances in human beings also.[24] Prolonged chronic noise can also produce stomach ulcers as it may reduce the flow of gastric juice and change its acidity. It may lead to abortions and other congenital defects in unborn children.[25]

In a separate study, data from a government health census in Seatle comparing mortality rates for those living near its airport with those of the city overall, found that infant mortality near the airport was 50% greater, heart diseases 57% greater, and cancer 37% greater.[26]

(c) Hearing Loss

In medical term, the loss of hearing is addressed by 'trauma' disease and the cause of this disease is the weakening of organ 'Corti' of human hearing mechanism. Hearing deafness depends upon three factors: (i) the level of noise; (ii) the pressure and frequency of sound waves; and (iii) the period of exposure to noise everyday. At one time, it was estimated that in the United States alone, 11 million adults and 3 million children suffer from some form of hearing-loss, on account of exposure to unreasonable noise.[27] Any noise, greater than 85 dB(A) can damage hearing power, if the human ear has been exposed to it over an extended period. Medical experts now believe that our hearing worsens with age partly because of exposures to the typical noise of our industrialized society. Dr. Samual Rosen, ear surgeon from Mount Sinal School of Medicine in New York, studied the Mabaans, a primitive African tribe living in quite environment. He found that Mabaan man of 75 can hear as much as the average 25 year old American man.[28]

Workers on noisy jobs must be made aware of the cumulative impacts of noise at work plus noise at home. At work, no worker should be exposed to sound levels in excess of the limits. For, noise exposure consisting of several periods of exposure at different levels, the daily noise dose 'D' should not extend unity. Since the daily noise dose to a worker, exceeds or approaches unity, worker may be risking permanent hearing damage. Further, if the worker comes home and uses power tools, or drive snowmobile or plays an instrument in a rock band, the added noise exposure heightens the risk of hearing impairment.

(d) Effects on Communication

External sounds are able to interfere with conversation and use of the telephone, as well as the enjoyment of radio and television programmes and like pastimes. It can thus, affect the efficiency of offices, schools and other places where communication has been of vital importance. The maximum accepted level of noise under such conditions has been 55 dB. 70 dB is considered very noisy and serious interference with verbal communications but so much noise is inevitable.

(e) Sleep Interference[29]

The sleep pattern is defined as a natural, regularly recurring condition of rest, and is essential for normal body and mental maintenance and recuperation from illness. Noise can affect the depth, continuity, duration and recuperative value of sleep. Chief among annoying noises have been those that interrupt sleep. Sleep is a human treasure, which is so important, that if it is broken in between, we may miss it for the whole night, which can further make individual short-tempered, weary and may yearn for a mid-day nap. In a social survey, carried out amongst people living in the vicinity of Palam Airport,[30] 22% people complained that they sometimes found difficulty in getting to sleep because of airport noises. In areas, where the noise level was particularly high, upto 50% complained about noise. Higher percentage stated that they got awakened by high intensity noises, usually early at night, when sleep was not yet deep, whereas medical science advocates that sound sleep is essential for physical as well as emotional health of each living being. Noise can interfere with sleep even when the sleeper has been not consciously awakened. Canadian scientists, studying the impact of noise on sleepers, exposed test subjects to a recording of the noise impact from a passing truck, plied at a selected peak level several times a night. At the level of 40 dB(A), they reported that there was a 5 percent probability of getting awakened by the subjects. At 70 dB(A) level, the same probability was recorded as 30%. However, when significant changes in the electro encephalogram records of the sleeping subjects had been taken into account, the probability of a shift in sleep level (up to and including awakening) rose to 10% at 40 dB(A) and to 70% at 70 dB(A). Also Dr. Colin Herridge, a British Psychiatrist, found in a two years study that persons living alongside London's Heathrow airport have a significantly higher rate of admission to mental hospitals then persons living in socially similar but quieter areas.[31] Here, it is worth to mention, if it is impossible to reduce external noises and it becomes too necessary to insulate swellings effectively to counteract it, many techniques for sound insulation are available today and can be applied at relatively modest expense.

(f) Speech Interference

A measurement has been worked out to determine the level at which noise interferes with speech. The speech interference level PSIL or SIL was developed to evaluate cabin noise in aircrafts. The PSIL is the arithmetic average of the sound pressure in the 500 Hz, 1000 Hz, and 2000 Hz octave bands. It is still being used in the aircrafts. It has also been used to evaluate the acoustics of rooms in homes, classes, auditoriums, and offices. Although, the PSIL is a useful technical tool. Noise in homes can be evaluated equally well with A-weighted noise ratings.[32]

(g) Hurts to Children

The loud music that children listen to on radio, stereos,

earphones, in discos, and at concerts, impairs their hearing. Studies show that noise interferes with learning and lowers reading and math scores. Children will be deprived of these skills and will be partially deaf by the time they are grown unless we act to lessen noise.

Noise can influence unborn babies, malformation in the fetus's nervous system that may affect behaviour later in life. Dr. Lester Sontag of the Fells Research Institute in Yellow Springs Ohio, found that starting sounds can quicken a human fetus's heart-rate and cause its muscles to contract. According to the national family health survey, the state of Rajasthan contributed 3% of all cases and 7% of deaths due to acute respiratory diseases (ARI) amongst children under the age of five years.[33]

Airport noise is harmful to the health and well-being of children and may cause lifelong problems.[34] According to the above referred study, the constant roar from jet aircraft can seriously affect, the health and psychological well-being of children. The health problems resulting from chronic airport noise, including higher blood pressure and boosted levels of stress hormones, the researchers say, may have lifelong effects.

"This study is probably the most definitive proof that noise causes stress and is harmful to humans," says Gary Evans, a professor of design and environmental analysis in Cornell's College of Human Ecology. This is, he says, the first longitudinal study of noise and human beings to look at the same group of individuals before and after noise pollution.

Other studies have been cross-sectional, comparing people exposed to noise and to well-matched controls who were not subjected to noise. Evans, an environmental psychologist and an international expert on environmental stress (such as noise, crowding and air pollution) and his German and Swedish colleagues, Monika Bullinger and Staffan Hygge, respectively, looked at 217 third- and fourth-grade children in rural areas 22 miles from Munich, Germany, before and after the opening of a new airport.

About half of the children, live in an area under the flight path of the new international airport; the others, who were matched for age, parental jobs, family size and socio-economic status, live in quiet areas. The children were tested for blood pressure, stress hormone levels and quality of life, six months before the airport was completed as well as six and 18 months after it opened.

The children in the chronic noise group experienced modest but significant increases in blood pressure and significant increases in stress hormones (epinephrine, norepinephrine and cortisol) while the children in the quiet areas experienced no significant changes. Eighteen months after the airport opened, the children exposed to the chronic aircraft noise also reported a significant decline in their quality of life.

"Although the increases in blood pressure were modest in the children living under the flight path, they may predict a greater likelihood of having higher blood pressure throughout adulthood," says Evans. There are indications, he says, that elevated blood pressure in childhood predicts higher blood pressure later in life.

Boosts in stress hormones also are of concern, because they indicate that noise induces physiological stress. These hormones are linked to adult illnesses, some of which are life-threatening, including high blood pressure, elevated lipids and cholesterol, heart disease and a reduction in the body's supply of disease-fighting immune cells.

Evans' and his colleagues' new study adds powerful evidence to cross-sectional and animals studies which have shown higher stress levels in children and adults working and living in chronically noisy environments. Also the study reveals that New York children living near an international airport tended to be poor listeners and did not read as well as matched children in quiet schools. The study was supported, in part, by the Society for the Psychological Study of Social Issues, the National Institutes of Health, the Nordic Scientific Group for Noise Effects, the Swedish Environmental Protection Agency and the German Research Foundation.

(h) Behavioural Effects

By lowering down the auditory sensibility of person, noise results in poor attention and concentration. It has been observed that the performance of school children is poor in 'comprehension' tasks, whose schools are situated in busy areas of a city and suffer from noise pollution. Noise causes irritations, which results in learning disabilities. Sudden noise distracts a person and can create nervousness in him. Housewives working in kitchen with all kinds of electric gadgets have been seen to get headache due to noise and vibrations of these gadgets.[35] According to Lehmann, studies show that workers in noisy environment tend to be more quarrelsome at work, than those doing equivalent jobs, but who are not subjected to similar noise stresses[36] Perhaps this may be the reason that our saints had always selected lonely place for meditation, away from residential localities and free from noise, preferably in the hilly unapproachable areas. Reports confirm that Astronauts subjected to a reproduction of 145 decibels of noise of a jet engine at full thrust, find difficulty in carrying out simple arithmetic operations and they were inclined to put down any answer in order to end the experiment.[37]

(i) Personological Effects Produced by Noise[38]

If, the injurious effects of noise tend to persist for longer period, it may cause stable mal-adoptive reactions in the individual, disturbing his total personality make up. The lowered performance level in children, may develop a feeling of inadequacy, lack of confidence, poor perception of one's own self, which may jeopardize optional personological development of a growing child. Once, the feeling of inaptness, worthlessness, and inadequacy are developed by a child in the growing age, its disastrous effects are not going to be removed easily for the whole life, without leaving their marks behind.

(j) Effects on Soldiers

The soldiers are also not unaffected from the harms, caused by the noise. They are exposed to noises caused by artillery practices, various equipments used by the military, vehicular movements, aircraft/ship engines, etc. It is a well-known fact that, the soldiers do not move in steps while crossing over bridge. Reason being, it could have produced dynamite results, if crossed in steps. During World-War II, the soldiers of Germany used noise, as a weapon. After surrounding the enemy, they caused so much noise, that the enemy soldiers surrendered then and there, without any battle.[39] In a recent judgment, Japanese Court found that ailments like stomach ulcers, sleeplessness and hearing difficulties are caused due to the noise of jet flights. The court while awarding the compensation to the people of Fukuto city, based its judgment on aforesaid findings relating to health hazards. In another case, Hachioji division of Tokyo district awarded compensation to inhabitants living in the area near U.S. Air Force base, on the ground of noise pollution, that disturbed their peaceful sleep. These facts certainly raise a question, against ill-effects of noise, on the health of soldiers. Once, the avionics-noise is proved detrimental to the health of people, residing near the airports/Air Force bases, one can understand the plight of the health of the soldiers, who not only reside within such installations, but also, regularly work at such highly noise causing sources itself. Therefore, there is a great need to pay attention and safeguard the health of those, who safeguard the boundaries of the nation.

(k) On Birds and Animals

The environmental pollution is known to produce eye and respiratory irritation in birds as well as animals, like in humans. Some empirical research conducted on pregnant female mice, reveals that aircraft's take-off which brings in 120-150 dB of noise, caused miscarriages in them. Several birds have been observed to have stopped laying eggs when subjected to excessive noise. Apart from this, the animals change their places. It is also observed that, there is a decrease of number in migratory birds to a place, if it is subjected to noise. Mankind has even made the use of the sensitivity of some animals to certain pollutants. For example, the use of canaries to detect poisonous gases in coal mines and nerve gasses near trains carrying it.[40]

Animals are susceptible to the effect of intense noise. Mink farmers can lose a majority of their animals in the killing frenzy, which the female minks undergo after being exited by a sonic-boom. Laboratory exposure of animals to short loud sounds can cause diverse effects, such as temporary rise in breathing and heart rates, a rise of blood pressure, or a lessoned flow of gastric juice. These responses, quickly subside on the cease of noise cause. Laboratory experiments have proved that sound with an intensity of 150-160 decibels is fatal to certain animals. The animals suffered from burn spasms and paralysis before dying. Sport fish are believed to be hype-sensitive to sound. Guinea pigs, exposed to short periods of abnormal, but supposedly tolerable noise, have developed swollen inside the membranes and vital auditory ear hair cells have been destroyed. Prolonged exposure to excessive noise has rendered the rats, to lose their fertility and eat their young ones. If loud enough, say for instance of 150 decibels, the noise eventually kills them through heart failures.[41]

A reference of English case, which shows the effects of noise on breeding system of birds, is quite relevant here. In this case, the plaintiff who was running the business of breeding silver foxes on their land, was granted injunction against the defendant (an adjoining land owner), restraining him from causing gun shots, on the ground that it adversely affected the foxes in their breeding seasons. When such foxes are disturbed by any loud noise, they stop breeding during that season, may miscarry or kill their own young ones.[42]

(I) On Acoustic Animals[43]

Imagine, if our world was full of blaring sound and intense light, then it would have been very difficult to find food or to locate our family. At any time, if the sound and light came so close, that we could become deaf and blind or even worse—the intense sound could cause internal hemorrhage leading to death. The above is equally true about the marine life. Most of the marine life relies on sound for their survival. For the last several years, the U.S. Navy has been moving ahead with plans to deploy Low Frequency Active Sonar, or LFAS—a new extended-range submarine-detection system that will introduce into the oceans of the world, a noise which is billion times more intense than that, known to disturb large whales. Now the National Marine Fisheries Service has proposed to introduce a permit system that would allow the Navy to proceed with LFAS deployment, and in the process, to harass, injure, or even kill marine mammals, while flooding the ocean with intense noise.

Active sonar, which floods the ocean with high noise, has been now suspected against previous standing. Analysis of the heads of several dead whales has enabled the scientists to confirm for the first time, the dangerous role of active sonar to a level of certainty, which even the Navy has not ignored. Not all, but one of the whales suffered hemorrhages in and around the ear, almost certainly, as a result of acoustic trauma. A marine scientist observed that at least one of the whale species that stranded in the Bahamas had virtually disappeared from the area. This raises the questions about the impacts of noise, well beyond the initial stranding and deaths.

(m) On Plants

Like human being, agriculture and horticulture also, are affected, by environmental pollution. The characteristic types of injury, caused by photochemical smog, have become so severe in some parts of the world, that it has become almost impossible to grow orchids, spinach, romaine lettuce, swiss-chard, and some other leafy plants. Even when pollution levels have been not high enough to produce noticeable injury, retardation of growth may occur. Some plants are more sensitive than others, to the pollution, be it air, water, or noise.[44]

A study by Denwar Dorothy, reveals that rock music has negative impact on the plants, whereas classical music shown positive effects on the same plants. The roots of the plants have been seen to divert, away the direction of sound and the growth of 'Pentunium plant' came almost into halt. On the other hand, 'Squash-wine plant' shown its love to music by way of wrapping around the radio, through which, sweat melodious classical music was being played. Even, pentunium plant started to bloom with six beautiful flowers in addition to becoming healthier alongwith its roots.[45] These results of Dorothy's study persuade the researcher and the same study was done second time, in which, the same was reiterated. The same was averred by Cratchman, Prof. of Agriculture Experiment Station in Ohio, and Dr. John Wilestern, an Agriculturist. Dr. T.C.N. Singh of Annamalai University, after various experiments, revealed that the growth of the plants get retardation once exposed to high sounds, i.e. noise pollution, whereas same plant has shown, not only the positive growth, but also increase in production capacity from 60%-100%, once exposed to sweat melodies at low volume.[46]

(n) On Non-Living Beings

The pollutants are able to accelerate the deterioration of material and constructions. Air pollutants, particularly sulfur dioxide gas, and the sulfuric acid aerosols, into which the gas is converted in the atmosphere, can corrode metals and building materials, increases the frequency of repair and replacements.[47] No one in India, is perhaps unknown with the dangers to the monuments like historic 'Taj Mahal', from the environmental pollution.

The high intensity of noise affects properties also, such as buildings, materials, and metals. The cracks in the city of the Recco Church, at Stemhausan, were caused by some booms. The damage has been noticed within structure of the aircraft itself, which produces high decibels of noise. However, the depreciation of the value of property for residential purposes near airports and other noisy areas is a fact, well-known to all.[48] The danger to the non-living beings, can be noticed from the fact that the British aircraft 'Concord' is not allowed to fly over India, because of the destructive cracks, found in the building of ATC, caused during its test flight.

(o) On Law and Order, and National Integration

Noise has created and may further create the problem of law and order also. There are reported cases, in which the noise of loudspeakers has resulted in to communal riots. Such type of incidents took place in the city of Meerut, in April 1987.[49] The incident was repeated second time in the same city, and created the problem of law and order. Indiscriminate use of loudspeakers from religious places and platforms instigated the people of one sect against another, and thrown the city into the flames of communal riots, resulting into the loss of innocent lives and destruction of public and private property. To control this situation, an order, u/s 144, CrPC, was issued by the Addl. District Magistrate, mainly to check and control the use of loudspeakers. It is pertinent to mention, that the situation in the city had become so critical that the popular 'Nauchandi Fair', a famous exhibition of northern India, had to be suspended. The incident had developed a feeling of insecurity among the people, around the city for a longer time.

Another incident of communal riots, due to the noise, was caused by the indiscriminate use of loudspeaker in Moradabad city, of same State (UP). On April 4, 1990, loudspeaker was being used at the place of worship, which was objected by the persons of other community. The communal riots resulted into the exchange of stone throwing and destruction of the property, of innocent persons. Several shops were looted and put to fire and disrupted the peaceful life of the people.[50] Further, it has also been noticed that in recent years, the frequent use of loudspeaker and use of musical appliances by the extremist, especially in the States of J&K and Punjab, has become a means of propagation of anti-national activities, threatening national integrity of the country.[51]

An incident of Criminal assault, on account of noise pollution, arose wherein high pitch of noise, caused by the audio CD Player of an autoriksha, became the cause of action. When traffic police asked to down-volume, another police constable, sitting inside the autoriksha, assaulted the noise-controlling officer. The incident resulted into a case of criminal assault and noise nuisance.[52]

Recently a petition has been filed before Supreme Court of India. The immediate provocation for filing the petition was that a 13 year old girl was a victim of rape whose cries for help sunk and went unheard due to blaring noise of music over loudspeaker in the neighbourhood. The victim girl, later in the evening, set herself ablazed and dead of 100% burn injuries.[52A]

It shows that the noise created by the indiscriminate use of loudspeakers has become nuisance in the normal life of the people besides creating a problem of law and order and that of national integration, which has posed a threat to the solidarity.

(p) Effects on Economy

The noise pollution has its impact on national economy also. Suresh Prabhakar Prabhu, when he was minister for environment and forests, estimated for treating the effects of environmental pollution on health in India costs 240 billion rupees annually. Long back in 1961, the *'Time'* Magazine estimated that the cost against noise pollution, which American industry, pays is 2 million dollars,[53] a day in the form of compensation, lost hours and diminished efficiency. Dr. Virendra of industrial city Kanpur has done an intensive study on 'noise and its evil effects'. The study reveals that, apart from the vehicles, the machineries are the second source of noise, which run continuously irrespective of day and night. These industries emit almost all kinds of pollutants including noise. The residents living in the vicinity of cotton industries are the most victims of noise. The intensity of noise has been recorded 105 dB in the shade of cloth manufacturing. It is a matter of shocking that the employee of these industries either have lost their hearing power or are suffering with the mental diseases on account of noise at work.[54] Another study[55] by scientist Dr. Shrivastav and Dr. Bihari of Industrial Poison Institute, Lucknow, heartens that industrial deafness has become a common disease among the industrial employees. The level of noise was ranging from 63 dB to 97 dB was caused to raug raug plant, breaker plant, and the molding plant of the paper mill. According to the study, the deafness has been the bonus paid to the employees of this mill, howsoever short may be period of his service. However, the employees, who have adopted ear protective devices, e.g. ear plugs, ear muffs, ear defenders have less impact of noise and therefore, lost lesser hearing power in comparison to others, who have not used any ear protective device. This study reveals that there is no relation between age and deafness as all employees have lost their hearing power irrespective of their age.

3. OBSERVATION

In nature there are neither rewards nor punishments—there are violent consequences, though slow.[56]

All of us, children and adults, are bombarded every day by noises and sounds that have a deleterious effect on our brain and well-being. Whether in the classroom, office or living room, our ears and brain constantly have to work hard to "tune out" these sounds in order to focus in on family, studies, or the task at hand. For sensitive children and adults, environmental noise pollution can be a constant source of stress. Imagine, being hypersensitive to specific frequencies of sound; having an auditory sequential processing problem; having a short attention span.

Now, imagine to filter out the sound of a jet plane flying over head, the car going down the street; your mother's breathing, your brother's rock music coming from upstairs; the hum of the computer, air conditioner and to top it all off, the noises coming from inside your own ears.

Conclusively, it can be said, that most of us in the society are now aware of the fact that noise can damage hearing power. Short of a threat, this disaster is certainly going to overtake the human race, if nothing is done to mitigate the malady of noise pollution. It is heartening and alarming to note the factual accuracy, which is broadcast by BBC Radio on September 23, 1999, that nearly a quarter of the police force, in the southern city of Bangalore, are suffering from hearing disabilities on account of multiplying noise pollution. A pilot study, conducted by Bangalore's Institute of Speech and Hearing, reveals that traffic constables at the city's main junctions are worst-hit victims of noise pollution. Sudden horning is one of the foremost causes of accidents on the road. 'Suniye', an institute for deaf, reports that daily on an average at least four persons are turning to total deafness in Delhi including one child in womb.[56A]

It is likely, that many people today are strongly motivated to do something about the problem. The reason being, that the ill-effects of noise do not allow for complacency or neglect any more. For instance, researchers working on children having hearing disorders are constantly reminded of the crucial importance of hearing to children. In early years, a deaf child, cannot learn to speak without special training. In this respect, there is a clear responsibility on parents to protect their children and employers' hearing power like their own eyesight. If no timely steps are taken, a significant percentage of future generations shall suffer from heavy hearing damage. It is horrible to imagine and predict, what will be the amount of total loss to whole human population.

Intensity of sound (in decibels)	Period of exposure (in hours)
90	8
92	6
95	4
97	2
100	$1\frac{1}{2}$
105	$\frac{1}{2}$
110	$\frac{1}{2}$

Colavita was unable to find a single student among the university students in his classes, who could hear a sound of 20 kHz, whereas, 20 kHz is an audible frequency, according to classical results drawn by Fletcher and Munson.

We can see, the table of the Noise Standards corresponding
to suggested periods of exposure, beyond which, it is detrimental
to hearing health.[57] As a precaution, none should, therefore, be
exposed to noise beyond these limits.

NOTES AND REFERENCES

1.   R.K. Sapru, *Environment Management in India-I*, p. 125.
2.   *Ibid.*, p. 89.
3.   Nilima Mishra, New Delhi (AP), *Green News*, Issue No. 60/98, July 11,
     1998, CSE fax 91-11-6985879 or email cse@cseindia.org.
4.   *Times of India*, January 15, 2002.
5.   Timmy Katiyar, *Environmental Pollution*, p. 13.
6.   Masroor, M. Gilani, *Green News*—Issue No: 60/98, Sat, 11 July 1998,
     masroor@greenpress.sdnpk.undp.org.
7.   *Ibid.*, No: 60/98, Sat, 11 July 1998.
7A. See, *Times of India*, New Delhi, April 29, 2005.
8.   *Times of India*, 1 May 2002.
8A. Asthma on Rise among children, *TOI*, December 12, 2004.
9.   Dr. Mahesh Mathur, *Legal Control of Environmental Pollution*, p. 182.
10. I. Mohan, *Environmental Pollution and Management*, p. 40.
11. AIR 1999 Cal 15.
12. *Supra* 9, p. 183.
13. *Supra* p. 126.
14. S. Chand, S.S. Dara, *A Text Book of Environmental Chemistry and Pollution
     Control*, p. 142.
15. *Supra* 1, Vol. I, p. 127.
16. N.S. Kamboj, *Control of Noise Pollution*, p. 19.
17. Pramod Singh, *Environment Pollution and Management*, p. 119.
18. Debi Prasad Tripathi, *Noise Pollution*, p. 11.
19. *Ibid.*, p. 60.
20. *Supra* 5, p. 42.
21. Interdisciplinary Minor in Global Sustainability, University of
     California, Irvine, Student papers, Spring 1998, Instructor: Peter A.
     Bowler, 'Cause and Effects of Noise Pollution' by Daniel G. Nunez,
     downloaded from internet.
22. *Supra*, 9, p. 204.
23. *Supra* 1, p. 128.
24. *Supra* 2, Vol. II, p. 89.
25. *Supra* 23.
26. *Times of India*, January 25, 2001.
27. *Supra* 9, p. 183.
28. *Supra* 17, p. 121.

29. R.K. Jain, L.V. Urban and G.S. Stacey, *Environmental Impact Analysis*, p. 277.
30. *Supra* 5, p. 226.
31. *Supra* 17, pp. 120-21.
32. *Encyclopedic Dictionary of Environmental Pollution*, p. 45.
33. *Times of India*, 1 May 2002.
34. Shows Cornell University's Study by Susan S. Lang, dated 4 March, 1998, Office: (607)255-3613,E-Mail-ssl4@cornell.edu).
35. Dr. Mahesh Mathur, *Legal Control of Environmental Pollution*, p. 184.
36. R.K. Supru, *Environment Management in India*, Vol. II, p. 89.
37. *Ibid.*, p. 185.
38. *Ibid.*, p. 90.
39. D.D. Ojha, *Noise Pollution* (Hindi), p. 68.
39A. *Times of India*, August 4, 2004.
40. *Supra* 5, p. 11.
41. *Supra* 9, p. 185 .
42. *Hollywood Silver Fox Farm Ltd.* Vs. *Emmett*, (1936)2 KB 46.
43. Compassionate Travelers Alert, June 2001, Stop the Navy's Whale-killing Sonar http://www.nrdc.org/wildlife/marine/nlfa.asp
44. Timmy Katiyar, *Environmental Pollution*, p. 11.
45. Akhand Jyoti, A Magazine published by Shantikunj, Haridwar, May 2002, p. 34.
46. *Ibid.*, p. 35.
47. *Supra* 5, p.13.
48. *Encyclopedic Dictionary of Environmental Pollution*, p. 46.
49. Originally it was alteration over the use of loudspeakers which was being used by one community on the occasion of 'jasuthan' ceremony of a newly born son. *The Navbharat Times*, April 17, 1987, New Delhi, see N.S. Kamboj, *Control of Noise Pollution*, p. 22.
50. *The Navbharat Times*, April 7, 1990, New Delhi.
51. Shri Jagmohan, former Governor of J&K, admitted in an interview that the indiscriminate use of loudspeaker had frequently been made from the religious places in state for raising anti-national slogans and indulging in anti-national activities and it could not checked due to the absence of any law in J&K to control the use of loudspeaker, *Sunday Magazine, Id*, June 17, 1990, New Delhi, see *supra* p. 16, p. 23.
52. *Rajasthan Patrika*, 4 July, 2002.
52A. C.W.P. No. 72/98 filed by Sh. Anil K. Mittal.
53. Dr. Mahesh Mathur, *Legal Control of Environmental Law*, p. 182.
54. *Ibid.*, p. 182.
55. *Supra* 39, pp. 69-70.
56. Robert G. Ingersoll, *Times of India*, Sacred Space, January 30, 2001.
56A. *Navbharat Times*, 25 August, 2003.
57. *Supra* 39.

Sustainable Development and Quality of Environment

The time has ripened to create a congenial atmosphere and environment to bestow 'sustainability of life' to all living creatures irrespective of their activities. There is a growing concern about the problems and challenges of sustainable development throughout the globe. The rationale behind this task is left with its content and meaning in real life situation. The advancement of science and technology and industrialisation has no doubt conferred many benefits, but at the same time, resulted in over drawl of natural resources and also brought in its trail, the problems of pollution of air, water and the noise, which is the enemy of human brain itself. While advancement and development is a must to every economy, it is also an essential to ensure that no irreparable damage is caused to ecosystems. It is the apprehension of destruction of the human race due to increasing pollution and irreversible depletion of natural resources, which has given birth to the concept of sustainable development and paved way for this approach. A specific concern is that those, who enjoy the fruits of economic development today, may be making future generations worse-off by excessively degrading the resources of the earth and polluting the environment. Hence, it becomes essentially desirable to know how environmental quality is being given up in the name of development? And how much development is being given up in the name of environmental protection? But it is a fact that too much quality of the environment is being sacrificed in the name of development.[1]

Sustainable development is not a new idea. Many cultures over the course of human history have recognized the need for harmony between the environment and economy. What is new is an articulation of these ideas in the context of a global industrial and information society. The concept of sustainable development was for the first time highlighted at Stockholm in June 1972 at the United Nations Conference on Human Rights. Besides India, various countries such as United States of America, Japan, Germany, and France have adopted this concept by way of enacting environmental laws. But, Progress on developing the concepts of sustainable development has been rapid since 1980s.[2] The term 'Sustainable Development' was brought into common use by the World Commission on Environment and Development, the Brundtland Commission, in its seminal 1987 report 'Our Common Future'. In 1992, leaders at the Earth Summit built upon the framework to create agreements and conventions on critical issues such as climatic changes, desertification and deforestation. Throughout rest of the 1990s, regional and sectoral sustainability plans have been developed. A wide variety of groups, ranging from businesses to municipal governments to international organizations such as the World Bank, have adopted the concept and given it their own particular interpretations. These initiatives have increased our understanding of what sustainable development means within many different contexts.

In simple terms 'sustainable development' argues the use of environment as a "waste sink" on the basis that waste disposal rate should not exceed the rate of (natural and managed) assimilation by the counter-part ecosystems. Sustainable development is an economic development that can continue indefinitely because it is based on the exploitation of renewable resources and causes insufficient environmental damage for this to pose an eventual limit.[3] Ecologically, sustainable development means using, conserving and enhancing the community's resources so that ecological processes, on which life depends, are maintained, and the total quality of life, now and in the future, can be increased.[4]

Sustainable development focuses on improving the quality of life for all of the Earth's citizens without increasing the use of natural resources beyond the capacity of the environment to supply them indefinitely. It requires an understanding that inaction has consequences and that we must find innovative ways to change institutional structures and influence individual behaviour. According to J. Coomer, the sustainable society is one that lives within the self-perpetuating limits of its environment.[5]

In broad sense, the concept of sustainable development encompasses:[6]

    (a) helping the very poor because they are left with no option other than to destroy their own environment;

    (b) the idea of self-reliant development, within natural resource constraints; and

    (c) the idea of cost-effective development, using different economic criteria of the traditional approach; that is to say, the development should neither degrade environmental quality, nor should it reduce productivity in the long-run.

1. SALIENT FEATURES OF SUSTAINABLE DEVELOPMENT

The concept of 'sustainable development' has grown since its inception at the international fora and it has acquired different dimensions in terms of economic growth, development, and environment protection. Some of the salient principles of 'sustainable development' as called out from Brundtland Report and other international document such as Rio Declaration and Agenda 21, are as under:

    (a) **Inter-Generational Equity**, i.e. the right of each generation to be benefited from the cultural and natural inheritance of the past generations as well as the "obligation" to preserve such heritage for future generations.

    (b) **Use and Conservation of Natural Resources**, i.e. the

use of the Earth's natural resources carefully and the natural resource base must be conserved and enhanced.

(c) **Environmental protection.**

(d) **The Precautionary Principles,** i.e. to ensure that a substance or activity posing a threat to the environment is prevented from adversely affecting the environment, even if there is no conclusive scientific proof of linking that particular substance or activity to environmental damage.

(e) **The Polluter Pays Principle:** The "Polluter Pays Principle" (PPP), as interpreted by the Supreme Court of India, means that the absolute liability for harm to the environment extends not only to compensate the victims of pollution but also the cost of restoring the environmental degradation. Thus, it includes environmental cost as well as direct cost to people or property. Remediation of the damaged environment is a part of the process of sustainable development and as such the polluter is liable to pay the cost to individual sufferers as well as the cost of reversing the damaged ecology. Under this principle it is not the role of government to meet the costs involved in either prevention of such damage, or in carrying out remedial action, because the effect of this would be to shift the financial burden of the pollution incident to the taxpayer.[7]

In 1972, the member-countries of Organization for Economic Cooperation and Development (OECD) agreed to base their environmental policies on a polluter pays principle (PPP). In the case of OECD, the guidelines on PPP were intended to discourage subsidies that could lead to distortions in trade. They promoted the principle when there was great public interest of environmental issues. At that time there was pressure built up on government and other institutions to introduce policies and mechanisms for the protection of the environment and the public from the threats posed by pollution in a modernized industrialized society. Since then there has been considerable discussion on the nature of PPP, but the precise scope of the principle and its implications for those, who are involved in polluting activities, have never satisfactorily agreed. There has frequently been dispute over its exact scope, especially over the limits on payment for damage caused. It is essentially a guide to satisfy in either European community or British environmental legislation. However, there is a very strong link between the principle and the idea it is vested with, i.e. 'the prevention is better than cure'. Further, the cost should include the full environmental degradation; not just the good for those that are immediately affected.

Principle 16 of the Rio Declaration also enunciates "PPP." The Supreme Court has clearly ruled that this principle may also be adopted by government, u/s 3 of the Environment (Protection) Act, 1986. Pertinent is that Sec. 3 empowers the government to 'take all such measures which it deems necessary or expedient for the purpose of protecting and improving the quality of environment'.[8] Thus, according to this principle it can be concluded that the responsibility to repair the environmental damage is the sole responsibility of the polluter only, and nonetheless.

(f) **Obligation to Assist and Co-operate:** The environmental problem is not the problem of one individual or of one country, but is a global problem and it has to be tackled with the assistance and co-operation of all.

(g) **Eradication of Poverty:** Brundtland Report has rightly pointed out, that poverty reduces people's capacity to use their resources in a sustainable manner and hence, it intensifies pressure on the environment. Most of the developing countries are under the stress of poverty. Therefore, it is necessary that the growth must be revived in developing countries where the link between economic growth, the alleviation of poverty, and environmental conditions, operate directly.

(h) **Financial Assistance to Developing Countries:** The people in developing countries strain their natural resources and over-exploit them to meet their basic needs. The developing countries also do not have the finances and modern technology to follow the path of development, which is sustainable. Therefore, the financial assistance and transfer of technology from the developed nations to the developing nations is a must, if we want to achieve the goal of sustainable development and environmental protection. In fact, this was one of the major demands of developing countries at the "Earth summit."[9]

2. WHAT, THE TERM 'SUSTAINABILITY' DENOTES?

Many dimensions are thereof the term 'sustainability'. First, it requires elimination of poverty and deprivation. Second, it requires the conservation and enhancement of resource-base, which alone can ensure the elimination of poverty permanently. Third, it requires broadening of the concept of development, so as to cover not only the economic growth, but also social and cultural development. Fourth and the most important, it requires unification of economics and ecology in decision-making, at all levels. A major challenge of the coming decades would be to learn, how long-term and large-scale interactions between environment and development could be managed in better way, so as to increase the prospects of ecologically sustainable improvements, for the well-being of mankind.

The core idea of sustainability is the concept, that current-decisions should not impair the prospects of maintaining or improving future living standards. This implies that our economic systems should be managed in such a order that we may enjoy the dividend of our resources, maintaining and improving the assets-base.[10]

More difficult to define is sustainability. The common use of the word "sustainable" suggests, an ability to maintain some activity in the face of stress, for example, to sustain physical exercise, like jogging or doing push-ups. Such a meaning appeals to everyone, as applicable technically. We thus, define agricultural sustainability, as the ability to maintain productivity, whether of a field, farm or nation, in the face of stress or shocks.

"Sustainability is a relationship between dynamic economic system and changing ecological system, so that human life continues indefinitely, individuals flourish, and culture develops.

A relationship, in which the consequences of human activities remain within bounds, and such consequences do not destroy the health and integrity of self-organizing systems.[11]

3. 'DEVELOPMENT'—IN CONTEXT OF SUSTAINABILITY

From molten mass of fire, we came into living-beings, from living beings to animals, and finally from animals to human beings. But still, this fast developing man could not be the crown of evolution and in course of time, social and political world of rapid developing man got divided into haves and have-nots. The major population lives below the poverty line. Teeming millions live in rags, tatters and tears. They ache-out a miserable existence to make two ends meet.[12]

Development is never ending improvement for the well being of mankind, raising of living standards, and improving of education, health, and equality of opportunity. Ensuring, political and civil rights is a broader developmental goal. The fact, that environmental damage hurts the basic life of people, in the present as well as future, also provides additional grounds of re-thinking for the measurement of our developmental progress. Indeed, it raises special concerns for education, health, nutrition and life expectancy, which tends to be improved by economic growth. Furthermore, the people suffering from the damage may be different from those enjoying the benefits of growth.[13]

The term 'development' encompasses, in its broad sense, all forms of exploitation of everything that is natural, i.e. flora and fauna, land, water, air and the rest. Dialectically, development is the process of self-motion from the lower (simple) to the higher (complex), revealing the internal tendencies and the essence of phenomena, and leading to the appearance of the new.[14]

4. SUSTAINABLE DEVELOPMENT: THE CONCEPT

The apprehension of destruction of the human race, on account of increasing pollution and irreversible depletion of natural resources, has given birth to the concept of sustainable development. Sustainable development means, keeping something ongoing, for an indefinite period. The concept is based on this realization that the earning does not belongs only to us but to our future generations as well.[15] Sustainable development may be defined here as a pattern of social and structural economic transformations, i.e. development, which optimizes the economic and societal benefits, available in the present, but without jeopardizing likely potentials and future benefits. The primary goal of sustainable development is to achieve a reasonable and equitably distributed level of economic well-being, that can be perpetuated continually for many generations.[16]

Sustainable development may mean different, to different people. But, the most frequently quoted definition, which first appeared in 1987 is:

"Sustainable development is that development which meets the needs of the present, without compromising the ability of future generations to meet their own needs."[17]

But what does this mean? What are the needs of the present? It will not take more than a minute to jot-down five to ten needs, that we have in our own life. We may list such needs that conflict with one another? For example, if our needs are simply confined to clean air to breathe or to live in noise-free peaceful environment, there is no conflict. But if we enlist, also a car or an aircraft for transportation, then our needs might conflict because we cannot move in a car or an aircraft without coming across noise. This conflict gets multiply, when whole community, city, country or the world is taken into account.

People, concerned about sustainable development suggest that, to meet the needs of future depends upon the fact that, how well we balance our social, economic, and environmental objectives, i.e. our needs, while making today's decisions. Sometimes these needs puzzle us like a puzzle-diagram. What social, economic, or environmental needs would we add to the puzzle? Studying the puzzle raises a number of difficult questions. What happens to the environment in the long-term, if a large number of people cannot afford to meet their basic household needs, today? If one does not have access to safe water, then one would resort to available water for which one would need wood or fuel to boil that, so as to avoid sickness. For this, one will not hesitate or worry to go to the extent of deforestation. Or, if a person had to drive a long distance to join his office, he will not be able to avoid environmental pollution including noise, caused by his car or by bus he travels through. Therefore, there is a need to balance all social, economic and environmental objectives in the short-term, so as to sustain our development in the long-term.[18]

5. ATTEMPTED DEFINITIONS: SUSTAINABLE DEVELOPMENT

The following are some definitions of sustainable development compiled for:[19]

Sustainable development is the maintenance of essential ecological processes and life support systems, the preservation of genetic diversity, and the sustainable utilization of species and ecosystems.[20]

Sustainable development is the development that is likely to achieve lasting satisfaction of human needs and improvement of the quality of human life.[21]

"Sustainable development is the development that meets the needs of the present, without compromising the ability of future needs. It contains within it two key concepts: the concept of needs, in needs of the world's poor, to which overriding priority should be given; and by the state of technology and social organization on the environment's ability to meet present and future needs."[22]

"Ecologically sustainable development can be thought of as changes in economic structure, organization and activity of an economic ecological system, that are directed towards maximum welfare and which can be sustained by available resources."[23]

6. SUSTAINABLE ECONOMIC DEVELOPMENT

The development is often taken to be a vector of desirable social objectives. Elements, which includes increases in real income per capita; improvements in health and nutritional status; education achievement; access to resources; a fairer distribution of income; and increases in basic freedoms.

Former Prime Minister of Britain, Margaret Thatcher had observed, "if every government espouses the concept of sustainable economic development, stable prosperity can be achieved throughout the world, provided the environment is nurtured and safeguarded."[24]

Economic growth means real GNP-gross national product per capita, which is increasing over time. But observation of such a trend does not mean that growth is sustainable. Sustainable economic growth means that real GNP per capita is increasing over time and the increase is not threatened by "feedback" from either biophysical impact.

Sustainable economic development is to find optimal level of interaction between three systems, the biological and natural resource system, the economic system, and the social system. The sustainable development concept constitutes further an elaboration of the close links, between economic activity and the conservation of environmental resources. It implies a partnership between the environment and the economy, within which a key element is the legacy of environmental resources, which is not unduly diminished. Sustainable development means basing developmental and environmental policies on a comparison of costs and benefits, and on careful economic analysis, that will strengthen environmental protection and lead to rising and sustainable levels of welfare.[25]

Sustainable development adjusts the economic growth so as to remain within bounds, set by natural replenishable systems, subject to the scope for human ingenuity and adaptation via careful husbanding of critical resources, and technological advance, coupled with the redistribution of resources and power, in such a manner that it guarantees adequate conditions of livability for all present and future generations.[26]

7. IMPORTANCE OF INDUSTRIALIZATION

Industrialization is the central dynamic force for most countries. It has been a key-growth objective of India's planned economy, with heavy investments. Labour productivity is at its highest, in manufacturing industries. This has assisted in raising national income at a faster pace. It is a precondition for agricultural development and it induces development in other sectors. The importance of industrialization in economic development is crucial for a growing economy with a large population like India.[27] So prosperity through industrialization has been a long-term strategy for the governments. Communities, businesses, and governments have enough debated on the results of industrialization, a debate that has ever continued to grow unabated. Being reliant on agriculture and having a large population base has made India impoverished, and hence industrialization is roughly a synonym for economic development as a means to conquer poverty and provide employment.

India's focus on economic growth, witnessed two problems. One is population and industrialization is the second. India realized that in order to become more self-reliant and increase economic-growth, some changes had to be made. Therefore, during 1980s, India had to move away from its planned market and had to emphasize on industrial growth.[28] Industrialization enables India to utilize its resources optimally, diversify the economic base, raise the living standard of people, and attain balanced regional-development through fiscal incentives and concessional finances for backward regions. But it is unfortunate, that these industries contributed significantly to increase environmental pollution. Small industries have contributed in the area of urban as well as rural establishments. Raising concerns on environmental grounds are seen not so much as a problem with large industries, as they are more supportive of environmentally protective issues, but more so in the case of small industries. These small industries seem to have acute environmental problems.

8. ROLE OF SMALL UNITS AND THEIR PROBLEMS, VIS-À-VIS ENVIRONMENT

As the industrialization gathered momentum, so did the increase in small-scale industries. Small units play an important role in the Indian economy, as they are labour-intensive and create job opportunities. They offer a higher productivity of capital than the capital-intensive enterprises, as they have low investment per worker. They help in dispersal of industries, rural development, and the decentralization of economic power. All this is required to increase and disperse economic growth.

In addition, small companies support entrepreneurial talent

and skills, stimulate personal savings, and help in developing innovative and appropriate indigenous technology, providing dynamism and contributing to competition. Therefore, these industries are supported by the government and have been actively encouraged; no public or private enterprise with more than 100 employees has been allowed to go out of business. The government to support this sector, not only for employment-generation, but also to enhance their competitive strength, has undertaken several policy initiatives and procedural simplifications. The government has also provided measures such as greater infra-structural support, more and easier availability of credits, lower rates of duties, technology up-gradation, and assistance to build entrepreneurial talent, facilities for quality improvement, and export incentives.

Contributions of Small-Scale Industries (SSIs) to India's industrial production, exports and employment are significant. About 3 million SSI units employing nearly 16.7 million persons account for 35% of India's total exports and about 40% of industrial manufacture.[29] In real terms, the small-scale sector recorded a growth rate of 10.1% in 1994-95 as against 7.1% in 1993-94 and 5.6% in 1992-93. By the year 2025, if not controlled, this sector will grow even more rapidly.

The government's prime role has been to encourage growth of these industries, often neglecting environmental considerations. Industrial effluent largely comes from the 3 million small- and medium-sized units that are scattered throughout the country, particularly in the production of paper, sugar, leather and chemicals. Unfortunately, only about half the medium to large-scale industries have partial or complete effluent treatment. Four-fold industrial growth from 1963 to 1991 resulted in six-fold growth in toxic release. Heavy industries, like iron and steel producers contribute nearly 70% of the toxic wastes released, but only 20% of industrial output. Industrial disposal of polluted effluent occurs via open drains into streams and reservoirs or through underground injection. Most industrial estates lack wastewater treatment systems.[29A] It stands highlighted in a report of the Comptrollers and Auditor General of India on River Yamuna for 2004 that even after a decade of symbolic Yamuna cleaning and expenditure of Rs. 872 crores, the river continues to be polluted due to the domestic and industrial sewage generated in Delhi.[29B]

Besides pollution problems, small-scale industries also have other kinds of problems. One is internal, that is, the techno-managerial and financial problems, that they encounter, and other is the external problem that, they confront due to non-compliance with regulatory and legislative measures.

Regulatory compliance has been a major issue for these units. Environmental legislation in India, although seemingly as tough as that in major developed nations, is not well enforced. Though multinationals and the large domestic companies are monitored, but poorly funded regulatory bodies find it nearly impossible to police the millions of small- and medium-scale units. Bribing, poorly paid inspectors, is reported to be common increasingly.

Environmentalists have viewed enforcement of environmental laws as lax, despite the regulatory framework and oversight authority of the Central and State Boards. There have been no incentives to invest in the pollution control efforts because of weak monitoring and enforcement of environmental regulations. It is mainly small industries, that continue to lack incentives to set-up treatment plant or to operate that equipment, if it already is installed, because operating that equipment has been more expensive than non-compliance.[30] Obviously, in India, scarcity of natural resources is of less concern than misuse of them. The pressure for profits predominates their decisions. The trade-off between economy and environment for production processes, customer needs, and technology is dynamic and complex. Porter and Linde suggest that, innovation-friendly regulations can improve resource productivity and competitiveness, but the problem is getting small industries to co-operate and to view it as a long-term solution rather than a short-term goal.

9. INCENTIVES FOR POLLUTION CONTROL:[31] THE ROLE OF CAPITAL MARKETS

It is often argued that firms in developing countries lack incentives to invest in pollution control efforts because of weak monitoring and enforcement of environmental regulations. But, it is assumed that the regulator is the only agent that can penalize a firm for poor environmental performance or reward it for good performance. Another possible source of incentive is capital market, which may react negatively to the announcement of an adverse environmental incident involving a firm such as a spill or a permit violation or positively to the announcement of greater pollution control effort (such as the adoption of cleaner technologies). To the extent that capital markets react to environmental news, the inability of regulatory institutions in developing countries to provide incentives for pollution control efforts may not be as serious matter, as is generally believed.

10. NOISE CONSCIOUSNESS ABROAD VIS-A-VIS DEVELOPMENT

The *Derby Evening Telegraph* in England has reported that a farm family in the Borough of Erewash, has sought permission to build up their own sound berm, in order to protect their farm from noise, created by the busy road along which the farm is located.[32] The *St. Petersburg Times* has published a letter to the editor from a reader who has legally questioned about the residential noise in Spring Hill, Florida neighbourhood.[33] The Sun-Sentinel reports, that the residents in Sunrise complain against the lack of action causing undue delay in constructing 8-foot noise barrier, to protect their homes from traffic noise and dust.[34]

The Hartford Courant reports that a group of residents in Suffield, Connecticut has decided to sue the state if noise on accounts of planes causing noise at Bradley International Airport is not controlled and reduced. According to the residents the noise has grown worse and have submitted a petition with 195 signatures asking that the noise be controlled.[35] Residents, near Montreal Area Airport protests that, the noise is unbearable, while officials show a deaf ear instead of sympathy.[36] The Associated Press reports that four helicopter tour operators have ceased from flying directly over the Strip in Las Vegas Nevada, because of noise complaints from hotel-casinos.[37] Residents and local Government officials strike out against plans to build a new stadium in Downtown Montreal.[38] The Montreal Gazette reports, that against the site proposed for the Expos baseball stadium, city officials and neighbours oppose tooth and nail. According to them, if the stadium was built up, the residents would face a 8-metre-high wall rather than the skyline view of the Radisson Hotel and the silvery Bell building they want to keep. In addition to the 35,000-seat stadium, the site would include residential and commercial space, 173 parking spaces and offices as high as 37 stories. The Capital of Annapolis, Maryland reports, Anne Arundel County residents are exposed to ever-increasing sources of noise. While many believe that their world is too noisy. Whereas, the experts say that everything depends upon, how people perceive it. Anti-noise groups ask UK government to fund their fight against Heathrow's Terminal.[39]

11. THE 7TH ANNUAL INTERNATIONAL SUSTAINABLE DEVELOPMENT RESEARCH CONFERENCE, 2001 (UNIVERSITY OF MANCHESTER UNITED KINGDOM)

The conference seeks to bring together an international interdisciplinary audience, to begin to tackle many of the issues connected with sustainable development, to share experiences and to begin to work towards solutions. By building informal partnerships and in offering opportunities to share ideas, this conference seeks to move this complex debate forward.[40]

12. NOISE PROTECTION ZONES NEEDED NEAR AIRPORTS[41]

The *Washington Post* reports that Stafford County and the Regional Airport Commission have planned, to create a number of noise protection zones, near the airport.

13. SUSTAINABLE DEVELOPMENT AND ROLE OF 'UNO'

(a) First Earth Summit,1992, Brazil

At the 20th anniversary of Stockholm Conference, the UN Conference on Environment And Development (UNCED), popularly known as Earth Summit, was held from 3 to 14 June 1992 at Rio-de-Janeiro in Brazil, wherein more than 150 countries participated. This was the largest UN Conference ever held, which had put the whole world on the path of sustainable development. The summit aimed at, meeting the needs of the present without compromising the ability for future generations to meet their needs. The Earth Summit was inspired and guided by a remarkable document of 1987—'Brundtland Report'. The summit forced the people to re-think worldwide, how their living affects natural environment and resources, and also to confront with new challenges in which they are going to live.

(b) The Commission on Sustainable Development

A significant institutional outcome of UNCED was the establishment of the Commission on Sustainable Development (CSD)[42] in December 1992, to ensure effective follow-up of UNCED; and to monitor and report on implementation of the Earth Summit agreements at the local, national, regional and international levels. The CSD is a functional commission of the UN Economic and Social Council (ECOSOC), with 53 members. It was agreed that a five-year review of Earth Summit progress would be made in 1997 by the United Nations General Assembly, meeting in special session. In June 1997, a Special Session of the United Nations General Assembly examined the progress of achieving sustainable development and there was a call for global collaboration, which would:

> ". . . halt and reverse the negative impact of human behaviour on the physical environment, and promote environmentally sustainable economic development, in all countries."

(c) Earth Summit + 5:[43]

The Special Session of the General Assembly held in June 1997 adopted a comprehensive document entitled Programme for further implementation of agenda 21 prepared by the Commission on Sustainable Development. It also adopted the programme of work of the Commission for 1998-2002.

The Commission on Sustainable Development consistently generates a high level of public interest. Over 50 ministers attend the CSD each year and more than one thousand non-governmental organizations (NGOs) contribute to its work. The Commission ensures the high visibility of sustainable development issues within the UN system and helps to improve the UN's coordination of environment and development activities. The CSD also encourages governments and international organizations to host workshops and conferences on different environmental and cross-sectoral issues. The results of these expert-level meetings enhance the work of CSD and help the Commission to work better with national governments and various non-governmental partners in promoting sustainable development world-wide. The 55th General Assembly session decided in December 2000 that the CSD would serve as the central organizing body for the upcoming 2002 World Summit.

(d) Kyoto Conference, 1997

On 11th December, 1997, delegates from 159 nations attended the World Conference reaching to a historic accord, and there was a calling for mandatory cuts in emissions of 'greenhouse gases', by the industrialized nations, in the next millennium to help save the planet, from potentially devastating global warming. The mandatory cut in emissions of green house gases, from the 1990 level, was decided to be 8% for Europe, 7% for America, and 6% for Japan between the year 2008 to 2012.[44] At the beginning, America was not ready to cut the emissions, more than the rate of 5%. But, later he had to accept the above figure of 7%. However, US sparked a world-wide uproar with its decision to abandon Kyoto accord, because it was likely to cost millions of US jobs. "Our nation must have economic growth, growth is also, what pays for investments in clean technologies, increased conservation and energy efficiency. We must encourage growth that will provide a better life for citizens, while protecting the land, the water and the air that sustain life", says US President George W. Bush. Japan acknowledged Bush's announcement but insisted on the establishment of a 'common rule in the future in which all countries including the US and developing countries participate'.[45] However, the developing countries like India shows their inability, based on critical financial condition, which is not sustainable to achieve these targets, hence they were exempted this time of the accord. The 'accord' came into force after ten days of UN Climate Conference in Kyoto (Japan) and was adopted in the form of a protocol.

A paragraph, calling for voluntary participation of developing nations in binding them into targets, had to face a strong opposition from India, China and other developing countries. The paragraph, therefore, had to be deleted from the final draft of the protocol. The opposing countries stood firm on their position that it was for the "major polluters" to cut down their heat-trapping emissions and help developing countries with advanced technologies and funds to promote clean industries.[46] In July 2005, while G-8 Summit at Gleneagles in Scotland, where India and China were special guests, a need was felt on consensus that all participating countries are to move forward to deal the issue in question.[46A]

14. SECOND WORLD SUMMIT, SOUTH AFRICA, 2002

After 10 years of Rio Summit, 1992, Johannesburg Summit 2002—the World Summit on Sustainable Development took place at Johannesburg in South Africa from 26 Aug. to 4 Sept., 2002. The summit focused on the world's attention and direct action towards meeting difficult challenges, including improvement on peoples' lives and conservation of the natural resources, in a world that is growing in population, with ever-increasing demand for food, water, shelter, sanitation, energy, health services, and economic security.

10 years later, the second Summit, 2002, presents an exciting opportunity for today's leaders, to take concrete steps and identify quantifiable targets for better implementing of the Agenda 21. A plan to restore the world's heavily depleted fish stock by 2015 was agreed upon by 189 nations, the first breakthrough in the negotiations.[47]

Some of the world leaders called the summit a failure in its totality, but calling for collective mobilization on a global scale, UN Secretary-General Kofi Annan said, that governments have agreed on an impressive range of concrete actions and commitments in this Summit for sustainable development. He further said, "Those who cause pollution, have to be there and become part of the solution. We have to work with business. Civil societies are our key partners but we need other stakeholders. Obviously, this is not Rio. Rio put sustainable development on the global agenda. This has instigated global action among a wide range of actors." According to Mr. Yashwant Sinha, the Foreign Minister of India, who represented India in this Summit, said, if sustainable development is more expensive than the development, it has to be separately financed.[48]

15. 'SUSTAINABLE DEVELOPMENT' IN INDIA: JUDICIAL TRENDS

India has always been on forefront, and has taken all possible steps for the protection and improvement of environment and is, constantly aiming at sustainable development. In UN sponsored three days Assembly, on Global Environmental Facility (GEF), held in April 1998, India appealed to the industrialized nations to enforce emission norms stringently, and to limit pollution levels, so as to save the world from an impending ecological disaster, on account of their high levels of economic activity and consumption, responsible for severe damage to the quality of environment.[49]

It is to be noted, that in India there has been a regular development of the environmental law. Neither environment nor the laws remain static. Both are dynamic in nature. But, the changing pace of the environment is so fast, that to keep and maintain the law on the same wavelength for a long time is very difficult. For this, either the laws have to be amended, quite frequently, to meet the new challenges or it has to be given new directions through the judicial interpretations. This becomes all the more important, in view of the ever increasing scientific and technological developments and advancements, the man has made. India has enacted various laws at regular intervals to deal with the problem of environmental degradation. At the same time, the dynamic judiciary in India has played a pivotal role in interpreting the environmental laws, in such a manner which not only helped in protecting the environment but also, in promoting the development in its sustainability. In fact, the judiciary in India has created a new environmental jurisprudence.[50]

It is true, that in developing countries like India, sustainable development is a necessary condition to have closest possible harmony with environment; otherwise there would be development, but no environment at all. This would certainly result into total devastation, however, this may not be felt in present, but in future it would have to be taken seriously and quite possible, that we are left with no choice, but with total devastation. In fact, there has to be a proper balance between the development and environment, so that both can co-exist without adversely affecting each other.[51]

16. DEMAND OF LIBERALISATION OF *LOCUS STANDI*

The common law traditions of India, and quest for restitution of its pristine environment, are often reflected in the pronouncements of its courts. Experience of developed nations, in their effort for a sustainable development, throws light on how India should act to combat environmental degradation. The liberal attitude of its courts towards *locus standi* in environmental matters, reflect the prevailing desire for a better environment.

By invoking the power under Art. 32 of the Constitution, the Supreme Court has provided relief to the individuals as well as environmental organizations. Casting aside its traditional posture of justice, the dynamic judiciary has disregarded the old and archaic concepts of *locus standi*, and has invented a new genus of litigation, viz. public interest litigation (PIL) for the protection of the fundamental rights of the people, and right to clean and healthy has been declared now a fundamental right of the citizen. The Supreme Court has, in its crusade against environmental deterioration, proceeded on the premise that a clean and wholesome environment is a prerequisite to enjoy the right to life enshrined in Art. 21 of the Constitution, as a fundamental right.

A series of PIL cases is a glorious precedent to accelerate the dynamism of sustainable development in India. In the recent PIL,[52] the Supreme Court focused its whole attention on the woes of the people living in a village full of sludge, a lethal waste, left out by the closed down chemical industries, which caused heavy damage to the environment.

Taking cue from the pro-active judgments of the Supreme Court, High Courts of the states too, have begun to invoke the power of the writ jurisdiction under Article 226 of the Constitution to protect the sustainable development and right to clean environment.

17. ENVIRONMENT MANAGEMENT IN INDIA: A BIRD'S EYE VIEW

There is a basic division of powers between the centre and the states in India, reflecting the federal nature of the Indian Constitution. To protect and improve the environment is the duty of both, central as well as state governments. Pollution monitoring and standards enforcement agencies in India— Central Pollution Control Board (CPCB) and State Pollution Control Boards (SPCBs) were created under the Water Act, in 1974. These boards were entrusted additionally to deal with the matters of air pollution in 1981 and now made responsible to monitor the noise levels in the country. Department of environment was created in 1980 for environmental management, which later became the part of Ministry of Environment and Forestry, established in 1985. The Environment ministry is contributing enough substantial, to protect and improve environmental quality. Further, Air Act, 1981 and Environmental Protection Act, 1986 are the statutes in India to meet with environment management. Some states have also shown their love for the environment, by way of creating departments of environment in their states on the pattern of centre. No doubt, formation of separate ministry of environments and forests is a good step towards environment management in India. Indian Judiciary is also contributing a lot by way of implementing and interpreting the laws most favourable to the environment. NGOs too, are energized to look into the environmental matters and to raise awareness among the public.

The mandate of the Central Pollution Control Board (CPCB) is to set environmental standards for all plants in India, lay down ambient standards, and coordinate the activities of the State Pollution Control Boards (SPCBs). The implementation of environmental laws and their enforcement, however, are decentralized, and are the responsibilities of the SPCBs. Anecdotal evidence suggests, wide variations in enforcement across the states.

Until 1988, the enforcement authority of the SPCBs was very weak. It was limited to criminal prosecution and seeking injunctions to restrain polluters. Now, however, SPCBs have the power to close non-compliant factories or cut-off their water and

114 Environmental Noise Pollution

electricity by administrative orders. But, it is a matter of concern that such powers are not with these Boards in respect with noise pollution.

Tamilnadu Pollution Control Board (TNPCB) has established awareness programmes and workshops on vehicular pollution, noise pollution control, hazardous waste management, solid waste management, biomedical waste management, plastic waste management, protection of ozone layer, etc. Special awareness campaigns are conducted against air and noise pollution during festival seasons such as Deepavali.

NOTES AND REFERENCES

1.   P. Ranjan Trivedi, *Encyclopaedic of Ecology and Environment*, p. 194.

2.   David Pearce, "Optimal Prices for Sustainable Development," in D. Collard, D. Pearce, and D. Ulph (eds.), *Economics, Growth and Sustainable Environment*, London: MacMillan.

3.   M. Allaby, *MacMillan Dictionary of the Environment*, 3rd ed., London: MacMillan Press Ltd.

4.   Australian Government, *National Strategy for Ecologically Sustainable Development*, Australian Government Publishing Service, Canberra, Dec. 1992.

5.   J. Coomer, "The Nature of the Quest for a Sustainable Society," in J. Coomer (ed.), *Quest for a Sustainable Society*, Oxford: Pergamon Press, 1979.

6.   *Supra* 3.

7.   Carolene Shellbourn, "Historic Pollution—Does the Polluter Pay", *Journal of Planning and Environmental Law*, See Environmental Law, By P.S. Jaiswal and N. Jaswal.

8.   *Nagar Palika Parishad Vs. National Newspaper and Paper Mill Ltd.*, Supp. (2) SCC 105.

9.   P.S. Jaswal and Nistha Jaswal, *Environmental Law*, p. 102.

10. R. Repetto, *World Enough and Time*, New Haven: Yale University Press, 1986.

11. p. 25, Norton, B.G. 1992, "A New Paradigm for Environmental Management," *Ecosystem Health: New Goals for Environmental Management* (Costanza, R., Norton, B.G., and Haskell, B.D., eds.). Washington, D.C., pp. 23-41.

12. Dr. Sampat Jain, *Public Interest Litigation and Judicial Activism*, Thesis presented, p. 4.

13. *Supra* 1, p. 194.

14. R. Kumar, *Environmental Pollution and Health Hazards in India.*

15. Sustainable Development, by Professor (Dr.) M.L. Mathur in Paryavaraan Sandesh, *A Quarterly News Letter of WWF* (I), Jodhpur Division.

16. R. Goodland and G. Ledoc, "Neoclassical Economics and Principles of Sustainable Development," *Ecological Modelling*, Vol. 38, 1987.

17. From the World Commission on Environment and Development's (the Brundtland Commission) report, Our Common Future (Oxford: Oxford University Press, 1987).

18. dep@worldbank.org.

19. murcott@mit.edu,AAAS Annual Conference, IIASA "Sustainability Indicators Symposium," *Seattle*, WA 2/16/97.

20. IUCN, WWF and UNEP, *The World Conservation Strategy*, Gland, Switzerland. 1980.

21. R. Allen, *How to Save the World*, London: Kogan Page, 1980, Summarizing the World Conservation Strategy.

22. World Commission on Environment and Development, 1987, Our Common Future, Great Britain: Oxford University Press (p. 43).

23. Braat, L.C. and I. Steetskamp, 1991, "Ecological-Economic Analysis for Regional Sustainable Development," *Ecological Economics* (Costanza, R., ed.), New York: Columbia University Press, pp. 269-88, p. 271.

24. Former PM Margaret Thatcher's Speech to the Royal Society on Sept. 27, 1988.

25. World Bank, *World Development Report, 1992: Development and the Environment*, Oxford University Press, New York.

26. Tim O'Riordan and Jill Yaeger, "Global Environmental Change and Sustainable Development," *Global Change and Sustainable Development in Europe*. Manuscript on file at the Wuppertal Institute, Nordrhein-Westfalen, Germany, 1994.

27. India's increasing population crossed the 1 billion mark in May 2000 (Vedantam, 2000) placing an additional burden on the Indian environment. The contrast between India's successful economic development and rapidly deteriorating environments, particularly urban-industrial environments, makes this country a test for the sustainable vision.

28. United States-Asia Environmental Partnership [US-AEP], 1996.

29. SIDBI report on small scale industries sector, 1999, p. 6.

29A. *Supra* 28.

29B. *Times of India*, 6 April, 2005.

30. Dasgupta, Laplante and Mamingi, 1998.

31. sdasgupta@worldbank.org.

32. *Derby Evening Telegraph*, April 15, 2000, Erewash, England.
33. Spring Hill, Florida Asks About Legal Rights Concerning Neighbourhood Noise, April 6, 2000, Florida.
34. *Lauderdale*, October 3, 1997, Sunrise, Florida.
35, *The Hartford Courant*, October 2, 1997, Suffield, Connecticut.
36. *The Gazette* (Montreal) October 2, 1997, Montreal, Canada.
37. *The Associated Press*, October 6, 1998, Las Vegas, Nevada.
38. *The Gazette*, October 7, 1998, Montreal, Canada.
39. Press Association Newsfile, May 14, 1998, London, England.
40. http://www.erpenvironment.org.
41. *The Washington Post*, October 7, 1998, Washington, DC.
42. http://www.un.org/esa/sustdev.
43. http://www.un.org/esa/earthsummit.
44. Dr. Jai Jai Ram Upadhyay, *Environmental Law* (Hindi), p. 247.
45. *Times of India*, February 10, 2001.
46. *Supra* 9, p. 94.
46A. *Times of India*, New Delhi, July 8, 2005.
47. *Hindustan Times*, August 29, 2002.
48. *TOI*, New Delhi, September 5, 2002.
49. "South must Check Pollution", *The Tribune*, 12 April, 1998.
50. *Supra* 9, p. 172.
51. See, *People United for Better Living in Calcutta* Vs. *State of Bengal*, AIR 1993 Cal 215 at 217.
52. *Indian Council for Enviro-legal Action* Vs. *Union of India*.

Legislation and Judiciary

Environmental degradation is a worldwide phenomenon, and a number of people are dying world-over, every year. But, very little has been done and is being done, to deal with environmental devastation, to which entire world is harping upon. The quality of environment is being lowered, day-by-day.

Noise pollution, an omnipotent and important component of air pollution, is assuming worldwide attention that is an inescapable by-product of industrial environment and is increasing very fast, with the technological advancements, industrialization and urbanization. It has challenged the very fundamentals of human survival and social well-being. It is a paradox that the industrialization and urbanization, which were once a symbol of progressive developed nations bringing revolutionary modernization in society, have brought manifold problems, unsafe for human race. To protect safe environment and to safeguard natural flora and fauna, has become one of the serious problems, of the present legal world. The attention of the world's governments at the national level and of UNO, at international level had been drawn towards the pollution of air and water. Various Conferences have been organized at international level. Numerous and varied laws have been enacted to control air and water pollution. The right to clean and green environment is recognized as a fundamental right by the courts in India.[1] Simultaneously, search and research has been and is being done to prevent and control air and water pollution. Comprehensive but distinct legislations have been passed in India on water and air pollutions, separately.

But to prevent and control noise pollution, no comprehensive legislation is yet enacted in India, which is a matter of great concern. Perhaps the reason thought for is, that the awareness about the noise pollution is of recent origin.[2]

Law is not merely a prescription or authorized guidance, or the direction to human conduct by virtue of a coercive mechanism, at the command of the state. It is also a means of social engineering and solidarity, and a part of progressive civilization and conservation of culture. In its ultimate analysis, law is a human contrivance, a part of man's scheme of survival on this earth, amidst all the threats and challenges to man's existence and safe-keeping. Therefore, with the extension of the province and functions of law, it can ill-afford to pay a scant regard to natural environment in which, human life itself is set and moves to action. Law is not only to be satisfied by balancing human interests for fruitful purposes; it has also to work for the maintenance of natural and physical environment by preserving ecological balance in its natural form and functions, without which human survival will be difficult.[3] Mens' survival on this planet, earth, depends on his harmony with the nature. Rule of law must defend the rule of life, and life will survive, only, when the biosphere is safe.

It is surprising that the 'noise' has been the most ignored pollutant by Indian legislators so far, whereas it is in no way lesser hazardous than the other pollutions. It has subtle effects on human body and properties. In spite of the fact that noise pollution incapacitates the psycho-power of mankind, our legislators could not devote their expressive attention to curb it. It is noteworthy that battle symptoms of this dire enemy of mankind, appear at the stage when it is beyond to cure. There is no central code on noise pollution. The express/implied law relating to noise is scattered in different legal statutes, viz. Constitution, I.P.C., Cr.P.C., C.P.C., Factories Act, Municipal laws, etc.

1. LAWS ON NOISE POLLUTION IN INDIA: A BRIEF MOMENTUM

In early days, before the development of Environmental jurisprudence, the Common law remedy of nuisance was the only means to provide remedy against noise pollution, and the same was wholly based on the discretion of the Judges. The movement against noise pollution could not find force with the people, because most of the people in India do not consider noise as a pollutant but take it as a part of routine, and of modern life. In order to curb noise pollution, it is essential that citizens should first realize its dangerous consequences and then to take some remedial measures. Available scant rules, regulations and few state laws have however addressed the issue of noise pollution but in part, confined to certain activities. The Indian Constitution under Art. 19 grants to every citizen a fundamental right to freedom of speech and expression, with reasonable restrictions on the grounds of decency, morality, security of State, defamation, incitement of offence, etc. The use of loudspeaker as a means of expression, is regulated by reasonable restrictions, so as to meet public order and peaceful atmosphere. The Judiciary, on its part, has come up with some interesting observations, as to the freedom of expression and right to religious practices, with that of noise-free environment. The Judiciary has thus, trying to maintain a balance between the needs of development and the health of peace loving citizens.

The scientists have been by and large conscious about noise pollution. National physical laboratory has surveyed the noise pollution country over and revealed that noise level in Delhi, Mumbai, Calcutta and Chennai was very high in dense populated areas. By publishing such survey reports, awareness has been aroused among the public who have started thinking that noise is also a serious kind of pollutant to be taken seriously. To invite official attention of the authorities, government and others, towards this malady, a Conference was held, with the joint efforts of National Physical Laboratory and Indian Acoustic Institution. This conference was attended by a large number of the scientists, engineers, construction architects, crafters, industrialists, transport officers, medical experts, advocates and defence officers. Many facets of noise pollution were discussed at length seriously and they all expressed their deep and great concern. Thus, the noise was raised against the noise pollution, collectively and individually.[4]

Through series of similar conferences, seminars, meetings, and workshops, it was experienced that this blazing problem is not confined only to the metro-cities but also has dimensions in other cities and industrial areas. After a survey in 1983, Indian Medical Research Council has warned, that the environmental noise can damage, the audio, bio, and psycho power of whole mankind, to a great extent.

Also, The Indian Acoustic Institute had prepared a detailed Report in 1985 and expressed the felt dire need for comprehensive Noise Pollution Law in India, to prevent and control such pollution in urban and industrial areas. As a result, thereof, Ministry of Environment and Forest had to appoint an expert committee, to study the present levels of noise in the country and to submit its report to pave way for legislation. But, Indian government without waiting long for the last submission of this committee till June 1987, recognizing the gravity and urgency of this malady, introduced an amendment to the Environment (Protection) Act, 1986. The noise was added as an environmental pollutant in the definition section, i.e. section 2 of EPA, 1986.

In 1989, the Ministry of Environment and Central Pollution Control Board constituted a technical committee to suggest measures to prevent and control noise pollution. The committee studied and classified various kinds of noises, caused by various sources, viz. high noise, domestic noise, traffic noise and industrial noise. While preparing its report, the committee kept in view not only the international noise standards of other countries and World Health Organization, but also took into account, the social conditions and the Indian way of life. The committee submitted its detailed Report in 1989, vide which, the following were considered as the sources of noise, that affect the mankind, inside as well as outside the homes:[5]

    (a) Industrial;
    (b) Traffic;
    (c) Domestic;
    (d) Airport; and
    (e) Telephonic.

2. NOISE POLLUTION UNDER THE ENVIRONMENT (PROTECTION) ACT, 1986 (EPA)

Amended Environment (Protection) Act, 1986 has two-fold bearing on noise pollution. First, sec. 6(2)(b) of the Act empowers Central Government to make rules prescribing maximum permissible limits regarding concentration of various environmental pollutants, including nose for different areas. Similarly, the rule-making power has been assigned to the central government by section 25[6] of this Act, and the noise is included, without its specific mention.

Rule 5[7] of the Environment (Protection) Rules, 1986 framed under EPA, restricts and prohibits the location of industries and to carrying on processes and operations, in different areas, which further depending on maximum permissible limits of concentration of various environment pollutants, including noise for that area.

3. NOISE POLLUTION (REGULATION AND CONTROL) RULES, 2000

Keeping in view the seriousness of health hazard from noise, the Government thought it fit to enact a special law in regulation to control Noise Pollution. It was 1999, when central government drafted the Noise Pollution (Control and Regulation) Rules,[8] inviting objections and suggestions from all the persons likely to be affected thereby. Consequently, in exercise of the powers conferred by clause (i) of sub-section (2) of section 3, sub-section (i) and clause (b) of sub-section (2) of section 6 and section 25 of the EPA, 1986 read with rule 5 of the EPR, 1986, the central government notified[9] the Noise Pollution (Control and Regulation) Rules in February 2000. These rules restrict the use of loudspeakers/public address system, and also lay down the ambient air quality standard in respect of noise. The rules have prescribed different levels of noise for different areas, i.e. noise level in industrial areas 75 decibels, commercial areas 65 decibels and in residential zones 55 decibels. These rules have entrusted the DC of the district to be the regulatory authority for its strict implementation. The rules mention of creation of *silence zones* to define the 100 meters from school, courts, educational institutions and hospitals. Rule 5(2) of Noise Rules restricts the use of loudspeakers, public address system at night. These devices can not be used even in day time without due permission u/r 5(1). The Supreme Court has observed in a case the breach of the rule and directed that wide publicity of the rule is to be given by the appropriate authority and SDMs to see the adherence to rule.[9A]

On 11-10-2002, the Government of India brought an amendment in the Rules. The amendment empowered the State Government to permit the use of loudspeakers or public address system during night hours (between 10 p.m. and 12 p.m. midnight) on our during cultural or religious occasions for a limited period not exceeding 15 days. Against this amendment, a writ petition was preferred before Kerala High Court but the same stood dismissed as being devoid of merits. Further, a special leave petition[9AA] was preferred before Supreme Court of India wherein the court has dealt the issue in detail at length and passed a historical judgment.

For violation of Rule 6 of Noise Rules, 2000, Delhi High Court had to issue direction to curb the noise in silence zone.[9B] The rules also fix different ambient air quality levels for firecrackers and industrial activities. As regarding use of loudspeaker, the rules stipulate that between 10 p.m. and 6 a.m., there cannot be use of loudspeakers except in closed premises.

Apart from the above, there are some other legal provisions, which deals directly or indirectly with the control of noise pollution, scattered in different statutes of India, which are discussed in detail at the appropriate place, under the same statute in this chapter of the treatise.

4. SCATTERED LAW ON NOISE IN INDIA

(a) Air (Prevention and Control of Pollution) Act, 1981

Among the present and advanced laws, environmental law is a newly emerging law and specially in our country. Available laws relating to environmental noise are scattered in different statutes. While addressing the first joint session of the seventh parliament, the President of India has very rightly stressed, the need for setting up specialized machinery, to maintain ecological balance. Accordingly, the Government of India on 23 February, 1980, constituted a high powered Committee under the chairmanship of the then Deputy Chairman of the Planning Commission, Mr. N.D. Tiwari, to recommend legislative measures and administrative machinery, for ensuring environmental protection. Submitting its report on September 15, 1980, the committee has recommended, not only the need to set up a separate department of environment but also, to enact a comprehensive law to improve ambient air quality in India.[10]

Under Art. 253 of the Constitution, the Air (Prevention and Control of Pollution) Act, 1981 was enacted, to implement (i) some of the recommendations of the Stockholm Conference, 1972; (ii) the outcome of the recommendations of Tiwari Committee; and (iii) the outcome of the debate on, "Rape of the Earth", initiated in Lok Sabha on August 11, 1980. The main objectives of the enactment, Air Act, 1981 are:

(i) To provide for, the prevention, control, and abatement of air pollution;
(ii) To provide for, the establishment of Central and State Boards, with a view, to implement the aforesaid purposes; and
(iii) To provide for, conferring on such Boards, the powers and to assign functions, relating thereto.

Originally, the Air (Prevention and Control) Act, 1981 was enacted exclusively for the control of air pollution, but by subsequent amendment, the problem of noise was also covered within the definition of air pollutants, under section 2(1)[11] of the Act. After this, the CPCB is empowered, under its plans and programmes for the abatement of air pollution, and further to lay down noise standards while issuing them for the quality of the air under sub-clause 2(h)[12] of the Act.

Similarly, after the inclusion of noise in the amendment, the state boards too are empowered under section 17(1)(a)[13] and have laid down the standards for noise and other air pollutants relating to industrial plants and automobiles, in exercise of their powers under sub-clause (1)(g) State Boards are duty-bound to consult CPCB and to follow the standard already issued by the Central Board. To ensure implementation of standards, against emissions of air pollutants from automobiles, State Boards are empowered u/s 20 of the Act, who shall, in consultation with control boards,[14] issue necessary instructions to the authorities, for compulsory registration of automobiles, under the Motor Vehicle Act, 1988.

For reference, some of the noise standards, and the rules relating to different noise pollutants, laid down by the Central Pollution Control Board in the exercise of its power under section 16(2)(h) are, categorically mentioned hereunder:[15]

(i) Ambient Noise Standards, for ambient air quality, in respect of noise;

(ii) Implementing agencies; and

(iii) Code of practice, for controlling noise from sources other than industries and automobiles.

Ambient Air Quality Standards in Respect of Noise[16]

Area Code	Category of Area/Zone	Limits in dB(A) Leq*	
		Day Time	Night Time
(A)	Industrial area	75	70
(B)	Commercial area	65	55
(C)	Residential area	55	45
(D)	Silence Zone	50	40

The Ministry of Environment and Forests has issued notification for these standards[17] and have included the noise pollutants, like motor vehicles, aircrafts, railways, construction works, loudspeakers, domestic appliances, and crackers.

Noise Exposure, Permissible for Industrial Workers

Noise in dB	Exposure time in hours
80	8
93	4
96	2
99	1
102	1/2
105	1/4
108	1/6
111	1/16
114	1/32
	(2 minutes or less)

Implementing Agencies for inside factory premises—

(i) Ministry of labour; and
(ii) State Department of labour.

Criticism

To err is human. In spite of the best efforts, which the lawmakers can put in, no legislation is possible, which is perfect and error-free. Some times, the legislators are hard-pressed, for the paucity of time. Even, the technicalities in law are, sometimes ignored by the legislators, because the fields are specialized. They may leave the technicalities to the experts in the field, who may not know much about legislation and the Air Act is no exception to it. Though, the Act is comprehensive and detailed in its contents, yet its scope is narrow and limited. A number of lacunae and loopholes have been noticed at the time of its implementation. It is imperative, therefore, to plug these loopholes, to remove the lacunae, and to overcome weaknesses, at the first opportunity, for the successful implementation of the Act. Wealth and power are no substitute for good health and happiness of a man. If on account of these loopholes, lacunas, or weaknesses in the Act, the man is further allowed to exploit the wealth of the nature unchecked, the man himself shall prove to be the Cancer, for this planet. These lacunas in Act are discussed below:[18]

(i) Noise Under Act

The noise pollution has been termed as the dire enemy, and first foe of the human brain, and is an insidious killer and a slow agent of death. Also, industrial and airport noise are becoming increasingly unbearable. Yet, the original texts of the Act, provided no legal check to prevent or control this fast increasing noise pollution. It was only in 1987, when the noise was included in the definition clause, as a pollutant by an amendment Act. Still, the Act including its amendment is not competent enough to curb this kind of pollution.

(ii) Exclusions under the Act

The Act, even after the amendment, has excluded the prevention and control of emissions from ships, aircrafts, and radioactive air pollution. By excluding these areas from the purview of this Act, its effectiveness has been undermined. For example, it is a well-known fact that the aircraft, flying at high altitude depletes the ozone layer and produces a high pitch of noise, while landing, take-off, and flying at low altitude. The check on emissions from ships and aircrafts is to be imposed through statutory legal sanctions.

(iii) Narrow Scope of the Act

The Act does not deal comprehensively with the prevention and control of noise pollution and only includes noise as a pollutant in its definition clause. Secondly, light pollution, which is becoming discernible, which causes discomforts and is harmful to sight and visual aesthetics, still remain unmentioned in the Act. Such glaring lights, which are the cause of traffic accidents, need to be nipped in the bud.

(iv) Offences Grave; Penalties Low

Many of the offences are, though laid down in the Act, but have inbuilt defences. Penalties are insignificant, as compared to the gravity of pollution offences and therefore unable to control pollutions.

(v) Overburdened Pollution Control Boards

Originally established under the Water (Prevention and Control of Pollution) Act, 1974, the Boards were assigned with a duty to improve the quality of water. After the enactment of Air (Prevention and Control of Pollution) Act, 1981, the same Boards were imposed with an additional duty to improve the ambient air quality. Now, the noise pollution, which also has become a matter of hue and cry, the same boards have been again assigned to monitor noise levels, in different zones of the country. It is also surprising that, initially full-time post of directors of these Boards have been converted into the part-time appointments by an amendment. During the interview with various State Pollution Control Boards, the author came across that these boards are being asked to undertake various pollutants to be controlled, with almost no increase in their infrastructures. On account of such multiple duties, with the same infrastructures, these Boards are unable to discharge their obligations, effectively. Further, the boards have no powers to enforce the prescribed noise standards; consequently their active involvement cannot be expected.

(b) Environmental Protection Act, 1986

Although, legislation like Water Pollution Act, 1974, Air Pollution Act, 1981 and several other Central and State enactments were already there to deal directly or indirectly with different aspects of the environmental pollution, yet it was necessary to have a legislation of general nature for environmental protection as some major environmental hazards remained out of the reach of these legislations. Therefore, there was a felt need of such Act, which could meet all the environmental problems in general. It was 1986, when a new Act, i.e., The Environmental Protection Act, 1986 was passed and assented to by the president on 23rd May, 1986 and came into force from November 19, 1986. The new Act was a welcome development in the legislative history of India and aims to fulfil:[19]

- (i) Aspirations of the people;
- (ii) Implement the directive principle of state policy mentioned in Article 48 of the Constitution;
- (iii) To make the people conscious of their fundamental duties under Article 51A(g) of Indian Constitution;
- (iv) To remove the defects of the earlier Acts;
- (v) To cover the environmental issues in its totality and generate community consciousness;
- (vi) To give integrated and comprehensive approach to the protection preservation and enhancement of environment;
- (vii) To develop strategy so that more and more people think in the direction of justice to nature and to homosapians;
- (viii) To have a direct law on the subject of environment protection, conservation of nature and natural resources;
- (ix) To bring harmony between the nature and man and thereby make the protection of environment a movement of masses and not classes;
- (x) To check blind and barbarous cutting of forests and

thereby to save the virgin earth, flora and fauna, lushes natural habitat, environment and biosphere; and finally;

(xi) To defend the Rule of law by defending Rule of Life.

The Environment (Protection) Act is an umbrella Act. Under this Act, the government is empowered to set standards for environmental quality and limits for emissions/discharges of pollutants from various specified sources. This Act empowers the government to prohibit and/or restrict certain activities, industrial or otherwise in specified areas to ensure protection of environment. It also confers enforcement agency with necessary punitive powers to restrict any activity detrimental to environment. The Supreme Court of India, under the provision of this Act, made the closure of 218 industrial units across the country and directed that the state government should strictly complied with the directions regarding closure of the industries operating without mandatory clearance from Union Ministry of Environment under this Act.[19A]

The Act is smaller than the earlier ones, comprising with 26 sections, divided into four chapters for prevention of hazards to human being and protection and improvement of environment. It is the first direct legislation passed by the government of India on the basis of the resolutions passed in 1972 at World Conference on Human Environment at Stockholm.

First chapter is preliminary and contains 2 sections. Section 2, which is definition section, has widened the definitions of environment, environmental pollution, pollutants and also of hazards substance so as to include not only water, air or land but it also covers human beings, other living creatures, plants, micro-organisms, property and their relationship.

Chapter 2 has 4 sections and deals with general powers of the central government. The Act empowers the central government under section 3 of the Act[20] to take all such measures, as it deems necessary or expedient for the purpose of protecting and improving the quality of the environment and controlling and abating environmental pollution. For this purpose Central Government may by notification under section 6(2)(a)(b)[21] of the Act, make rules to regulate environmental pollution. These rules may include the standards of quality of air, water and the maximum allowable limits of the concentration of various environmental pollutants (including noise) for different areas.

For carrying out the purposes of the Act, under section 3, there is a provision in section 4 for the appointment of an officer with such designations as central government thinks fit. The central government may in the exercise of its powers and performance of its functions under this Act, issue directions, in writing, to any person, officer or any authority and such person, officer or authority shall be bound to comply with such directions. Section 6 gives rule-making power to the central government for the better working of the Act.

The central government in exercise of its power under aforesaid sections 6 and 25 of the Act, enacted the Environmental Protection Rules, 1986. Under Rule 5(1)(ii) of these rules, central government may restrict or prohibit the location of industries, which may ultimately restrain them from carrying on their business in certain areas. Further the central government in exercise of its power under aforesaid sections 6[22] and 25 of the Act and for giving effect to the objectives mentioned under Rule 3 of the Environmental protection through its notification adopted some rules about the noise standards which are known as "Ambient Air Quality Standards in respect of Noise." For this purpose Schedule III has been added to the aforesaid Environmental Protection Rules.

NOISE STANDARDS AND GUIDELINES[22A]

Noise Standards for Domestic Appliances and Construction Equipment at the Manufacturing Stage

(as notified under Environment (Protection) Rules, 1986, by G.S.R. 742(E), dated 30.8.90 and subsequently amended by G.S.R. 422(E), dated 19th May, 1993)

Category of Domestic Appliances/Construction Equipment	Noise Standards
(a) Window air conditioners of 1 tonne to 1.5 tonne	68 dB(A)
(b) Air coolers	60 dB(A)
(c) Refrigerators	46 dB(A)
(d) Diesel generator for domestic purposes	85-90 dB(A)
(e) Compactors (rollers), Front loaders, Concrete mixers, Cranes (movable), Vibrators and Saws	75 dB(A)

Standards/Guidelines for Control of Noise Pollution from Stationary Diesel Generator (DG) Sets

(as notified under Environment (Protection) Rules, 1986, by G.S.R. 7, dated 22nd December, 1998)

(A) Noise Standards for DG Sets (15-500 KVA)

The total sound power level, Lw, of a DG set should be less than $94 + 10 \log_{10}$ (KVA), dB(A), at the manufacturing stage, where KVA is the nominal power rating of a DG set.

This level should fall by 5 dB(A) every five years, till 2007, i.e. in 2002 and then in 2007.

(B) Mandatory Acoustic Enclosure/Acoustic Treatment of Room for Stationary DG Sets (5 KVA and above)

Noise from the DG set should be controlled by providing an acoustic enclosure or by treating the room acoustically.

The acoustic enclosure/acoustic treatment of the room should be designed for minimum 25 dB(A) Insertion Loss or for meeting the ambient noise standards, whichever is on the higher side (if the actual ambient noise is on the higher side, it may not be possible to check the performance of the acoustic enclosure/acoustic treatment. Under such circumstances the performance may be checked for noise reduction up to actual ambient noise level, preferably, in the night time). The measurement for insertion loss may be done at different points at 0.5 m from the acoustic enclosure/room, and then averaged.

The DG set should also be provided with proper exhaust muffler with Insertion Loss of minimum 25 dB(A).

(C) Guidelines for the Manufacturers/Users of DG Sets (5 KVA and above)

1. The manufacturer should offer to the user a standard acoustic enclosure of 25 dB(A) Insertion Loss and also a suitable exhaust muffler with Insertion Loss of 25 dB(A).

2. The user should make efforts to bring down the noise levels due to the DG set, outside his premises, within the ambient noise requirements by proper siting and control measures.

3. The manufacturer should furnish noise power levels of

the unsilenced DG sets as per standards prescribed under (A).

4. The total sound power level of a DG set, at the user's end, shall be within 2 dB(A) of the total sound level of the DG set, at the manufacturing stage, as prescribed under (A).

5. Installation of a DG set must be strictly in compliance with the recommendations of the DG set manufacturer.

6. A proper routine and preventive maintenance procedure for the DG set should be set and followed in consultation with the DG set manufacturer which would help prevent noise levels of the DG set from deteriorating with use.

Noise Standards for Fire-crackers

(as notified under Environment (Protection) Rules, 1986, by G.S.R. 682(E), dated 5th October, 1999)

A. (i) The manufacture, sale or use of fire-crackers generating noise level exceeding 125 dB(AI) or 145 dB(G)$_{pk}$ at 4 meters distance from the point of bursting, shall be prohibited.

   (ii) For individual fire-cracker constituting the series (joined fire-crackers), the above mentioned limit be reduced by 5 $\log_{10}$ (N) dB, where N = number of crackers joined together.

B. The broad requirements for measurement of noise from fire-crackers shall be—

   (i) The measurements shall be made on a hard concrete surface of minimum 5 meter diameter or equivalent.

   (ii) The measurements shall be made in free field conditions i.e., there shall not be any reflecting surface up to 15 meter distance from the point of bursting.

   (iii) The measurement shall be made with an approved sound level meter.

C. The Department of Explosives shall ensure implementation of these standards.

Noise Limit for Generator Sets Run with Petrol or Kerosene (as notified under Environment (Protection) Rules, 1986, by G.S.R. 742(E), dated 25th September, 2000)

1. Noise Limit for New Generator Sets

Noise limit for new generator sets run with petrol or kerosene shall be as given below:

	Noise limit from	
	September 1, 2001	September 1, 2002
Sound Power Level L_{WA}	90 dBA	86 dBA

Chapter III has 11 sections and deals with prevention, control and abatement of environmental pollution. Section 7 prescribes the powers of the central government to lay down standards regarding discharge of the pollutant. Section 8 provides with the safeguards to be complied with by the industries, which are dealing in hazardous substances. It is obligatory on the parties, polluting the environment, u/s 9, to inform about any accident and to provide all necessary information and to take remedial measures to mitigate the pollution. Section 10 provides wide range of powers of inspection of industrial plants, register and other documents and if any person fails to give proper information, he is made punishable under the penal provisions of the Act. Section 11 deals with the power to take sample and procedure to be followed in connection therewith. Sections 12 to 14 deals with the analysis of the sample taken u/s 11. Sections 15, 16 and 17 are the penal sections and therefore, provide the punishments for the offence committed under the Act. Section 15 advocates that whoever fails to comply with or contravenes any of the provisions of this Act, or the rules made or orders or directions issued thereunder shall in respect of each such failure or contravention, be punishable with imprisonment for a term which may extend to five years or with fine which may extend to one lakh rupees, or with both and in case the failure or contravention continues, with additional fine which may extend to five thousand rupees for every day during which such failure or contravention continues after conviction for the first such failure or contravention.[23] If the failure or contravention referred to in sub section (1) continues beyond a period of one year after the date of conviction, the offender shall be punishable with imprisonment for term which may extend to 7 years.[24] This penal provision of punishment to the wrongdoers, is superb provision and can be said to be the very heart of the Act, as this will bring a fear psychosis in the minds of the polluters or potential polluters. The novel feature of this Act is of entitling the private citizens also to file complaint in the court of law in his individual capacity.[25] Sections 16 and 17 deals with the offences committed by the companies and Government departments respectively.

Chapter IV titled 'Miscellaneous' consists 9 sections, i.e. from sections 18 to 26. The Act certainly provides for the proceeding against government department but at the same time, it does provide protection to these government servants, who have done anything in good faith, or in case such director, manager or secretary of the company, or the officer of the government department proves that the offence was committed without his knowledge or that he exercised all due diligence to prevent the commission of such offence. These provisions have been inserted with a view to keep the moral of the officers so that they may take action against wrong doers, without any fear of self-prosecution, suit or other legal proceedings against polluters or potential polluters.[26]

Section 19 empowers the government as well as private individual to prosecute the polluters. This is significantly a good provision, bringing the government and the individual at one pedestal in respect of filing of complaint against polluter or apprehended polluter. This is truly a novel features of the Act, distinguishing this Act with earlier Acts of entitling private citizens also to file complaint in the court of law in his individual capacity.[27] This is a new power given under the Act which we do not find in prior legislation.

The provision of section 20 is another notable thing, which states that 'the central government may, in relation to its functions under this Act, from time to time, require any person, officer, state government or other authority to furnish to it or any prescribed authority or officer, any reports, returns, statistics, accounts and other information and such person, officer, state government or other authority shall be bound to do so'.

Under section 21 of the Act, all the officers or other

employees working or acting in pursuance of this Act/rules made thereunder, have been deemed as public servants within the meaning of section 21 of IPC. By making them public servants, they have been given all the privileges and immunities to which a public servant is entitled; hence it is a good provision.

It is a reality that without delegation of powers no authority can either work properly or achieve the desired goals or complete the target, which it intends to achieve. It was, therefore, thought essential by the parliament that the Act should also have a delegation of power clause attached to it so that power may be delegated to the persons or authorities as per the requirement of the Act. Section 23 has completed this novel task by incorporating delegation of power clause in the Act and thereby made the Act live and workable.

As the parliamentarians have no technical expertise in each and every sphere; therefore, every Act provides for rule-making power so that the ideals cherished in the Act may be realized. Sections 6 and 25 deals with rule-making power and also contains an exhaustive list of guidelines to be observed by the delegated authority while making rules. It is often seen and observed that in spite of having guidelines; the delegated authorities works in an arbitrary manner by overusing, abusing and misusing this delegated power. Not only this, sometimes in spite of their genuine desire; not to make rules beyond the powers assigned to them by the parent Act; because of lack of expertise in legislation making; they frame the rules which go beyond the limit assigned. With the aim of curbing this double lacunae, section 26 has been inserted in the Act, which provides that the rules passed or framed under this Act shall be laid before each house of parliament for its approval and these rules will be effective only after their approval. This is also a welcoming provision, as on one hand it saves the time of the parliament, which otherwise may be busy in other important matters and on the other hand helps in bringing the excessive legislation to an end. This section in fact strengthens the concept of Rule of Law by way of putting checks on arbitrariness while making rules and fulfilling its objectives to a maximum possible extent.[28]

Though, there is no hesitation in saying that this Act provides for speedy, effective and planned strategy for preventing and integrating environmental pollution and is a step forward towards a profound co-operative movement for justice to nature and homosapians. But no Act howsoever perfectly and meticulously drafted can remain free from ambiguities, drawbacks, shortcomings or lacunae and this umbrella Act is not an exception to it. The Act drafted with utmost caution, care, planning/keeping the lacunae and drawbacks of the previous legislation in mind, is far better than earlier Acts, projecting wider perspective for preservation, protection, conservation and enhancement of environment; and acts as a living and dynamic legislation in curbing environmental pollution and disaster management. Still it has certain de-merits, which requires immediate attention and remedial measures to be adopted by the parliament for smooth functioning of the Act. These de-merits are discussed below:

(i) As evident from section 2 of the Act, the malady of noise pollution is not dealt with as needed. The Act does nothing to curb noise pollution except including the noise as only the pollutant in its definition clause. It seems that Act is unaware with the health hazards of the noise and that is why this Act is called 'two steps forward and one step backward'.[29]

(ii) Under section 6, a specific mandatory provision is needed for industry to prepare and submit a suitable environment impact assessment report before the location chosen is approved and noise pollution impact needs specific mention.

(iii) The period of 60 days for notice under section 19(b) needs to be reduced to the bare minimum, so as to lift up an unnecessary obstacle in the way of the community moved by nation-wise programmes of environmental protection and promotion, to actual efforts in this direction.[30]

At one point at least section 19(b) may be appreciated, i.e. the party, who is served with notice, gets his source of pollution cleared by removing all the defects within statutory period of 60 days. It may be because of the penal liability or pecuniary liability or otherwise, but at least we find an establishment free from environmental pollution. The rule-making environment free from pollutants may be accelerated, if the period of notice is reduced and therefore, the victims of environmental pollution will have to wait and bear for lesser time. Due to these provisions of the Act, PIL movement also got set back.

(i) One could locate an other drawback under section 24(2) which states as under:

'Where any acts or omission constitutes an offence punishable under this Act and also under any other Act, then the offender found guilty of such offence shall be liable to be punished under that Act and not under this Act'. It seems to be strange and hackneyed provision taking life out of the new enactment. This Act seems to be a provision that reduces the law into a 'barking dog' that never bites[31] and reduces the deterrent effect of enhanced fine and takes the wind out of the sail of the law.[32] and hence appears like a king Kobra with large fangs but having no venom. It also takes away life out of the law and turns it into a dead law from that of a living law by making it unenforceable through clause (2) of section 24.

(ii) Section 15 dealing with penal provision suffers from one more glaring defect and that is no minimum sentence is prescribed.[33] It is true that provision provides for higher punishments against the wrong doers but wide discretion has been placed in the hands of the judges and courts in the matter of sentencing, which might weaken the intended deterrent impact of EPA. It is therefore, most humbly submitted that section 15 must provide, some minimum punishment so that violators may have apprehension of such minimum punishment even in case of his smallest offence. Wide discretion in the hands of the judges and courts is also against the basic tenets of law or Rule of Law, because personal likes and dislikes may play a vital role while punishing a wrong doer, therefore, this rider of minimum punishment 'was' and is must.[34]

(iii) The Act can also be criticized on the ground that it is absolutely silent with respect to civil liability. New Motor Vehicle Act, 1988 has a provision for compensation and civil liability so that the victim of the accident may not be in financial hardship. Financial assistance to the victim or family is a solace and a step forward to ensure minimum amount of safety, security and means of livelihood. It is also a fundamental principle of Rule of Law and of natural justice that why the victim or his family should suffer because of no fault of him and therefore, in each and every case, victim must be compensated. Therefore, a like provision should be inserted in EPA also.

(c) Indian Penal Code 1860 (45 of 1860)

The Indian Penal Code, 1860 (hereinafter referred to as IPC) was enacted to provide a general penal code for India.[35] The IPC of 1860, the earliest legislation of the nation, drafted by first Law Commission, under the headship of Lord Maccauley, contains provisions relating to offences affecting the public health, safety, convience, decency and morals. The deepest doctrinal roots of modern environmental law are found in the common law principles of nuisances.

The deterioration of environment in India is held to be penalized under IPC for certain types of acts termed as nuisances. The chapter XIV of the Code covers various kinds of pollutions under the different forms of public nuisances, namely, spreading of infection,[36] fouling of water, making the atmosphere noxious to health,[37] adulteration of foods, drugs and drinks, negligent in handling of poisons, combustibles and explosives,[37A] negligent with respect to machinery,[38] buildings,[39] animals,[40] spread of obscenity.[41]

Public nuisance is of two kinds, viz. public and private. The public nuisance may be considered as offences against the public, either by doing a thing, which tends to annoyance of all the king's subjects, or by neglecting a thing which the common good requires.[42] Since the spread of noise pollution definitely annoys the subjects and is not of the common good, hence, the problem of noise pollution is covered under the offence of nuisance dealt with section 268 of IPC, which states:

"A person is guilty of a public nuisance who does any act or is guilty of an illegal omission which causes any common injury, danger or annoyance to the public or to the people in general who dwell or occupy property in the vicinity, or which must necessarily cause injury, obstruction, danger or annoyance to persons who may have occasion to use any public right."

Further, this section advocates that a common nuisance is not excused on the ground that it causes some convenience or advantage. According to the above provision, the noise, which causes annoyance is undoubtedly covered under public nuisance. The question, under which circumstances the act of noise amounts to public nuisance under IPC, came before Punjab High Court in *Kirorimal Bishambar Dayal* Vs. *State of Punjab*.[43] The petitioner set-up a factory of flourmill in the outskirts of Rewari town located far considerable from the inhabited area. The old running factory was reformed into metal factory manufacturing brass utensils. Mean time, the factory area developed into a residential locality and the inhabitants complained that the noise caused by the factory interfered unreasonably with the comforts and enjoyment of the private property. Also, the vibrations caused by the heavy machinery were contended to shatter the foundation of the buildings. The trial court convicted the factory owner for public nuisance, which was upheld by the higher court in appeal. In another case of *Metropolitan Properties Ltd.* Vs. *Jones*,[44] it was held, if some heating apparatus, installed in a house, was causing excessive noise due to its operation with an electric meter, the same was considered to be the nuisance under section 268 of IPC and hence actionable under section 290. Noise from a paddy husking machine at night, was also held to be an actionable nuisance under IPC.[45] In *Rapier* Vs. *London Tramway*,[46] the noise caused by the Stable of horses to run tramways was considered to be the nuisance and the defendant was issued with an injunction. In a recent case, *Nayan Bihari Dass* Vs. *State of Orissa*,[47] the Orissa High Court held the use of multi-horns as public nuisance and directed the state authority to prohibit the same and give wide publicity to this directive through TV and press.

The annoyance caused by the noise differs with the persons and their likings; attitudes, mental state and the circumstances at that moment, viz. the sweat melody in the morning may cause annoyance to those, who still wish to be in bed. Ivour Hyden's is the case[48] in which the court excused the act of playing radio loudly on the ground that the act is of trivial nature. But, this decision seems to be erroneous and needs fresh look, because the playing of radio at moderate volume may be tolerable but not at a high frequency of voice, which becomes certainly objectionable by the man of ordinary prudence. More so, if the noise nuisance is permitted at such pretexts, the noise generated by the radios, TVs, or loudspeakers will definitely, ill affect that locality. Therefore, the possibility of an amendment in IPC, prohibiting expressly the noise pollution, cannot be ruled out.

(d) Environment Protection under Law of Torts

Before independence, Indians were governed by Common law principles, and in common law a person can sue for nuisance, when an act endangers his life, health, property, or comfort, or when such an act obstructs him in the enjoyment of the common rights. As envisaged, the environmental pollution materially affects the human health, and property too. Similarly, in India too, the problem of environmental pollution in general and noise pollution in particular, has been covered under the law of nuisance in torts. Public nuisance affects the subjects generally, whereas private nuisance affects only individuals, and therefore, it is the affected community at large, to initiate action against the polluters, in case of public nuisance. Individual is the right prosecutor in case of private nuisance.

A tort may be defined as a civil wrong, to constitute which, an act must be wrongful, resulting into damage to another and giving rise to a legal remedy, i.e. an act would not amount to civil wrong unless it violates some one's legal right. Thus, a noisy act does not amount to civil wrong, till it encroaches upon the legal rights of peaceful living of others. Since it does not need medical evidence, that the excessive noise disturbs the mental state of human being, and renders him to irritate, annoyance, nervousness, and heart-ailments. The act, undoubtedly amounts to nuisance under the law of torts. As it has been established that it infringes the legal rights of a person, such as right to peaceful living, right to peaceful sleep without disturbance, right to carry on ordinary conversation, right to read, right to hear by maintaining hearing power and the like.

Noise, when Amounts to an Actionable Nuisance

In *Metropolitan Properties Ltd. Vs. Jones.*[48A] It was held that if some heating apparatus is installed in a house and the operation of the same was with an electric meter, causes lot of noise. Such noise was considered to be a nuisance, which is actionable. Sameway, in *Halsey Vs. Esso Petroleum Co.,*[49] the noise of 83 decibels, caused by the movement of defendant's tankers, near plaintiff's residence, was considered an actionable nuisance.

Public and private nuisances are not, in reality, the species of same genus.

Theory of Substantial Damage

It has been recorded, in many decisions of the courts that an act of noise would amount to an actionable nuisance, only if it has violated the standards of comfort (i.e. caused substantial damage) of an ordinary person, which is to be judged according to the standards of that locality and not the position of the complainants. The standard of comforts of the locality becomes the question of discussions and forms the substance of decisions, which may invite the erroneousness.

The noise is declared detriment to human health, not only by medical experts, but also is affirmed by the victims of noise, during interview with the author. Still, proof of 'substantial damage' is needed under law of torts, to remedy.

However, the courts have observed and accepted, that the noise is destroying the ecosystem, consuming the quality of environment, and also capturing the psycho power of mankind. In this regard, Justice B. Upadhyay observes:

> "I am unable to accept the contention that it is essential in a case like this[50] either to prove that the property has been damaged or the health of the inhabitants or the plaintiff's house has been proved to be impaired. It is enough, that such discomfort is caused to the plaintiff, on account of noise and vibrations caused by the mill, that the plaintiff couldn't enjoy his residence in a reasonable manner, and is put to substantial inconveniences."

In wake of the above vague theory of 'substantial damage', it is suggested that, to bring the noise pollution within the ambit of actionable nuisance under law of torts, the substantial damage or discomfort should not be the criteria for the prosecution, but the level of noise should be recorded and if it exceeds the limits, the case becomes fit for judicial process for a civil remedy. This way, the 'noise-cause' should not only be removed, but the initiation of legal consequences should also follow. Thus, the judicial energy to be used, to decide the question of discomfort (substantial damage), may be saved. Therefore, to decide the cases of noise pollution, the substantive base should be the violation of 'permitted noise standards' for the source and the locality of its use. It may bring the drastic fall in court cases of noise pollution, because readily available remedy through enforcement machinery against high noise levels will have to be exhausted first.

However, in *Dhannalal* Vs. *Chittar Singh*,[51] MP High Court has framed some guidelines to be followed, given below:

(i) Constant noise if abnormal or unusual can be an actionable nuisance, if it interferes with one's physical comforts.

(ii) The test of nuisance causing physical discomfort is the actual local standard of comfort and not an ideal or absolute standard.

(iii) Generally, unusual or abnormal noise on defendant's premises, which disturbs public sleep or occupants of the plaintiff's house during night or which is so loud during day time that due to it one cannot hear ordinary conversation in the plaintiff's house or which cannot allow the occupants of the plaintiff's house to carry on their ordinary work, is deemed to be noise which interferes with one's physical comfort.

(iv) Even in a noisy locality, if there is substantial addition to the noise by introduction of some machine, instruments or performances at defendant's premises which materially affects the physical comforts of the occupants of the plaintiff's house, then also the noise will amounts to actionable nuisance.

(v) If the noise amounts to an actionable nuisance the defence that the defendant is making a reasonable use of his own property, will be ineffectual. No use of one's property is reasonable if it causes substantial discomfort to one's person.

(vi) If the defendant is found to be carrying on his business so as to cause a nuisance to his neighbours, he is not acting reasonably as regards them and may be restrained by injunction, although he may be conducting his business in a proper manner and according to rules framed in that behalf either by the municipality or by the government. The latter defence can be effective in case of public nuisance, but not in that of a private nuisance.

(vii) If an operation on the defendant's premises cannot by any care and skill be prevented from causing a private nuisance to the neighbours, it cannot be undertaken at all except with the consent of those injured by it.

After analyzing the case law, it can be observed that Indian courts remained reluctant in awarding damages and have preferred to grant the relief, by way of injunction. No doubt, the law relating to nuisance under the law of torts in India is based on common law of nuisance, even than the Indian courts find it difficult to assess the damages in cases of noise. Whereas, under common law of nuisance, damages have frequently been awarded by British Courts in the cases of noise pollution. Not only in England, in most of the industrialized countries, the damages have become one of the common reliefs, in cases of noise nuisances. For instance in Fukuto city, near Tokyo, a large number of 507 residents complained, against the noise caused by the flights of military as well as civilian jet aircrafts. After three years of filing suits, 319 residents were awarded $ 1.59 million.[52] In another case a damage of above 330 million Yen was awarded by Tokyo District Court to 596 people, living near Yokota, the U.S. Air base, because of the noise pollution from its jet aircrafts.[53]

This practice of Indian court i.e. to grant injunction, does not have any deterrent effect upon the noise creators, because in case of injunctions, they have only to stop the cause of noise and the matter becomes over. Whereas, in cases of damages, he has to compensate the loss occurred on this account, in addition to seizure of the cause of noise. Hence, it is submitted that theory of awarding damages may prove more effective, than injunction theory, for mitigating the nuisance of noise, to an extent.

(e) Tamilnadu Towns Nuisances Act, 1889

Previously, section 3(10) of this Act provided that use of any sound amplifier except at such times and places and subject to such conditions as shall from time to time be allowed by an officer of the police department not below the rank of a DSP, is an offence and whoever in any public place commits the said offence shall be liable on conviction to fine not exceeding fifty rupees or to imprisonment of either description not exceeding eight days. But Tamilnadu Act IV of 1975, sub-section (10) of sec. 3 was omitted and sec. 3-A was inserted which is given below:

"Sec. 3-A (1): Whoever plays any music or uses any sound amplifier except at such times and in such area and subject to such conditions as shall, from time to time, be allowed by an officer of the police department not below the rank of an Inspector of police shall be liable on conviction to fine not exceeding five hundred rupees or to imprisonment which may extend to three months.

(2) Any police officer referred to in sub-section (1) may subject to such rules as may be made in this behalf, seize any sound amplifier used in contravention of the terms and conditions of a licence granted under sub-section (1) and the court trying an offence under this section may also direct the forfeiture of any sound amplifier as seized."

Thus, the above statutory provisions empower the police officers referred to therein to impose conditions from time to time upon user of sound amplifier. However, the State Government has issued orders under the said provisions from time to time prescribing conditions for grant of licences and permission also for the use of loudspeakers.[54]

(f) Police Act, 1861

The Police Act, 1861 covers the problem of noise pollution arising from music, an aspect of noise pollution. It authorizes the Superintendent of Police to regulate the extent to which music may be used in streets on the occasion of festivals and ceremonies.[55]

Sec. 30: This section of the Act provides for the regulation of music in streets. Under this section, the SP or ASP may regulate the extent to which music may be played in the streets on the occasion of festivals and ceremonies.

Sec. 31: Police to keep order on public roads, etc.—It shall be the duty of the police to keep order on the public roads, and in the public streets, thoroughfares, ghats and landing places, and at all other places of public resort, and to prevent obstruction on the occasions of assemblies and processions on the public roads and in the public streets, or in the neighbourhood of places of worship, during the time of public worship, and in any case when any road, street, thoroughfare, ghat or landing place may be thronged or may be liable to be obstructed.

Thus, if the problem of law and order is disturbed on the places mentioned in the above section due to environmental pollution, it is the duty of police to prevent the same. It is pertinent to note that the noise has resulted many times into the problem of law and order, hence noise created nuisances definitely lies under this provision.

Sec. 32: Penalties for disobeying order issued under last three sections, etc.—Every person opposing or not obeying the orders issued under the last preceding section, or violating the conditions of any licence granted by the District Superintendent or Assistant District Superintendent of Police for the use of music, or for the conduct of assemblies and processions shall be liable, on conviction before a Magistrate, to a fine not exceeding two hundred rupees.

Sec. 34: Punishment for certain offences on roads, etc.— Any person who, on any road or in any open place or street or thoroughfare within the limits of any town to which this section shall be specially extended by the State Government, commits any of the following offences, to the obstruction, inconvenience, annoyance, risk, danger or damage of the residents or passengers shall, on conviction before a Magistrate, be liable to a fine not exceeding fifty rupees, or to imprisonment with or without hard labour not exceeding eight days; and it shall be lawful for any police officer to take into custody, without a warrant, any person who within his view commit any of such offence, namely (here only the provisions relating to environmental pollution are being mentioned)—

(i) **Slaughtering cattle, furious riding, etc.**
Any person who slaughters any cattle or cleans any carcass; any person who rides or drives any cattle recklessly or furiously, or trains or breaks any horse or other cattle.

(v) **Throwing dirt into street**
Any person who throws or lays down any dirt, filth rubbish or any stones or building materials, or who constructs any cowshed, stable or the like, or who causes any offensive matter to run from any house, factory, dung-heap or the like.

State Amendments

Pondicherry
(1) After Section 34, the following sections shall be inserted, namely:
34-B. Penalty for certain offences in public place.— "Whoever, in any public place, . . . beats a drum of tom-tom, or blows a horn or trumpet or beats or sounds any brass or other instrument or utensil or plays any music or uses any sound amplifier except at such time and place and subject to such conditions as may be specified in licence issued in this behalf by the Inspector-General of Police or by any authority authorised in this behalf by him, shall be punishable with fine which may extend to fifty rupees or with imprisonment for a term which may extend to one month.[56]

Sikkim
In its application to the State of Sikkim after Section 34, insert the following section, namely:
34-A. Power to prohibit, restrict, regulate or impose conditions on the use of microphones, etc.—(1) If, in the opinion of the Magistrate of the district or Superintendent of Police of the district or Sub-Divisional Police Officer, it is necessary so to do for the purpose of preventing annoyance to, or injury to the health of, the public or any section thereof, or for the purpose of maintaining public peace and tranquillity, he may, by order, prohibit, restrict, regulate or impose conditions on the use or operation, in any area within his jurisdiction or in any vehicle

within such area, of microphones, loudspeakers or other apparatus for amplifying human voice or for amplifying music or other sounds.

(2) The State Government may, on its own motion or on the representation of any person or person aggrieved, modify, alter or cancel any order made under sub-section (1).

(3) A police-officer not below the rank of Sub-Inspector, may take such steps or use such force as may be reasonably necessary for securing compliance with any order made under sub-section (1) or and such order as modified or altered by the State Government under sub-section (2) and may seize any microphone, loudspeaker or other apparatus used or operated in contravention of the order.

(4) A police officer, who seizes any microphone, loudspeaker or other apparatus under sub-section (3), may also at the same time seize any vehicle in which such microphone, loudspeaker or other apparatus is being carried or conveyed or is being kept at that time:

Provided that any police officer of the police-station within the limits of which the vehicle is seized, not below the rank of Sub-Inspector, may release such vehicle on a bond for such sum not exceeding five hundred rupees as he deems reasonable being executed by the owner of the vehicle in favour of the State Government to produce the vehicle at the time of investigation or the trial, and to surrender the vehicle, if detached to be forfeited under sub-section (5).

(5) Any person who contravenes any order made by the Magistrate of the district or Superintendent of Police of the District or any Sub-Divisional Police Officer under sub-section (1) or any such order as modified or altered by the State Government under sub-section (2), shall, on conviction before a Magistrate, be liable to a fine which may extend to one hundred rupees and the Court trying an offence under this section may also direct the forfeiture of any microphone, loudspeaker or other apparatus seized under sub-section (3) or any vehicle seized under sub-section (4) or released under the proviso to that sub-section.

(6) The provisions of this section shall be in addition to and not in derogation of the powers conferred by any other section of this Act.[57]

West Bengal

After Section 34, the following sections shall be inserted, namely:

34-A. Power to prohibit, restrict, regulate or impose conditions on the use of microphones.—(1) If, in the opinion of the Magistrate of the district or any Sub-Divisional Magistrate, or Magistrate of the first class, it is necessary so to do for the purpose of preventing annoyance to, or injury to public health or any section thereof, or for the purpose of maintaining public peace and tranquillity, he may, by order, prohibit, restrict, regulate or impose conditions on the use or operation, in any area within his jurisdiction or in any vehicle within such area, of microphones, loudspeakers or other apparatus for amplifying human voice or for amplifying music or other sounds.

(2) The State Government may, on its own motion or on the representation of any person or persons aggrieved, modify, alter or cancel any order made under sub-section (1).

(3) A police officer not below the rank of Sub-Inspector, may take such steps or use such force as may be reasonably necessary for securing compliance with any order made under sub-section (1) or and such order as modified or altered by the State Government under sub-section (2) and may seize any microphone, loudspeaker or other apparatus used or operated in contravention of the order.

(4) A police officer who seizes any microphone, loudspearker or other apparatus under sub-section (3), may also at the same time seize any vehicle in which such microphone, loudspeaker or other apparatus is being carried or conveyed or is being kept at that time:

Provided that any police officer of the police-station within the limits of which the vehicle is seized, not below the rank of Sub-Inspector, may release such vehicle on a bond for such sum not exceeding five hundred rupees as he deems reasonable being executed by the owner of the vehicle in favour of the State Government to produce the vehicle at the time of investigation or the trial, and to surrender the vehicle, if directed to be forfeited under sub-section (5).

(5) Any person who contravenes any order made by the Magistrate of the district or any Sub-Divisional Magistrate, or Magistrate of the first class under sub-section (1) or any such

order as modified or altered by the State Government to produce the vehicle at the time of investigation or the trial, and to surrender the vehicle, if directed to be forfeited under sub-section (5).

(6) The provisions of this section shall be in addition to and not in derogation of the powers conferred by any other section of this Act.[58]

Delhi Police Act, 1978

The commissioner of police under Delhi Police Act has been empowered to prevent any annoyance, disturbance, discomfort or injury to the public or to any person. For this purpose, he can issue directions against any person enquiring him for preventing, prohibiting, controlling or regulating any vocal or instrumental music or sound caused by the playing, beating, clashing, or use of loudspeakers causing disturbance or carrying on any trade, avocation resulting into noise.[59]

Bombay Police Act, 1951 (22 of 1951)

The problem of noise resulting from the musical instruments, horns, or other noisy instruments undoubtedly lies within the provisions of the Bombay Police Act.[60]

The commissioner of police and district magistrate have been empowered under the Act to make rules for licensing, controlling or prohibiting the playing of music or the beating of drums, tom-toms (Indian drum) or other instruments and blowing or sounding of horns or other noisy instruments in or near streets or public places.[61] They have also been empowered to regulate the conduct and behaviour or action of persons constituting assemblies and processions on or along the streets or public places wherein the noise caused by public processions may be covered.[62] Further, the Act also empowers them to prescribe the procedure in accordance with which any license or permission is to be obtained under the Act.

Section 33(1)(r)(iii): The Commissioner and the District Magistrate in areas under their respective charges or any part thereof, may make, alter or rescind rules or orders not inconsistent with this Act for licensing or, in order to prevent obstruction, inconvenience, annoyance, risk, danger or damage of the residents or passengers in the vicinity prohibiting the using of a loudspeaker in or near any public place.

Section 33 of the Act confers upon the officers mentioned therein powers to make rules or orders for the use of a loudspeaker in or near a public place. The powers conferred are three in number, viz (i) the power of licensing; (ii) the power of controlling; and (iii) the power of prohibition. The authorities on whom the powers are conferred are the Commissioner and the District Magistrate.

In exercise of the power conferred under the provisions of the Act, the police commissioner of Ahmedabad enacted certain rules for regulating the conduct and behaviour of the processions. The validity of these rules was challenged in *Himat Lal Vs. Police Commissioner.*[63] The Supreme Court held that Rule 7 of section 33(1)(a), which prescribed that no public meeting with or without loudspeaker would be held on the public street within the jurisdiction of the commissioner of police, Ahemedabad, unless necessary permission in writing had been obtained, was struck down as it gave arbitrary powers to the police commissioner and gave no guidance about the refusal of the permission.

Madras City Police Act, 1887

Section 71 of this Act empowers the Commissioner or, subject to his orders, any police officer above the rank of head constable, to regulate assemblies, meetings and processions in public places, etc. Sub-section (i) enables him to issue licences and regulate or prohibit the use of music or sound amplifiers in any area. Sub-section 8 makes the section inapplicable to any assembly or meeting of a purely religious character held in a recognized place of worship, any assembly or meeting gathered together purely for the purpose of taking part in sports, any procession on the occasion of any wedding, funeral or similar domestic occurrence, or of any religious ceremony, or to any public meeting held under any statutory or other express legal authority, or public meeting convened by the Sheriff, or to any public meetings or class of public meetings exempted for that purpose by the State Government by general or special order.

Sec. 71-A: "(1) Whoever plays any music or uses any sound amplifier except at such times and in such area and subject to such conditions as shall, from time to time, be allowed by the Commissioner or subject to his orders, any police officer above the rank of a Head-Constable, shall be liable on conviction to fine not exceeding five hundred rupees or imprisonment which may extend to three months.

(2) Any police officer referred to in sub-section (1) may subject to such rules as may be made in this behalf, seize any sound amplifier used in contravention of the terms and conditions of a licence granted under sub-section (1) and the court trying an office under this section may also direct the forfeiture of any sound amplifier so seized."

(g) Railway Act, 1890 (Act IX of 1890)

Railway engines and carriages cause a huge amount of noise pollution. Study reveals that the noise health hazards, on account of railway, is observed on the people, who resides near the railway stations, rail-tracks, and workshops. This is a matter of concern that there is no check to curb this noise pollution under the Railway Act, 1890. The railway engines have statutory protection and hence, it appears, that nobody can get any relief against noise pollution caused by railways.

Rule 5.16 or section 16 of Railway Act, 1890 has empowered railway administration for the use of locomotives. The section/rules states that the administration may, with previous sanction of the central government, use locomotives engines or other motive power and rolling stock to be drawn or propelled thereby, to produce noise as much as they can and there is no check upon them.

The above provision of Railway Act reveals that neither railway administration nor the government is serious to curb the noise pollution caused by the railway. However, recently some steps in this direction have been taken, one of the instances adoption of continuous welded rail (CWR). Railway engineers have decided to weld the joints left earlier for thermal expansion, which may contribute to reduce the noise caused by the rail and wheels. Yet there is an urgent need to control this unbridled pollutant caused by railway.

During interview with railway authority, the author observed that there is no major action plan to curb railway noise. Even railway authorities are reluctant to accept that the railway is a major source of noise. They say that railway noise is inevitable and hence can't be curbed. Whereas, in other countries like that of Japan, many steps have been taken up to curb railway noise. There is some special type of material, used on the contacting surface of railway tracks and wheels so as to bring the noise level to bare minimum. Apart from replacement of steam and diesel engines by electric engines, it is submitted that Railway Act needs to be amended and appropriate provision be incorporated to curb the rail noise. A lot of noise can be reduced if shunting operations are done far away from the residential areas. The entry of hawkers, beggars, or musicians must be ceased immediately inside the railway installations. The limits of noise levels in the engine cabins, coaches, workshops, etc. must not only be laid down but also be implemented.

Fast running trains must be slowdown while passing thick residential localities. Use of earmuffs should be made imperative for the railway drivers and the employees of workshops. Awareness to be raised accordingly about the noise health hazards. Annual audio medical examination must be carried out so as to record the reduction in audio power of railway employee. The seeing-off practice at railway platforms needs to be ceased-off so as to bring the noise level down at railway stations/platforms. Maximum one or two persons should be allowed to accompany the traveler and that to only in guanine cases. For this, however, railway has to sacrifice the revenue collected on account of platform tickets' sale.

(h) Workmen's Compensation Act, 1923

Workmen's Compensation Act, 1923 creates the liability of employers to pay compensation to their workers in case of injuries caused in the course of employment.[64] The injuries include "absolute deafness"[65] and "hearing impairment caused by noise."[66] As absolute deafness and hearing impairment caused by noise affects on earning capacity of the workers, the problem of noise in factories needs be controlled to some extent through aforesaid provisions of the Act provided compensation regarding injuries is made more.

(i) The Motor Vehicles Act, 1939 (4 of 1939)

Laws to control vehicular pollution need periodic revisions of emissions regulations, dealing with vehicles and fuel quality. The Central Motor Vehicle Act of 1939 was amended in 1988 to regulate vehicular emissions. Although Air Act, 1981 and Environment (Protection) Act, 1986 provide for the prescription of automobile emission standards by CPCB or Ministry of Environment and Forests, yet the implementation and enforcement of these standards is the responsibility of Union Ministry of Surface Transport or the Transport Commissioner at the state level as the case may be.

In addition to containing various provisions relating to licensing of motor vehicle's driver, control of transport vehicle, control of traffic, insurance of motor vehicle, etc. The Motor Vehicles Act, 1939, empowers the State Governments to frame their rules for the upkeep of motor vehicles and control of noise produced by them in their jurisdiction. However, a close examination of motor vehicles rules made by various states, reveals that there is nothing substantial to control the pollution of noise except a small control on 'Horns' and 'Silencer' produced noise.[67] Motor Vehicles Act, 1988[68] covers the problem of air and noise pollution caused by motor transport. The Act empowers the central government under section 110(h)[69] to frame the Rules for the reduction of noise, emitted by the vehicles. There are provisions, u/s (iii)(b)(c) and (g)[70] for State Government to frame rules of regulating intensity of audible signals, radios, tape recorders, audiovisuals, etc. which shows that there are statutory ways to control the vehicular noise.

Though, Motor Vehicles Act, u/ss 20, 21 J, 41, 68, 68 (i), 70, 90 & 111A empowers the State Government to frame the rules for the upkeep of motor vehicle. Section 70 specifically deals with problem of noise pollution and empowers the Government to frame the rules for reduction of the vehicular noise.[71] But it is a matter of notice that the power conferred by this Act has not been fully utilized by the State Governments to control noise pollution as a whole, as the rules framed by the States are mostly centered to curb the noise on account of horns and silencers only. Some of the provisions made by the State Government are discussed below:

(j) Tamilnadu Motor Vehicles Rules, 1989

Rules 402 and 403 of Tamilnadu Motor Vehicle Rules, 1989 read as under:

Rule 402, "No driver of motor vehicle shall sound the horn or other device for giving audible warning, with which the motor vehicle is equipped, or shall cause or allow any other person to do so to an extent beyond that which is reasonable necessary to ensure safety."

Rule 403, "The Commissioner of police in the city of Madras and elsewhere the Superintendent of Police may, by notification in the official Gazette and by the erection in suitable places of traffic sign No. 7 as set forth in Part A of the Schedule to the Act, prohibit the use of any horn, or other device fitted on a motor vehicle for giving suitable warning within such locality and during such hours as may be specified in the notification."

Provided that when the Commissioner of Police or the Supdt. of Police as the case may be, prohibits the use of any horn, or other device for giving audible warning during certain specified hours, he shall cause a suitable notice in English and setting forth the hours within which such use is so prohibited, to be affixed below the traffic sign. In M.S. Appa Rao's case,[72] the court also has issued the appropriate directions to enforce the same.

(k) Bengal Motor Vehicles Rules, 1940

Rules 114(d) of Bengal Motor Vehicles Rules, 1940 contains a provision that no transport vehicle can be fitted with any other form of horn excepting a bulb horn. Also the transport authorities were held responsible, under statutory obligation and duty u/s 112 of the Motor Vehicles Act, 1939, to punish the person who contravened the Provisions of above Rule 114(d) of the BMVR, 1940.

(l) Central Motor Vehicles Rules, 1988

Sections 119 and 120 of the Rules deal with the noise caused by the motor horns and read as under:

Rule 119

(1) Every motor vehicle shall be fitted with an electric horn or other device conforming to the specifications of the Bureau of Indian Standards for use by the driver to give audible and

sufficient warning of the approach or position of the vehicle.

(2) No motor vehicle shall be fitted with any multitioned horn giving a succession of different notes or with any other sound-producing device giving an unduly harsh shrill, loud or alarming noise.

(3) Nothing contained in sub-rule (2) shall prevent the use on vehicles used as ambulance or for fire fighting or salvage purposes or on vehicles used by police officers of Motor Vehicles Department in the course of their duties, of such sound signals as may be approved by the registering authority in whose jurisdiction such vehicles are kept

Rule 120

(1) Every motor vehicle shall be fitted with a device, which by means of an expansion chamber or otherwise reduces as far as practicable, the noise that would otherwise be made by the escape of exhaust gases from the engine.

(2) Every motor vehicle shall be so constructed and maintained so as to conform to noise standards, as notified under Environment Protection Act, 1986.[73]

(m) Delhi Motor Vehicles Rules, 1940

Rule 5.5: Horn

(1) Every motor vehicle shall be fitted with a horn or other approved device available for immediate use by the driver of the vehicles and capable of giving audible and sufficient hearing of the approach or position of the vehicles.

(2) No motor vehicle shall be fitted with any multitioned horn giving a succession of different tones or with any other sound producing device giving an unduly harsh, shrill loud or alarming noise.[74]

(3) Nothing in sub-rule (2) shall prevent the use of vehicles used as ambulances or for fire fighting or salvage purposes or on vehicles used by police by a provisional Government.

(4) Every transport vehicle shall be fitted with a bulb type horn, taxis and motor cycle, auto-rikshaws would however, be provided with either two electric horns with switches or one electric horn and one bulb type horn.

Rule 5.6: Silencers

(1) Every motor vehicle shall be fitted with a device which by means for an expansion chamber or otherwise reduces as far as may be reasonable and practicable the noise that would otherwise be made.

(2) Every motor vehicle shall be so constructed that the exhaust gases from the engines are discharged downwards so as to impinge on the road surface.

Rule 5.9

Every motor vehicle shall be so constructed and maintained as not to cause undue noise when in motion.[75]

(n) Uttar Pradesh Motor Vehicles Rules, 1940

Rule 115 of above said Rules of State of Uttar Pradesh provides that horn or approved device should be capable of giving audible and sufficient warning of the approach or position of the vehicle.

(o) Bihar and Orissa Motor Vehicles Rules, 1930[76]

Rule 21: Horn

(1) Every driver of a motor vehicle shall not sound the horn for any purpose other than that ensuring safety in the traffic and shall not sound it continuously.

(2) No cut out exhaust whistles, siren, electric horn and similar appliances of any description shall be used on any motor vehicle in such areas as may be notified by the district Magistrate in this behalf.

From the above provisions of Motor Vehicles Act and the Rules framed thereunder, it is observed that the attention mainly has been paid to the control of noise caused by the horns or silencers, whereas the noise caused by the faulty engines, body, mismatching of the parts, loose fittings, doors, windows, etc. music whether fitted to the vehicle or otherwise, crying in loud voice to attract the passengers at private terminals, finds often no place. To control such noise, it is recommended that a specified limit needs to be fixed for the engine of each type of vehicle as well as supportive appliances/devices for their operation or maintenances. Overall noise caused by the type of vehicle and the terminals from where these are being plied is also to be gone into. These limits, so fixed needs strict enforcement. The vehicle, causing noise beyond the limit should not be allowed to ply on the road. Perhaps, the periodical check of the noise, caused by the vehicle, may be introduced along with exhaust emission's periodical checks. The 'Pollution Under Certificate' should also reflect the decibels of noise caused by that vehicle. It is pertinent to mention that the way the private agencies, which have been authorized in this behalf, are checking the engine exhaust emissions and issuing the certificates to that affect, is unsatisfactory. The pollution under control seems the tiger of that certificate and not that of fact. It has been observed many times that the vehicle apparently emitting a high quantity of smoke, does also has valid certificate for pollution under control. It shows, either the pollution has not been measured correctly or the measuring instrument may be faulty or the certificate has been issued without measurement. Therefore, the transport authority should look into this aspect afresh, so as to curb the pollution and keep it under control in deed. The Central/State Pollution Control Boards may be the effective monitoring/controlling agencies. It would be fruitful if these pollution control boards crosscheck the calibration of pollution measuring instrument.

Further, it also has been observed by the author himself, while interviewing the traffic controlling agencies, that there is a felt need of knowledge of pollutions caused by the vehicles and the portable (preferably pocket size) instrument for their measurement.

Category of Vehicle	Maximum permissible Noise Levels in dB(A)
Two-wheelers (petrol driven)	80
All passenger cars, all petrol driven three-wheelers and diesel driven two-wheelers.	82
Passenger or light commercial vehicles including three-wheeled vehicles fitted with diesel engine with gross vehicles weight up to 4,000 Kgs.	85
Passenger or commercial vehicles with gross vehicle weight above 4,000 Kgs and up to 12,000 Kgs.	89
Passenger or commercial vehicles with gross vehicle weight above 12,000 Kgs.	91

However, under Central Motor Vehicles Rules, 1989, it has been notified,[77] that every motor vehicle shall be construed and maintained so as to conform to noise standards as indicated in the foregoing table and these standards shall be tested as per Indian Standards IS: 3028.

For the sake of comparison, in Europe, EC noise emission limits for selected vehicles and products are given below:

Vehicle Category	1972	1982	1988/90	1995/96
Passenger Car	82	80	77	74
Urban Bus	89	82	80	78
Heavy Lorry	91	88	84	80

Two and Three-wheelers

Motorcycles and Three-wheelers	1980	1989	Proposal
< 80 cm^3	78	77	75
$> 80 < 175$ cm^3	80-83	79	77
> 175 cm^3	83-86	82	80

It is also to be noted that Under Environment (Protection) Rules, 1986, it has been notified,[78] that the following noise limits for vehicle shall be applicable from the 1st day of the year (i.e. 1st January) 2003. The test method to be followed shall be IS: 3028-18.[79]

Category of Vehicle	Maximum permissible Noise Levels in dB(A)
Two-wheelers	
Displacement more than 80 cm^3	75
Displacement more than 80 cm^3 but up to 175 cm^3	77
Displacement more than 175 cm^3	80
Three-wheelers	
Displacement up to 175 cm^3	77
Displacement more than 175 cm^3	80
Passenger car	75
Passenger or Commercial Vehicles	
Gross vehicle weight up to 14 tonne	77
Gross vehicle weight more than 4 tonne but up to 12 tonne	80
Gross vehicle weight more than 12 tonne	82

Although, it is an uphill task to maintain the above noise standard on roads, terminals or in workshops, but it can be made achieved, if the states enforce the rules strictly, made therein for the purpose. The states, which have not yet framed the said rules, should also frame and enforce in their true sense.

(p) Factories Act, 1948

It is a paradox, that the industrialization and urbanization, which were once a symbol of progressive/developed nations and revolutionary modernization in society, have brought manifold problems, which are unsafe for human race. Environmental noise pollution is one of them.[80] In beginning, no concrete and effective steps were taken to curb or control the evil effects of pollution, may be either due to ignorance, lack of technology, paucity of legislation, absence of legal obligations or deemed unnecessary cost expense. But, now increasing graveness of noise health hazardous warranted an urgent attention to prevent and control industrial noise.

It is very surprising, that India, being one of industrially advanced states, does not provide any direct protection to the workers from noise pollution in any of its laws, specially out of a long series of industrial laws. More amazing is, that the protection to the eyes of an employee is provided under section 35 of Factories Act, but his ears are left unprotected to be deaf, along with other more many maladies caused by environmental noise. It is only section 11 of Factories Act, 1948, which could deal with this kind of pollution. Sec. 11 states:

> "Every factory shall be kept clean, and free from effluvia (foul discharge) arising from drain, privy, or *other nuisance. . . . .*"

As evident from above texts of section 11 of the Act, one could locate the coverage to remedy noise pollution, only under the term "other nuisance", and it, therefore becomes the statutory duty of the industrialists to adopt and provide, adequate measures for the control of noise menace. However, this Act puts an obligation on medical practitioner as well as occupier of factory, to inform chief inspector regarding any of noticeable diseases, detected by him, alongwith all other relevant information. Failure to this has been made a punishable offence, under Sec. 90 of this Act.

Sec 88A. **Notice of certain dangerous occurrences:** Where in a factory, any dangerous occurrence of such a nature as may be prescribed, occurs, whether causing any bodily injury, or disability or does not; the manager of the factory shall send a notice thereof, to such authorities and in such form, and within such time, as may be prescribed.

Third Schedule, to Secs. 89 and 90 specifically mentions about 'Noise induced hearing loss' (exposure to high noise levels).

Under the Act, occupier of every industry is required to report about the name and diseases of the patient among the workers in the factory. The diseases caused on account of noise pollution, should also be diagnosed and be made strict imperative of Secs. 89 and 90. It is a matter of concern, that section 11 of Factories Act has been provided with five substitutions/insertions in 1976 but, no one could devout any insertion to curb industrial noise.

This Act is said to be the donor of term 'occupier' to all the pollution laws and the definition of 'hazardous process' under Sec. 2(cb)[81] of the Act[82] describes two outcomes of process: (i) medical impairment to health of the person engaged in or connected therewith; (ii) problem of general environment. If the industry is as noisy as to produce hearing impairment, then the problem of noise undoubtedly lies, well within the ambit of section 2, and employer is liable to be penalized u/s 41(b)(c) accordingly, in response to the hazardous process.

Protection Against Noises in Work Zone Area (As Prescribed in Schedule XXIV of Model Rules under Factories Act, 1948)

In every factory, suitable engineering control, or administrative measures shall be taken to ensure, so far is reasonably practicable, that no worker is exposed to sound levels exceeding the maximum permissible noise exposure levels specified, in table given on next page.

Table A: Permissible Exposure in Cases of Continuous Noise

Total time of exposure per day (in hours)	Sound pressure level in dB(A)
8	90
6	92
4	95
3	97
2	100
1½	102
1	105
¾	107
½	110
¼	115

Notes: (i) No exposure in excess of 115 dB(A) is to be permitted.

(ii) For any period of exposure falling in between any figure and the next higher or lower figure as indicated in column 1, the permissible sound pressure level is to be determined by extrapolation on a proportionate basis.

Table B: Permissible Exposure in Cases of Impulsive or Impact Noise[82A]

Peak Sound Pressure Level (In dB)	Permitted number of Impulses or Impacts per day
140	100
135	315
130	1,000
125	3,160
120	10,000

Notes: (i) No exposure in excess of 140 dB peak sound pressure level is permitted.

(ii) For any peak sound pressure level falling in between any figure and the next higher or lower figure as indicated in column 1, the permitted number of impulses or impacts per day is to be determined by extrapolation on a proportions basis.

For the purposes of this schedule, if variations in noise level involve maximum at intervals of one second or less, the noise is to be considered as a continuous one and the criteria given in Table 'A' would apply. In other cases, the noise is to be considered as impulsive or impact noise and the criteria given in Table 'B' would apply.

When daily exposure is composed of two or more periods of noise exposures at different levels their combined effect should be considered, rather than the individual effect of each. The mixed exposure should be considered to exceed the limits value, if the sum of the fractions is C1/T1+C2/T2+....Cn/Tn, exceeds unity.

Where,

'C' indicates the total time of actual exposure at a specified noise level; and

'T' denotes the time of exposure permissible at that level. Noise exposure of less than 90 dB(A) may be ignored in the above calculation.

Where, it is not possible to reduce the noise exposure to the levels specified in sub-rule (1) by reasonably practicable engineering control or administrative measures, the noise exposure shall be reduced to the greatest extent feasible by such control measures, and each worker so exposed shall be provided with suitable ear protectors so as to reduce the exposure to noise to the levels specified in sub-rule (1).

Where the ear protectors provided in accordance with above rules and adopted by a worker cannot still attenuate the noise, reaching ear, as determined by subtracting the attenuation value in dB(A) of the ear protectors concerned from the measured sound pressure level to a level permissible under Table 'A' or Table 'B' as the case may be; the noise exposure period shall be suitably reduced to correspond to the permissible noise exposures specified in sub-paragraph (1).

In all cases, where the prevailing sound levels exceed the permissible levels specified in sub-paragraph (1), there shall be administered an effective hearing conservation programme which shall include among other hearing conservation measures, pre-employment and periodical auditory surveys conducted on workers exposed to noise, exceeding permissible levels, and rehabilitation of such workers either by reducing the exposure to the noise levels or by transferring them to places where noise levels are relatively less or by any other suitable means.

Every worker employed in areas where the noise exceeds

maximum permissible exposure levels specified in sub-rule (1), shall be subjected to any auditory examination by a Certifying Surgeon within 14 days of his first employment and thereafter, shall be re-examined at least once every 12 months. Such initial and periodical examinations shall include tests which the certifying surgeon may consider appropriate and shall include determination of auditory thresholds for pure tones of 125, 250, 500, 1000, 2000, 4000, and 8000 cycles per second.

Need of 'Polluter Pays Principle' Against Industrial Noise

'Polluter Pays Principle' warrants that it is the industrial world, which has polluted the environment most, and it is the industrialist who are to pay for its up-gradation too. It is an appeal to all industrialists that, this planet earth is our home, our only home in this life, we have no other home. We will have to suffocate till death, if it is polluted beyond the limits. The level of noise has also increased and will increase more, if left unchecked.

(q) Air Craft Act, 1934

The Air Craft Act, 1934 provide no specific provision for the control of noise pollution caused by aircrafts. However, it may be covered under section 5, which empowers the government to enact rules for the protection of public health, manufacture, possession, use, operation, sale, import or export of any aircraft and hence the airport noise can be checked by this enactment. The Code of practice, prescribed by the 'Central Pollution Control Board' can be referred here, which bans the constructions of airports in inhabited area, and also prohibits the flight-paths over such places. Further, to reduce the noise, mounting of potable silencers has been recommended by these rules.

It may be a valuable suggestion, to adopt latest developed technologies, right at the designing and manufacturing stages, for the control of avionics-noise despite an immediate enforcement of ear protective devices.

(r) Madhya Pradesh Control of Music and Noises Act, 1951

Though, the sweet music, if listen with concentration, is to restore subtle mental imbalances and to relieve the boredom of mind. Musical vibrations may convey moods and emotions and

·shape our consciousness.[83] According to a famous psychiatrist Dr. Sanjay Chugh, the music therapy has shown good results to cure insanity and brain hemorrhages. Pt. Shashank Katti of Mumbai, a researcher of music therapy, opined that, music may cure disease of arthritis, sugar, blood pressure and migraine.[84]

Though the music has the capability to stimulate the mind but the excess of the same may be miserable for that mind. Moreover, one's music may be the pollution for another and hence, may increase the mental agonies. The agony of society is perhaps the compulsion for enacting Madhya Pradesh Control of Music and Noises Act, 1951

The object of the Madhya Pradesh Control of Music and Noise Act, 1951[85] is to prohibit loud music on public streets and private places after midnight and before 4 a.m. On the other hand, it allows the soft music. The musical noise emitted from hotels, shops and restaurants adjacent to public streets also lies within the purview of the Act.[86] The musical instruments under the Act include sitara, sarangi, ektara, violin, bansi, bin, veena, sarod, piano, harmonium, gramophone, tabla khanjari, dholak, dhol, band and radio other than the nocturnal noise. The district magistrate has been empowered to declare any noise as nocturnal and to prohibit it in certain areas or localities.[87] Under the Act, the use of loudspeakers or amplifiers for broadcasting any speech, sermon, music or gramophone has specifically been prohibited after midnight till 4 a.m.

Further a provision for penalty has also been made under the Act. In case any person is found violating any of the provisions of the Act, he shall be punished up to one month's imprisonment or with fine up to Rs. 100 or with both.[88]

No doubt, the problem of noise of musical instruments including loudspeaker lies within the provisions of the Act, but the critical aspect of the Act is that it merely covers the noise after midnight and has nothing to do, if the musical note arises in late night hours. According to medical science, a sound body needs minimum 6 to 8 hours sleep for sound health, whereas this Act protects it from noise only from midnight to 4 a.m., i.e. only 4 hours, which is certainly insufficient to keep the body in sound health. Further, the Act prohibits the noise emitted from the streets, shops, restaurants adjacent to the streets, whereas the excessive noise is hazards to mankind irrespective of its place of origin. Therefore, each locality needs to be protected from the increasing menace of noise pollution. The ultimate and important need of the hour is that; the enforcement machinery under the Act is to be made more vigilant to come heavily on the violators and incorporation of an amendment in the Act as discussed above.

Thus the Act cannot be said as an effective even for the control of musical noises. This Act is silent on the limits of decibels, above which a sound turns into the noise.

(s) Punjab Instrument (Control of Noises) Act, 1956 (Act 36 of 1956)

Punjab Instrument (Control of Noises) Act, 1956 has been passed to control the use and play of instruments such as loudspeakers, microphones and amplifiers. The Act states that the indiscriminate use of loudspeakers, amplifiers and such other apparatus omitting and transmitting sound, is a great source of nuisance causing obstruction in streets and lanes, annoyance and injury to neighbours, especially student community, in endangering health of aged and infirm, who cannot enjoy sound sleep.[89] Out of total 6 sections, below given are the provisions of the Act, which deal with the use of noise causing instruments.

Section 3 (For Punjab): Restriction on the use of Instrument

No person shall use or operate any instrument:

    (i) in or upon any premises at such pitch or volume as to be audible beyond the precincts thereof, and

    (ii) on any road, street, thoroughfare or other public or vacant place, (except under the written permission of the district Magistrate or any officer authorized by him in this behalf and under such conditions as may be attached to it).

Section 3 (For Haryana): Restriction on the use of Instrument

No person shall use or operate any instrument:

    (i) in or upon any premises at such pitch or volume as to be audible beyond the precincts thereof, and

    (ii) in or upon any street of bazaar or open space (except

under written permission of the District Magistrate or any officer authorized by him in this behalf and under such conditions as may be attached to it).

Section 4: Limitation on the Use of Instruments

No person shall use or operate any instrument between 10 'O' clock in the night and 6 'O' clock in the morning, except with the written permission of the District Magistrate or any officer authorized by him in this behalf and under such conditions as may be attached to it.

Section 4A: Fee

No permission under section 3 or 4 shall be given unless the application for permission bears a court fee stamp of the value, calculated at the rate of five rupees for every day or part thereof in respect of which the permission is sought:

Provided that, where the permission is either refused or given for a period which is less than one applied for, the amount of fee shall be refunded wholly or proportionately as the case may be.

Section 5: Penalty

Whoever contravenes the provisions of the Act, shall be liable to be punished with imprisonment of either description for a term, which may extend to six months or with fine that may extend to 1,000 rupees or with both.

Section 6: Offences to be Cognizable

Notwithstanding anything contained in the Code of Criminal Procedure, an offence punishable under this Act shall be cognizable.

Thus, it may be observed that Punjab Instrument (Control of Noise) Act covers the problem of the noise of loudspeaker, amplifier and other apparatus provided it amounts to nuisance or creates obstruction in streets or causes annoyance to neighbours. Further, the Act also protects the interest of student community and the health of the people against the noise.[90]

The Act prohibits the use of instrument if it is inaudible beyond the premises except with the permission of the District Magistrate who can attach necessary conditions to such permission.[91] Further, the Act prohibits the use of instrument between 10 p.m. and 6 a.m.[92] A provision of penalty has also been prescribed under this Act. In case of violation of the provisions of the Act, an imprisonment up to six months and a fine up to Rs. 1000 or both can be imposed.

The constitutional validity of the Act was upheld by the Supreme Court in *Bedi Gurcharan* Vs. *State of Haryana.*[93]

The author is of the view that the Act, undoubtedly has provisions to curb noise pollution and protects the persons from excessive noise, but does not protects the persons who are present in the precincts thereof, where the loudspeakers or amplifiers are being used. These persons may be bearing high pitch sound either due to unawareness of the health hazards of noise pollution or under some other compulsions. Therefore, in addition to the restriction under section 3 that no person shall use or operate any instrument in or upon any premises at such pitch or volume as to be audible beyond the precincts thereof, it is submitted that by appropriate amendment in section 3 of this Act, maximum decibel of sound must be prescribed, below which it is to be maintained inside the precincts in which sound-amplifying device is used irrespective of its purpose.

(t) Ajmer (Sound Amplifiers and Loudspeakers Control) Act, 1953

Ajmer Sound Amplifiers and Loudspeaker Control Act[94] was enacted to control the problem of noise caused on account of the use of loudspeakers in the state of Rajasthan.

However, this Act and other corresponding laws are not in force now, in any part of the State, as the Act itself has been repealed under section 10 of the Rajasthan Noises Control Act, 1963.

(u) The Rajasthan Noises Control Act, 1963 (Act No. 12 of 1963)

The Act provides for the control of noises caused by various sources, in the State of Rajasthan. The Act consists of 10 sections.[95] Section 1 relates to the applicability of the Act and Section 2, provides definitions. According to section 2, a 'loudspeaker' or a 'sound amplifier' means, an instrument whereby soft sound, whether vocal, instrumental or recorded, are augmented. 'Public place' is defined as a place, (including road, street or way whether a thoroughfare or not, and a landing place), to which the public has access or has a right to resort, or over which the public has a right to pass.

Section 3: Declaration and Prohibition of Nocturnal Noise (Noise caused by a picture or song of the night scene)

(1) In any area, to which this section may be applied under sub-section (4) of section 1, the District Magistrate or any other officer, empowered by the State Government in this behalf, may by notice, given in such manner as may be prescribed and in such other manner, as he thinks fit, declare any noise produced during such hours of the night as may be specified in the notice, whether vocally or by loudspeaker or a sound amplifier or otherwise which, in his opinion, is likely to cause annoyance or serious inconvenience to the public, to be nocturnal noise.

(2) Nocturnal noise shall be prohibited by notice, given by the District Magistrate or by any other officer empowered by the state government in this behalf, in such manners as may be prescribed and in such other manners as he thinks fit.

Section 4: Restriction Against the Use and Play of Loudspeakers

No person shall use or play a loudspeaker or a sound amplifier, for broadcasting any speech, sermon, music or radio programme, or shall attach the same to any wireless receiving set, or gramophone within such distance as may be prescribed:

(i) from a hospital or from a building in which there is a telephone exchange; or

(ii) from any educational institution managed, maintained, recognized or controlled by the State Government, or a University established under any law for the time being in force, or a local authority, during the hours of working of such institution; or

(iii) from any hostel, maintained or recognized by the State Government, or a University, or a local authority, when such hostel is in the use of students; or

(iv) From a building, in which a court or Government office is held during the hours of working, of such court or office; or

(v) Between the hours of 11 p.m. and 5 a.m. without the permission in writing, of the authority prescribed:

Provided that nothing in this section shall apply, to the use in a place, other than a public place, of a sound amplifier, which is a component part of a wireless apparatus, duly licensed, under any law for the time being in force.

Section 5: Power to Prevent Noises, Irrespective the Time and Place

The District Magistrate or any other person, authorized by the State Government in this behalf may, on being satisfied that in his opinion it is necessary in the public interest to do so, may by an order in writing and recording reasons, prohibit noise of any kind whatsoever, including the amplification thereof, in any place and at any time. To maintain peace at public and other places, DC, Jodhpur has banned the use of sound amplifying devices. This order, which is issued u/s 5 of this Act, prohibits the use of loudspeakers, radio, transistor, microphone, gramophone, etc. near educational institutions, colleges, university, government or semi-government offices, without prior permission from District Collector. No transport operator to play the horns for a longer period. However, the order is issued for a limited period.[96]

Section 6: Penalties

Whoever contravenes or attempts to contravene or abets the contravention of the provisions of this Act or acts contrary to any order lawfully made under this Act, shall, on first conviction be punished with fine, which may extent to two hundred and fifty rupees and on second or subsequent conviction be punished with imprisonment of either description, which may extent to one month or with fine, which may extend to two hundred and fifty rupees, or with both.

In a PIL, filed under this section, the High Court of Jodhpur has directed DC and SP city Jodhpur, to produce an action report before the court, taken on the earlier directives of the court, for ensuring non-existence of noise pollution in the city, caused by the loudspeakers, without prior permission. The impact of this petition is prominently seen, when many directives have been issued by District Collector of Jodhpur city thereafter, banning the use of loudspeakers. Even the signboards for 'no horns' are being seen nowadays.

Section 7: Procedure

An offence under this Act shall be cognizable, bailable and triable by a Magistrate of the first class.

Section 8: Power of Police to Arrest

It shall be lawful for a police officer, not below the rank of sub-inspector, to require any person, acting contrary to the provisions of this Act, or any order lawfully made thereunder, to abstain from so doing; and in case of refusal or disobedience, to arrest such person, as if he has committed a cognizable offence.

Section 9: Power to make Rules

(1) The State Government may, subject to the condition of previous publication, make rules generally for carrying out the purposes of this Act and, in particular, for providing for matters which, under any provision of this Act, may be or are required to be prescribed, or for which, under such provision, rules may be or are required to be framed.

(2) All rules finally made under this Act, shall be laid, as soon as may be, before the House of the State Legislature, while it is in session, for a period of not less than fourteen days, which may be passed in one session or in two successive sessions, and if before the expiry of the session in which they are so laid, or of the session immediately following, the House of the State Legislature, makes any modification in any of such rules or resolves that any such rule should not be made. Such rule shall thereafter have effect only in such modified form or be of no effect, as the case may be, so however, that any such modification or annulment shall be without prejudice to the validity of anything previously done thereunder.

Section 10: Repeal

The Ajmer (Sound Amplifiers and Loudspeakers Control) Act, 1953 (Ajmer Act III of 1952) and other corresponding laws against noise, in force in any part of the State are hereby repealed.

UP Municipal Act, 1916

In pursuance with the empowerment u/s 298 of UP Municipality Act, 1916, the government of Uttar Pradesh has framed its model rules for regulating the use and the control of loudspeakers on November 14, 1968, which were subsequently amended in 1969 and thereafter in 1970.[96A] The constitutionality of these rules has also been upheld by the court of state in *Rajnikant* Vs. *State of UP.*

According to these rules, everyone, who wants to use loudspeakers for public meeting, marriages, musaira, Kavi Sammelan, musical-nights, sport events, stage dramas, religious ceremonies, kirtans and election campaigns, etc. has to get the license issued by the executives of municipal boards. These rules strictly restrict the use of loudspeakers between 8 a.m. to 10 p.m. in the winter season and between 7 a.m. to 11 a.m. for the season of summer. Loudspeaker shall not be used for the period other than mentioned in the rules, without prior permission of district magistrate on request made to him. The license for the use of loudspeaker is issued with an undertaking that the noise of these would not be audible beyond the premises of its use and same undertaking has to be annotated on the letter of permission. The provision of sound governor with the loudspeakers has been made a condition precedent so as to regulate the volume of the sound emitted by these loudspeakers. To grant permission for private use, has been made the discretionary power of authority concern, depending upon the interest, security and convenience of the public and it may be withdrawn or amended if needed for the public good.[97] Despite detailed model rules, some district municipality boards are indifferent and failed to percept the gist of the rules. For instance, the city board of Muzaffarnagar has amended Rule 2(3)[98] of aforesaid rules, through a resolution and permitted the use of loudspeakers for religious purposes causing thereby religious noise, which is definitely against the rules.

Industrial Licensing Policy in UP

After enactment of Air Act, the licensing policy applicable for the small scale industries have gone under an important change. The mandatory consent of the State Pollution Control Boards has been made as condition precedent for registration of any proposed industry because section 21(i)[99] of Air Act provides that—

> "Subject to the provisions of this section, no person shall, without the previous consent of the State Board, establish or operate any industrial plant in an air pollution control area."

It is well appreciated that the State Pollution Control Board (SPCB) issues NOC for the establishment of new industry, only after the submission of 'noise abatement programme' adopted by the prospective industrialists with a view to keeping noise levels within the permissible limits. But there are non-hazardous small-scale industries, enumerated in a list named as A-179, for which no consent of SPCB is required in UP. These enterprises are like *atta chakki* (flour mill), oil ginning expelling, wood furniture, handloom weaving which usually operate within the municipal limits of any city and the respective municipality boards have been made controlling agencies for them including the workshops operated usually in residential areas viz. denting shops, vehicle repairing centers, etc.

The Municipality Act of the states empowered their respective municipality boards to frame their own rules[100] to control the conduct of trade and business, therefore, these municipal boards may play a very important and effective role to curb the noise pollution caused by such activities within their jurisdiction. However, the noise standards, prescribed by the Ministry of Environment and Forestry, in consultation with the CPCB may be applied by the states also with some tolerance limits depending upon the type, situation, activity, place and locality.

In wake of increasing religious noise, it is submitted that the permission sought for religious purposes needs a hard look in tune with the gist of Arts. 14, 19 and 21 of Indian Constitution and hence section 268 of the Municipal Act, 1916 of UP should accordingly be amended. Secondly, the condition for the use of loudspeaker that the noise so caused should not be audible beyond the premises of its use needs to be amended. This condition does not protect the ears of the person who happened to be the part of that premises either by way of some compulsion or otherwise. Here, it is submitted that the condition should be based on the decibels produced by such loudspeakers and not its audibility beyond the premises. If noise level of the premises goes higher than the permitted one, the permission should be withdrawn and the user should be asked either to bring down the noise level otherwise not to use them. Confiscation of noise source along with further legal proceedings should take place for non-compliance.

(v) Hyderabad Municipal Corporation Act, 1955

Section 521(1)(e)(ii) of the Act deals with the environmental matters, which reads:

> "Certain things not to be kept, and certain trades and operations not to be carried on, without a licence.— (1) Except under and in conformity with the terms and conditions of a licence granted by the Commissioner. (2) No person shall carry on, allow to be carried on, in or upon any premises, any trade or operation which in the opinion of the Commissioner is dangerous to life, health or property, or likely to create a nuisance either from its nature, or by reason of the manner in which, or the conditions under which, the same, is or is proposed to be carried on."

It is not to establish that the noise is dangerous to life, health, property, and hence is the genus of nuisance under the Act, causing irritation, annoyance. Therefore, under the above provision, police commissioner is empowered to regulate the levels generated by the trade of operations mentioned therein. But, in *A.P. Bankers & Pawn Brokers' Association* Vs. *Municipal Corporation of Hyderabad*,[101] Andhra Pradesh High Court held:

> "If there are no terms and conditions which can be imposed by the Commissioner or the Municipality in respect of a particular trade or operation then even if the Commissioner is of the opinion that the trade or operation is dangerous to life or health or property or that it is likely to create a nuisance, he would not be able to regulate or control that trade or operation. Maintenance of cleanliness, deciding location and regulating noise pollution would not fall within section 521(1)(e)(ii)."

In this case, the appellant filed a writ petition in the High Court of Andhra Pradesh, challenging the notification issued by the commissioner on 11-4-1987, *inter alia*, on the ground that Section 521 of the Act in question, did not empower the Commissioner to notify the trades of money-lending and pawn-broking as being trades for which a license is necessary. Single Judge of the High Court dismissed the writ petition. Against the judgment of the learned Single Judge, the appellant filed an appeal. The appeal came to be dismissed by the impugned judgment. By the impugned judgment, the learned Judges have disagreed with the Single Judge and held that the business of money lending or pawn-broking is not dangerous to property. They have, however, held that these are the operations, which are likely to create a nuisance *inter alia*. A copy of the license issued by the respondent had been produced. On a perusal of the license it was clearly made out that there was not a single term or condition, in that license, which could apply to this trade or occupation. Hence, it was held that the maintenance of cleanliness, deciding location and regulating noise pollution would not fall within Section 521(1)(e)(ii).

It is unfortunate that this decision came at such a time, when whole world is harping with problem of environmental pollution caused by various trade affluent. The recent Earth Summit held, in Johannesburg from 26 August to 4 September, 2002, on Sustainable development is the blazing trail to show that the environmental quality is deteriorating day by day due to fast technological advancements, industrialization, urbanization and other rampant activities. This judgment does not seem to be in the spirit of getting clean environment in the industrial world. It was, however, sought to be submitted that, there were blank spaces provided in the license wherein terms and conditions regulating such trades and operations were hand-filled before a licence was issued. Further, the license was stamped, that the offices should be kept clean and later was stated that the regulation is to the extent of deciding the location, maintenance of cleanliness and regulating noise pollution. Besides this, court held that the maintenance of cleanliness, deciding location and regulating noise pollution would not fall within Section 521(1)(e)(ii).

The decision seems to be erroneous and hence needs fresh

look. It is not to establish that the noise is dangerous to life, health, property, and is the genus of nuisance causing irritation, annoyance. Therefore, under the above provision, police commissioner must be empowered to regulate the levels generated by the trade of operations mentioned therein.

Also, this case warrants that our Honb'le judges need a special training to deal with the cases of environment. Since, the environmental noise is the problem of very recent origin and might not be included within the ambit of terms and conditions of the license in question. But once, it was included later, by way of stamp or hand filled, it should have been taken in its true spirit. At last, it is humbly and respectfully, submitted that no activity should be allowed which is prone to cause environmental pollution of any kind.

(w) Bihar Control of the Use and Play of Loudspeakers Act, 1955

The State of Bihar has shown an example to control the noise nuisance by enacting Bihar Control of the Use and Play of Loudspeakers Act, 1955 at early stage. The Act[102] is meant exclusively for the use and control of the loudspeaker, which is one of the main major sources of noise pollution. The Act not only restricts the timings for the use of loudspeaker, but also the places for its use. The use of loudspeaker, near educational institutions, university, hostels and the court during working hours, has been prohibited under section 3 of the Act, which provides that "No person shall use and play a loudspeaker:

(a) Within such distance as may be prescribed from a hospital or a building in which there is a telephone exchange; or

(b) Within which distance as may be prescribed from any educational institution, maintained, managed, recognized or controlled by the State Government or University established under any law for the time being in force or a local authority or admitted to such university or any hostel maintained, managed or recognized by such institution or hostel is in the use of students.

The use of loudspeakers between 10 p.m. to 6 a.m. has not been allowed without due permission. The Act also provides that the use of loudspeakers would not be made unless the permission has been sought and prescribed fee is paid. But, its use for humanitarian purposes or for the purposes connected with the maintenance of law and order have been exempted from the charge of any fee.[103] The Act also provides penalty up to one month imprisonment or fine of Rupees 100 or both in case of violation of any of the provision of the Act.[104] Section 6 of the Act clarifies that the cognizance of the offence under this Act would be on a complaint made by or at the instance of the person aggrieved by such offence or upon a report in writing made by any police officer.

No doubt, the Act regulates the use of loudspeaker by way of putting restriction on the timings and the places of its use, but it fails to put any effective control on the volume of the sound of the loudspeakers, which ultimately becomes the cause of noise pollution. Therefore, the Act is inadequate to control the problem of the noise of loudspeaker in all respects. The Act requires an amendment to lay down the permitted noise levels under it and the measures of their strict enforcement.

(x) Criminal Procedure Code (Cr.P.C.) 1973 (2 of 1974)

Though, the Code of Criminal Procedure, 1973, provides the procedure, yet it also contains some specific provisions of the nature of substantive law. For example, Chapter X of the Code deals with the procedure for the abatement of public nuisances. The term 'public nuisance', in reference with environmental pollution, has already been defined under the provisions of I.P.C., 1860, hence need not repeat here. All types of nuisance, resulting from the environmental pollution, including *noise*, can be controlled or removed under the provisions of this code, enshrined in this chapter. Injunction may be granted by the District Magistrate/Sub-Divisional Magistrate/Executive Magistrate under Sec. 133 of the code, which states as:

"Whenever a District Magistrate or a Sub-Divisional Magistrate or any other Executive, specifically empowered in this behalf by the State Government, on receiving the report of the police officer or other information and on taking such evidence (if any) as he thinks fit, considers;

(i) that any unlawful obstruction or nuisance should be removed from any public place or may be lawfully used by the public; or

(ii) that the conduct of any trade or occupation, or the keeping of any goods or merchandise, is injurious to the health or physical comfort of the community, and that in the consequences, such trade or occupation, should be prohibited or regulated or such goods or merchandise should be removed or the keeping thereof regulated; or

(iii) that the construction of any building, or, the disposal of any substance, as is likely to occasion configuration, or explosion should be prevented or stopped; or

(iv) that any building, tent or structure, or any tree is in such a condition that it is likely to fall and thereby cause injury to persons living or carrying on business in the neighbourhood or passing by, and that in consequence the removal, repair or support of such building, tent or structure, or the removal or support of such tree, is necessary; or

(v) that any tank, well or excavation adjacent to any such way or public place should be fenced in such manner as to prevent danger arising to the public; or

(vi) that any dangerous animal should be destroyed, confined or otherwise disposed of.

As such, magistrate may make a conditional order requiring the person causing such obstruction or nuisance, or carrying on such trade or occupation, or keeping any such goods or merchandise, or owing, possessing or controlling such building, tent, structure, substance, tank, well or excavation, or owing or possessing such animal or tree, within a time to be fixed in the order—

(i) to remove such obstruction or nuisance; or

(ii) to desist from carrying on, or to remove or regulate in such a manner, as may be directed, such trade or occupation or to remove such goods or merchandise, or regulate the keeping thereof in such manner as may be directed; or

(iii) to prevent or stop the construction of such building or to alter the disposal of such substance; or

(iv) to fence such tanks, well or excavation; or

(v) to destroy, confine or dispose of such dangerous animal in the manner provided in the said order.

If he objects so to do appear before himself or some other Executive Magistrate subordinate to him at a time and place to be fixed by the order, and show cause, in the manner hereinafter provided, why the order should not be made absolute.

(2) No order duly made by a Magistrate under this section shall be called in question in any Civil Court.

Explanation.—A "public place" includes also property belonging to the State, camping grounds and grounds left unoccupied for sanitary or re-creative purposes.

Here, it is the matter of notice that the nuisance cases of urgent nature are dealt under the provisions of section 144 of Cr.P.C., which empowered the executive magistrate to issue orders to prevent any annoyance or injury to any person or danger to human life health or safety or disturbance of public tranquility, riot or any affray. The object of such order is to force the problem of law and order temporarily as the duration of such order is merely of two months. In addition to the adverse effects on human health, sometimes the communal noise caused by riots or the like, alarms the sickness or causes the irreparable loss to the student/examinee, who has to study for very next morning.

Thus, from the text of sections 133 and 144, it is evident that the executive magistrate, empowered under this statutory provision, either on police report or on other information, may remove, prohibit or regulate any public nuisance or any trade/ occupation injurious to health or physical comfort of the community. Noise some times amounts to public nuisance and also may cause physical discomfort to the people,[105] hence, the nuisance caused by the noise certainly lies within the ambit of the aforesaid sections of the code and warrants emphatic action.

In *Dwarka Prasad* Vs. *B.K. Roy*,[106] the question, whether the nuisance of noise resulting from the ice-making machine lies under section 133 of Cr.P.C., came up for consideration before the Hon'ble High Court of Calcutta. In this case, the noise, caused by a running ice-making machinery (refrigerator) in a shop was alleged to be a public nuisance whereas; the owner of the machine denied the same. The magistrate passed an order to restrain the work from this machine for a certain period, which was later confirmed by the session court. However, the High Court set aside the order of the magistrate and observed that—

> "In this case there is really no evidence to show that anybody was affected by the sound of this machine, except some persons living in the same house. The evidence of some witnesses that the noise constituted a public nuisance is really evidence of opinion and as such is not admissible."[107]

As a procedure u/s 133 of Cr.P.C., if the magistrate, empowered in this behalf by the state government, on receiving the report of a police officer or other information with or without evidence, thinks that the existing cause of public nuisance (including noise source) needs be removed, prevented or obstructed, may order or summon the nuisance creator to remove that cause or to appear and show the cause[108] for its continuance. Under section 135, the person in question is to act within the stipulated time and the manners, specified in the order or to appear and show cause against the same, otherwise he shall be liable to be punished in accordance with section 188 of I.P.C., i.e. the imprisonment to the extent of 6 months or with the fine which might extend to 1000 rupees or both. If a person against whom the show cause summon is served, appears and files objection, the magistrate should not dispose of the case under section 136 but should make an enquiry by giving opportunity of being heard and satisfy himself, by evidences on record, that the order passed by him is reasonable and proper and then only should make the order 'absolute' with or without modification as he considers necessary. However, if the magistrate is not so satisfied, further proceedings shall be dropped as in fructuous. It is worth mentioning that, if the person, against whom the order has been made, appears and questions the legality of order whether by recourse to legal rights, title or otherwise, then the magistrate should refer the matter to the competent court and stay the proceedings accordingly. The magistrate is also empowered to get the matter investigated by such person as he thinks fit.[109]

When an order has been made absolute u/s 136 or section 138, the magistrate shall give notice of the same to the person against whom the order was made, and shall further require him to perform the act as directed within the stipulated time, so fixed, and also inform him that, in case of disobedience, he will be liable to be penalized under section 188 of I.P.C.[110] If such act is not performed within the fixed time, the magistrate may cause it to be performed and may recover the cost of such performing, either by the sale of any building, goods or other property removed by his order, or by the distress and sale of any other moveable property of such person within or without such magistrate's local jurisdiction and if such other property is without such jurisdiction, the order shall authorize its attachment and sale when endorsed by the magistrate within whose jurisdiction, the property to be attached is found.[111] Any act done in good faith under this section is protected from legal liability.[112] An immediate injunction,[113] if enquired, may also be issued by the magistrate during the pendency of order u/s 136 for which he will not be liable if done in good faith.[114] It is matter of satisfaction that Indian Code of Criminal Procedure does not only removes, prohibits or injuncts the public nuisance but also prohibits the repeatance or continuance of the same under its section 143.

The urgent cases of such nuisance are dealt u/s 144 of this code, which empowers the magistrate to issue orders, in danger to human life, health or safety or disturbance of public tranquility, riot or affray. The object of such order is to tackle with the problem of law and order temporarily as the duration of such order is only for two months and even can be passed *ex-parte*, if the circumstances warrants so and there is no time to serve notice or summon. The respective orders made by the magistrate or government may be rescinded or altered, on the application of aggrieved person or on its own motion, as the case may be.

Besides various health hazards, the noise may lead to the problem of social insecurity, by way of causing communal riots, and hence may invite this provision of the procedural code to control through the prohibitory orders. It shows that the aforesaid provisions of the Code, though not a permanent answer to the growing problem of noise pollution, but is certainly being proved a good weapon to control the noise nuisance.

It is observed that Indian code of procedure is competent to deal with the rising problem of pollution in general and of noise in particular, which is evident from the judgment of Madhya Pradesh High Court through justice V.D. Gyani in *Krishna Gopal* Vs. *State of MP*.[115] In this case Mrs Tripathi filed a complaint against the manufacturer of a glucose saline factory (operated in residential area of Indore) that the noise caused by the vibrations of the boiler of the factory was aggravated the illness of her husband by disturbing his sleep, who is a heart patient. It was contended by the petitioner that noise pollution emitted by the factory was resulting into deleterious effects on the residents of the locality and therefore the court was prayed to remove that public nuisance of noise pollution. The respondent (factory owner) contended that the petitioner is only the lady who has made such complaint and further he has already obtained no objection certificate from the concerned authorities. Rejecting the contentions of the respondent, the court observed "Merely because one complaint has come forward to complain about the nuisance can not be said to be not a public nuisance contemplated by section 133 Cr.P.C. The court appreciating the women's efforts not only accepted her appeal but also asked the respondent to pay the cost of litigation to the petitioner."

In the case of environmental pollution, the application of principles of "Polluter Pays" and "absolute liability" needs strict implementation because under Cr.P.C, the polluter manages to escape on the pretext of *mens-rea* or otherwise. The court has also observed—"a vagrant, committing a petty theft is punished for 5 years of imprisonment, while a billion dollar price fixing, executive comfortably escapes the consequences of his environmental crimes."[116] The court went on saying that—

"Society is shocked when a single murder takes place, but the atmospheric pollution is merely read as news without any perturbence, till people fall ill, go blind or die in distress, on account of pollutants, that too resulting in filling of the pockets of few."[117]

(y) The Union Territory of Delhi Loudspeakers (Licensing and Controlling) Regulations, 1980

The Commissioner of Police, with the previous sanction of the Administrator of Union Territory of Delhi and in exercise of powers conferred by section 28(1)(s)(iii) read with section 28(2) and (3) of Delhi Police Act, 1978, has made these regulations with a view curb Noise Pollution in Delhi caused by the loudspeakers. There are total 13 regulations out of which sections 3 to 7 provides conditions under which the loudspeakers can be used. Rule 8 empowers the police to visit the place of use of loudspeakers, whereas u/s 9 Commissioner of Police, Delhi may cancel the license issued under regulation 3. The details of the regulations are made appendix B to this book.

5. INTERNATIONAL LEGISLATION ON NOISE POLLUTION: A BRIEF ACCOUNT

The harmful effects of environmental noise have compelled many nations to curb this problem, by introducing various legislative measures. In ancient world, the Romans had enacted the first prohibitory law, when by a popular decree, chariots were banned from moving in the streets and on roads at night. It was a calculated measure to control noise pollution so that the citizens rest in peace and may sleep sound in the night, in calm environment.

USA

The United States of America, being one of the most developed countries, industrially and technologically, is facing the grave problem of environmental pollution. The concern for environmental protection has its genesis in the 1960s, when many laws to this affect were passed by several states of USA. The president of USA signed the National Environmental Policy Act on 1st January, 1970. It was a very significant piece of legislation.

The aforesaid policy not only recognizes the right of man to enjoy a healthy environment but also, imposes on him a responsibility to contribute for the preservation and enhancement of the environment.[118] In fact, the Noise Control Act in the US was passed as early as 1955, but the US Noise Control Act of 1972, amended by Quiet Communities Act, 1978, is a major breakthrough in the Federal attempt to eliminate the excess noise of every level. Its main concern is to protect the health and safety of the citizens. Manufacturers and others who do not conform to the standards are subject to heavy fines and imprisonment.

The first significant federal regulation of occupational safety and health occurred in pursuant to the Walsh Healey Act of 1936.[119] The Walsh Healey Act requires the government contractors to certify that none of the materials manufactured or furnished by the contract were manufactured under working conditions that were unsanitary, hazardous or dangerous to the health and safety of any employee engaged in performance of the contract.

Subsequently, the Occupational Safety and Health Act, 1970 provides no specific standard that an employee must follow; instead it authorizes the Secretary of Labour to promulgate occupational safety and health standards.[120] When the Act was drafted, the U.S. Congress considered the noise as a serious health hazard, its continuing concern about the dangers of noise apparent from enactment of the Noise Control Act, 1972.[121] Under the Act, the Congress while declaring U.S. Policy, expressed its concern that inadequately controlled noise presents a growing danger to the health and welfare of nation's population particularly in urban areas, imposed the primary responsibility for the control of noise on state and local government and declared the policy of the US to promote the environment for all Americans free from noise that jeopardizes their health and welfare.[122] In 1974, the Secretary of Labour under the authority of the Occupational Safety Health Act, 1970 promulgated occupational safety and health standards relating to safety and health of the workers. Among these standards the occupational noise regulations, which had previously been promulgated under the Walsh Healey Act were included. These are shown in the table given below:

Duration per day hours	8	6	4	3	2	1½	1	½	¼
Sound level dBA slow response	90	92	95	97	100	102	105	110	115

It shows that at 90 dB(A) level of exposure for 8 hours, the amount of sound energy observed, is taken as the limit of exposure which will not cause any hearing loss. The statistics indicate higher sound levels with corresponding permissible exposure times that will not induce any damaging effects than 8 hours of 90 dBA. Therefore, workers in any industry must not be exposed to sound levels greater than 115 dBA for any amount of period.

6. NEW YORK CITY NOISE CONTROL CODE, 1972

In New York, an early attempt to attach a fine schedule for noise offenders grew out of an ordinance in 1935. Further, in 1954, Milwauko established that no vehicle could exceed 95 dB level of noise, when measured from a distance of 20 feet from the right rear wheel of the vehicle in motion. However, more practical rules regarding the control of noise for various sources were made applicable in New York City, Noise Control Code,[124] which intends to reduce the ambient noise level in the city as to promote public health, safety and welfare and also to maintain peace and comfort of the inhabitants and to prevent injury to plant, animal life or property. The Act prohibits the use of any sound reproduction device for commercial or business or advertising/sale purposes, in front of or outside any building, place or premises, or adjacent to a public street, park or palace. Further, it directs not to operate or use any radio, phonograph or tape recorder in or on rail, road or omnibus in such a manner, that it is audible to another person.[125] The noticeable point of this Act is that even the noise of bird and animal has been brought within its scope and no person is permitted to cause their noise while they are under his control.[126] The persons have been prohibited to cause noise adjacent to hospitals, schools, and the courts while in session.

7. CHICAGO NOISE CONTROL REGULATIONS, 1971

In Chicago, some of the most recent sweeping Noise Control Regulations[127] were put into effect from July 1, 1971. The project to silence Sh-h-h-h-icago has brought numerous environmental sounds under control. In one highly published incident that involved the ringing of church bells, a resident of the neighbourhood of a church complained to city hall and the noise ordinance was brought to bear on the priest and the bells were made silent. The Chicago ordinances on noise also set forth a schedule for the continuing reduction of various noise sources.

8. CONNECTICUT HIGHWAY NOISE CONTROL ACT, 1971

Connecticut Highway Noise Control Act provides that every motor vehicle should be equipped with a horn in good working order and capable of emitting sound under normal conditions. Further, it directs that motor vehicles and the devices like siren, whistle, bell therein should be so operated as to prevent unnecessary or unusual noise.[128] The Act establishes decibel levels for motor vehicle producing noise exceeding the established limit, which has been applied after January 1, 1975.[129] The established limit reads as follows:

(a) 90 dB(A) in 1973 and 1974, 88 dB(A) in 1975 and 1976, and 86 dB(A) in 1977 and thereafter, for noise emitted by vehicle operated in the state; and

(b) 85 dB(A) in 1975 and thereafter for vehicles sold or offered for sale in the state.

The commissioner of motor vehicles on the advice of the commissioner of environment protection has been empowered to establish the procedure for checking such decibels, which will be measured at fifty feet from the centerline of the vehicle. The Act also prescribes the punishment by way of fine not less than twenty-five dollars and not more than one hundred dollars.

Thus, in the United States of America, the problem of noise pollution simultaneously lies within the control of federal government and that of state governments and political sub-divisions thereof. But the noise emission level issued by them should not in any way violate the permissible standards laid down by the central authorities of the country.

8A. LAW OF THE PEOPLE'S REPUBLIC OF CHINA[129A]

The law of the people's Republic of China on prevention and control of pollution from environmental noise was adopted on 29 October 1996.

This Law is enacted for the purpose or preventing and controlling environmental noise pollution, protecting and improving the living environment, ensuring human health and promoting economic and social development.

For purposes of this Law, "environmental noise" means the sound that is emitted in the course of industrial production, construction, transportation and social activities and that impairs the living environment of the neighbourhood.

The competent administrative department for environmental protection under the State Council shall, in accordance with the national standards for acoustic environmental quality and the State's economic and technological conditions, fix national limits for environmental noise emission.

Every project under construction, renovation or expansion must conform to the regulations of the State governing environmental protection.

The industrial noise emitted to the living environment of the neighbourhood within an urban area shall be kept within the limits set by the State on emission of environmental noise within the boundary of an industrial enterprise.

The construction noise emitted to the living environment of the neighbourhood within an urban area shall be kept within the limits set by the State on the emission of environmental noise within the boundary of a construction site.

It is forbidden to manufacture, sell or import automobiles that emit noise beyond the limits set on noise level.

All units and individuals are forbidden to use high-pitch loudspeakers in urban areas where noise-sensitive structures are concentrated.

Any unit or individual suffering from the hazards of

environmental noise pollution shall have the right to demand the polluter to eliminate the hazards; if a loss has been caused, it shall be compensated according to law.

9. JAPAN

In Japan, the 'Anti-pollution Basic Law' covers noise pollution. A National council has been established in Japan under the chairmanship of the Prime Minister. This council controls the quality of air, water, noise and vibrations caused by construction work and land support vehicles. It takes firm steps to check noise. Under the Japanese Noise Regulation,[130] the perfectural governors have been empowered to designate residential areas, schools, hospital zones and other areas for the purpose of preserving living environment through prevention of noise. While designating such areas, perfectural governors shall establish "regulatory standard for specified hours in respective zones within the standards set forth by the Director General of the Environmental Agency. The Director General has also been empowered to establish the maximum permissible level of noise, produced by the operation of motor vehicle. The perfectural governor is responsible for the monitoring of noise levels in designated areas. The local government has also been authorized to regulate the noise of loudspeakers and that of the bars, restaurants operating during night hours.[131] The regulation also prescribe the permissible noises levels for the various areas as well as the time period between which noise-emitting machines can be used. The regulation also deals with restrictions upon operating-ours in accordance with physical and social conditions.

10. UK

In the United Kingdom, laws for the pollution control are as old as their history. Even in the 13th century, controls were imposed on the activities, which presented an immediate threat to health. In the 19th and early 20th centuries, noise under the English law was considered as a nuisance. The Noise Abatement Act, 1960 of the UK has provision for the control of noise and vibrations with a view to their abatement. Department of Environment (DOE) in UK is responsible for policy on environmental matters (including noise pollution and noise other than transport or occupational noise) as well as local government while the department of transport is responsible for control of road vehicles (traffic noise).[132] The acceptance of noise as a form of pollution requiring the control by statute has been fairly recent. In 1936, when statutory provision was made by Parliament for the abatement of certain specified types of nuisance under the Part III of Public Health Act, it was not thought necessary to make such provisions in respect of noise.[133] However, it was for the first time that London County Council Act, 1937 provided that any excessive, unreasonable or unnecessary noise which is injurious or dangerous to health, would be a noise nuisance which might be dealt with summarily under the Public Health Act, 1936.[134] It was not in fact until the passage of the Noise Abatement Act, 1960 that noise became treatable as statutory nuisance at least by three or more aggrieved persons was made essential.[135]

In 1970, the Government set-up the Noise Advisory Council under the chairmanship of the Secretary of States for environment "to keep under review the progress made generally in preventing and abating the generation of noise, to make recommendations to Ministers with responsibility in the field and to advise on such matters as they refer to the council. In 1971, it reported on the working of the Noise Abatement Act, 1960 and made recommendations for new legislation. Many of these recommendations are incorporated in Part III of the Control of Pollution Act, 1974, which replaced the Noise Abatement Act, 1960. The noises resulting from construction sites, loudspeaker, and certain premises in noise abatement zones have been covered under the Control of Pollution Act, 1974. The local authorities have been held responsible for the control of environmental noise from any premises whether industrial, commercial or domestic.

10A. AUSTRALIA[135A]

In New South Wales (NSW) no single government authority has the responsibility or capacity to be able to minimise all forms of noise pollution. The State is excluded from control of noise in a number of areas by commonwealth legislation. These include aircraft noise, where noise limits could affect trade, and the setting standards for noise emissions from new vehicles. In areas where the State does have powers to control noise the Environment Protection Authority (EPA) has an overall responsibility for environmental noise (as distinct from occupational noise), under the *Noise Control Act*, 1975. The Act deals with the prevention, minimisation and abatement of noise and vibration and empowers the EPA, the Waterways Authority, local government and the police for these purposes.

The EPA controls noise from scheduled premises those required by the Noise Control Act to have a licence and noise associated with rail traffic and the construction or upgrading of freeways and toll roads. The Police and local council are generally responsible for neighbourhood noise issues and have authority to issue noise abatement directions to control noise from premises and for noise from burglar alarms. Local council have an essential role in minimising the effects of excessive noise, particularly in their local residential areas, from smaller factories, non-scheduled premises and public places. The Waterways Authority has specific responsibilities in relation to noise from vessels in navigable waters.

Under the provisions of the *Noise Control Act*, 1975 in NSW the railway system is classified as scheduled premises and as such the EPA has a regulatory role, and seeks to achieve noise targets for rail operations throughout the State to minimise the impact on local residents.

The EPA issues licences for the management of scheduled premises. When issuing a licence the EPA sets initial noise limits that are achievable with the operation of plant and equipment currently installed, operated and maintained effectively. To achieve further improvements in noise exposure to residents, negotiations with the licensed premises are carried out and can be incorporated in the licence as Pollution Reduction Programs (PRPs). The EPA is currently working with industry to reduce noise levels from major sources.

The Noise Control (Miscellaneous Articles) Regulation, 1995 was introduced to cover community noise issues not covered by previous legislation. It includes limitations on burglar alarms for both residential and commercial premises. Changes have been made to the night-time control of common domestic noise sources such as power tools, air conditioners, amplified music and lawn mowers. Under the new regulation only one warning to the offender is required and the warning is valid for 28 days. If an offence is committed within this period a fine can be issued without further warnings. The previous regulation warning was only active for 12 hours which meant it was not very effective with repetitious offences typical in sub-urban areas.

The Noise Control (Motor Vehicles and Motor Vehicle Accessories) Regulation, 1995 controls the noise of individual motor vehicles. It includes a provision to control noise from a range of accessories including horns, alarms, refrigeration units and sound systems. It also places responsibility to ensure compliance of repairs/modifications of vehicles on the vehicle repairers.

In addition to the measures introduced to reduce the source and transmission of noise, measures can be undertaken to noise proof buildings thereby reducing the occupant exposure to noise.

10B. MONTGOMERY COUNTRY NOISE CONTROL ORDINANCE[135B]

The Montgomery Country Noise Control Ordinance allows for normal activities during regular hours; however, it does attempt to eliminate interference from noise when most of us want to rest and relax. It also seeks to control disturbing and unhealthy levels of noise in general. Key provisions of the Noise Control Ordinance:

(i) Provide day/night sound legel limits.

(ii) Establish "quiet hours."

(iii) Define sounds that constitute noise disturbances.

(iv) Establish a "nuisance provision" that prohibits certain noises at any time.

A noise disturbance, as defined by the ordinance, is any sound that is unpleasant, annoying, or loud; abnormal for the time or location; and prejudicial to health, comfort, property, or the conduct of business. Under the ordinance, it is unlawful to create a noise disturbance anywhere during "quiet hours," including multifamily buildings and townhouses. The "nuisance provision" prohibits some noise disturbances anywhere at any time.

The Montgomery Country Noise Control Ordinance promotes peace and quiet for everyone by covering a wide variety of residential and business situations. The Ordinance does not cover noise from aircraft and railroads or motor vehicles on public roadways, as Federal and State governments supersede local regulation. Also exempt are emergency operations by public utilities.

Among other provisions, the Montgomery Country Noise Control Ordinance makes it illegal to:

  (i) Operate, or allow to be operated, a radio, television, or other electronic sound-producing device on public or private property if the sound exceeds 55 decibels at the receiving property line.
 (ii) Create a noise disturbance during "quiet hours" in a residential zone or multi-family structure.
(iii) Operate any equipment that exceeds the receiving property line sound level limit.
 (iv) Allow an animal or fowl to create a noise disturbance at any time.
  (v) Load or unload material during quiet hours.
 (vi) Create a noise disturbance across property lines during "quiet hours" by operating power equipments mounted on a motor vehicle, for example refrigerated trucks or commercial vacuum cleaners.
(vii) Permit construction noise to exceed 75 dB with allowances for higher decibel levels under an approved "Noise Suppression Plan."

11. ISRAEL

Even a small country like Israel has taken initiative in this field by enacting legislation to control pollution. The Kanowitz Law (1961) of Israel prohibits from causing any considerable or unreasonable noise, smell or pollution of air from source whatever, if the same disturbs or is likely to disturb a person in the vicinity or a passerby. This law entitles citizens to file complaint to prosecute the offender and seek retribution for damages.[136]

12. EVOLUTION OF ENVIRONMENTAL LAW IN INDIA

Nature is the common heritage of humankind, irrespective of any boundary, in land, water or space, and it is the nature, which constitutes the environment or the ecology for the man. Environmental protection is not the problem and duty of single nation, but is a matter of global consideration. The air, which blows irrespective of boundaries, is the part of common heritage. Not only the beauty, which the nature has gifted, but also the very existence of life depends upon nature and that is the reason of its worship by our ancestors. Nature provides everything to everyone as a matter of her children. For example, the tree of Tulsi and Pipal are worshiped in India, because of the popular belief that the Gods inhibit on such virtuous trees. Such pious plants, apart from faith and spiritualism, scientifically provide the diet to human survival like oxygen through atmosphere, round the clock. Surya Namaskara, a kind of worship, is the part of almost all the religious ceremonies, like Yoga and Shastras. Besides, giving light to the whole world, it protects our environment in many ways. It is worth-mentioning, that the world's oldest major religions including Hinduism, begin with Vedic scriptures and forest book Aryankas, are believed to be written by the sages living in the forests. The culture of the forests fueled the culture of India.

Environmental pollution is as old as the evolution of 'homosapien' on the planet, which emerged as the dominating species about 40,000 years ago.[137] The problem facing is not new, but, what is new, is only urgency of the problem.

13. IN ANCIENT INDIA

In ancient time, every individual was taught that natural resources must be preserved and ecology should not be disturbed. Five basic elements of existence, the 'earth', 'water', 'air', 'light', and cosmos, were considered to be the angels and hence were worshiped with utmost devotion.[138]

The environmental protective devices and the rules, are traceable from times immemorial in ancient India and following are some of the instances, evidential to it:

(i) Even before Christ, as early as in 4th century, the rules pronounced by Chanakya, to be followed by the administrator for city administration, testify that the ancient rulers were keen on maintaining hygiene and cleanliness.[139] Manusmriti, Chapter 3 and 4, No. 56 mentions for the maintenance of ecological balance.[140] Laws against the fouling of water, was declared a sin, to be visited with penance and fine.

(ii) Arthashastra prosecuted the persons, who threw inside the city, the carcass of animals like cats, dogs, mongoose and snakes, and punished them with three panas (money unit). Stringent punishment of fifty panas was inflicted, if the carcass was of the animal such as ass, camel, mule or corpse.[141]

(iii) It is perhaps the sole example in global history wherein, the Bishnoi sect of environment loving-people, did not hesitate for sacrificing their own lives, not only for the protection of environment, but also to stop the cutting of trees and killing of deers to protect wildlife, a sacred tree named 'Khejri' in Rajasthan, found on the barren land of the state. Actual happening was, that the then king of the State ordered cutting of the said tree for preparation of royal furniture for his palace. Bishnoi sect, after their protest becoming to no avail, were left with no alternate other than to get themselves wrapped with each tree and sacrificed their lives against the wrath of the King. The king could, no longer overlook this state of killing of the subjects, and he had to withdraw his orders of cutting the trees. This example of unique love of Indian humanity with nature and protection from the dire exploitation of natural environment is marked with a historic event in the history of the World.[141A]

After evolution of democratic states, the protection of wildlife and forests has been taken seriously and the legislations are enacted to protect them. In a recent case, known country wide for cruelty against the wildlife, i.e. killing of hirans—'Chinkara' took place near the city of Jodhpur and the popular bollywood film actor

Salman Khan is facing trial in law court of Rajasthan at Jodhpur.

(iv) The commentary on 'Holy Quran' by M.M. Ali, also reveals that Holy Quaran is not indiscriminate with the environment but has the reference for not making the mischief in the earth.[142] Likewise, the 'Christians' are baptized in water as a sign of purification and the 'Guru Granth Saheb' too emphasizes the composition of human being with five basic elements of nature, i.e. earth, air, water, fire, and sky, and hence they be respected accordingly.[143] "Ahimsa", the non-violence, the basic tenets of Budhism, is a good conservator and protector of natural environment, by way of eliminating consequences caused by the killing of human beings, as well as of wild life. Same way is the Jainism, which has the reference of minimum destruction of living as well as of non-livings. Ashoka, the great emperor, accepted as his duty and made all efforts for the preservation of animal life, plant and trees. He prohibited the killing and haunting of animals for food and game.

14. PRE-INDEPENDENCE ERA

In pre-independence era, efforts had started to overturn the old concept of environmental protection in India. Successive invasions and a long period of subjugation to foreign rule with different philosophical and ideological beliefs, influence of Buddha and Ashoka started weakening. The Britishers, continued with the exploitative policy, which resulted in the depletion of forests, wild life and the eco-balance.

Besides, the environmental hazards caused by World Wars, the population explosion is proving, a third world war for India. Uncontrollable population growth in India is deteriorating the environment in all the spheres of its walk, i.e. air, water, noise, solid wastes, as the environmental pollution and depletion of the natural resources is directly proportional to the population, as well as to development of science and technology. Here, if we accept this ratio, the improvement of the environment must also be in the same proportion, because the contributory strength is increased in the same proportion. But it is a matter of concern that one who is responsible for causing such deterioration, does not want to do anything substantial for the up-gradation of environment. Whereas, he himself selfishly wishes to live in a clean environment, free from all kinds of pollutions. Here, it is pertinent to submit, that on account of nation's environment, everyone of the country be made responsible to contribute, based on the principle of 'polluter pays', either monetarily or otherwise, in proportion to population. The funds so recovered or collected may be utilized for making the environment clean and hygienic.

After the advent of industrial revolution, rapid development of science in western countries and its consequential impact crept into India. This brought a radial change in the relationship of man with nature.[143A] The threat of pollution of environment was obviously realized first in western countries, which were the fathers of modern industrialization and civilization. However, at that time India was almost on threshold of pollution era. The Indian society—a believer of renunciation, meditation, Dharma and Moksha, started converting into society of culture of consumption, Artha, and Kama. This resulted in change of general outlook of nation and public, towards environment and nature. This time was the turning point for India towards scientific and technological developments. In this race of rapid development, whole mankind has literally become blind and unconscious of consequences of his activities. Population kept on increasing. Civilization, urbanization, and industrialization continued putting out the stresses on natural resources like soil, water, forests, mineral wealth, and sea. Thus, a chain of action and reaction started.[144]

The laws passed in India during British era, had a reflection of lurking danger in their contents. Though, this regime could not legislate much notable for the protection of environment, yet the period is not barren, because in I.P.C. 1860, there are many provisions to this effect, apart from other statutes. The Shore Nuisance (Bombay & Kolaba) Act, 1853, The Oriental Gas Company Act, 1873, The Northern Canal & Drainage Act, 1873, The Madras River Conservancy Act, 1884, The Indian Explosives Act, 1884, The Indian Fisheries Act, 1884, The Bengal Smoke Act, 1905, The Indian Ports Act, 1908, The Destructive Insects and Pests Act, 1914, The Indian Forests Act, 1923, The Petroleum Act,

1934, The Motor Vehicles Act, 1939 (Amended in 1988), The Drug and Cosmetic Act, 1940 are many examples of contemporary context.

15. POST-INDEPENDENCE ERA

After Independence in 1947, the activities related to economic development got momentum and greater emphasis was given to increase of agriculture produce and industrialization. Use of fertilizers, insecticides, and pesticides came on increase and the country, where even the needle was the article of import, became the owner of heavy industries in various fields, viz. steel, fertilizers, petroleum, refineries, ferrous and non-ferrous metals, mining, and heavy chemicals, etc. Perhaps, the environmental protection was also the base of the ideology of the father of nation, Mahatma Gandhi, relating to non-industrialization. But the national progress, development, better living, and technological backwardness were perhaps the factors responsible for prevailing wave of industrialization and development of science and technology. It is true that our country was in need of fast development to be at par with the world, but this blind race of advancement turned the blue sky into the black, and became so serious and complicated issue that it threatened the very survival of life.

16. MODERN ERA

Pollution is not a new phenomena, it is as old as the civilization itself is. It was also conceived the day Adam dawned on the earth. Many centuries ago, the idea of interaction between man and environment was also given by Avicenna, an Egyptian of 5th century A.D., who emphasized the need to keep atmosphere free from pollution. But, the environment was a new discovery to the politicians of 1965. All of a sudden, the buzz word in Washington was "Environmental Quality." Realising the importance of environmental pollution, United Nations also established Scientific Advisory Committee in 1968, to consider a conference on Human Environment, which could be later held in Stockholm from 5th to 16th June 1972. This UN Conference on human environment and development, to which India is a signatory member, is considered as 'Magna-Carta' of environment protection and sustainable development. It was for the first time, that the world community got together to deliberate on an important issue of environmental protection and sustainable development. It proclaimed that man is both, creator and molder of his environment, which gives him physical sustenance and afford him the opportunity of intellectual, moral, social and spiritual growth. Both aspects of man's environment, the natural and man-made, are essential to his well-being and to the enjoyment of basic human rights, even the right to life itself.[145]

This UN Declaration of seventies, on human environment at Stockholm, fueled the India's environment concern of sixties and kept on giving momentum to it during seventies and eighties, and even is influencing today. As a result thereby, after the enactment of Wild Life (Protection) Act, 1972, amended in 1983, 1986 and 1991 and CrPC, 1973, India considered the importance of water pollution first, and enacted 'The Water (Prevention and Control of Pollution) Act, 1974', followed by the Water (Prevention and Control of Pollution) Rules, 1975, The Water Pollution (Procedure for Transaction of Business) Rules, 1975. The Water (Prevention and Control of Pollution) Cess Rules, 1978. Though, during 1950s and early 1960s, several states had taken steps to pass legislation on water, viz. The Orissa River Pollution Act, 1953, The Punjab State Tubewell Act, 1954, West Bengal Notification No. 7, Regulation-Control of Water Pollution Act of 1957, Jammu & Kashmir State Canal and Drainage Act, 1963, The Maharashtra Water Pollution Prevention Act, 1969. It is also a matter of satisfaction that India took note of all these integrated environmental problems and the concern was for the first time articulated in its fourth Five Year Plan, 1969-74. The plan drew our attention to the environmental issues in the following words:

> "It is an obligation of each generation to maintain the productive capacity of land, water, air and wild life in a manner, which leaves its successors some choice in the creation of healthy environment ... planning for harmonious development recognizes this unity of man and nature. Such planning is possible only on the basis of

comprehensive appraisal of environmental issues, particularly economic and ecological. There are instances in which timely specialized advice on environmental aspects could have helped in project design and in averting subsequent adverse effects on environment, therefore, to introduce the environmental aspect into our planning and development."[146]

Further, the word environment kept on reflecting from the paper of subsequent five-year plans.

17. CONSTITUTIONAL AMENDMENTS, 1976

The original constitution of India, which came into force in 1950, was silent in this regard. But, the decisions taken at the Stockholm Conference, 1972, compelled the Indian Government think it necessary to amend the Constitution so as to bring constitutional mandate for the protection of environment. India was one of the first countries in the world, to introduce an amendment into its Constitution allowing the state to protect and improve, the environment for safeguarding public health, forests and wild life. The 42nd amendment was adapted in 1976 and went into effect on January 3, 1977. By amending Articles 48 and 51, the two-fold provisions were made. On one hand it gives directive to the state for the protection and improvement of environment. On the other hand, it casts a duty on every citizen to help in the preservation of natural environment. An important subtlety in the directive's language is the provision, that the Article "shall not be enforceable by any court, but it shall be the duty of state to apply these principles in making laws." This allows the directive to be an instrument of guidance for the government.

18. TIWARI COMMITTEE, 1980

National Committee on Environmental planning and Co-ordination-NCEPC, was set-up in 1972, by the Department of Science and Technology with a view to identify and investigate the problems of preserving and improving human environment and to propose strategic solutions for environmental problems.

However, a National Committee on Environmental Planning replaced this Apex body-NCEPC.

The Government of India constituted a high-powered committee under the chairmanship of the then deputy chairman of the Planning Commission Shri N.D. Tiwari. This committee submitted its report in September 1980, with far reaching recommendations. The committee noted that:[146A]

(i) many of the laws related to environment are outdated;

(ii) they lack statements of explicit policy objectives;

(iii) they are mutually inconsistent; and

(iv) there is absence of procedure for reviewing the efficiency of laws.

In the aftermath of the Water Act, and on the recommendations of Tiwari Committee, the Department of Environment (DOE) was created in 1980, which performed an oversight role for the central government. DOE did environmental appraisals of development projects, monitored air and water quality, established an environmental information system, promoted research, and coordinated activities between federal, state and local governments. However, DOE was criticized by the environmental groups who recognized, that with its small political and financial base the agency was very weak and symbolic in nature, and would essentially serve as an advisory body with few enforcement powers.[147]

19. THE AIR (PREVENTION AND CONTROL OF POLLUTION) ACT, 1981

The air was the next area of focus, following the passage of Water Act, 1974. This legislation was another cognizance to the decisions which were taken at the UN Conference on human environment held in Stockholm, in which India participated and owed the obligation to take appropriate steps for the preservation of the natural resources of the earth, including preserving of quality of air and control of air pollution. This legislation had an interesting component, as for the first time, private citizens were given the right to file cases against non-complying factories. A private citizen may file a complaint, however, only after giving notice of at least 60 days prior to the concerned authority of his/ her intentions.

Originally the Air (Prevention and Control of Pollution) Act, 1981,[148] was enacted exclusively for the control of air pollution but, by the subsequent amendment of 1987, the problem of noise pollution also was covered within the ambit of definition of air pollutants, u/s 2(i) of the Act. Perhaps, it was the first instance at the part of central government, when noise was recognized as the pollutant in modern India. However, the citizen's Report,[149] mentioned the noise as a pollutant along with other various kinds of pollutants.

20. THE FORMATION OF POLLUTION CONTROL BOARDS

The Water Act of 1974, established the various Pollution Control Boards, at the center as well in the states. Each Board, central or state, consists of a chairman and other such number of persons as nominated by Central and State Governments according to the provisions of the Act. The Central Pollution Control Board (CPCB) was made a legal entity with a name of perpetual succession and a common seal.

Under section 3 of Air (Prevention and Control of Pollution) Act, 1981, it was provided that CPCB constituted u/s 3 of the Water Act, 1974, shall without prejudice to the exercise and performance of its powers and functions under this Act, exercise the powers and performs the functions of the Central Board for the prevention and control of air pollution also. Whereas, section 4 of the same statute states that, in any state in which the Water Act is in force and the state government has constituted for that state, a State Board for the prevention and control of water pollution u/s 4 of that Act, that state board shall be deemed to be the state board for the prevention and control of air pollution also u/s 5 of Air Act, and accordingly the board for the prevention and control of water pollution, shall without prejudice to the exercise and performance of its powers and functions under that Act, exercise the powers and performs the functions of the state board for the prevention and control of air pollution under this Act.

The state boards have similar responsibilities as that of CPCB, although, they play an important subsidiary role of doing plant level inspections, monitoring, and advising the central pollution control board, of problems and trends at the local level plants. SPCB members also have unfettered access to any plant site at any reasonable time. In situations, where a state board believes that immediate action is necessary, it has the authority to prevent further discharges, and can also approach to a judicial magistrate for restraining order. In the case of emergency, state boards are empowered to take any remedial measure, whatever they deem necessary.[150]

It is very amazing that in case of noise pollution, the pollution control board is only the monitoring agencies, as the enforcement authorities designated by the central government are police commissioners.[150A] The author, during his visits at CPCB and various SPCBs, observed that providing adequate infrastructure and funds might accelerate their function, as SPCBs are not getting the cess collected under the Water Act. Also, the pollution control boards needs wide publicity, as very few are aware about their functions and whereabouts. Perhaps, this unawareness is the sole reason for poor response from the citizens towards complaints of existing pollutants. It is heartening to note that Meghalaya State Pollution Control Board could register only a sole complaint on account of noise pollution and that was against the community noise caused by the huge gathering in a field, near the residence of the complainant. It is submitted that the enforcement power may be assigned to these boards in respect with the industrial noise pollution also as is the case with that of air and water pollution. However, the Delhi Pollution Control Committee will now set-up its own monitoring of air, water and noise pollution for which adequate financial assistance is reported to be provided to it for strengthening and modernisation of its laboratory.

21. FORMATION OF THE MINISTRY OF ENVIRONMENT AND FOREST (MOEF)

The Ministry of Environment and Forest (hereinafter referred as MoEF) was set-up in January 1985 and the Department of

Environment created in 1980, was made the part of it. It is the nodal agency in the administrative structure of the central government, for the planning, promotion and co-ordination of environment and forestry programmes. The principal activities undertaken by MoEF, consists of conservation and survey of flora, fauna, forests and wild life, prevention and control of pollution, forestation and regeneration of degraded areas and protection of environment, in the framework of legislations. The organizational structure of the ministry covers various divisions, ancillary body of associated offices and autonomous agencies. Since the enactment of Environment (Protection) Act, 1986, several actions have been taken by MoEF to create comprehensive legal and institutional infrastructure for safeguarding the environment, the policy and law division of this ministry deals with the framing of rules, notifications of standards, notifications of environmental laboratories, delegation of powers, identification of agencies for management of hazards councils, in the states, etc. Besides this, the existing laws, rules are also amended from time to time.[151] The MoEF provides technical assistance and limited grants to promote central affluent treatment plants.

It is a matter of observance that noise standards notifications and issue of Noise (Control of Pollution) Rules, 2000, are neither, comprehensive legislation on noise pollution, nor the enforcement of noise standards in India has been assured. Therefore, there is a need to create a separate cell in the MoEF to deal with noise pollution.

22. ENVIRONMENT (PROTECTION) ACT, 1986

Though, the Water, Air and other pollution Acts were passed immediately after the Stockholm Conference, but the comprehensive legislation covering all aspects of preservation of environment was not enacted. The then existing laws were, generally, focused on specific types of pollution or on specific categories of hazardous substances, leaving some major areas of environmental hazards uncovered. Because of a multiplicity of regulatory agencies, there was a need for an authority which could assume the leading role for studying, planning and

202 Environmental Noise Pollution

implementing long-term requirement of environmental safety and to give direction to and co-ordinate a system of speedy and adequate response to emergency situations, threatening environment.

Keeping the above facts in view, and to give effect to the decisions taken in Stockholm Conference, 1986, post-Bhopal gas tragedy, Indian parliament was motivated to address environment pollutants in general. In 1986, with only casual resistance from powerful industries and business interests the Government enacted 'The Environment (Protection) Act, 1986'.

Though, Ranbir Singh, a reader of faculty of Law, MD University, Rohtak, called this Act as one step forward and two steps backward, but the Umbrella Act definitely goes beyond the scope of Water and Air Acts and deals with the problem of environmental disasters from hazardous industries.

23. INCLUSION OF NOISE POLLUTION UNDER EPA

The Act has two-fold bearing on noise pollution. First, section 6(2)(b) of the Act empowers the central government to make the rules regarding maximum allowable limits of concentration of various environmental pollutants including noise, for different areas. Similarly, the rule-making power has been assigned to the central government by section 25 of this Act, under which, the noise is also said to be included without specific mention to the word noise.

Rule 5 of the Environment (Protection) Rules, 1986 framed under the EPA also prohibits and restricts the location of industries and carrying on processes and operation in different areas depending upon maximum allowable limits of concentration to various environment pollutants, including noise for that area. It is pertinent to mention here that the Noise Pollution (Regulation and Control) Rules, 2000 have been notified under the provision of the EPA & EPR.

The rule of strict liability, in *Ryland* Vs. *Fletcher*[152] case, had been handling the field, for over a century until the pronouncement of path breaking judgment, in *Oleum Gas Leak Case*.[153] This decision is significant, as it brings to fire various aspects of law governing hazardous substances. It was held, that enterprise, which is engaged in hazardous or inherently dangerous activity must provide highest standard of safety and if any harm resulted from such activity, the enterprise must be absolutely liable to compensate. In final pronouncement of this case, some of the doctrines developed by the court have attracted debate. The court ruled, that no exceptions to the rule of strict liability as laid down in *Flether's case*, would apply in such cases. Adapting the 'deep pocket theory', the court said that the amount of compensation to be awarded would depend upon the magnitude and capacity of the enterprise, because such compensation must have a deterrent effect.

In the *Bhopal Gas Leak Case*,[154] tort litigation took a new turn in India regarding the rule of liability. However, the Supreme Court missed a chance to decide about the liability principles, instead a settlement was arrived at, for a sum of US $ 470 millions with the liability on past, present and future claims remaining open. The mixed verdict in these two cases, has also brought to force the question of extent of compensation to be given to the victims of an industrial disaster. Though, the absolute liability principle attracted currents and cross-currents, but the Supreme Court has repeatedly ruled it as a settled law of the land.

24. PUBLIC LIABILITY INSURANCE ACT, 1991

Keeping in view, the Apex Court's above-mentioned observations, regarding liability, it was inevitable to ensure how the liability was translated into relief for victims. Thus, the issue of insurance, which had attracted the intention of the West, stood considered by the legislature in our country too. This is the reason why Public Liability Insurance Act (PLIA), was enacted by the parliament in 1991 to provide public liability insurance, for the purpose of providing immediate relief to the persons affected by the accidents occurring while handling the hazardous substances and for matters connected therewith, or incidental thereto. The Act provides that the owner shall be liable to suitable relief where death or injury to any person or property has resulted from an owner who has been defined as a person having control over the handling of the substance. Though, the Act makes it mandatory for every owner to frame out the insurance policies, to insure himself against liability to give relief to affected persons, before he starts dealing with any hazardous substance. But the Act being the outcome of Bhopal Tragedy, deals with the liability arose from the harm of hazardous substances only. Being it established, that the noise is so hazardous to the health that it does not only confiscate one's hearing power but also capture his psycho power, in absence of which one can hardly do anything, neither for him nor for the nation. It is, therefore, recommended that noise also be brought under the hazardous substance of the Act and the victims of noise, be provided relief accordingly including the relief from environmental relief fund, which has been established by an amendment to the Act in 1992.

Further, the UN Conference on Environment and Development (UNCED), popularly known as 'Earth Summit' was the most important and largest UN Conference ever held, which put the world on the path of sustainable development, and aimed at meeting the needs of the present, without limiting the ability of future generations, to meet their own needs. The earth summit forces the people worldwide, to re-think how their lives affect natural environment and their resources. This earth summit is of utmost importance to Indian Environmental law, because to implement the decisions of this summit, India had to enact The National Environmental Tribunal Act, 1995 (NETA). This Act was enacted *inter-alia* (i) to providing for strict liability for damage arising out of any accident occurring while handling any hazardous substances; (ii) for the establishment of a National Environmental Tribunal for effective and expeditious disposal of cases, arising out from such accident; and (iii) for giving relief and compensation, for damages to persons, property and the environment and for matters connected therewith or incidental thereto.[155] It is a matter of concern that like Public Liability Act, 1991, here also the noise has not been considered hazardous and therefore, has not been covered under this Act.

Keeping court verdicts in view, MOE&F had to issue a draft notification on 21st June, 1999 known as Environment (Siting of Industries) Rules, 1999. Accordingly, the National Environment Appellate Authority Act was passed in 1997 with the object 'to provide for the establishment of a national environment appellate authority, to hear appeals, with respect to the restrictions of areas in which any industry, operation, process or class of industries, operations or processors shall not be carried out subject to certain safeguard under the EPA, 1986 and for matters connected therewith or incidental thereto. Thus, besides environment tribunal, another forum for settlement of disputes, i.e. the National Environment Authority, has also been constituted.

Consequently, in exercise of the powers conferred by clause (i) of sub-section (2) of section 3, sub-section (i) and clause (b) of sub-section (2) of section 6 and section 25 of the EPA, 1986 read with rule 5 of the EPR, 1986, the central government notified the Noise Pollution (Control and Regulation) Rules, 2000. These rules restrict the use of loudspeakers/public address system, and also laid down, the 'ambient air quality standard' in respect of noise.

The Bio-diversity Bill, 2000 is of recent origin in India. This landmark legislation following the Bio-diversity convention on the Earth Summit, aimed at protecting India's bio-assets and ensuring equitable benefit shoring by the users and the owners. The bill is intended to provide for conservation of bio-logical diversity, sustainable use of its components and equitable sharing of the benefits arising out of the use of biological resources and for matters connected herewith or incidental thereto.

25. ENFORCEMENT OF POLLUTION LAWS

Pollution laws have achieved little success. The courts have been slow to respond to enforcement actions sought by State Pollution Boards. The Boards themselves have been poorly funded and charges of corruption have been regular and widespread. However, large industries have achieved pollution compliance more easily than small industries.[156] The reason is that they are afraid of taking risks. On identifying the driving force for better environmental performance, it was revealed that the implied current efforts in environmental management is driven largely by a fear of the penalty, that can be imposed by the government when environmental laws are violated.[157]

The 'Hindu', reports from Tiruvananthapuram, that the Report of the Comptroller and Auditor General of India for 2000-2001 has brought out serious deficiencies in enforcement of pollution control laws in the State. It is noted that the policy on abatement of pollution and the environment policy drafted by the State Government in 1993 and 1994, respectively were not adopted. There was heavy shortfall in monitoring the emission of even consented units. Stock monitoring was done only in a few industries. Surprise inspections in 19 industrial units, disclosed major shortcomings in pollution control measures in these units, the report said. The deficiencies in the implementation of National Ambient Air Quality Monitoring Project, pointed out by the Central Pollution Control Board remained un-rectified. The CAG report 2004 also reveals that despite Rs. 872 crore expenditure, Yamuna remains still polluted.[157A]

Though the Noise Pollution (Regulation and Control) Rules, 2000 came into force in February 2000, but classification of areas in the State and prescribing the enforcement agency was not decided by the State Government as of October 2001. It is also to note that in case of noise pollution particularly, the SPCBs are only the monitoring agencies and do not have the enforcement power like air and water. They say that their monitoring is of no use, once defaulters cannot be dealt-with, by them. Moreover, the suitable noise meters are yet to be provided to the concern agencies.[158]

In a PIL filed by public spirited lawyer, Jodhpur High Court directed the District Collector (DC) and SP city, on 10 Feb. 1999 to assure the non-existence of noise pollution sources in the region on account of loudspeakers and other sound amplifying systems so that people are not devoid of their right to live in noise free environment. They were directed to come heavily on the defaulters.

The concerned officers did not take the above court directive seriously, hence another PIL had to be filed in the same court for its enforcement. The Bench comprising N.N. Mathur and D.N. Joshi, JJ., directed the DC and SP, to produce action report, along with an affidavit, on the implementation of the orders in question dated 10 Feb., 1999.

However, DC, imposed a ban on indiscriminate use of loudspeaker. None to use loudspeakers for the purpose of social, religious, marriages, industrial, public or personal use, without the prior permission.[159]

However, traffic police prosecuted vehicle owners on account of noise pollution caused by the use of unauthorized pressure horn. Secondly, on 11 December, 2001, the action was initiated against two autorikshaw for causing noise pollution by playing audio cassette player at high pitch of sound.[159A] Still, noise pollution is failed to find its place in all the traffic police programmes against the polluter vehicles.

Protection of environment now tops the agenda of many countries including India, which the judiciary ought to be familiar. A panoramic view of environmental laws bring to fore the ancient Indian heritage which lies embodied in Upanishads, Puranas, and Arthashastra which prescribed it as a moral duty of every human being, to maintain conducive environment in his habitat. Kautilaya's sense of environmental sanitation, health and hygiene for the people, was the same. India is a cradle of various religious thoughts. Reverence for nature and its creations, are the unifying ethical principles in the religions of India. All of these keep nature above the man and may be considered to be a precursor of customary international law. Despite such strong traditions, the environmental law in India has not been successful in real sense of the term.

In independent India, various legal measures have been taken to protect and improve the environment. Besides the constitutional provisions, a survey of these Indian laws reveals, that these numerous enactments passed, either by the central or the state legislators, have not been able to check environmental degradation and eco-system imbalances. Though, courts in India have played a pivotal role and created an environmental jurisprudence, which seek to strike a balance between environmental protection and the sustainable development. The law-makers lack sufficient awareness of environmental problems, which restricts formulation of comprehensive legislation on environment. The National Environment Tribunal Act, 1995 is yet to be enforced and the constitution of Tribunals is awaited and also a comprehensive legislation on environment known as the National Environmental Laws (Amendment) Bill, 1999 is under consideration of the Ministry of Environment and Forest, Government of India.[160] However, taking wing on a request from the Apex court, made in December 2000, it has been reported[161] that the Law Commission in India will be reviewing the whole range of environmental legislation for the object of consolidation and codification. It is expected that Law Commission would pay adequate attention on the malady of noise pollution in the country, which is the need of the hour. Sanctions are to be registered and greater responsibilities are to be imposed on authorities to implement laws. Laws in action have to be legislated expeditiously to check impending harm to the mankind. Encouragement and incentive for promoting better environment, both amongst the rural and urban populace, would be a better substitute to the penal sanctions.

It is true that law alone cannot serve the purpose, except increasing the thickness of the statute book, if they are not enforced strictly. In this direction, we are still far behind in achieving our goal. The Planning Commission Steering Committee on Environment for the Tenth Plan, for instance, has suggested a revamp of environmental laws to ensure effective implementation, training of judicial officers in environment law and strengthening the enforcement mechanism.[162]

It is also imperative that there should be a guinine public participation in environmental decision-making body. The citizens can play crucial role in the form of people's movement in order to protect the environment. This social obligation has been emphasized on every citizen by the court also in *Rural Litigation Entitlement Kendra* Vs. *State of U.P.*[163]

26. ENVIRONMENTAL POLLUTION AT INTERNATIONAL PERSPECTIVE AND UNITED NATIONS

International concern toward deterioration of environment may be recorded from the fact that world bodies had to think for compensating Malaysia, but not to allow cutting of forests in any case. It is pertinent, that Malaysian Government itself started to cut vast reserves of forests, for exporting wood to other countries and thereby causing ecological imbalance. As, it was not the concern of Malaysia alone, but of the entire World. Hence, the world bodies were of the view that the Malaysian Government was digging graves for its countrymen and it became the duty of every homosapian on this earth, to stop such homicidal attempt, at once. The Heads of Common Wealth Nations met at Kualalumpur, the capital of Malaysia, from 18th to 24th October, 1989, taken note of it and requested Malaysian Government to stop denuding the forests. "Awake and aware, before it is too late", warned Common Wealth to Malaysian Government at Lankawi.[163A]

It is true that environmental pollution is the problem of no continent, no hemisphere, no race, no system or no individual, but is a collective and joint problem of entire world, which is not to be handled alone, but by each and everyone on this earth. Realizing this collective and joint responsibility, UN had to hold a Conference on Human Environment, in June 1972 at Stockholm.

Following the Stockholm Conference on the Human Environment, many countries developed a substantial body of environmental law and regulations, dealing with the protection of the environment and the management of natural resources. Widespread public concern over pollution, led to legislation to curb emissions of effluents and airborne pollutants, while concerns over the depletion of natural resources, led to legislation for resource conservation and the preservation of areas of special biological value.

In many South East Asian Nations, this legislation was more comprehensive. Laws and regulations were revised, updated and expanded, to cover areas concerning pollution control, nature conservation, protection of public health the control of toxic substances and hazardous wastes. In Thailand, in addition to being institutionalized, many environmental regulations were included in the Constitution of 1997 to make them more binding, and easier to implement. In Philippines, the administration of water resources and sewage management systems has been handed over to the private sector. Cambodia, the Lao People's Democratic Republic and Myanmar are all at the initial stages of strengthening institutional framework. But, the challenges associated with this new legislation have arisen from conflicts between environmental protections, resource conservation, need for rapid economic growth, and fast development. The full and effective enforcement of environmental legislation and sanctions for non-compliance, remain elusive goals. This is due to lack of political will, the relative weakness of environmental institutions, inadequate funds, and technical expertise.

Monitoring, and enforcement of standards in East Asia, has been generally weak. In Japan, legislative initiatives in late 1960s, including the establishment of an Environment Agency, were compromised by rapid industrial growth and economic development. However, by the end of 1980s, Japan's growing international role and generally poor state of national environment, forced a re-evaluation of environmental and developmental goals. New legislations were enacted, e.g. a separate legislation to reduce vehicle emissions. By 1993, the government had established a Basic Environmental Plan, environment agency of Japan, 1994, which outlined policies, policy instruments, and defined the roles of each sector of society. Industries were made responsible for self-monitoring and evaluation of pollution.

Similarly, after adopting the same fast track of developmental path, as in Japan, the Republic of Korea also encountered severe environmental degradation and has responded with comprehensive legislation and environmental action.

Recent efforts of the Chinese government, to implement environmental laws and regulations, have culminated in a comprehensive Environmental Protection Law, which focuses on implementation and enforcement. The law defines accountability, legal responsibility, and imposes sanctions for non-compliance. A standard constitute a major component of environmental policy and now embraces every aspect of environmental quality, pollution discharge, environmental management, and even monitoring methodology. Recent amendments to the criminal law have greatly strengthened this mandatory aspect of environmental protection. At the institutional level, significant progress is reported in implementing unified monitoring, inspection and management systems throughout the country, through a wide range of local and central environmental bodies. Growing numbers of environmental professionals are now also employed in both, the state and the private industrial sectors.[163B]

Environmental policy responses, and law in Australia have attempted, particularly in recent years, to incorporate the guiding principles of ecologically sustainable development.[163C] Coordination for environmental management is effected mainly through the Council of Australian Governments and the relevant Ministerial Councils.[163D]

Laws and institutions dealing with New Zealand's environment were reduced in number and made more coherent in the late 1980s and early 1990s. The philosophical center-piece is the Resource Management Act, 1991, which places most environmental decisions, making in the hands of locally-elected authorities and requires them to develop policies and plans, governing use of air, land and water. Central government still has primary responsibility for environmental issues, where there is a clear national interest, and it can also set national policies, standards or guidelines to ensure that local authorities manage environmental issues in ways, that are of national consistent. One of the greatest policy challenges of the decade is, to promote liberal trade, while maintaining and strengthening the protection of the environment and natural resources. Trade and investment have been the principal engines of economic growth but they have resulted in serious environmental degradation. A number of governments are now taking action to reconcile trade and environmental interests, through the use of trade-environment-related policies and agreements, such as product standards, enforcement of the polluter pays principle, health and sanitary standards related to food exports, and eco-labeling. On this issue, ASEAN has recognized that any measures to promote better environmental management, must be consistent with General Agreement on Tariffs and Trade (GATT) principles. It, therefore, calls for trade arrangements that support environment and development policies and seeks to improve capacity in trade-environment policy analysis, planning and evaluation[163E]

The problem of environmental pollution does not recognize any territorial barrier, its control needs a collective action of all the nations. In fact, the action and behaviour of the family of nations are mainly regulated through U.N Treaty, 1945. One of the objectives of this treaty is to promote social progress and better standards of life.[164] The significance of such human rights has been recognized by the General Assembly through Universal Declaration of Human Rights, 1948 which lays down common standard of achievement for all the people and nations. The declaration not only recognizes the right to life of every person under Article 3 but stresses the quality of life also under Article 25 wherein the right to standard of living, adequate for the health and well-being of himself and his family, has been guaranteed.

The object behind the principles of this declaration is to promote the conditions for the full development of human personality and dignified life, the fulfilment of which depends upon the existence of any healthy environment, but the same would not be so possible, if natural atmosphere is disrupted by human activities. Therefore, the protection and preservation of environment is quite essential for the family of nations for human existence.

Besides several other international treaties, some conventions also deal with the problem of environmental protection in fragmentary manner. No doubt, these conventions mainly relate to the problem of disarmament but the ultimate object is to control the problem of environmental pollution. For instance, Partial Test Ban Treaty, 1963, Outer Space Treaty, 1967, Treaty for the Prohibition of Nuclear Weapon in Latin America, 1967, Treaty on Non-Proliferation of Nuclear Weapons, 1968, The UN Convention on the Law of the Sea, 1982, are some examples of such conventions, which deal with the pollution problem and noise pollution lies well within their ambit.

27. STOCKHOLM CONFERENCE ON HUMAN ENVIRONMENT

In 1968, UN established a scientific advisory committee to consider the question of holding a conference on Human Environment, which was later, held in Stockholm from 5 to 16 June in 1972. This historic conference was attended by the delegates world over, including the then Indian Prime Minister Late Smt. Indira Gandhi. The conference adopted '26-point declaration' of principles including controversial reference to nuclear weaponry besides providing certain recommendations as guidelines for the further conduct of states in environmental matters.

The Stockholm declaration proclaims that man is both creature and molder of his environment. Due to the rapid growth of science and technology man has acquired the power to transform his environment in countless ways and on an unprecedented scale. The natural and man-made environments are essential to his well-being and to the enjoyment of basic human rights, even the right to life itself.[165] While stressing the qualities of life of human beings, the declaration mandates that every man has a right to adequate conditions of life in an environment of quality, which permits the life to dignity. Further a responsibility to protect and improve the environment for present and future generation has also been imposed over every individual.[166] Besides, a duty on the states has also been imposed to prevent pollution in sea, which is liable to create hazards to human health and to marine life as well. The conference has also directed the member-states to make such environmental policies as to enhance their present and future development. In case of any economic difficulties arising in application of such policies, states and international organizations have been directed to take appropriate measure.[167]

28. INTERNATIONAL LABOUR ORGANISATION (ILO) AND NOISE CONTROL

The object of ILO is to look after the welfare of the labour and also to indicate international standard of policy for them. To this end, General Conference of ILO adopted a convention to protect the workers against health hazards resulting from noise and vibrations.[168] Under this convention, each member has been directed after consultation with the representative organization of employers and employees to accept the obligation of this convention separately in respect of air, noise and vibrations. The term 'noise' used in the convention includes all sounds, which result in hearing loss and harm the health. The convention also creates an obligation on the member-states to take measures for prevention and control against occupational hazards, in working environment resulting from air, noise and vibrations and to enforce them through their national laws or regulations. The employers have been made responsible to comply with aforesaid direction in prescribed manner.[169]

In view of aforesaid convention, International Labour Organization amended its Constitution and 'protection of workers against occupational hazards in the working environment due to noise pollution and vibrations 1977', was inserted within its chronological table at serial number 148, for guidance of the member-states to enforce it through their respective national legislation. The convention has also been made applicable to all the branches of economic activity. A responsibility has been cast upon the employers to import the conditions of monitoring air pollution, noise and vibration in the working environment. For this purpose, employer would arrange equipment, and apply regularly. The employer has been directed to ensure the regular inspection and maintenance of machines and installations with respect to the emission of harmful substance, dust, noise and vibration. In this context the supervision of the workers health would include pre-assignment medical examination on regular basis.

29. WORLD HEALTH ORGANISATION (WHO)

The role of World Health Organisation (WHO) for the control of noise pollution is also noteworthy. It is to raise the standard of health of the people. Although, WHO is not an authority to prescribe the limits of noise, yet it recommends some permissible limits of noise, which are just advisory for its member-states. The documents prepared by WHO on noise recommends that in case of working environments, there is not risk of hearing damage as noise level of less than 75 dB(A)[170] Leq (8 hrs). For higher level, there is an increasing predicable risk and this must be taken into account when setting occupational noise standards. As per WHO, bed-room noise level 35 dB(A) is desirable level of noise to prevent any significant community annoyance. According to a report, WHO has fixed 45 dB as the "Safe noise level." But, during Diwali, noise levels recorded at a distance of about 12 meter away from the point of bursting crackers were found to be as high as 120 dB. Think of what this could do to our ears. However, WHO on 24 March 2006, has released its new guidelines, which calls for gradual reduction in pollution levels. Many countries in Europe are willing to enforce the guidelines in three to four years.[170A]

It shows that aforesaid convention and declaration of UN and that of its agencies lay down the guidelines for the member-states to control the problem of environmental pollution and that of noise pollution through their respective laws.

30. UNITED NATIONS ENVIRONMENT PROGRAMME (UNEP)

To meet the expectation of the Stockholm Conference, General Assembly established, Governing Council of UNEP consisting 58 members based on equitable geographical distribution, the council was to keep under review the world environmental situation in order to ensure that emerging environmental programme is of wide international significance. A provision for additional financing "Voluntary Fund" for environmental programme was also established with effect from January 1, 1973. One of the greatest contributions of the Governing Council of UNEP was the holding of United Nations Conference on Human Settlement—popularly known as HABITAT, which urged for special emphasis on balanced development, for all regions.

Thus, UNEP has become a basic international instrument for coordinating environmental operations among the countries and in developing a global environment monitoring system, to deduct impending environmental changes, man-made or natural. In the worlds of Mustafa:[171]

> "UNEP has become the environmental conscience of the UN system and its environmental advocates to the world."

World Charter for Nature, 1982

In 1982, UN General Assembly adopted a new Charter namely, "World Charter for Nature"[172] through which it was unanimously decided that nature shall be respected and its essential processes shall not be impaired. It was further resolved to conserve all areas of earth, and man will fully recognize the urgency of maintaining the quality of environment and conservation of natural resources.

Third UN Convention on Law of Sea, 1982 also imposes an obligation on states, to protect and preserve the marine environment and to take all necessary measures to reduce and control marine pollution.

31. WORLD COMMISSION ON ENVIRONMENT AND DEVELOPMENT (WCED)

In 1984, the UN made another significant achievement in the field of environmental development, and it was the formation of World Commission on Environment and Development (WECD). The commission was to examine the problems of environment, which the world was facing with the prospective of the year 2000 AD. The legal experts of WECD drafted a long and exhaustive list of 22 Articles, in which the right to environment was discussed at length. The principles contained in these 22 Articles were approved by the participants at the meeting of WCED held at Peace Palace, in Hague in June 1986. Entire world community was of the view that "Environmental problem is not the problem of an individual or nation but is a problem, which no nation, no continent, no hemisphere, no race, no system can handle alone.[173] It is a problem of entire human race which required joint action.

32. INTERNATIONAL COURT OF JUSTICE (ICJ)

ICJ, in its Report to UN General Assembly, 1986 declared its willingness and readiness to deal with the cases of environment and said:

"The doors of ICJ are always open to welcome consideration of any request for settlement of environmental disputes."

33. UNITED NATIONS CONFERENCE ON ENVIRONMENT AND DEVELOPMENT, 1992

It was for the first time down the history of environmental protection that the representatives of 178 countries participated under the auspices of U.N. Conference on environment and development for "Earth Summit-1992 at Rio De Janerio, Brazil. It adopted a convention on "Bio-diversity", consisting of 27-points along with 40 chapters of Agenda 21, known as Rio Declaration. The convention not only reflects the spirit for reaching responsibility and commitment of the states but also stresses to co-operate in a global partnership to conserve, protect and restore the health and integrity of the earth's ecosystem.

It devolves and spells a set of specific liabilities on the countries at national and international level. For example, under principle 9 of the convention, member-countries have been called upon to enact laws for liability and compensation for the victims of pollution and other environmental damages. Further, it enjoins the states to ensure exchange of scientific and technological knowledge in order to help indigenous capacity building for substantial developments. The convention also requires the countries under its principle 10, to initiate the participation of the citizens on development issues and to ensure their right to access the information relating thereto. It also makes obligatory for the countries to facilitate and encourage public awareness about environmental matters and to provide them effective access to judicial and administrative proceedings for the same.

However, the disappointing feature of the convention is that it has failed to raise enough funds for a new global environment facility and for launching the ambitious Agenda-21, the plan action for 21st century. The refusal of United States of America to sign the convention is also another setback to it.

No doubt, the Rio Declaration cannot be said of much success, but environmental movement has gained a new momentum and a new sense of direction.

34. JOHANNESBURG SUMMIT, 2002

After 10 years of Rio Summit, Johannesburg Summit, 2002— the World Summit on Sustainable Development took place at Johannesburg in South Africa from 26 August to 4 September 2002 and focused world's attention to direct their action towards meeting difficult challenges, including improving people's lives and conserving the natural resources in a world that is growing in population, with ever-increasing demands for food, water, shelter, sanitation, energy, health services and economic security.

At Earth Summit, 1992, in Rio, the international community adopted Agenda 21, an unprecedented global plan of action for sustainable development. But the best strategies are only as good as their implementation. Ten years later, the Johannesburg Summit presents an exciting opportunity for today's leaders to adopt concrete steps and identify quantifiable targets for better implementing Agenda 21.

Though, some of the world leaders called the summit, as failure in its totality but, calling for collective mobilization on a global scale, UN Secretary-General Kofi Annan said that governments has agreed on an impressive range of concrete actions and commitments at the World Summit of Sustainable Development. He quoted:

"... those who cause pollution have to be there to be part of the solution. We have to work with business. Civil society are our key partners but we need other stakeholders."

35. ENVIRONMENT AND INDIAN CONSTITUTION

Legislation is one of the major and the most effective measure, available for the regulation of environment, provided the provisions are enforced in their true sense and spirit. To achieve this purpose and to protect mankind from the hazards of polluted environment, the executive machinery has to be sensitized for the enforcement. Letters of the law become meaningful only when they are enforced and consequently the public opinion is also generated for the obedience of the law. The illustration is not far to seek. The rules of the road regarding drivers of two-wheelers to wear crash helmet are in existence for a longer period, but were not enforced so far. Only a few months before the city police administration became very particular to enforce the said rule. Now, the citizens have also become aware of the rules and sincerely started obeying them. Thus sincere enforcement has fostered sensible public opinion. This proves the above fact that law in action sensitized the citizens to obey.

The International concern for the global environment is of recent origin. It was in the year 1972 at Stockholm, when United Nations in its important conference on human environment took place and wherein India was one of the signatories out of 113 countries and was represented by the then Prime Minister of India Late Mrs Indira Gandhi. In this conference signatory nations took responsibility to protect and improve the environment. This Conference was the result of resolution passed by the Economic and Social Council of United Nations. Next, movement came in 1974, in the form of Charter of Economic Rights and Duties of States, 1974. The combined effect of these two International resolutions was that India decided to bring necessary changes in its basic charter, i.e. Constitution of India, as original text of this pious statute was free from even the term environment.

The Chapter on Directive Principles in the Indian Constitution indirectly could locate the protection of environment under Art. 47, which casts a primary duty upon the state to improve public health along with raising the level of nutrition and standard of living of its people. But this Article categorically did not provide for the protection and improvement of environment in particular. But the serious concern to enforce this directive is of more recent origin. It is the cardinal principles that a Constitution to be living, must be growing. However, the specific provision has been included in the Constitution in 1976 by 42nd Amendment, i.e.. Article 48A and Article 51A(g). Article 48A mandates that state shall endeavor to protect and improve the environment and to safeguard the forest and wild life of the country. Art. 51(A)(g) imposes a fundamental duty upon every citizen of India to protect and improve the natural environment including forests, lakes, rivers and wild life, and to have compassion for living creatures. Art. 51A(g) further qualifies the environment to be natural and imposes a fundamental duty upon the citizen to keep the environment 'natural'. It has been well observed in *Kinkri Devi's case*, that these two Articles serve as constitutional pointer to both, the state as well as citizens, who have a constitutional duty, not only to protect the environment but also a step further, 'to improve' the environment, and to preserve and safeguard the same in its natural form. But again our Constitution is silent as to what machinery shall be employed to enforce citizen's duty to keep environment natural. In spite of the fact that the state is empowered to invent any legislative or executive procedure or any other device of its own to enforce the duty of citizens, yet the state has not exercised its power.

In *Masud Alam's case*, the question before the Calcutta High Court was whether the use of electric loudspeaker, which disturbs the whole locality and the neighbourhood, could be justified on the ground of being for religious purpose to enjoy the right to freedom of religion under Art. 25. The brief facts of the case clarify the whole situation. In this case the Commissioner of police had banned the use of loudspeakers for calling the Azan five times a day. One of the contentions of the petitioner was that India is a secular state and under Art. 25, all persons are at liberty to freely practice and propagate their religion; and that such liberty was curtailed by the suppression of the use of loudspeaker to propagate the Azan. It was held that the use of loudspeaker, which caused disturbance in the area, could not be justified on the ground that the same was in connection with a religious purpose. This shows that the constitutional mandate was rightly applied in the interest of human environment. The right to use loudspeaker, mike, is not a fundamental right in itself. It is the eco-friend Indian Constitution under whose shade our Supreme Court could recently ban firecrackers with a high decibel of bursting noise and held that such restriction is not violative of religious rights u/s 25 of the constitution.[173A]

36. JUDICIAL ACTIVISM ON ENVIRONMENTAL EDUCATION

Supreme Court under Article Art. 51(A)(g) of the Constitution has directed the State Government and Union Territories to put a condition on licenses to all cinema halls, touring-cinemas and video-parlours, that at least two slides or messages on environmental understanding should be shown free of cost, as a part of each show which is to be provided by the Ministry of Environment and Forest. Simultaneously the court directed the Ministry of Information and Broadcasting to start producing short-films, which shall deal with the environmental pollution. One such film will be shown, as far as practicable in one show every day, by the cinema halls. All India Radio and Doordarshan will take steps to make and broadcast interesting programmes on environmental pollution. The Attorney General has said that five to seven minutes can be devoted to these programmes, each day on these Radio/TV stations. The UGC will take appropriate steps to require Universities to prescribe a course on the environment. They should consider making this course a compulsory subject. As far as education up to college level, every State Government and every Education Board concern with education up to the matriculation stage ; as well as Intermediate college, is required to take steps to enforce compulsory education on environment, in a ground way. It shows that the Constitution of India, does not only cast a duty on its citizens to improve and protect the environment, but also raises environmental-awareness amongst them, through its judicial svstem.

37. FUNDAMENTAL RIGHTS AND THE ENVIRONMENT

The Constitution of India, in its Pre-amble, ensures to secure justice to all its citizens; social, economic, and political. Every one has, therefore, a fundamental right to get social justice.

Hence, to provide pollution-free environment is also the part of social justice without which the survival of mankind would be too difficult. Thus, right to health becomes primary to all the fundamental rights and enjoyment of all other fundamental rights like right to equality, freedom, religion, becomes dependent upon right to healthy environment. To remain healthy, one is closely associated with clean environment, free from all types of pollutions. Here it is submitted that, by a new amendment into the IIIrd Part of Indian Constitution, it becomes imperative to incorporate the fundamental right to health categorically.

38. ARTICLE 19

Part III of Indian Constitution, deals with all fundamental rights guaranteed to both citizen and non-citizens. Art. 19(1)(a) makes provision for all the citizens to have right to freedom of speech and expression and 19(1)(g) provides right to practice any profession, or to carry on any occupation, trade and business. In Art. 19(2) state is empowered to impose reasonable restrictions by making any law for this purpose. But in spite of the constitutional restrictions, the indiscriminate use of loudspeakers, mike or other sound amplifying devices violate the freedom of speech and expression and the right to practice any profession and right to carry out any trade or business under Art. 19(1)(g) is infringed by establishing such industries and practicing such professions which pollute the environment. The use of loudspeakers for the purposes of conducting rallies, meetings, religious and social ceremonies, election campaigns, advertisements, are the instances where the whole locality could be compelled to become a captive audience of the noise, caused in the name of freedom of speech, expression and religion. In *Jacob* Vs. *Supdt of Police*,[174] it was held that right to speech implies the right to silence also. It implies freedom of, not to listen, and not to be forced to listen too. The right is subordinate to peace and order. Freedom of speech and expression, guaranteed under Art. 19(1)(a) of the Constitution of India includes by necessary implication, freedom not to listen, and/or to remain silent. One can not exercise this right at the cost and in total deprivation of others' rights. A right cannot be conferred by the authority concerned, upon a person or a religious organization to exercise their rights, suspending and/or taking away the rights of others.[175]

Our dynamic Judiciary declared public interest to be on priority than the individual freedom. The court said that it is erroneous to bring unrestricted freedom causing pollution within the ambit of Art. 19. Being custodian of the constitution, the conscious judiciary had gone up to the extent of closing down the sources of environmental noise,[176] e.g. industries causing pollution in spite of the fact that such entrepreneurs were a strong revenue source for the nation as well as national development.[177] However, in few instances, individual could succeed to convince the judiciary to prefer their individual rights over the public right to health. In Ivour Hyden's,[178] the High Court of Andhra Pradesh has excused the act of playing radio on loud voice as being the act of trivial nature.

Not only in India, but also in United States, the US Supreme Court has opined that the restriction on use of loudspeakers was against the right to freedom of speech. But in its later decision in a case, it changed its view and held that reasonable restriction on amplifier does not violate constitutional rights of speech.

To conclude we can say that the mixed decisions of judiciary on Art. 19 have added fuel to the fire, making environment further noisy. It is therefore, suggested that either the judiciary should give definite decisions or Art. 19 be amended to add in Art. 19(2), some qualifying words, e.g. freedom of speech and expression shall be subject to reasonable restrictions not to pollute environment so as to rule out any further possibility of causing pollution on the pretext of these freedoms by way of convincing judiciary or otherwise. It is also pertinent to mention that the said amendment would also avoid litigations on environment and hence it will save judicial energy and time.

However, our dynamic judiciary has recently held that nobody can take shelter behind Article 19(1)A and claim a fundamental right to create noise by amplifying the sound of his speech with the help of loudspeakers. While one has right to speech, others have a right to listen or decline to listen. The court further held that nobody can be compelled to listen and nobody can claim that he has a right to make his voice trespassing into the ears or mind of others. Nobody can indulge into aural aggression.[179]

39. 'RIGHT TO CLEAN ENVIRONMENT': AN ATTRIBUTE OF 'RIGHT TO LIFE'

Art. 21, enshrined in Part III of the Constitution provides to its citizens, the right to life and liberty. This right has been transformed into positive right by the activist judicial interpretation. Until the advent of *Maneka Gandhi's case*, all the fundamental rights were considered to be negative in nature, imposing only negative obligation on the state, which prohibited the state to interfere with the enjoyment of these rights. But in *Maneka Gandhi's case*, the Supreme Court for the first time transformed it into a positive right by imposing an affirmative duty on the state. The post-Maneka era has witnessed an unprecedented judicial activism in the country, elevating Art. 21 to the position of "a brooding omnipresence" and converting it into a sanctuary of human values.[180]

The main question, in the context of Part III of Constitution may be raised whether it guarantees a fundamental right to a hygienic environment? If it does, the next question may be—where can it be located? The answer to this has been given by Hon'ble Justice Bhagwati, while delivering a historic judgment in *Francis Carolie Mullien* Vs. *Delhi Administration*[181] for the import of the right to life:

"The right to life enshrined in Art. 21 can not be restricted to mere animal existence. It means something more than just physical survival. The right to life includes the right to live with human dignity and all that goes along with it, namely, the bare necessities of life such as adequate nutrition, clothing and shelter over head."

Now, it has been held by the court that the preservation of sanitation and environment falls under Art. 21. In *Rural Litigation and Entitlement Kendra* Vs. *State of UP*,[182] a bench, presided over by the then Justice P.N. Bhagwati, Sen, J. and Justice R.N. Mishra through their order, who observed:

"This is the first case of its kind in the country involving issues relating to environment and the ecological balance while dealing with limestone quarries in Dehradun. Held, where the court finds that due to working of limestone quarries there is imbalance to ecology or hazard to healthy environment, then in that case the court will order their closure. If due to closure of these quarries the lessees of limestone quarries would be thrown out of business in which they have invested large sum of monies and expanded considerable time and efforts, would undoubtedly cause hardship to them. But it is a price that has to be paid for protecting and safeguarding the right of the people to live in healthy environment with minimal disturbance to ecological balance and without avoidable hazard to them and to their cattle, homes and agriculture land and undue affection of air, water and environment."[183]

40. RIGHT TO HEALTHY ENVIRONMENT u/a 21 AND 47 BOTH (*State of Punjab Vs. Ramlubhaya Bagga*)[184]

It also has been stated by the court, that maintenance of health, preservation of the sanitation and environment falls within the purview of Art. 21 as it adversely affects the life of the citizen and amounts to poisoning and reducing the life of the citizen because of the hazards created, if not checked. Right to peaceful sleep, right to breathe in free and fresh air, right to drink contamination free water, right to reside, walk and travel in noise free environment is guaranteed by Art. 21 to all the residents of India. In *Maulana Mufti Md. Syed Noorur Rahaman Vs. State of West Bengal,*[185] the court has maintained that the right to leisure, right to remain silent, right to listen, right to rest, right to read, right to speak, right not to listen, right to read for examination, are within the ambit of Art. 21. The court, in *State of Himachal Pradesh Vs. Umed Ram Sharma,*[185A] had gone to the extent of saying that right to easy access to road in hilly areas is also a fundamental right, covered under Art. 21.

The right to live in an atmosphere free from noise pollution has been upheld as one guaranteed by Article 21 of Indian Constitution. These decisions of the courts are pronounced in the case of *Free Legal Aid Cell Shree Sugan Chand Agarwal @ Bagwati Vs. Govt. of NCT of Delhi and others*[185B] and *P.A. Jacob Vs. Supritendent of Police,* Kottayam.[185C]

Article 25: *Noise Pollution* Vs. *Right to Religion*

In fact, the freedom of speech and expression under Art. 19(1)(a) and freedom of religion under Art. 25 of the Constitution are inseparable, as one cannot be enjoyed without the exercise of another. Thus, if any one wishes to propagate his religious ideas, as guaranteed by Art. 25, it could only be possible through the exercise of the right to speech and expression. Art. 25(i) guarantees to every person freedom of conscience and right to profess, practice and propagate religion.

India being a secular country, the architects of its Constitution, perhaps drafted the Art. 25, intending to make India really secular in its true sense by way of giving equal opportunity to each religion to practice and propagate its own religion.

Loudspeaker Noise Vs. Right to Religion

The Calcutta High Court on November 21, 1996 banned the use of loudspeakers at all places of worship, irrespective of religion. A division bench of Justice Bhagabati Prasad Benerjee and Justice A.K. Chakraborty in their ruling stated that as India is a secular state, the ban would cover all religions and hence the steps to control noise pollution should cover all religious communities. The ban, which minimized noise levels in the city, during the Durgapujas and Kalipujas, would also cover gurudwaras and Mosques also. On December 25, 1996 in the evening *Milad-un-nabi* (religious programme) was held with loudspeakers in the Masjid campus, near Gate No. 1, in Dum Dum Airport area of Calcutta Officials of the State Pollution Control Board, found that the sound of the mike-system was 85 decibel, whereas, 65 decibel was the limit prescribed by the Court. The matter was reported to the High Court, which issued a contempt of court notice against the Masjid committee for violating its order. The court found them guilty and imposed a penalty of Rs. 2500 to be deposited with the board. Nearly two dozen Durgapuja, Kalipuja and Jagadhatripuja Committees of Calcutta, also were charged with the contempt of court for violating the noise pollution order and fined Rs. 1000 each.[186]

Once the ban order is enforced in West Bengal, it would gradually be extended to other states in the country. But in practice, this Article could also be violated by way of causing loudspeakers generated noise pollution. While propagating, the people could neglect the sentiments in their neighbourhood, causing much inconvenience to them. Loudspeakers with their high pitches and loud voices have become the associated part of religious ceremonies, of all religions. Though, the spiritual benefits of kirtan, prayers and mantras may be good for the praying mind, yet their loud voice may certainly cause disturbance to a student preparing for the exams, to ailing patients, sleep of the aged persons and also those who are not interested to listen to such kirtans during those moments. Also, against the victimization by the indiscriminate use of loudspeakers for religious purposes, the High Court of Himachal Pradesh had to comment in *Yoginderlal* Vs. *Municipal Corporation, Shimla:*[187]

> ". . . that though the condition imposed on the use of loudspeakers are laudable indeed, they are mostly being observed in the breach. We may also record that in our courtroom many times, we have to stand the noise of the loudspeakers used by religious institutions. It appears that some religious institutions are bent upon insisting, the fear of God in the society by using loudspeakers, in such a way that these can be heard over the maximum people of the town. It seems that in their zeal, the religious institutions are following the principles of home delivery services."

Against the menace of noise pollution entering into the court rooms, court itself has observed, that the right to use a loud-speaker is not a fundamental right in itself. Noise pollution is an accepted danger to health and therefore, indiscriminate use of loudspeakers cannot be permitted. A loudspeaker is a lively symbol, through which vibrates the robust as well as virulent notes emanating from Art. 19(1)(a) of the Constitution; both are unnecessary to sustain openness in a democracy. The untrammeled blare of loudspeakers, in the premises of a courtroom is a menace, which hampers the administration of justice.

In *Rajnikant* Vs. *State of Uttar Pradesh,*[188] the petitioner challenged the by-laws of Allahabad Municipal Board, under which the permission from the executive officer was necessary before any use of loudspeaker. The plea of right to freedom of

speech and expression and right to religion, supported by Art.
19(1)(a) and Art. 25 respectively, were taken in his favour by the
petitioner for this purpose. But the court, while dismissing the
petition, expressed following views:

> ". . . use of mechanical instruments like loudspeakers and
> amplifier is not covered by the guarantee of the freedom of
> speech and expression under Art. 19(1)(a) and hence is not
> the absolute right under Art. 25."

Right to religion under Art. 25(i), like other constitutional
rights, is not absolute. This right is subject to public order,
morality and health and to the other provisions of Part III of the
Constitution. Also, under sub-clauses (a) and (b) of clause (2) of
Art. 25, the state is empowered by law:

   (a) To regulate or restrict any economic, financial, political
      or other secular activity which may be associated with
      religious practice; and
   (b) To provide for (i) social welfare and reform, and (ii) to
      throw open Hindu religious institutions of public
      character to all classes and sections of Hindus.

In yet another case of *Masud Alam Vs. Commr. of Police*,[189] it
was held that the use of loudspeakers, causing disturbance in
the area, could not be justified for the religious purposes and
the ban on its use was upheld. Likewise, in *Maulana Mufti Md.
Syed's case*,[190] the precedence has been laid down to the
imposition of restriction on use of microphone and loudspeaker
for the purpose of calling Azan is not violative of right to religion
guaranteed by the Art. 25 of Indian Constitution.[191] In this case
court observed that the Azan is not a form of propagation but it
is an essential and integral part of religion to meet at the prayer
from a call being made through Azan. Traditionally and
according to the religious order, Azan is to be given by the Imam
or the person in charge of the Mosques through their own voice,
this is sanctioned under the religious order. In *Church of God in
India Vs. KKR Majestic Coloney Welfare Association*,[192] the court has
observed that the noise pollution in some area of a city/town,
might be exceeding permissible limits prescribed under the rules,

but that would not be a ground, for permitting others to increase the same, by beating of drums or use of voice through amplifiers, loudspeakers or by such other musical instruments. Therefore, rules prescribing reasonable restrictions, including the rules for the use of loudspeakers and voice amplifiers, framed under the Madras Town Nuisance Act, 1889 and also the Noise Pollution (Regulation and Control) Rules, 2000, requires to be enforced. Lack of awareness among the citizens is to be removed by raising a comprehensive environmental-awareness education. The spiritual leaders and religious preachers are required to understand the noise health hazards and further also to cause awareness among their followers by way of inspiring them not to make loud noise on any of the occasions, be it social, religious, political or any other. Every citizen, must therefore note that his drum beat's noise in the name of enjoying his right, may increase some one's heart beats and mental agony, further adding to the sufferings of others, resulting thereby defeating others' right to life. The court recently held that loudspeakers and amplifiers or other equipments or gadgets which produce offending noise once detected as violating the law, should be liable to be seized and confiscated by making provisions in the law in that behalf.[198A]

Articles 32 and 226

The Art. 32 is said to be the heart of Indian Constitution, and the same has been uttered by Dr. B.R. Ambedkar, chairman of the drafting committee of the Constitution. In his words:

> "If I was asked to name any particular Article in this Constitution as the most important one, without which this Constitution would be a nullity-I could not refer to any other Article except this one . . . it is the very soul of the Constitution and the very heart of it."

If a person is conferred with the right to enjoy the fruits of Kalpvraksh, planted at a specified place, but is not provided the way to reach there, then this right would only prove futile to him. Similar would have been the fate of the fundamental rights, conferred by the Constitution to its subjects, if Article 32/226 would have not provided the way to enforce one's constitutional rights through the prerogative writs issued by the courts. It is, therefore, worth-mentioning that these prerogative writs do not require any specific forms or technicality, to be followed, to have access to the courts under Arts. 32/226. It is to be noted that Art. 32 enforces the fundamental rights through the Apex Court, whereas a person can knock the doors of High Court under Article 226, against the infringement of any constitutional rights. Thus the jurisdiction of Article 226 becomes wider than that of Article 32.

The Supreme Court in Oleum Gas Leak Case-III,[193] held that under Article 32(1) of the Constitution it is free to devise any procedure appropriate for the particular purpose of the proceeding, namely, enforcement of a fundamental right and also has the power to issue direction, order or writ as may be necessary in a given case including all incidental and ancillary powers, necessary for the enforcement of the fundamental rights. The power of the Supreme Court is not only injunctive in ambit, that is preventing the infringement of fundamental rights, but also, it is remedial in scope and provides relief against breach of these rights, which has already been committed. In the circumstances, the Court has the power to grant compensation in appropriate cases. The Court also said that compensation could be awarded against Shriram Food and Fertilizer Corporation, thereby bringing private corporations within the purview of Article 32 of the Constitution.

It is worth recognition that the birth of PIL in the modern era of judicial activism in India could become possible only due to these both articles on the face of the supreme law of the land. It is PIL concept, which could bring out the various pollutants causing hazards to health and could force the executive and judiciary to look into the state of environmental pollution in the nation. It would not be amazing if these prerogative writs are called legal Brahamastra in PIL Tarkash of judiciary. These writs are much contributory to maintain the judiciary as the custodian of the Constitution and to bridge the gaps left by the executive having failed in their constitutional duties. Justice Krishna Iyer was of the opinion that purpose of PIL concept is to wipe out every tear from every eye. But this movement has been bitter hard to be digested by the executives and the politicians, as they allege that judiciary is usurping the powers of executive through this movement. It has been observed, that PIL movement has made the administrators and the citizens alert and duty conscious to a great extent and environmental protective duties are not exception to it. But still, much is required to be done in this direction. In fact, it is we, who pollute the environment, and it is we, who should protect and improve the same, without inviting any provision of law, to remind us of our own duties. If we want to survive on this globe, pollution-free environment is necessary, otherwise day is not far when every one will have to suffocate in this polluted world. It is the principle of 'polluter pays' which also advocates the same.

In US, sale of fire works is banned by the most states because they cause noise pollution. Display of Fireworks is allowed only under close controlled conditions of the professionals and Fire brigades. In Canada also, the retail sale of fireworks is banned to the children and is only available to the adults after production of necessary certificate of competency. In Japan, the minors are not allowed to buy fire-crackers, the permitted fire-crackers should contain only a small quantity of explosive mixture.

There are strict legal controls on the sale and use of fireworks in several other countries also. Similarly, in India too, apart from restricting the indiscriminate use of sound producing devices, the active and dynamic judiciary, in very first year of new millennium, has issued detailed directives for the sale and use of fire-crackers in the country. But still the noise levels were found too higher than the permissible limits during the Diwali festival in the year 2001. However, it is a matter of concern that this legal directive could not find much force. Overriding them some Government organizations are still conducting well-planned shows of fire-crackers, bursting them at very high intensity. It is also a PIL filed by Patanjali Shiksha Sanstha, an NGO, wherein Delhi High Court has asked Municipal Corporation, Delhi to ban all illegal activities in public parks/ streets and ensure a complete ban on the use of loudspeakers at these places during social functions.[193A]

Directive Principles for States

In *Sachidanand Pandey* Vs. *State of West Bengal*,[194] it has been stated by the court, that when the court is called upon to give effect to the directive principles and the fundamental duty, the court is not to shrug its shoulders and say that priorities are a matter of policy and so it is the matter left for the policy-makers. The ecological balance shall be maintained by the courts in spite of the fact that such duty imposed on the government is merely a directive principle of state policy under the Part IV of the Constitution.

If Article 42, enshrined in Part IV of the Constitution is applied in the above real sense and the term 'humane conditions of work' is interpreted accordingly, it could contribute much to keep the work place free from environmental pollutions, as it advocates that the state should make provisions for just and humane conditions at work.

Similarly, Art. 39(e) states that health and strength of workers, men and women, and the tender age of children are not to be abused. But the industrial pollution is certainly causing the health hazards to them irrespective of sex or age. Hence, this directive principle needs correct interpretation and enforcement. Likewise, there are other directive principles of state policy in Indian Constitution, which have bearing on the environment and hence need attention accordingly.

Article 43 advocates the good conditions, i.e. hygienic environment for life and goes on to states that security of living wages is not enough, state should endeavor to ensure decent standards of life also.

Article 47 casts duty upon the state to raise the level of nutrition and standard of living and to improve public health and public health, in turn is closely related to the pollution-free environment in which the individuals should reside. Since the state has a duty to protect and improve environment in view of Art. 47 and 48A, it must be taken that citizen has a right relating to same under Art. 21.[195]

Also, Article 49 casts a positive duty upon the state to protect every monument of national importance and place of historic interest, from spoiliation, disfigurement, destruction, etc. Since, it has scientifically been proved that environmental pollution (including noise pollution) has its deleterious effects on trio, human, animal and properties. Hence, this directive principle has a bearing on the protection of environment from pollutants.

Art. 51A: Fundamental Duties

Art. 51(A)(g) poses a duty to protect the environment. Therefore, it requires every citizen to protect and improve the natural environment, including forests, lakes, rivers and wildlife, and to have compassion for living creatures. But, to fulfil these obligations to the environment, people need to be better educated about the environment.

With regard to the environmental provisions of our Constitution, Articles 249, 252 and 253, though not directive principles of state policy, but in some context have bearing on environment, they deal with the enactment of law in India and environmental legislation is not bar to it.

41. THE ROLE OF PUBLIC INTEREST LITIGATIONS

Change is the rule of nature. Nothing is permanent, except the change itself. Everything is in the process of change. Times are never static; the situations do change and therefore, law has also to be dynamic in nature. Law has to keep pace with the felt necessities and changing needs of society. Environmental problems, environmental awareness and 'environmental litigation' were unknown to most of us, barring few exceptions. The subject was treated so dry, that no body wanted to talk of it. But, with the adverse changes in environment, during last few years, environmental quality has become a matter of global concern. It is true beyond doubts that without pollution-free environment, very survival of mankind is at stake and it has become a matter of life and death. Once, there is a great hue and cry for clean environment at national as well as international level, how could the judiciary remain a silent spectator, when the subject has acquired so high importance, and is a matter of caution as well as judicial cognizance. It is nothing, but the newly-invented concept of 'Public Interest Litigation', which became a powerful weapon, in armory of the courts with which, the courts came foreword and intended to make the environment, free from the pollutants, viz. air, water and the noise. It has been declared that right to life is not the mere existence, rather animal existence, but to live with dignity. Right to clean environment, which certainly includes right to peaceful living, in a noise-free environment, has been now accepted as an attribute of right to life, under Art. 21. Also, the right to health, hygiene and pollution-free environment, right to sleep, right to read, right to road, right not to listen, and right not to hear are brought within the ambit of constitutional provisions. Once, right to speech is a fundamental right under Art. 19, then right not to speak, i.e. right to silence or peace definitely lies within that ambit.

'Public Interest Litigation' (hereinafter, referred to as 'PIL') has become a revolutionary step or a great cause to ameliorate miseries of masses through the court system. PIL is a great challenge to the judicial system. Judicial activism and PIL are two sides of the same coin. They go hand in hand. It is the most striking innovation in the recent past in the delivery of legal services. Judicial activism is the moving force behind the movement, and PIL is the media, through which this great mission 'the cause' is being advanced. PIL in India is major break-through in the delivery of social justice,[196] a new constitutional jurisprudence, based on necessity to give new meaning to the rights of the socially and economically disabled masses, a strong arm of legal aid movement, which is intended to bring justice within the reach of poor masses, who constitute the low visibility area of humanity; a silent movement in judiciary to create a new juristic horizon, and a movement which is changing the entire fabric of law.[197] PIL is a device of organized social action for the purpose of bringing about socio-economic changes. In *Bihar Legal Support Society* Vs. *CJI*,[198] it was observed that the strategy of PIL has been evolved by the courts with a view to bringing justice within the easy reach of the poor and the disadvantaged sections of the community. The court specifically observed that the court has the same treatment with a 'small man' or the 'little man', which it gives to the big industrialists rather the concern shown to the poor and the disadvantage is greater than that shown to the rich and well to do because the latter can on account of their dominant social and economic position and large material resources, resist the aggression on their rights, whereas the poor and the deprived just do not have the capacity for the will to resist and fight. The real inspiration for social litigation flows from the preamble of Indian constitution itself and was not required to seek support from any country. The Council for Public Interest Law set-up by Ford Foundation, has opted for an inclusive and broad definition in its report and has defined Public Interest Law as:

> "Public Interest Law is the name that has recently been
> given to the efforts, to provide legal representation to
> previously un-represented and under-represented groups
> and interests in the legal process. Such efforts have been
> undertaken in recognition that the ordinary market place for
> legal services fail to provide such services to significant
> segments of the population and to significant interests. Such
> groups and interests include the poor, environmentalists,
> consumers, racial and ethnic minorities, and others. These
> include, not only the poor and the disadvantaged, but also
> the ordinary citizens, who can not afford to engage lawyers
> to represent their cause and hence lacked access to the
> courts, administrative agencies, and other legal forums in
> which basic public decisions affecting their interests are
> made."[199]

The use of term 'public interest litigation' was originated
in U.S.A. and assumed wide currency in 1960. Perhaps, the main
reasons for this innovation were two-fold, firstly, the failure of
administrative agencies to protect public interests; and secondly,
the representation of diffused interests. The environmental
matters were so diffused rights that no individual liked to invest
their time and efforts on this behalf.

During the 19th century, the courts were reluctant to give
access into the court, unless one had a particular grievance of
one's own. He had to show individually that he had some legal
right which had been infringed or some property of his own that
had been injuriously affected. But, the environment, being no-
one's own property, could not be brought forth by any one,
except by the authenticated representative body. The quantum
of damages on account of environmental pollution cannot be
ascertained and therefore, it is not easy to establish. Particularly,
the noise pollution has its subtle ill-effects, which cannot even
be noticed at their preliminary stages. Apart from these ill-effects,
the noise pollution is a serious health hazards to human brain,
and once the balance of the brain has gone out of order, it may
not restore back or may sometimes prolong even till death.

During 20th century also, 'Relator Action Theory'—

representation by the Attorney General, did not have a notable bearing on environmental matters. Even the available statutes did not provide any access to the individual citizen or public-spirited bodies, to knock the doors of judiciary, for the protection of noise-free environment. However, slowly, the position changed and the courts evolved the theory of 'Sufficient Interest'. But, this theory also proved illusive in matters of environment and to maintain it free from all kinds of pollutions. It was yet to be worked out by the courts.

In England, the court of appeal, mainly through Lord Denning, had liberalized the rules of standing to admit public-spirited persons to maintain actions to preserve and check breaches of the law by persons and authorities exercising governmental function, which were continuing unchecked. In Blackburn cases and in McWhirter case, the court opined that it could not listen to a busybody, who was interfering in things, which did not concern to it. But it would listen to an ordinary citizen, who came asking that the law should be declared and enforced even though he was only one of hundred, or one of a thousand, or one of millions, who were affected by it. As a result, therefore, 'action-popularis' or citizen action came as a new procedure, which proved the boon to the society to take the environmental pollution cases to the courts directly. In India, green lawyer, Mr. M.C. Mehta borrowed this concept first and applied in the field of environment, which was further inspired and accelerated by the activist green judges. In respect with the activist judges, Lord Serman in *Duport Steel Ltd.* Vs. *Sirs*[200] commented upon that the great judges are in their different ways judicial activists. Thus, a new era, to protect and improve the environment through public interest litigation, started in India. Many cases were filed countrywide and various kinds of pollutants were prosecuted including noise.

The Supreme Court in its crusade against environmental deterioration, proceeded on the premise that a clean and wholesome environment is a prerequisite, to enjoy right to life, enshrined in Indian Constitution, as a fundamental right. Right to life is more than the life itself. It guarantees life in its many splendoured facets, emotional, spiritual, and aesthetic. The right to clean environment is a part of it observed Sankaran Nair, J., in *Mathew Lukose* Vs. *Kerala State Pollution Control Board*.[201]

Rural Litigation and Entitlement Kendra Vs. *State of U.P.*[202] can be said to be the harbinger of the new trend of PIL era. In that PIL case, the Apex court of India ordered certain quarrying activities to be closed down, because their activities were solely accountable for environmental pollution. In a few subsequent PIL cases also, the court recognized the right to environment and invoked the power under Article 32 of the Constitution, to issue appropriate orders and directions. *Chandigarh Admn.* Vs. *Namit Kumar* is the PIL[202A] wherein the Court has taken various steps to bring down air and noise pollution and to overcome the traffic congestion and unsystematic functioning of various authorities in Chandigarh.

It was 1976, when a new Article 39A was introduced in Part IV of the Constitution, incorporating a Directive Principle to that effect, "the State shall secure, that the operation of the legal system promotes justice, on a basis of equal opportunity and shall, in particular, provide free legal aid by suitable legislation or schemes or in any other way to ensure that opportunities for securing justice are not denied to any citizen by reason of economic or other disability."

The credit goes to this PIL era only, that Indian environmental NGOs found the most rewarding moment when the Supreme Court on 12 February, 1997 issued a direction to the Ministry of Environment and Forests, to take necessary steps by 1st April 1997, to implement the relevant laws, banning the use and dumping of hazardous and noxious substances, by industrial units throughout India. In its order on a PIL filed by an NGO-Research Foundation for Science, the Supreme Court warned the Ministry, that if the top officers concerned, did not measure up to their duties and enforce the provisions of the Environment (Protection) Act, 1986, the court would be constrained to record a 'judicial finding of failure to perform their duties against them' and that the court would also ensure that the judicial finding is recorded in their service records.[203] Thus, this decision of conscious dynamic Apex Court of India, transmits a signal to the executives, to be loyal to environmental laws, otherwise judiciary will have to bridge the lacunae.

42. PIL AGAINST CRACKER'S NOISE

The Diwali, it is the festival of lights ushering in prosperity and happiness, but for someone, it may be painstaking routine of endless visits to the doctors and a fight for every breath. Diwali has become the festival of pollution and also the cause of traffic jams on pre-Diwali days which further excuse more automobile exhaust fumes/noise decibels. According to CPCB, 95% of the crackers available in the market, violate noise and air pollution norms. The noise level on Diwali day in 2003, increased at 8 locations in Delhi and remained same at only one location as compared to Diwali day 2002. The average noise values ranged from 69 to 90 Leq dB(A) against the previous year's average values of 66 to 88 Leq dB(A).

Keeping in view, the noise pollution caused by crackers on Diwali occasion, Delhi High Court has put a blanket ban, on production of high noise-making crackers, and made it mandatory for the manufacturers to mark their products with the level of pollution caused by them.

Restricting the bursting of crackers during Diwali, Dussehra, and other festivals between 6.00 p.m. and 11.00 p.m., a Division Bench, comprising of Justice Anil Dev Singh and Justice M.K. Sharma ordered, that no cracker when exploded, should make a noise more than 125 DB at 4 meter distance from the point of its bursting.[204]

Despite the above clear cut direction by the court, the noise menace prevails everywhere. Recently, for example, the former Lt. Governor of Delhi, B.L. Joshi has complained that he is victimised of not only noise pollution but also of other nuisances on account of Farm House parties that blatantly violate the noise rules.[204A] Further in a case,[204B] the Delhi High Court spoke through Arijit Pasayat, C.J. and D.K. Jain, J. and observed various evil effects of noise pollution and gone to the extent of laying down as under:

(i) The prescribed standards regarding noise by Government of India may by enforced strictly in letter and spirit.

(ii) Separate Courts regarding noise pollution may be established.

(iii) The cases should be decided within a prescribed time limit.

(iv) All District Magistrates and Sub-Divisional Magistrates should be empowered to issue prohibitory orders under Section 144 of the Code of Criminal Procedure, 1973 limiting the hours of loudspeakers in religious places and for other social gatherings and functions.

(v) The subject of environment protection may be made compulsory at school, college and University levels.

(vi) The press and media should play a constructive role to highlight disastrous effects of noise pollution and its remedy.

(vii) The District Administration and the concerned Pollution Control Boards should work out the modalities to prevent catastrophic effect of noise pollution by ensuring strict compliance with the statutory provisions, scanty though they are.

(viii) Both Central Government and State Government should consider the desirability of having adequate legislative measurers to prevent this fast growing menace which though appears to be 'silent' has in fact potentialities of producing a future generation of deaf persons.

(ix) Permanent monitoring bodies should be appointed to make periodic review of the situation and suggest remedial measures. The composition of such body has to be determined by the State/Central Government.

(x) Use of fire-crackers in religious festivals, marriage processions, etc. should be regulated properly. It should be ensured that they are used in residential areas in such a manner that there is no likelihood of danger to life and property. In marriage processions, use of fire-crackers on the public streets shall be prohibited. Use of fire-crackers like anars, phuljaris and the like which do not have wider danger potential may, however, be permitted in restricted manner. It may be permitted at the place of marriage in the open area comprising not less than 100 metres around it.

(xi) Use, if any, permitted should also be between specified time-periods and should not be permitted in silence zones, hospitals, nursing homes and other health centres.

(xii) Periodic display in Press and electronic media should be made about the desirability of young children not using dangerous fire-crackers and safe use thereof.

(xiii) Rule 5(2) of the Noise Pollution Rules restricts the use of loudspeakers, public address system at night, i.e., between 10.00 p.m. to 6.00 a.m., except in dosed premises, like auditorium, etc. These devices cannot be used even during the day without obtaining permission in terms of Rule 5(1) but experience shows that the rule is more observed in breach than in observance. We direct that the Authority empowered to take action under the said rules shall give vide publicity to the rule by inserting appropriate advertisements in at least six national daily newspapers. It will be the responsibility of the area S.D.Ms. to see that the rule is strictly adhered to in letter and spirit. Any default in this regard will be treated as misconduct and the defaulting officer shall be liable for disciplinary action, besides action for disobeying Court's order.

In a PIL[204C] the Supreme Court has opined that total restriction on bursting firecrackers between 10 p.m. and 6 a.m. must continue without any relaxation in favour of anyone. The court also observed that firecrackers that only increase the ambient noise level but also contribute significantly in increasing air pollution by means of toxic gases and particles due to their blast wave resulting from a rapid release of energy.

It is only the PIL[204D] wherein Delhi High Court through Justice Vijendra Jain and Rekha Sharma took stern view and directed Municipal Corporation Delhi to take strict action against not only the illegal constructions but also against the farm wedding and indiscriminate use of loudspeakers.

43. CONSTITUTION OF OTHER ASIAN COUNTRIES[205]

I. Bangladesh

Parts II[206], III[207] and IV[208] of Constitution of the People's Republic of Bangladesh[209] contains the provisions on environment, which are as follows:

Article 23

The state shall adopt measures to conserve the cultural traditions and heritage of the people and so foster and improve the national language, literature and the arts, that all sections of the people are afforded and the opportunity to contribute towards and to participate in the enrichment of the national culture.

Article 24

The state shall adopt measures for the protection against disfigurement, damage or removal of all monuments, objects or places of special artistic, or historic importance or interest.

Article 31

To enjoy the protection of law, and to be treated in accordance with the law, and only in accordance with the law, is the inalienable right of every citizen, wherever he may be, and of every other person for the time being within Bangladesh, and in particular no action detrimental to the life, liberty, body, reputation or property of any person shall be taken except in accordance with the law

Article 32

No person shall be deprived of life or personal liberty save in accordance with the law.

Article 102

1. The High Court Division, on application of any person aggrieved, may give directions or orders to any person or authority, including any person performing any function in connection with the affairs of the Republic, as may be appropriate for the enforcement of any of the fundamental rights conferred by Part III of this Constitution.

2. The High Court Division may, if satisfied that no other equally and efficacious remedy is provided by law—

    (a) on the application of any person aggrieved, make an order:

        (i) directing a person performing any functions in connection with the affairs of the Republic or of a local authority, to refrain from doing that which he is not permitted by law to do or to do that which he is required by law to do or;

        (ii) declaring that any act done or proceeding taken by a person performing functions in connection with the affairs of the Republic or of a local authority has been done or taken without lawful authority, and is of no legal effect.

II. Cambodia

Appended below are the provisions enshrined in the Constitution[210] of the Kingdom of Cambodia for the protection of environment.

Article 32[211]

Every Khmer citizen shall have the right to life, personal freedom and security. ...

Article 39[212]

Khmer citizens shall have the right to denounce, make complaints or file claims against any breach of the law by State and social organs or by members of such organs committed during the course of their duties. The settlement of complaints and claims shall reside under the competence of the courts.

Article 54[213]

The manufacturing, use, storage of nuclear, chemical or biological weapons shall be absolutely prohibited.

Article 58[214]

State property notably comprises land, mineral resources, mountains, sea, underwater, continental shelf, coastline, airspace, islands, rivers, canals, streams, lakes, forests, natural resources, economic and cultural centers, bases for national defense and other facilities determined as State property. Law shall determine the control, use and management of State properties.

Article 59[215]

The State shall protect the environment and balance of abundant natural resources and establish a precise plan of management of land, water, air, wind, geology, ecological system, mines, energy, petrol and gas, rocks and sand, gems, forests and forestry products, wildlife, fish and aquatic resources.

Article 109[216]

The Judiciary power shall be an independent power. The Judiciary shall guarantee and uphold impartiality and protect the rights and freedoms of the citizens. The Judiciary shall cover all lawsuits including administrative ones. The authority of the Judiciary shall be granted to the Supreme Court and to the lower courts of all sectors and levels.

Article 122[217]

After a law is promulgated, the King, the Prime Minister, the President of the Assembly, 1/10 of the assembly members or the courts, may ask the Constitutional Council to examine the Constitutionality of that law. Citizens shall have the right to appeal against the constitutionality of laws through their representatives or the President of the Assembly as stipulated in the above paragraph.

Article 128[218]

The National Congress shall enable the people to be directly informed on various matters of national interests and to raise issues and requests for the State authority to solve.

III. China

China paid a sensitive attention to legislative work on environment and has now established an environmental statutory framework that takes the constitution of the People's Republic of China as the foundation and the environment protective law of the land and also can be called the cardinal law for the environmental protection in China.[219]

The constitution of the People's Republic of China stipulates: "the state protects and improves the living environment and the ecological environment, and prevents and remedies pollution and other public hazards," and "the state ensures the rational use of natural resources and protects rare animals and plants. The appropriation or damage of natural resources by any organization or individual by whatever means is prohibited."[220]

Since the land in the cities is owned by the state, hence, the users of land in China whether organization or individual are under a constitutional mandate for not making any irrational use of it and pollute the environment.[221] Under Article 12 of Chinese Constitution, the state protects socialist property and appropriation or damage of state or collective property by any organization or individual by whatever means is prohibited. The natural resources of China are also protected by its Constitution which states that Mineral resources, waters, forests, mountains, grassland, unreclaimed land, beaches and other natural resources are owned by the state, that is, by the whole people, with the exception of the forests, mountains, grasslands, unreclaimed land and beaches that are owned by collectives in accordance with the law.[222]

China has enacted and promulgated many special laws on environment as well as laws on natural resources related to environment, e.g. Law on the Prevention and Control of Water Pollution, Law on the Prevention and Control of Air Pollution, Law on the Prevention and Control of Environmental Pollution by Solid Wastes, Marine Environmental Protection Law, Law on the Protection of Wild Animals, Grassland Law, Law on Water and Soil Conservation, Fisheries Law, Agricultural Law and Land Administration Law.

The Chinese government has also enacted the regulations for the protection of environment including the regulation for the prevention and control of Noise Pollution, which has been adopted at the 22nd meeting of the Standing Committee of the Eighth National People's Congress on 29 October, 1996 and promulgated by the president of the nation on same date.[223] The purpose of this law is to prevent and control environmental noise pollution, protect and improve the living environment, ensuring human health and to promote economic and social development.[224]

IV. Indonesia

Constitution of the Republic of Indonesia has straight forward and clear-cut prohibition from polluting the environment in which the present generation lives and future to bloom. Article 50 enshrined in Chapter IV of the Constitution states that protecting the environment in which the present generation lives and in which future generations will develop socially is considered a public responsibility in the Islamic Republic. Therefore, economic activities, and other activities, which may pollute the environment or destroy it irrevocably, shall be forbidden.

V. Nepal

In a paper presented by four Nepalese scientists two years back had shown some grave facts about noise pollution in 30 noise producing industries in Kathmandu Valley. The noise pollution in different industrial locations in Kathmandu is posing health hazards to the workers. The machines and the processes causing impact, vibration or reciprocation movements, friction and turbulence in air or gas streams,[225] cause indoor noise in the industries.

The Constitution of Nepal[226] is not the moot spectator of environmental degradation but has the provision[227] that the social objective of the Panchayat System shall be to establish a harmonious social life, based upon morality, by eliminating the obstacles, that may arise in the process of mobilising the general public for setting up of a society as envisaged by clause (1) and to maintain national unity with due regards to the existing mutual harmonious tolerance upon the cultural and traditional values of Nepal adhered to by the Nepalese citizen from time immemorial as the prosperity and glory of Nepal as well as their national character.

By taking the over polluted air of this bowl shaped valley into consideration, the Supreme Court last year ordered the Ministry of Environment to set-up thresholds for air emissions, noise levels, effluent discharges into rivers, sewage and radiation from industries located across the country. Not only this, the Supreme Court of Nepal by its sweeping ruling, ordered the government to immediately stop the import of Indian vehicles not meeting Euro-I emission standards and hence an agreement was signed between India and Nepal during Koirala's visit to India for allowing the Indian made vehicles in Nepal with a certificate of "environment friendly" given by its manufacturer and not the government. It is pertinent to note here that Nepal's Environment Protection Act, 1997 mitigate the environmental pollution within the specified thresholds and limitations for polluting exhausts decided by the government.[228]

VI. Thailand

Article 56 of Constitution of the Kingdom of Thiland, states that Individuals are guaranteed the right to cooperate with state and local communities to conserve and benefit from natural resources and bio-diversities; and to protect, promote and maintain the quality of the environment so that the communities may continue to live in an environment which is not hazardous or threatening as provided by the law.

Any activity or project, which can seriously affect the quality of the environment, is prohibited unless an environmental study and evaluation is undertaken. The study must receive endorsement from independent agencies, which include representatives from environmental non-governmental organizations and university academics, as provided by the law. Individuals are guaranteed the right to file lawsuits against government agencies, state enterprises, local administrative organizations and other organizations to require them to not violate the first and second paragraphs.[229]

VII. Sri Lanka

There is a growing awareness in Sri Lanka that environmental considerations must be taken into account in all spheres of economic development and the cooperation and involvement of all sectors is an essential factor to achieve sustainable environmental management objectives. The Constitution of the Democratic Socialist Republic of Sri Lanka is also the document which contains the provisions to protect environment[230] and guarantees that the state shall protect, preserve and improve the environment for the benefit of the community.[231]

In addition to the exercise and enjoyment of rights and freedoms, every one in Sri Lanka is cast upon with two-fold constitutional duty firstly to preserve and protect public property, to combat misuse and waste of public property[232] and secondly, to protect nature and conserve riches.[233]

The natural resources in Sri Lanka are conserved in its national policy too adopted in 1980. A separate Ministry of Forest and Environment was set-up by Sri Lankan government in 1990 with subsequent National Environmental Action Plan policy intervention relating to land and water, forest and biodiversity, coastal and marine resources, industrial and urban pollution and the energy and mineral sector.

VIII. Pakistan

Constitution of the Islamic Republic of Pakistan does not have any direct bearing on the protection of the environment. To save the environment from further degradation and to face the dire mankind of human (environmental pollution) one could locate the provision under Articles 9 and 14 enshrined in the part II of the constitution of Pakistan.[234] Article 9 states that "no person shall be deprived of life or liberty save in accordance with law", whereas Article 14, under its clause (1) says that "the dignity of man, subject to law, the privacy of home, shall be inviolable."

IX. Vietnam

In Vietnam all acts of exhaustion of natural wealth and to cause damage to the environment are strictly forbidden. Article 29 of the Constitution[235] of Vietnam advocates the rational use of natural wealth and says that State organs, units of the armed forces, economic and social bodies, and all individuals must abide by State regulations on the rational use of natural wealth and on environmental protection. All acts to bring about exhaustion of natural wealth and to cause damage to the environment are strictly forbidden.

Article 17[236] makes communities of the nation responsible to protect, maintain and secure the national resources/assets/wealth whether natural or otherwise by stating that "The lands, forests and mountains, rivers and lakes, water sources, underground natural resources, and other resources in the territorial seas, on the continental shelf, and in the air space; capital and assets that the state invests in the various enterprises and projects falling under different economic, cultural, social, scientific—technical, diplomatic, and national security and national defense programmes and other property defined by law as belonging to the state are under the ownership of the entire people."

On the use of land according to set goals and rational exploitation the verdict of the constitution is that all lands are put under unified state management according to plans and laws to ensure that they are utilized according to plans and laws to ensure that they are utilized according to set goals and bring about results. The state allots land to the various organizations and individuals for use on a stabilized and long-term basis. Organizations and individuals involved have the responsibility to protect, replenish, and exploit such land in a rational and economical fashion. They may transfer the right to the use of land allotted to them by the state as stipulated by law.[237]

X. Philippines

The Constitution of the Republic of the Philippines which was adopted on 15 October, 1986 has the following provisions related to the environment:

(a) Protecting the life, liberty, and property of everyone in the country section 5 of Article 2 states that the maintenance of peace and order, the protection of life, liberty, and property, and the promotion of the general welfare are essential for the enjoyment by all the people of the blessings of democracy. Further section 16 protects and advances the right of the people to a balanced and healthful ecology in accordance with the rhythm and harmony of nature.

(b) Article 3, through section 7 guarantees the right to information by way of providing every citizen the access to official records, documents, and papers pertaining to official acts, transactions or decisions, as well as to government research data used as basis for policy development, subject to some limit

(c) Owing the responsibility of all natural resources of the nation and ensuring no alienation of them, the constitution speaks that all lands of the public domain, waters, minerals, coal, petroleum and other mineral oils, all forces of potential energy, fisheries, forests or timber, wildlife, flora and fauna, and other natural resources are owned by the State. With the exception of agricultural lands, all other natural resources shall not be alienated. The exploration, development and utilization of natural resources shall be under the full control and supervision of the State.[238] After classification of the lands of public domain into agricultural, forest or timber, mineral lands and national parks[239] as well as accounting the requirements of conservation, ecology and development (subject to the requirements of agrarian reform), the congress shall determine, by law, the size of lands of the public domain which may be acquired, developed, held, or leased and the condition therefore. Also the Congress shall, as soon as possible, determine by law the specific limits of forestlands and national parks, marking clearly their boundaries on the ground. Thereafter, such forestlands and national parks shall be conserved and may not be increased nor diminished, except by law.[240] Subject to the provisions of this Constitution and national development policies and programs, the state shall protect the rights of indigenous cultural communities to their ancestral lands to ensure their economic, social, and cultural well-being.[241]

(d) The law on social justice and human rights is embodied under Article 13 of the constitution as "the State shall, by law, undertaken an agrarian reform programme..To this end, the State shall encourage and undertake the just distribution of all agricultural lands, subject to such priorities and reasonable retention limits as the Congress may prescribe, taking into account ecological, developmental, or equity consideration.."[242]

(e) Under the mandate[243] of the constitution, the state of Philippines is bound to protect the rights of subsistence of fishermen especially of local communities, to the preferential use of the communal marine and fishing resources, both inland and offshore. . . . The State shall also protect, develop and conserve such resources.[244]

XI. Myanmar (Burma)

As adopted on 3 January 1974, the Constitution of the Socialist Republic of the Union of Burma is also not the moot spectator of the environment deterioration but has a provision on its face under Article 132(i) enshrined in Chapter X which advocates that the People's Council at different levels are Local Organs of State power and they shall implement the task of preserving, protecting and developing pf natural environment within the framework of law.[245]

44. JUDICIAL TRENDS

The idea behind analyzing the judicial trend is to see whether the judiciary in India has maintained *status quo* by remaining static or activated itself, by evolving new interpretations, principles, and norms to deal with the problem of environmental pollution and invented a new 'environmental jurisprudence' or not? More important is, that the world community is in dire need of evolution of an environmental jurisprudence of recent origin, i.e. 'jurisprudence of noise pollution; as it has become *sine qua non*, to maintain the balance of human brain in this very world, which is every moment becoming more and more noisy.

While deciding a PIL case,[245A] the court observed that "like an industry, which can not pay minimum wages to its workers, can not and should not be allowed to exist. Likewise, if an establishment, which can not set anti-pollution plant, can not be permitted to continue to be in existence, at the cost of public health."

In another PIL case, Hon'ble Justice K.N. Singh, while taking note of the problems such as the unemployment and loss of revenue, aroused by the closure of industries, on account of non-compliance with the environmental standards, held:

"We are conscious, that closure of such industries may bring unemployment and loss of revenue. But the life, health and ecology are of greater importance to the people."

In series of PIL cases, instituted by a public-spirited lawyer, Mr. M.C. Mehta, the Supreme Court has set a glorious precedent. In one of these cases, which concerned the closing down of a chlorine plant of Shriram Industries. This well-known case, also known as 'Oleum gas leakage case', decided by a Constitutional Bench of 5 judges, granted *locus-standi* to the petitioner and held, that the exceptions to the rule in *Rylands* Vs. *Fletcher*, like natural use of the land are, no longer applicable in India, in cases of the industries, which are engaged in hazardous or inherently dangerous activities.

In next important 'Ganga Pollution case', which concerned the discharge of effluents into the pious and holy river Ganga by the tanneries and chemical industries, Supreme Court ordered that the tanneries, which did not have pre-treatment plants, approved by the Pollution Control Board, to stop the discharge of affluent of their such plants. In yet another case, involving the issue, whether the petitioner, who was not a riparian owner, could be granted standing to move for prevention of nuisance for pollution in river Ganga. The court allowed the riparian owner, and held it reasonable, to allow any person to take proceedings, on behalf of the community at large.

In a PIL, *Indian Council for Enviro-legal Action* Vs. *Union of India*, the Court focused its attention on the woes of the people, and their suffering seriously, who were living in a village, full of sludge, lethal wastes, left out by the closed-down chemical industries, causing heavy damage to the environment. Viewing the case as "social action litigation," the court ordered that remedial action be taken and compensation be given, for the silent tragedies, in line with the 'absolute liability' principle.

It is apparent, that law, justice, and public authority had compromised with the technological advancements, unplanned urbanization, and rapid industrialization. There are two views about it. One is that technology has become an end in itself; that it subjects man to its demands, rather than serving his needs; that it is inherently destructive of personal freedom; and that it will make the world totally uninhabitable or at least deprive it of all hopes and beauties. The other view is that technology is a universal solution, which has not only liberated man from the bondage of poverty and disease but, will assure global prosperity and universal happiness for generations to come, if applied vigorously.

The attitude of the Judiciary towards noise nuisance too has been lukewarm. The courts ordinarily admitted the defence of accused for the enjoyment of their constitutional rights. It seems that judges are not fully aware of the health hazards of environmental pollution. Courts, usually, took it very lightly. The courts generally do not regard noise as a public nuisance, unless it affects the whole locality or individual with specific damages. For instance, in *Ivour Hden's case*[246] court excused the act of playing radio loudly, on the ground that the act was of trivial nature. Whereas, the careful reading of section 95 of IPC shows, that only that harm is excusable, which is not expected to be complained by the person of an ordinary temper and prudence. This decision of the court seems to be erroneous and needs a fresh look, because the playing of radio at a moderate voice, may be tolerable, but not at a high pitched frequency of voice, which is certainly objectionable by the man of ordinary prudence. Moreover, if the affected person is busy with any mental work, such noise is definitely very offending to him.

In another case, *Health* Vs. *Mayor of Brighton*,[247] the court refused to grant injunction, against a buzzing noise from defendant's power station and observed that the noise did not cause annoyance to any other person, but the incumbent, nor was the noise of such nature, that it could detract the attention of a prudent person, attending the church.

Though, it need not establish, that the noise is dangerous to life, health, property, and is the genus of nuisance, which causes irritation, annoyance, and other bodily harms. But, in a very recent case *A.P. Bankers & Pawn Brokers' Association*, Vs. *Municipal Corporation of Hyderabad*,[248] Andhra Pradesh High Court has held:

> "If there are no terms and conditions, which can be imposed by the Commissioner or the Municipality in respect of a particular trade or operation, then even if the Commissioner is of the opinion that the trade or operation is dangerous to life, or health, or property, or that it is likely to create a nuisance, he would not be able to regulate or control that

trade or operation, maintenance of cleanliness, deciding of location, and regulating noise pollution."

In this case, the appellant filed a writ petition in the High Court of Andhra Pradesh, challenging the notification issued by Commissioner, *inter alia*, on the ground that Section 521 of A.P. Municipality Act, 1955 did not empower the Commissioner to notify the trades of money-lending and pawn-broking, as being trades for which a license is necessary. Judges held that the business of money lending or pawn-broking is not dangerous to property. They have, however, held that these are the operations, which are likely to create a nuisance *inter alia*. it was held that the maintenance of cleanliness, deciding location, and regulating noise pollution would not fall within Section 521(1)(e)(ii).

It is unfortunate, that this decision came at such a time, when the whole world is harping with the problem of environmental pollution, caused by various trade affluent. The recent second 'Earth Summit' held in Johannesburg, from 26 August to 4 September 2002, on Sustainable Development, is the blazing trail to invite world attention towards deteriorating environmental quality day-by-day. This judgment does not seem to be in the spirit of making environment, free from the pollutants. It was, however, sought that, there were blank spaces provided in the license, containing the terms and conditions of licence and produced before the court for perusal. The terms and conditions, regulating such trades and operations, were hand-filled in these blank spaces, before a licence was issued. Not only this, before issue, the license was stamped, that the offices should be kept clean, and later, also stated that the regulation is to the extent of deciding the location, maintenance of cleanliness and regulating noise pollution. Still the court held that the maintenance of cleanliness, deciding location and regulating noise pollution does not fall within Section 521(1)(e)(ii).

This case warrants, that our judges need a special training to deal with the environmental pollution cases, a global problem. Since the environmental noise is the problem of very recent origin, and might not be included within the ambit of old terms and conditions of the licence, in question. But once, it was included later, by way of stamp or hand filled, it should have been taken in its true spirit. It may be submitted that no activity should be allowed, which is prone to cause environmental pollution of any kind, even in future.

The concept of *locus standi*, prior to post-emergency era was too narrow, to bring forth the diffused rights, such as right to noise-free environment. The public, officials, and even the judiciary took water and air pollution on priority, but kept noise on the lowest priority. However, by some judgments, the liberation from ghost of *locus standi*, reflects the activism of judiciary, to look into the menace of noise. But still, the Indian courts and citizens are not much serious, to free environment from noise, and make it worthwhile for a peaceful living. They lack knowledge, about all the 'noise health hazards', and also relevant provisions of the law to curb it. The recent report in *Sunday Times*,[249] is of relevance here. It has been reported, that over 200, State and Central laws, in India, pertain to environment, but many are unknown even to the judges. Thus, leading to their often failing to understand environmental problems, in their true perspective. This was asserted in a programme, organized by Centre for Advancement in Environmental Law (CAEL), in collaboration with Orissa High Court and State Pollution Control Board, which was attended by over 50 judges from different primary courts, who came to learn laws on environment.

Justice Holmes observed, that law must be interpreted in terms of felt necessities of the people, in order to achieve social justice. For this, a study of some more decided cases on noise is imperative, so as to know the present trends of Indian judiciary, if it has interpreted the laws in favour of nature, public health, or otherwise. However, the noise in India, is the newly recognized pollutant and, therefore, only few judicial precedents are available on it:

(a) In *Kishorimal Bishambar Dayal* Vs. *State of Punjab*,[250] a penal action was initiated u/s 290 of IPC for causing, noise and vibrations by operating heavy machinery in the residential areas. Also the same action was initiated for causing noise at night, by paddy husking machine.[251]

(b) Noise and vibrations, by running of a mill, caused the inconveniences and serious discomforts to the plaintiff and the residents thereof, was considered to amount private nuisance and hence could not be permitted.[252]

(c) *D. Anant Prabhu* Vs. *The District Collector, Ernakulam and Others*.[253] In this case the permission was sought by the petitioner from the District Administration to celebrate the annual ceremony of RSS. But, the permission was granted on condition, not to use loudspeakers. Against the imposition of this condition, the case came before the Court under Articles 14 and 19 of the Constitution. The court observed:

". . . a right, which is guaranteed by Art. 19(1)(a), is not merely a right to express and propagate one's views, but also includes in it, the right to circulate one's views to others by all such means as are available to the citizens to make known those views. Under the circumstances, in our judgment, any legislation or order, which puts a ban on the use of a loudspeaker, which helps the citizens in circulating his views, to as large audience as he can, will be *prima-facie* infringement of his fundamental right to freedom of speech and expression, unless the infringement is justified by clause (2) of Art. 19."

This judgment is very damaging as it results into the multiplication of noise pollution. However, similar judgments in two cases were also delivered, in which a condition of banning the use of loudspeaker was held unreasonable and hence not justifiable under Art. 19(2).[254]

(d) In *Rahib Mukherjee* Vs. *State*,[255] a Public interest writ petition was filed against the nuisance of noise pollution, created by the transport operators by indiscriminate installation and use of electric and air horns, which caused unduly harsh, shrill, loud, and alarming noise. A *mandamus* was sought to command the authorities to enforce the provisions of Rule 114 of the Bengal Motor Vehicle Rules, 1940. The court held that Rule 114(d) of Bengal Motor Vehicle Rules contained a mandatory provision that no transport vehicle can be fitted with any other form of horn except a bulb horn. The court pointed out that the transport authorities were under a statutory obligation and owed a duty, under section 112 of the Motor Vehicles Act, 1939, to punish a person, who contravened the provision of Rule 114(d) of the Rules and issued appropriate directions to enforce the said rule.

(e) In *Jacob Vs. The Supdt. of Police*,[256] it was observed that a person is at liberty, to decline to read a publication, by switching off his radio, or his television set, if he does not want to listen. But, how can he prevent the sound, coming from a loudspeaker in vicinity and reaching him against desire? One cannot be forced to hear, what he wishes not to hear. That will be an invasion on his right to be alone and enjoy his peaceful life. No one has a right to commit trespass on the mind or ear of another, and commit an auricular or visual aggression. Limits must be drawn for liberties, lest they turn into licence and the antithesis of liberty, in its true sense.

(f) *Election Commission of India* Vs. *All India Dravida Munetra Kazkhgam and Others*.[257] In this writ petition, a political party contesting the two bye-elections in state, assailed the constitutional validity of Order, made by the Election Commission under Art. 324(i) of the Constitution. The order imposed certain restrictions on the duration on loudspeakers use, mounted on mobile vehicles for the election campaigns. The relevant and operative part of the Commission's order reads:

"After considering all aspects of the matter, the Commissioner, in exercise of its powers conferred by Article 324 of the Constitution and all other powers enabling it in this behalf, hereby DIRECT that the use of loudspeakers at future elections shall be strictly regulated as follows:

(i) The use of loudspeakers fitted on vehicles of any kind whatsoever for the electioneering purposes during the entire election period starting from the date of announcement of election and ending with the date of declaration of result shall be permitted only between 8.00 a.m. and 7.00 p.m. No moving loudspeakers shall be permitted to be used before 8.00 a.m. and after 7.00 p.m. in any area.

(ii) If for the purpose of any public meeting or processions any loudspeakers, which are fully static are to be used beyond the said hours; specific prior written permission shall be obtained from the Government authorities concerned."

Indeed, the court was persuaded to the view that an interlocutory intervention of the High Court cannot be supported. The *prima-facie* position and the balance of inconvenience seem to be in favour of public good, in a matter, which cannot be said to be unrelated to the powers of the Election Commission, under Art. 324. The interlocutory order made by the High Court was set aside. But, the impugned order, which prohibits the use of loudspeakers on mobile vehicles between 7 p.m. and 8 a.m. be modified to read 10 p.m. and 6 a.m. However, the Chief Minister of the State of Tamil Nadu, who was under the 'Z Plus' category of security, shall remain exempt from the restrictions contained in the order of the court and be entitled to address election meetings, beyond the restricted hours from the stationary vehicles, equipped with loudspeakers without the requirement of prior permission.

It may be appreciated, that our dynamic judiciary interpreted the order, made under Art. 324 of the Constitution, in favour of public good, by imposing the restrictions on the use of loudspeakers for the purposes of electioneering. But, the exemption of the Chief Minister of the state from these restrictions does not ram down the throat. Because, the noise pollution is equally hazardous to the health and is inconvenient to the public, whether it is caused by the chief minister or by an ordinary citizen.

In a landmark decision, *M.S. App Rao Vs. The Government of Tamilnadu and Others*,[258] first of such Writ petitions, was for issue of a *mandamus*. It was for directing the State Government to impose strict conditions, for obtaining licence for the use of amplifiers and loudspeakers under Secs. 41 and 71-A of Madras City Police Act, 1888 and Sec. 10 of Madras Towns Nuisance Act, 1889. It was to ensure, that the licences do not violate the conditions thus imposed, and do not cause noise nuisance.

In another petition, filed by the same person, the prayer was for issue of *mandamus*, to direct the State Government to issue appropriate order, and to impose a total ban on the use of loudspeakers, amplifiers, and air horns, by automobiles.

The court, victimized itself by noise pollution, commented in this case as under:

"In fact, this court has often been the victim of noise pollution. If we can put it mildly, it would be practically impossible to hear the arguments of the counsels. For example, on the 30th ultimo, which supposed to be a 'Sarvodaya Day' or Martyrs' Day', when the whole nation is supposed to pay homage to its Father, the authorities concerned had permitted public agitation by Bank employees on the public road abutting the High Court compound, who were using loudspeakers and sound amplifiers without any restrictions, for over five hours continuously, during the court's working hours. We were somewhat surprised, if not shocked, that the concerned authorities were not aware of a notification issued under sections 6 and 25 of EPA, 1986, by the Ministry of Environment and Forest, New Delhi in 1989,[259] prescribing ambient air quality standards in respect of noise with regard to different categories of areas or classified areas as industrial, commercial, residential and the silence zone. Also, the court in this case, framed and issued guidelines for the use of loudspeakers, and a need to set-up a separate Cell in the office of DC and SP, to monitor the noise pollution and said that, with regard to the use of air horns, the commissioner of police in the city of Madras and the SP in each district, shall act in accordance with Rules 402 and 403 of Tamil Nadu Motor Vehicles Rules and enforce strict compliance of Rule 119 of the Central Motor Vehicles Rules. The said authorities shall notify, that the action will be taken under sections 53, 54, 177, 179 or 184 of the Motor Vehicles Act against the persons, who violate Rule 119 of the Central Motor Vehicles Rules.

In *M.C. Mehta* Vs. *Union of India and Others*,[260] a PIL under Arts. 32 and 21 of the Constitution, was filed by an environmentalist lawyer, for seeking a direction against the Haryana Pollution Control Board to control pollution, caused by the stone crushers, pulverizes (a noisy machine, which crushes into dust), and mine operators in Faridabad. Supreme Court directed, State Pollution Control Board to inspect and ascertain the impact of mining operations, on the ecologically sensitive area of Badkal Lake and Surajkund. Also, the report was obtained by Court from another expert body, viz. National Environmental Engineering Research Institute (NEERI). In its report, NEERI stated that the noise levels were measured by the inspection team and found beyond the prescribed limits. Noise levels were also measured during blasting, when 820 gms. of explosive was used in four holes of 1.2 mts. depth. The noise level of 59.5 dBA was recorded at a distance of 500 mts. from the blast site.

Further it was also recommended that green belt should also be developed on either side of the roads in the mining area, to minimize the effects of dust and noise pollution.

The Calcutta High Court, in November 1996 banned the use of loudspeakers at all places of worship, for all races. The court, through Justice Bhagawati Prasad Benerjee and Justice A.K. Chakraborty, spoke, that India is a secular state, and hence the ban would cover all religions. The ban, which minimized noise levels in the city, during the festivals Durga-puja and Kali-puja, would also cover Gurudwaras and Mosques. But, on December 25, 1996, Milad-un-nabi (religious programme) was held in Masjid campus, near Dum Dum Airport, Calcutta. When loudspeakers were used, officials of the State Pollution Control Board, found that the sound of the mike-system was 85 decibel, whereas, 65 decibel was the limit prescribed by the Court. The matter was reported to the High Court, which issued a contempt of court notice against the Masjid committee for violating its order. The court found them guilty and imposed a penalty of Rs. 2500. Nearly, two dozen, Durga-puja, Kali-puja and Jagadhatri-puja Committees of Calcutta, were also charged with contempt of court, for violating the noise pollution order, and were fined with Rs. 1000 each.

It is a really appreciable mile stone verdict, delivered by the judiciary, for curbing noise pollution, caused in the name of religions. Though, the law was present in the state to deal with such noise, but no executive could ban, such indiscriminate use of loudspeaker and to arouse the wrath of state's religious sects. It is, undoubtedly a good beginning, initiated in West Bengal, and is expected that it would gradually be extended to other states in the country.[261]

In *Nayan Behari Das Vs. State of Orissa*,[262] the court observed that the use of multitioned horns, or similar devices giving unduly harsh, shrill, loud, and alarming sound is not permissible. It was observed that a scant view was being paid to these provisions by the operators of the vehicles in general, by owners of motor cars, and surprisingly, even by two-wheelers, who think it quite fashionable to use peculiar and loud sound producing devices as horns. In spite of Rules, prohibiting its use, the use of multitioned horns and other similar devices are on the increase, and as such drastic steps are required to be taken by the appropriate authorities for strict enforcement of these provisions. The court also observed that there is no prohibition on the manufacturers of such devices. Hence, there is need for it. Further the penalty provided is not stringent, therefore, a person is not bothered about the prohibitions. It is, therefore, clear that prohibition imposed by rules is not enough to deter the bus operators and transporters, to refrain from using such sound producing devices.

In *Moulana Mufti Syed Md. Noorur Rehman Barkati Vs. State of Bengal*,[263] it was claimed, that the use of microphone for the purpose of 'Azan' is a part of the religious right, guaranteed under Art. 25. But, the court held that the public cannot be forced to be a captive audience or forced listeners, who are unwilling to bear the sound, music, or the communication made by the loudspeakers. It was declared that a citizen has a right to leisure, right to sleep, right not to hear, right to remain silent, right to read, right to speak with others, right to worship, right to meditation, right to live alone in peace and silence, and right to think of any matter. The use of microphone, certainly infringes these rights of citizens. Further, the court viewed, that the time has come, when everybody has to think either, to survive or to perish. If the pollution is not controlled, the human beings cannot survive in long-run. It is evident, that unpalatable sound is one of the recognized modes of creating pollution, and this kind of pollution has to be controlled by all means. One may like sound, but he has no right to take away or abridge the right of others. There is no religious freedom in this country excepting the provision of Art. 25 of the Constitution, which is subject to public order, morality, health and other provisions of Part III including Art. 19(1)(a). The framers of the Constitution intended to make India a secular country, and provided freedom of religion, but made it subject to others freedoms guaranteed under Art. 19. Hence to maintain the secular character, this court is bound to maintain and follow secularism, as clearly laid down in the Preamble of the Constitution of India.

Church of God in India Vs. *KKR Majestic Coloney Welfare Association*,[264] the Court has observed that the noise pollution in some areas of a city/town, might be exceeding permissible limits, prescribed under the rules, but that would not be a ground for permitting others to increase the same, by beating of drums or use of sound amplifiers, loudspeakers, or by some other musical instruments. Therefore, rules prescribing reasonable restrictions including the rules for the use of loudspeakers and voice amplifiers framed under the Madras Town Nuisance Act, 1889 and also the Noise Pollution (Regulation and Control) Rules, 2000, are required to be enforced.

In *Salva* Vs. *National Capital Territory of Delhi*, the Court observed the violation of Noise Rules, 2000 wherein SHO, Lajpatnagar filed status report and the Court passed directions to curb the noise in silence zones.[264A]

In Free Legal Aid Cell *Shri Sugan Chand Aggarwal* Vs. *Govt. of NCT*,[264B] the court has not only observed the evil effects of noise pollution but also passed many guidelines in order to curb it.

To protect health from noise pollution, M.P. High Court held in a PIL, *Syed Maqsood Ali* Vs. *State of Mahdya Pradesh*[264C] held that noise infringes the fundamental rights of peaceful living in vecinity. It is pertinent that this PIL was filed by an ailing heart patient, residing near a Dharamshala where use of loudspeaker was usual frequent nuisance.[264D]

In re: Vs *Noise Pollution*, The Supreme Court shown its love to pollution free environment and issued various directions so as to curb noise pollution. The court has discussed various laws, rules, causes, impediments and case law with a view to bring in the dynamism in environmental jurisprudence.[264E]

From the threadbare analysis of above important cases on noise pollution, it can be well inferred, that Indian judiciary, particularly, the Supreme Court of India, which was often accused of being obstructive to social reforms and insensitive to environmental issues, has shown its dynamism, in refreshing contrast to such allegations in the past. Casting its archaic rules of procedure and throwing away traditional adjudicatory posture, Supreme Court of India became the Supreme Court for Indians. The activist judges have shown their keen love for nature and have come forward to protect it from various kinds of pollutions. Not only this, the judiciary sometimes came out heavily on the executives, and has bridged the gaps or lacunas by directing authorities to enforce the environmental laws. In cases of necessity, the court itself has framed the schemes or guidelines and issued them, in 'public green good'.

It is observed that in earlier cases relating to noise caused by loudspeakers was not objected primarily to curb the noise pollution, but to protect the right to religion or right to speech and expression. The post-emergency era of PIL and judicial activism, energized the public-spirited and social-minded citizens' associations, lawyers and activists judges, to sow new seeds, so as to free the environment from pollutants. Ban on indiscriminate use of loudspeakers, air horns, noisy machineries, injunctions against noise nuisance, etc. are some examples of new dimensions in the field.

There is still ample scope for such dynamism to protect the world from being polluted. The applicability of the principle of master's liability, for making good the loss caused to his servants, has been laid down, in *Thompson* Vs. *Smiths Shiprepaiarers (North Shields) Ltd.*,[265] needs to be applied in India too. In this case, plaintiffs were employed as labourers, in shipbuilding and repairing yard, over a long period from 1940 to 1970. During the course of employment their hearing power was impaired, due to exposure to high noise. The employer knew about such noise, but failed to provide any protection till early 1970s. In 1963, the pamphlets were issued by the Ministry of labour, on industrial noise, and only thereafter, protective devices were made available to the employers, to be distributed amongst and used accordingly.

In 1980 and 1981, plaintiff labourers brought action against their employers for negligence in failing to provide protection against noise, in yard. It was well established that substantial part of the damage had occurred before 1963 and after that it had merely aggravated the existing damage and accelerated hearing disability.

The court determined that the employer was negligent and failed to take initiatives in seeking knowledge about the facts. It was held that the employees were entitled to recover compensation from the employers.

The US courts have even gone further deep and have co-related the right of privacy with noise. And in *Bernard Carey* Vs. *Roy Brown*,[266] the court has held that the State's interest in protecting the well-being of the citizens, and their right to tranquility and privacy in home, is certainly a right of the highest order, in a free and civilized society.

In another US case, *Frisby* Vs. *Schultz*,[267] the court has further emphasized on the importance of right to privacy, and has said, that the individuals are not required to welcome unwanted speech into their own homes, and the government must protect the said freedom, because 'no one has a right to force one's speech into the home of an unwilling listener. Recently at Manhattan in New York, Sir Sean Connery has been sued for 15 million dollar by his neighbours for being too noisy and a disturbing influence. A family in the neighbouring New York apartment stated that he plays loud music round the clock.[267A]

In this wake, judiciary being the custodian of people's rights, should not betray the confidence of the people and their trust in justice through court system, by shirking their shoulders from great responsibilities, but should come foreword promptly and provide relief, in cases of need. Also, the court should put into its best efforts to protect the rights of the citizens, may be in flagrant disregard of the personal wrath, comfort, or inconvenience to any sect, and to protect and improve the environment from being polluted. The Delhi High Court rightly has rejected the petition of a generator manufacturing company and ordered the manufacturers to provide an acoustic enclosure while making diesel generators. This enclosure is to ensure that the minimum permissible sound pressure of a generator is 75 dB. The court further held that the consumer has a right to drag generator manufacturers to consumer court if there is no acoustic enclosoure.[268] Similarly the Supreme Court of India has judiciously rejected a petition *inter alia* prayed for giving retaxation in the busting of crackers and use of loudspeakers.

The Apex Court of India has ordered the closure of 218 industrial units and mines across the country saying that these can not be allowed to function at the cost of protecting the environment.[269]

Ordinary legal remedies, provided by long and ordinary procedure are absolutely inadequate to meet the growing need of effective control of noise pollution. Civil remedies under the law of torts against nuisance and outdated municipal laws are insufficient safeguards to protect individual rights, public health, and safety against the inroads to noise pollution. Such quieting process, adopted by courts to satisfy the citizens cannot break a new ground, unless individual outlook itself changes by conviction. Unless, the individual is fully informed and realizes, that unwanted noise is a serious threat to his health, the law alone cannot control the noise malady, operating on a wide scale. The individual has to be educated that noise is not just an unpleasant irritant to be tolerated and digested, but to strongly react against this serious health hazard which is the cost, one has to pay for the blind race of technological advancements, the man is after in the name of progress. Therefore, the concept of 'sustainable development', which is an urgent need of the time before planning any activity of development or modernization. The psychology of individual needs change. Public pressure could be a very effective catalyst for securing legal protection against all specific sources, producing noise.

But unfortunately, ours is the country of ignorant citizens and passive executives and therefore, the sword ultimately is to ply by the judiciary to win the battle and to prove that:

'The court is the symbol of "cure"; if the green to 'prosperity'; white to 'peace', and brown to 'barrenness'.

NOTES AND REFERENCES

1. *Subhash Kumar* Vs. *State of Bihar*, AIR 1991 SC 420. Also see *Damodar Rao* Vs. *Municipality Hyderabad*, AIR 1987 AP 171.
2. *Curbing Noise Pollution Through Law*, Tilak Raj Advocate.
3. An Article written by Dr. S.R. Jain, Prof., JNVU, Jodhpur.
4. D.D. Ojha, *Noise Pollution*, p. 82 (Hindi).
5. *Ibid.*

6. Sec. 2(b), is mention with the word noise but the word noise is missing from the text of section 25.
7. Rule 5 (II) of EPR perhaps is the persuasion for amendment to Air (Amendment) Act, 1987 so as to include the noise as the pollutants.
8. See S.O. 528 (E) dated 28th June, 1999.
9. See Notification S.O. 123 (E), dated 14th February, 2000 and further amended by S.O. 1046 (E), dated 22nd November, 2000.
9A. 2001 AIR (Del) 455.
9AA. C.A. No. 3735/2005 arising out of S.L.P. No. 21851/03.
9B. *Salva Vs. NCT of Delhi*, 2003 AIR (Del) 73.
10. I. Mohan, *Environmental Pollution and Management.*
11. N.S. Kamboj, *Control of Noise Pollution*, p. 162.
12. *Ibid.*, p. 105.
13. *Ibid.*
14. *Ibid.*
15. *Ibid.*
16. (a) Day time shall mean from 6.00 a.m. to 10.00 p.m.
    (b) Night time shall mean from 10.00 p.m. to 6.00 a.m.
    (c) Silence zone is defined as an area comprising not less than 100 metres around hospitals, educational institutions and courts. The silence zones are zones which are declared as such by the competent authority.
    (d) Mixed categories of areas may be declared as one of the four above mentioned categories by the competent authority.
    dB(A) Leq denotes the time weighted average of the level of sound in decibels on scale A which is relatable to human hearing.
17. G.S.R. 1063 (E) in the Gazette of India Extraordinary, Part 2, sec. 3(i), December 26, 1989, See *Supra* 11, p. 106
18. R.P. Anand, *Law, Science and Environment*, pp. 106-08.
19. Chetan Singh Mehta, *Environmental Protection and the Law*, p. 15.
19A. *TOI*, February 23, 2005.
20. *Supra* 11, p. 111.
21. *Ibid.*
22. Under 6(b), such rules may provide the maximum allowable limits of concentration of various environmental pollutants (including noise) for different areas. The use of this provision has been made by the Government vide related notification and maximum noise level has been fixed for different localities for day and nights viz. residential, commercial, industrial and silence zone.
22A. Noise Pollution Regulations in India; Pollution Control Law Series: PCL 106/2001-02 by Central Pollution Control Board, Delhi.
23. Section 15(1).
24. Section 15(2).

25. Section 10.
26. Chetan Singh Mehta, *Environmental Protection and the Law*, p. 23.
27. *Ibid.*, pp. 24-25.
28. Krishna Iyer, J., *Environmental Protection and the Law*, p. 105
29. Chandra Shekhran N.S., Environmental protection—two steps forward and one step back, *J.I.L.I.*, No. 2, Vol. 30 (198), p. 192.
30. Upendra Baxi, *Environmental Protction Act*—An Agenda for Implementation I.L.I. (1987), p. 39.
31. *Supra* 29.
32. Leela Krishnan P., *Towards Better Regime of Environment*, National Seminar Faipur, p. 27.
33. Upendra Baxi, E.P.A.—An Agenda for Implementation I.L.I. (1987), p. 41.
34. Chetan Singh Mehta, *Environmental Pollution and the Law*, p. 27.
35. See preamble to IPC.
36. *Winfield on Tort*, 7th Edition, p. 19.
37. Sec. 278 of IPC.
37A. I. Mohan, *Environmental Issues and Programmes*, pp. 284-86.
38. Sec. 287, IPC.
39. Sec. 288, IPC.
40. Sec. 289, IPC.
41. Sections. 292-295.
42. *Russel on Crime*, 11th Ed., p. 1589.
43. AIR 1958 Pun 11.
44. (1939) 2 All ER 202.
45. AIR 1919 Cal 539.
46. (1982) 2 CH 589.
47. AIR 1998 Orissa 39.
48. 1984 Cr L J (NOC) 16 AP.
48A. (1939) 2 All ER 202.
49. (1961) 1 WLR 683.
50. N.S. Kamboj, *Control of Noise Pollution*.
51. *Supra* 11, p. 91.
52. *Ibid.*, p. 56.
53. *Ibid.*, p. 57.
54. G.O.Ms. No. 1643, dated July 1, 1969, 1023 dated April 4, 1972, G.O. Ms. No. 849, dated 15 May, 1975 and G.O. Ms. No. 3485, dated 29 December 1977.
55. *Supra* 11.
56. Pondicherry Act VI of 1966 and VII of 1968.
57. Sikkim Act 7 of 1980.
58. West Bengal Act, XXXVIII of 1963.
59. Section 32(i)(a)(b) of Delhi Police Act, 1978.

60. Act No. 22 of 1951.
61. Section 33(i) of Bombay Police Act, 1951.
62. Sub. Cl. (o)(a) of Bombay Police Act, 1951.
63. *Supra* 11.
64. Section 3.
65. Sl. No. 6, Sch. I.
66. *Supra* 11.
67. R.K. Sapru, *Environment Management in India-II*, p. 93.
68. Act No. 59 of 1988.
69. *Ibid.*
70. *Ibid.*
71. Section 70(2)(i).
72. *M.S. Appa Rao Vs. Govt. of TN*, 1995 AIHC 4168, also see *Rahib Mukherjee Vs. State of West Bengal*, 1995 Cal 222.
73. G.S.R. 742(E) dated 25th September 2000.
74. R.K. Sapru, *Environment Management in India*, Vol. II, p. 103.
75. G.K. Nagi, M.K. Dhiloon, G.S. Dhaliwal, *Noise Pollution*, Ist Ed., p. 147.
76. *Supra* 11, p. 117.
77. G.S.R. 338 (E), dated 20 March, 1993.
78. G.S.R. 742 (E) dated 25th September, 2000.
79. *Source:* Noise Regulations in India, Pollution Control Law series: PCLS/06/2000-01, issued by Central Pollution Board, East Arjun Nagar, New Delhi, pp. 13-15.
80. Dr. Mahesh Mathur, *Legal Control of Environmental Pollution*, p. 187.
81. Definition of hazardous processes.
82. Definition—Any process or activity in relation to an industry specified in schedule 1 of the Act which produces two results viz. (a) material impairment to health of the person engaged in or connected therewith, and (b) problem of general environment.
82A. *Supra* 11, p. 16.
83. *Employment News*, New Delhi, 26 January-1 February, 2002.
84. *Dainik Bhaskar*, Jodhpur, February, 24, 2002.
85. Act No. 14 of 1951.
86. Section 3.
87. Section 5.
88. Section 10.
89. Statement of objects and reasons of the Act.
90. Section 1.
91. Section 3.
92. Section 4.
93. *Supra* 11.
94. Act No. 3 of 1958.

95. Sections 3 to 8 came into force, w.e.f. 16 January, 1976 in the municipal areas of Sojat, Sadri, Sumerpur, Nimba, Takhatgargh and Jaitaran town of Pali district and w.e.f. 26 March, 1976 in the towns Dunagaragh and Taranagar vide Notification No. S.O. 258/F 11(4) Home/5/75, dated 16 January, 1976, published in Rajasthan Gazette, Part IV-C(II) Extraordinary, dated 16 January, 1976 and Notification No. Ss.O. 308/F1 (13) (1) Home/Gr. 5/76, dated 26 January, 1976 published in Rajasthan Gazette, Part IV-C (II), extraordinary dated March 26, 1976 respectively.

96. *Rajasthan Patrika*, October 5, 2001.

96A. G.O. Letter No. 1162B/11-Kha-853/68 issued on May 12, 1970.

97. Rule 2.

98. *Supra* 11.

99. Subs. by Act 47 of 1987.

100. Such rules should be consistent with the Act and their object should be to promote/maintain the health, safety and convenience of the inhabitants of that municipal area.

101. Civil Appeal No. 1691 of 2001, decided on 2 March, 2001.

102. Act No. 12 of 1955.

103. Section 5.

104. Section 9.

105. *Supra* 11.

106. AIR 1950 Cal. 345.

107. *Ibid.*, p. 350.

108. Section 135 of Cr.P.C.

109. Sec. 139 of Cr.P.C.

110. Sec. 141(i) Cr.P.C.

111. Sec. 141(2), Cr.P.C.

112. Sec. 141(3) Cr.P.C.

113. Sec. 142.

114. Sec. 142(3).

115. 1986 Cr.L.J. (396).

116. *Krishna Gopal* Vs. *State of MP*, 1986 Cr.L.J. (396).

117. Chetan Singh Mehta, *Environmental Protection and the Law*, p. 82.

118. *Supra* 11.

119. *Ibid.*

120. *Supra* 11.

121. *Supra* 11.

122. *Ibid.*

123. *Ibid.*

124. *Ibid.*

125. *Ibid.*

126. *Ibid.*

127. *Ibid.*
128. *Ibid.*
129. *Ibid.*
129A. An extract from the judgment in RE: Noise Pollution 2005(5) SCALE.
130. Noise Regulation Law—Japan.
131. *Ibid.*
132. *Ibid.*
133. *Ibid.*
134. *Ibid.*
135. *Ibid.*
135A. Extracted from a judgment in RE: Noise Pollution, 2005(5) SCALE.
135B. *Ibid.*
136. *Supra* 75, p. 194.
137. I. Mohan, *Environmental Issues and Programmes,* p. 279.
138. Dr. Mahesh Mathur, *Legal Control of Environmental Pollution,* p. 136.
139. Compendium on Environmental Protection Laws, Published by Rajasthan State Board for Prevention and Control of Water Pollution, Jaipur, see *Legal Control of Environmental Pollution,* Mahesh Mathur, p.137.
140. *Journal of The Indian Law Institute,* Vol. 43, No. 3, 356.
141. P.V. Kane, I, *History of Dharam Shastra,* p. 538 (1968).
141A. *Supra* 138, p. 137.
142. *Journal of the ILI,* Vol. 43, No. 3, July-September 2001, p. 359.
143. Guru Nanak uttered in Jap Ji Saheb that the air is vital force, water the progenitor, the vast earth, the mother of all, days and nights are nurses fonding all creation in their lap, also see page 359 of *Journal of the ILI,* Vol. 43, No. 3, July-September, 2001.
143A. Sundarlal Bahuguna, *Technology Vs. Ecololgy, The Hindustan Times,* Februray 1986, also see, *Legal Control of Environmental Pollution* by Mahesh Mathur p. 138.
144. *Supra* 138, pp. 138-39.
145. *Journal of the ILI,* Vol. 43, No. 3, July-September, 2001.
146. An Overview—B.R. Sharma in R.K. Sapru, *Environment Management in India,* p. 158.
146A. See Tiwari Committee Report.
147. Indian Pollution Regulations and Background by David Sharma down loaded from internet.
148. *Supra* 11, p. 106.
149. Citizen's Report was published in 1982 by the Center for Science and Environment, New Delhi, see pp. 1-99.
150. India's Environmental Background, David Sharma down loaded from internet.
150A. See Noise Control Rules, 2000.

5 tk

95. Sections 3 to 8 came into force, w.e.f. 16 January, 1976 in the municipal areas of Sojat, Sadri, Sumerpur, Nimba, Takhatgargh and Jaitaran town of Pali district and w.e.f. 26 March, 1976 in the towns Dunagaragh and Taranagar vide Notification No. S.O. 258/F 11(4) Home/5/75, dated 16 January, 1976, published in Rajasthan Gazette, Part IV-C(II) Extraordinary, dated 16 January, 1976 and Notification No. Ss.O. 308/F1 (13) (1) Home/Gr. 5/76, dated 26 January, 1976 published in Rajasthan Gazette, Part IV-C (II), extraordinary dated March 26, 1976 respectively.
96. *Rajasthan Patrika,* October 5, 2001.
96A. G.O. Letter No. 1162B/11-Kha-853/68 issued on May 12, 1970.
97. Rule 2.
98. *Supra* 11.
99. Subs. by Act 47 of 1987.
100. Such rules should be consistent with the Act and their object should be to promote/maintain the health, safety and convenience of the inhabitants of that municipal area.
101. Civil Appeal No. 1691 of 2001, decided on 2 March, 2001.
102. Act No. 12 of 1955.
103. Section 5.
104. Section 9.
105. *Supra* 11.
106. AIR 1950 Cal. 345.
107. *Ibid.,* p. 350.
108. Section 135 of Cr.P.C.
109. Sec. 139 of Cr.P.C.
110. Sec. 141(i) Cr.P.C.
111. Sec. 141(2), Cr.P.C.
112. Sec. 141(3) Cr.P.C.
113. Sec. 142.
114. Sec. 142(3).
115. 1986 Cr.L.J. (396).
116. *Krishna Gopal* Vs. *State of MP,* 1986 Cr.L.J. (396).
117. Chetan Singh Mehta, *Environmental Protection and the Law,* p. 82.
118. *Supra* 11.
119. *Ibid.*
120. *Supra* 11.
121. *Supra* 11.
122. *Ibid.*
123. *Ibid.*
124. *Ibid.*
125. *Ibid.*
126. *Ibid.*

172. UN Resolution No. 37/7, dated 28 October, 1982.
173. Krishna Iyer J., *Environmental Pollution and The Law*, p. 102, Dr. Kurt Waldheim in Stockholm Conference, 1972.
173A. *In RE*: Noise Pollution, 2005(5) SCALE.
174. 1992 (2) KLT 238.
175. *Supra* 11, p. 72B.
176 *M.C. Mehta* Vs. *UOI.*
177. *Rural Litigation and Environmental Kendra* Vs. *State of UP*, AIR 1985 SC 652.
178. 1984 Cr L J (NOC) 16 (AP).
179. *In RE*: Noise Pollution, 2005(5) SCALE.
180. R.P. Anand, *Law Science and Environment*, pp. 189-90.
181. AIR 1981 SC 746.
182. AIR 1985 SC 652 and *Devi Nandan Pandey* Vs. *UOI.*
183. Chetan Singh Mehta, *Environmental Protection and the Law*, p. 101.
184. (1998) 4 SCC.
185. AIR 1999 Cal 15.
185A. 1986 (I) Scale-182.
185B. AIR (2001) Delhi 455 (D.B.).
185C. AIR (1993) Kerala 1.
186. http://www.islamicvoice.com/may97/#Top.
187. AIR 1984, NOC 137 HP.
188. AIR 1958 All. 368.
189. *Supra* 11, p. 72.
190. AIR 1999 Cal 15.
191. *Hindustan Times*, November 4, 1998.
192. 2000(3) KLT 651 = 2000 JT (9) 575.
192A. *Supra* 179.
193. *M.C. Mehta* Vs. *Union of India*, AIR 1987 SC 1026.
193A. *Hindustan Times*, Delhi dated 14 January 2006.
194. AIR 1987 SC 1109.
195. *M.C. Mehta* Vs. *UOI*, 1998 (9) SCC 589.
196. N.R. Madhava Menon, Public Interest Litigation, a Major Breakthrough in the Delivery of Social Justice. J.B.C.I., p. 150.
197. *Public Interest Litigation*, Dr. Sampat Jain, Introduction, p. 1.
198. AIR 1987 SC 38
199. *Public Interest Litigations*, by Sampat Jain, Director ASC, JNVU, Jodhpur, p. 31.
200. 1980 (1) All ER 529 p. 551.
201. 1990 (2) KLT 686.
202. AIR 1985 SC 652.
202A. (2004) 8 SCC 446.
203. (dhanush@giasmd01.vsnl.net.in).

203A. Towards a Pollution Free Diwali, *TOI*.
204. *The Navhind Times*, Panaji, Friday, September 1, 2000.
204A. *Times of India*, 29-3-2005.
204B. *Free Legal Aid Cell Shri Sugan Chand Aggarwal* Vs. *Govt. of NCT of Delhi*, 2001 AIR (Del) 455; See Delhi High Court Case Law Search System.
204C. *In RE*: Noise Pollution, 2005(5) SCALE.
204D. PIL filed by Patanjali Siksha Sanstha; *TOI*, Delhi, January 14, 2006.
205. This matter as an extract of the Constitution of some Asian Countries has been taken from the Compendium prepared by UNEP following SACEP/UNEP/NORAD symposium on the Role of Judiciary in promoting the Rule of law in the Area of Sustainable Development, held in Colombo, Sri Lanka, 4-6 July 1997. Downloaded from Internet.
206. Articles 23 and 24.
207. Articles 31 and 32, in *Dr. Mohiuddin Farooque* Vs. *Secretary, Ministry of Communication, Government of the Peoples' Republic of Bangladesh and 12 others* (1995), remedy for mitigating air and noise pollution was sought under Articles 31 and 32 of the Constitution in conjunction with the Motor Vehicles Ordinance, 1983 and the Supreme Court of Bangladesh directed Respondent No. 2 (Chairman, Bangladesh Road Transport Authority) and Respondent No. 4 (Commissioner, Dhaka Metropolitan Police) to show cause as to why they should not take effective measures, as provided in the Motor Vehicles Ordinance, 1983, to check air pollution caused by motor vehicle emissions and noise pollution resulting from audible signaling devices.
208. Article 102.
209. As amended in 1986.
210. Constitution of 1993.
211. See Chapter III of the Constitution of the Kingdom of Combodia.
212. *Supra.*
213. See *Constitution of the Kingdom of Cambodia*, Chapter IV.
214. *Supra* Chapter V.
215. *Supra.*
216. *Constitution of the Kingdom of Cambodia*, Chapter IX.
217. *Supra* Chapter X.
218. *Supra* Chapter XII.
219. Compendium prepared by UNEP following SACEP/UNEP/NORAD symposium on the Role of Judiciary in promoting the Rule of law in the Area of Sustainable Development, held in Colombo, Sri Lanka, 4-6 July 1997.
220. Article 26 of the Constitution of People's Republic of China.
221. Article 10 of the Constitution.

222. Article 1 of the Constitution.
223. Became effective as of March 1, 1997.
224. Article 1 of the Constitution.
225. The Rising Nepal, *National Daily*, Kathmandu, 29 April, 2001.
226. As amended in 1980.
227. Article 19(3) under Chapter IV.
228. The Rising Nepal, *National Daily*, Kathmandu, 29 April 2001.
229. The Compendium of Summaries of Judicial Decisions in Environment Related Cases prepared by UNEP following the SACEP/UNEP/NORAD Symposium on the Role of the Judiciary in Promoting the Rule of Law in the Area of Sustainable Development, held in Colombo, Sri Lanka on 4-6 July 1997, and is included herein with the permission of UNEP.
230. Amended in 1984.
231. Article 27 enshrined in Chapter VI of the Constitution of the Democratic Socialist of Sri Lanka.
232. Article 28(d) (Chapter VI).
233. Article 28(f).
234. *Supra* 205.
235. Constitution of the Socialist Republic of Vietnam, 1992.
236. Article 17 enshrined in Part II of Constitution of the Socialist Republic of Vietnam.
237. Article 18.
238. Article 12, Section 2 of the Constitution of the Republic of the Philippines.
239. Section 3.
240. Section 4.
241. Section 5.
242. *Supra* note 3.
243. Article 13, Section 7.
244. *Supra* Compendium prepared by UNEP.
245. *Ibid*.
245A. AIR 1988 SC 1037.
246. 1984 CrLJ (NOC) 16 (AP).
247. (1998) 98 LT 718: 24 TLR 414.
248. Civil Appeal No. 1691 of 2001, decided on 2 March, 2001.
249. *Times of India*, New Delhi, January 13, 2002.
250. AIR 1958 Punjab 11.
251. AIR 1919 Cal 539.
252. *Messers Dutta Mal Chiranji Lal* Vs. *L. Ladi Prasad and Others* (AIR 1960 All 632).
253. AIR 1975 Kerala 117.
254. See AIR 1971 SC 2486 and AIR 1973 SC 87.

255. AIR 1985 Cal 222.
256. AIR 1993 Kerala 1.
257. Civil Appeal No. of 1994 (Arising out of SLP (C) No. 9059 of 1994), decided on May 12, 1994.
258. 1995 AIHC 4168.
259. See G.S.R. 1063 (E), dated 26 December, 1989.
260. 1998 (9) SCC 589.
261. http://www.islamicvoice.com/may97/#Top.
262. AIR 1998 Orissa 39.
263. AIR 1999 Cal 15.
264. 2000 (3) KLT 651 = 2000 JT (9) 575.
264A. 2003 AIR (Del) 73.
264B. 2001 AIR (Del) 455
264C. 2001 AIR MP 220.
264D. *Rajasthan Patrikia*, Sept. 18, 2002.
264E. 2005(5) SCALE.
265. AIR 1968 P&H 399.
266. 447 US 455.
267. 447 US 447.
267A. Noisy Country sued in New York, *Times of India*, February 24, 2005.
268. HC Tightens Services on Generator Manufacturers, *TOI*, April 8, 2004.
269. *Times of India*, February 23, 2005.

6

Role of Non-Governmental Organizations (NGOs) and the Duties of Citizens

The last three decades have seen an unprecedented rise in the number of Voluntary Organisations and Non-Governmental Organisations (NGOs) in India, particularly in some states. The growth of NGO movement is attributed to the failure of public institutions to address social and environmental problems.[1] According to Dr. Veena Jha,[2] the NGOs and grass-root institutions in India do not exclusively deal with environmental issues, but they follow an integrated approach by linking poverty, social justice, inequality, rural development and health issues. NGOs differ from each other in their diversity of roles, ideologies, approaches, management styles and organisations. However, Judicial interventions and activism of NGOs have together made the industries more aware of environmental concerns. For example, in the State of Maharastra such activism has been decisive in enforcing environmental rules and regulations. NGOs and peoples' organisations have, through careful analysis of procedures organisational factors; functioning style and policies have achieved some breakthrough in the erstwhile secretive and non-co-operative government institutions and agencies. Governments have responded to NGO pressure by simplifying unenforceable laws and cumbersome procedures. While governments may be reluctant to enforce cumbersome and onerous environmental legislations on trans-national corporations (TNCs), NGOs have acted as the watchdogs on TNCs. In a milieu, where governmental efforts are mostly directed towards attracting TNCs, whereas public interest litigation and NGOs have directed their efforts on ensuring that TNCs confirm to high environmental standards. While it is to be expected that NGOs would be more active in states such as Bihar, with weak administrative and governance structures, surprisingly they have surfaced in larger number of states such as Maharastra and Tamil Nadu, where governance structures are relatively stronger. This appears to indicate that strong governance structures are more conducive to building higher levels of public awareness, on issues such as environment. Such States appear to be relatively wealthier than the states, which do not have a strong NGO presence. Of course, number of TNCs in these states is also higher. While urban Indians favour TNCs, rural Indians are still hostile to their presence.

1. NON-GOVERNMENTAL ORGANISATIONS (NGOs)

There is no common definition of an NGO, acceptable to all. The term carries different connotations in different circumstances. Nevertheless, there are some fundamental features. Clearly, an NGO must be independent from the direct control of any government. In addition to above, there are three generally accepted characteristics of NGOs, which distinguish them from other particular types of bodies. First, an NGO shall not have any political affiliation, i.e. with any political party. Second, it shall be a non-profit-making organization, purely service oriented or social welfare body. Third, it must not be a group of criminals to pursue some criminal activities for selfish ends and of non-violent nature. These characteristics apply in general, because they match with the conditions laid down by the United Nations for their recognition.[3]

NGO is defined as an independent voluntary association of

people acting together on a continuous basis, to achieve some common goals, other than what the government wants to pursue, or to make money or to carryout illegal activities.

A 1994 document of United Nations, describes an NGO, as a non-profit entity, whose members are citizens or associations of citizens of one or more countries and whose activities are determined by the collective will of its members in response to the needs of the members of one or more communities with which the NGO cooperates. This formulation embraces every kind of group, except for private businesses, revolutionary or terrorist groups, and political parties. Other popular substitutes for the term NGO are private voluntary organizations, civil society organizations, and independent sectors but such terms are almost vague. To know and judge an NGO, one shall have to examine and focus on its goals, membership, funding sources, and the like. Still, there is not a universal agreement on what NGOs exactly are?

2. BRIEF HISTORY OF NGO MOVEMENTS

The term 'Non-Governmental Organization' or NGO was not in currency before the establishment of United Nations. In 1910, 132 international associations decided to co-operate with each other at the international level under the label of Union of International Associations. After its formation, the League of Nations officially referred to the Union of International Associations as "liaison with private organizations." Many of such unions and bodies liked to call themselves, as International Institutes, International Unions or simply International Organizations. The First Draft of the UN Charter did not make any mention for maintaining co-operation with private bodies. A variety of groups, mainly but not solely from USA, lobbied to rectify this at the San Francisco Conference, by which UN was established in 1945. Many diverse types of bodies are now described as NGOs.[4] Professor Peter Willetts, City University, London is of the view that the term, "non-governmental organization" or NGO, came into currency in 1945 because of the need for the UN to differentiate in its Charter between participation rights for inter-governmental specialized agencies and those for international private organizations.[5]

Many protest and activist NGOs[6] largely emerged in response to an imminent attention to local environments that would otherwise have remained un-addressed by policies and regulations. Most were passive and rarely violent. Many of these were issue-based protest NGOs and formed with external assistance, external leadership, and management inputs. Some protest and activist organizations joined established networks or formed alliances and addressed problems collaboratively (like the National Alliance of People's Movement). Other NGOs were individualistic in addressing issues of their particular interest; some NGOs are small and others large; some focus on policy issues only, others target projects; some are region specific, others are cause issue specific, or localised in influence; some address broader interdisciplinary issues like environment, human rights, health, land reforms, while others specifically focus on natural environment; many depend on corporate sponsorship, some on private charity and a rare few on government funding. Several organisations are single person-based institutions with a short life span. In 1980's two remarkable developments in the Indian legal system provided a strong impetus to judicial activism in India. There was a broadening of existing environmental laws in the country and judicial activity through public interest litigation began in India. These two developments gave more scope to citizens and public interest groups to prosecute a corporation or a TNC, which violates environmental norms.

Until the enactment of Environment Protection Act, 1986, only the Government could initiate prosecution under Indian environmental laws. Public interest groups and citizens had no statutory remedy against a polluter who discharged effluents or emitted the pollutions beyond permissible limit. But under section 19 of The Environment Protection Act, 1986, a citizen could prosecute the polluter, provided a 60-days notice is given of his/her intention to prosecute. Other provisions allowing citizens to participate in the enforcement of pollution laws are now found in section 43 of the Air Act, as amended in 1987, and in section 49 of the Water Act as amended in 1988. Both these Amendments require the Pollution Control Board to disclose internal reports to citizens seeking to prosecute a polluter.

3. NGOs AND THE UNITED NATIONS

According to the UN Charter, the participation of NGOs to the UN is limited to the work of ECOSOC.[7] It is ECOSOC that establishes procedures of accreditation and suspension for NGOs. In July 1996, ECOSOC reviewed and expanded its arrangements for consultation with NGOs and recommended that the General Assembly to examine the question of "participation of NGOs in all areas of work of the UN." Thereafter, member states began negotiations, but these soon stalled. The Secretary General wrote two reports but nothing substantial has happened. Former German President, Richard von Weizsäcker, argues in favour of new social and economic institutions to help the UN face new challenges. Despite Secretary General Kofi Annan's efforts to increase the dialogue between the UN and civil society, many states still see NGO's as a threat to their sovereignty. However, the Rio Summit is often seen as a turning point in the relations between NGOs and the UN. In July 2001, there were 2091 NGOs in consultative status with the Economic and Social Council (ECOSOC) in three different categories: General, Special and Roster.[8]

4. SETTING OF AGENDAS

NGOs have long played a key role in forcing leaders and policy-makers to pay attention on the social matters, and clean environment is not bar on them. In 1945, NGOs were largely responsible for inserting human rights in the UN Charter and have since then put almost every measure of human rights issue on the international agenda. Likewise, NGO activism since 1960s and 1970s has successfully raised the profile of global environmental issues. Instead of holding marches or hanging banners off buildings, NGO members now use computers and cell phones to launch global public-relations blitzes that can force the top policy-makers to activate upon.

5. SOLUTIONS EMERGING FROM NGOs' EFFORTS

Even the impossible solutions, which the government cannot or will not like to attempt, NGOs have made them possible by their persistent efforts, judicial or otherwise. Some humanitarian and development NGOs have a natural advantage because of their transparency, impartiality, perceived neutrality and experience. International NGOs have also played critical roles in translating international agreements and norms into domestic realities. After the Stockholm Declaration on Human Environment, 1972, perhaps one of the most vital roles of NGOs is, to promote the societal changes, needed to make the glob free of environmental pollutants.

The Noise Pollution Clearing House is such a national non-profit organization, with extensive online noise related resources. The mission of this house is to create more civil cities and more natural rural and wilderness areas, by reducing noise pollution at the source itself.

The Ministry of Environment and Forestry has decided to have a series of interactive meetings with concerned government agencies, NGOs, experts and citizens, with the objective of defining a plan of action to combat the problem. The outcome of these meetings is White Paper on Pollution in Delhi, with an Action Plan covering various aspects of pollution control, including noise pollution, vehicular and industrial pollution, and solid waste management.[9] Even the World Bank recognizes the important role that non-governmental organizations can play and have played, in making the clean environment as an essential human right, pacing with new technological developments.[10]

The Forum of Environmental Journalists of India (FEJI) is a strong environmental journalist forum with representation across India's diverse regions. Most of its office bearers are freelance journalists, allowing them more time to concentrate on forum work. Some of FEJI's activities include, to provide a resource support network for Indian journalists, organizing educational workshops and field trips, educating media groups and editors on environmental issues and taking part in environmental seminars and conferences on local, regional and international levels.[11]

The success of India's environmental programme depends greatly on the awareness and consciousness of the people, which is being aroused, to a good extent by the NGOs. National environmental awareness campaign has been launched to sensitise the people to the environmental problems through audio-visual programmes, seminars, symposia, training programmes. 'Paryavaran Vahinis' have been constituted in 184 districts, involving the local people to play an active role in preventing, poaching, deforestation and environmental pollution. 4000 NGOs have been financially assisted for creating environmental awareness among the people. An Environmental Information System (ENVIS) network has been set-up to disseminate information on environmental issues. India has a large network of NGO's, which are involved in transmitting the message of sustainable development and the quality of environment. The website of the Ministry of Environment and Forests[12] provides latest information about the new policy initiatives, legislations, and projects given environmental clearance.

6. NGO ACTIVISM THROUGH PIL

The Bhopal gas tragedy gave environmental and factory enforcement agencies[13] a major cause for concern and highlighted the lacunae that existed therein. This led to a boost in NGOs' activity. In cases where cities developed primarily around industries (mostly textile and dyeing units, chemical plants, or factories), the question of their safety became critical.

Effective awareness building tools, which may spawn undesirable second-order effects, are protests. Many NGOs protest through vocal and verbal communication to educate and lobby for people and institutional support. Commonly used protest mechanisms like *dharna* (sit-in demonstrations), *morchas* (processions) and *padyatras* (marches and processions) are effective to increase public awareness and activate agencies and institutions to community interests. The mechanism aims to deter on-going projects by revealing to society the options that would have lost for otherwise inexplicable reasons—a means to bring their legitimate complaints before a quasi-judicial body (like the Green Bench or SPCBs to settle issues through dialogue).[14]

Since 1985, most of the environmental cases have been brought before the court, in the form of writ petitions, normally by the NGOs acting on a *pro bono publico*. Petitions are generally lodged in the Supreme Court and High Courts. Here technical expertise for examination and assessment is largely absent. In such a case, the court may decide to appoint an independent committee in consultation with parties.

For the protection of environment, the Government has introduced a new device of 'public hearing' through which the NGOs are allowed to voice the cause of the community. Public hearing has now proved a powerful legal instrument in the hands of community through NGOs. Through this new movement, the NGOs are successful in educating public on environ-legal issues and bringing forth the initiatives among people to organise themselves so as to protect their environmental rights. But, unfortunately the public is not sufficiently well informed about this movement. In January 1994, such public hearings were made mandatory under the Environmental Impact Assessment (EIA) Notification for 29 different classes of hazardous industries. These industries, according to this notification, were required to obtain clearance certificate from the Central Government (mainly the Ministry of Environment and Forests), prior to the commencement of work. Environmentalists allege that due to the powerful industrial lobbies, public hearing on EIAs was diluted and made optional in May 1994. This option had an adverse effect and the result was that there were no public hearings on EIAs, from May 1994 to March 1997.[15]

This led to a severe criticism and had to face NGOs strong environmental protection movement, and the government in April 1997 had to amend EIA notification to make public hearing mandatory for all EIAs projects.[16] Impact of NGOs Activities on Institutional Reforms and Laws Enforcement

Vigilant people's institutions have challenged, and have enquired into the role played by the state institutions, their authority and powers, through an authority superior to them, i.e. dynamic judicial agencies and policy directives by higher governmental authorities. This has, in turn, reinstated the powers of the state institutions that was corroded and eclipsed on account of culture of corruption and inertia.

The efforts of NGOs have not only clarified and crystallized the scope of official discretion, but also have helped in the simplification of rules and regulations, and have enhanced accountability and transparency to a great extent. Over the past few years, government agencies have been asked to partake and share responsibilities with the NGOs and the community at large.

This reform of government institutions has helped to increase the legitimacy of institutions and democratization of the process through participation, as well as to increase the efficiency and effectiveness of their services and policies. This has led to achieve a broad objective of increasing and strengthening accountability on the part of the government.

Liberalization of the economy and increasing NGO activities forced the government agencies to implement rules and regulations more particularly. Under the circumstances, how long the defaulters and law-breakers will escape and would expose and penalize. To combat corruption, prevalent in the state agencies, is now far more easier, on account of widely available information and increasing education of the stakeholders, i.e. NGOs, industries, and trade bodies.

To conclude, the role of NGOs, has emerged to address the issues of environmental management in varied industrial areas, is a development of recent origin, not only in India but also in other countries. In India, most of the NGOs are partners in development rather than to serve as the watchdogs. Industrial symbiosis has emerged in industrial areas, in regions like Thane-Belapur, Pimpri-Chinchwad and Patalganga, where inter-industry and industry-NGO co-operation has increased to a vast extent.

Despite all its merits, the role of NGOs is questionable. NGOs are so diverse and controversial that it is not possible to support, or oppose, all NGOs. They may claim to be the voice of the people and to have greater legitimacy than governments, but this may be a plausible claim, only under authoritarian governments. Often, NGOs address environmental and developmental issues from an emotional rather than an informed view. The weakness in NGOs approaches, arise because of lack of scientific and technical perspectives. One main deficiency, which persists in entire environmental movement, is the lack of *scientific inquiry*. NGOs lack scientific capacity and technical know-how to understand industrial ecology. Also, industries and Pollution Control Boards make little effort to publicize their Environmental Impact Assessments—EIAs, project plans and environmental reports, which make the role of NGOs suspicious. State Pollution Control Boards—SPCBs too, lack technical staff and facilities to assess each project and industry. Despite, tremendous demonstration capacity of NGOs to perform well, their increasing organizational power, has exposed them to heightened criticisms. However, some of them are justified. One recent study on NGOs in Bosnia, playing a major role of peace-building is criticized because of their misuse as advertising agency, such as signboards of T-shirts. Such misuse, as the study has noted, is for a maligned purpose of denigrating local rebuilding efforts. Questions are also being raised that where the NGOs actually put their money? According to a popular daily newspaper of Rajasthan, 40% NGOs do not have the account of their money. Whereas, SOM Committee, a committee constituted for uniform tax policy, revealed that Central Government bears a loss of more than three thousand crores of rupees on account of tax exemption given to these NGOs. In the state of Rajasthan, 89 NGOs have been blacklisted on account of not repaying the loans, non-submission of accounts, and misappropriation of allotted money.[17] The latest report of year 2005 reveals that 295 of NGOs working in rural area blacklisted as they took funds from the government and failed to deliver on projects proposed by them.[17A] In Sudan and Somalia, NGOs have subsidized warring factions by making direct and indirect payments to gain access to areas, needing assistance. The UN High Commissioner for Refugees has already warned in 1996, that if national governments continue to blindly favour NGOs over multilateral agencies, in donor assistance, they may undermine important systems of coordination and cooperation in large-scale emergencies.

But to strike the balance, the record of such NGOs is certainly no worse, than that of governments. NGOs are aware of such weaknesses. They have started taking measures, therefore, to curb them by adopting codes of conduct and are pledging to "do no harm."[18]

Lastly, it is very heartening to note, that there are many NGOs, which are taking up the issue of environmental pollution, in general but rare of them are initiating to prevent and control the noise pollution, in particular. It is observed that instead of active action plan, the NGOs are limiting themselves only to the delivery of lectures on noise pollution. Whereas, it is proven fact, that noise pollution is in no way less hazardous, than other kinds of pollutions. Therefore, every NGO needs to be appealed, to take up the noise pollution on equal footing, with other pollutions.

Duties of Citizens and the Environment

According to Salmond: "A duty is an obligatory act. That is to say, it is an act opposite of which would be wrong. Duties and wrongs are co-relatives. The commission of a wrong is the breach of a duty and the performance of a duty is the avoidance of wrong."[19] It is a debatable question whether rights and duties are necessarily co-relative. According to one view, every right has a corresponding duty. Therefore, there can be no duty unless there is someone to whom it is due. There can be no right without a corresponding duty or a duty without a corresponding right. Author is also of the view, that as there can be no husband without a wife or a father without a child, similarly there can be no right without its corresponding duty and right to have clean environment is no bar to it. If some one has a right to live in unpolluted and peaceful environment, another is under duty, not to pollute or to make it noisy. If some one has right to sleep, others have a corresponding duty not to cause noise and disturb his sleep. Here, it may be concluded that if everyone becomes duty-conscious sincerely, no one shall have to fight for his rights, because it will automatically come to him in the form of other's duty.

Duties are of two kinds. One is legal and moral is another. Legal duty is commanded by the law to be performed. Moral duty is dictated either by the internal compulsions from consciousness or from the expectations of the society, we live in. It is, therefore, 'to protect and improve the environment is the duty cast upon the citizens by the Indian Constitution under Article 51A(g). Environmental laws cast a legal duty upon everyone not to pollute environment. But the moral duty comes from the society or from within, therefore, it needs to educate the people to make them aware about their moral duty for keeping the environment clean or raising the awareness about the health hazards of environmental pollutions. And such a duty is not cast by any statute, but is the moral duty of every citizen. In *L.K. Koolwal's case*, unsatisfactory sanitary conditions, were challenged. The High Court of Rajasthan held that Art. 51A of the Constitution casts a duty on citizens to maintain a clean environment. It also creates a right in the favour of petitioner to move the court to see that the state performs its duties.[20]

Clean Environment: A Neglected Human Right and Citizen's Ignored Duty

Man lives in environment around him and the right to have clean surrounding, free from pollution, dirt and squalor is the birth right of all human beings. But unfortunately, those who clamor for human rights seldom have paid attention to the need for environmental protection. The human rights, we talk about nowadays are mainly political and social rights. Right to live in to unpolluted environment has yet to find a place even amongst the Universal Declaration of Human Rights (UDHR). It is noted that the UDHR was formulated in 1948 and in those days the adverse impact of environmental harm was not of much felt. Industrialization and development of economy only were the prime concern of the nations. In the quest for economic development, environmental protection was relegated to a place from where it was viewed only as a matter of neglected importance or as a mere duty of poets and writers to advocate. Today's citizen is mostly running behind technological development and modernized industrialization, desiring for economic liberty, but he is unaware that the ill-effects of industrialization on the nature do not confine to the places of their origin, but transcend the national boundaries. The acid filled clouds, generated by the British and European industries, traveled far towards the northern hemisphere and caused acid rains in the Scandinavian countries. The victimized countries voiced their concern against the destruction of forests and aquatic lives due to such acid rain. Because of their efforts, that the first UN Conference on Human Environment could be convened at Stockholm in 1972.

However, the international instruments pertaining to human environmental rights during Pre-Stockholm era, were confined to the right to life of human beings. The UN Convention on Civil and Political Rights (1966) provided that "every human being has the inherent right to life." The UN Covenant on Economic, Social and Cultural Rights (1966) guarantees the rights to "a satisfactory standard of living" and to enjoy "the highest attainable standard of health." In the wake of growing concern for environmental protection, the later international agreements began to give increasing importance to environment. All these provisions required interpretation in such a way as to make them appear to have some semblance of the right for a clean environment.

Clean environment as the right of human beings finds now a place in some regional treaties. Art. 24 of the African Charter on Human and People's Right (1981) expressly provided that "all people have the right to a general satisfactory environment, favourable to their development." Art. 11 of the Protocol of San Salvador to the American Convention on Human Rights provides individual human right "to live in a healthy environment," which is not in force now. Another global convention too expressly acknowledges the health hazards environmental pollution. Art. 24 of the Convention on the Rights of the Child (1989) recognizes the "right to combat disease . . . took into account, the dangers and risks of environmental pollution."

A very important and historical petition was filed before the Supreme Court of Filipinos on behalf of some school children against the excessive logging in that country. Their contention was that they are being deprived of the right to enjoy the benefits from the trees, as the future citizens. The Supreme Court in a ground breaking judgment in that case, popularly known as the *OPPOSA decision*, held that state owes a duty to the present generation to preserve the environment from deterioration due to excessive and mindless exploitation of the same and that the future generation has a right to have the present environment protected for the posterity. The court applying the principles of intergenerational equity allowed the case of the school children and prohibited the logging operations.

Though, several nations have also recognized the need for environmental protection in their Constitutions. Some countries including Spain, Portugal, Turkey, Slovakia, Slovenia, Hungary, Poland and South Africa have explicit provisions for environmental rights. But, the countries like Germany, Netherlands, Greece, Sweden, India, some African and Arab countries recognize only the environmental duties. In India, the newly incorporated Art. 51A recognizes the environmental protection as a fundamental duty. It says that:

> "It shall be the duty of every citizens of India to protect and improve the natural environment including forests, lakes, rivers and wild life, and to have compassion for living creatures.

The Indian Constitution, therefore, categorically and specifically mandates that the citizens have a responsibility to "protect and improve the natural environment including forests, lake, rivers and wildlife, and to have compassion for living creatures." Further, Art. 48A added to the Directive Principles of State Policy, declaring that the State shall endeavor to protect and improve the environment and to safeguard the forests and wildlife of the country. The above provisions are enforced by the Indian Courts in their totality while deciding many cases on environmental matters.

It is heartening to note that despite the introduction of above clear cut Articles, i.e. Articles 48A, 51A, and the Article 32 which provides remedy to enforce these rights, remained as dead letters for about the next 15 years from their inclusion in the Constitution in 1976.

Environmental Rights—The Administrators' Abhorrence Duty

Giving full recognition to the environmental human right is still a dilemma for the policy-makers. One of the reasons for not giving full-fledged right to a clean environment is that the term 'environment' is very vague. Viewing from different perspectives, the term has different meanings. It takes in air, water, land, noise, bio-diversity, climate and even the natural surroundings of human and other life forms. It will be too difficult for the policy-makers and legislatures to adopt a comprehensive meaning of the term 'environment'. The imprecise nature of the term makes it difficult to enforce, if environmental right is given legal recognition.[21]

NOTES AND REFERENCES

1.   www.cbs.dk/departments/ikl/cbem.
2.   Dr. Veena Jha the project co-ordinator of UNCTAD (United Nations Conference on Trade and Development) in New Delhi affiliated to the International Trade Division of UNCTAD, Geneva. She has undertaken projects for many UN and bilateral agencies under various inter-agency co-operation frameworks of UNCTAD or as an independent consultant. She holds a doctorate in Economics from the Queen's College, University of London.
3.   Learning to Live with NGOs By P.J. Simmons.

4. UNESCO Encyclopaedia Article 1.44.3.7 Non-Governmental Organizations.

5. By Professor Peter Willetts, City University of London.

6. Baxi U. (1986), Activism at Cross-roads with Signposts, Social Action, Vol. 36.

7. Economic and Social Council of the United Nations: one of the 'principal organs' specified in the UN Charter and the body to which NGOs are accredited.

8. http://www.globalpolicy.org/visitctr/membersh.htm.

9. http://enfor.nic.in/divisions/c polls/c poll.html.

10. http://www.worldbank.org/search.htm.

11. http://www.oneworld.org/slefj/index.htm.

12. http://envfor.nic.in/

13. Environmental policies are enforced by the Pollution Control Boards, but in addition the Factories Act is enforced by factory enforcement agencies.

14. *Time of India*, Green Groups Mobilize Public Opinion, Nov. 24,1994, p. 7.

15. I. Mohan T. 1998, *Of Participatory Democracy, Public Hearings and Projects*, CAG Report, May-June 1998, Consumer Action Group, Chennai, India. Since amending the notification involves public participation, the Environment (Protection) Rules, 1986, were amended on 16 March, 1994 (for which no public participation is required) so as to do away with the process of public participation in formulating/amending notifications. Using this amendment to the Rules the Notification was amended.

16. MOEF 1997, The Gazette of India, *Extraordinary*, 10th April, 1997.

17. *Rajasthan Patrika*, 20 August, 2002.

17A. *Times of India*, New Delhi, February 20, 2005.

18. http://www.foreignpolicy.com.

19. V.D. Mahajan, *Jurisprudence & Legal Theory*, Vth edition, p. 283.

20. http://www.city.yokohama.ip/ne/info/generalE.htm.

21. http://www.nic.in/map/map.map.

Control of Noise Pollution: Constructive Suggestions

In nature, neither there are rewards nor punishments, but only the consequences. Violence begets violence. Nature obeys this principle.

The post-independent era has witnessed rapid industrial development due to the farsighted vision of the then Prime Minister Pt. Jawaharlal Nehru. Industrial development led to the growth of numerous urban centers. The cities became metropolis and small towns became big cities. New townships were developed near the places of industrial growth centers. Today, India ranks amongst the ten most industrialized nations of the world.[1]

Before 1972, environment was the exclusive preserve of sanitary engineers and health officers. But from 1972 onwards, the thinking changed and it was realized that to cater to the perpetuation of the living systems (including human kind) on this planet, conservation of life support system became more essential.

To save present and coming generations from extinction, now we have to solve three 'P's grave problems, namely, population, poverty and pollution. Environmental pollution is the gravest and most dangerous problem among all the three, like cancer, in which death is sure but slow, and therefore, it requires most urgent attention. Man's capacity to become master of his surroundings and his quest to enhance the quality of life, has caused incalculable harms to human beings and environment. Man has relentlessly explored the nature's resources but, his exploration can safely be termed as Ecocide. Our mad race for economic development through industrialization on the cost of environment would ultimately lead to disaster. If the present rate is not checked, the man will breathe, eat and see the pollution only.[1A]

1. NOISE POLLUTION

All of us, children and adults, are bombarded every day by various kinds of noises and sounds that have a deleterious effect on our brain. Whether in the classroom, office or living room, our ears and brain constantly have to work hard to tune out these sounds in order to focus on family, studies, or the task at hand. For sensitive children and adults, environmental noise pollution is a constant source of stress. Short of a threat, this disaster is certainly going to overtake the human race, if nothing is done to mitigate the malady of noise pollution. It is heartening and alarming that, nearly a quarter of the traffic police force, in the southern city of Bangalore, are suffering from hearing disabilities on account of multiplying noise pollution.[2]

Like air pollution, noise pollution also reduces rainfall. According to Robert Koch, a Noble prize-winner, German bacteriologist, "A day will come when man will have to fight with merciless noise as the worst enemy of health." According to him "noise like smog, has been a slow agent of death."

The importance of hearing power is known from the children, having hearing-disorders, constantly remind of the crucial importance of hearing. If no timely steps are taken, a significant percentage of future generations shall suffer from heavy hearing damage. It is horrible to imagine and predict, what will be the amount of total loss to whole human population. Colavita was unable to find a single student among the university students in his classes, who could hear a sound of

20 kHz, whereas, 20 kHz is an audible frequency, according to classical results drawn by Fletcher and Munson.[3]

At least 11 million children of the world die every year, on account of poisons in their homes, in the form of contaminated drinking water, polluted air and noisy environment, which is definitely avoidable. International study of pollution in cities, reveals that New Delhi is one of the world's most polluted 15 cities and of Asia's 13 such cities. Report 2002 reveals that tuberculosis and disease of the respiratory tract cause the highest number of deaths and a good percentage of it is due to the environmental pollution.[4]

Not immediately visible but the consequences of noise pollution are definite, leading to deafness, poor concentration, irritation, nervousness, aggressive social behaviour, anxiety, heart diseases and high blood pressure are recorded, which develop at the later stage. Consequently, further it leads to the temporary or permanent elimination of the workforce through sick leave or early retirement, and as a consequence, the nation suffers a great economic loss.[5]

On the basis of medical reports, court observed that noise pollution causes interruption of sleep, loss of efficiency, hearing loss or deafness, high blood pressure, depression, irritability, fatigue, a gastrointestinal problems, allergy, distraction, mental stress and annoyance. It does not spare the animals, birds, plants, and wildlife also. The extent of damage depends upon and is in proportion to the duration and the intensity of noise. Sometimes it leads to serious law and order problem. It is revealed by Dr. Lester Sontag of the Fells Research Institute in Yellow Springs Ohio, that high noise can quicken a human foetus, heart rating and causes the muscles to contract. If, the injurious effects of noise tend to persist for longer period, it causes stable mal- adoptive reactions in individual, disturbing thereby his total personality make up. The lowered performance level in children, develops a feeling of inadequacy, lack of confidence, poor perception of one's own self.

Even the buildings and properties do not remain unaffected by noise pollution. Concord, supersonic jet aircraft of British Airways, produces so high noise that it cracked the structure of aircraft itself and hence its flight over India, is not permitted. Its sound caused the cracks into the glasses of buildings at Mumbai

International Airport, during its test flight. The flight of this 1000-seated aircraft having from London to Singapore, was diverted over Hind-Mahasager, in place of Indian air space. In New York also, it is permitted to land only from Sea end of the runway.[6]

About the health hazards of airport noise, in a study in UK, at Heathrow airport, it was found that there were more number of mental patients in comparison to other socially similar but quieter places. Similar was revealed in a social survey conducted at Palam airport in Delhi.[7]

Empirical researches conducted on pregnant female mice, reveal that aircraft's taking off which brings in 120-150 dB of noise levels has caused miscarriages in them. Several birds have been observed to stop laying eggs. If the rule of generality is applied, high noise is capable to create these disturbances in human beings also.

It is a matter of concern that only little can be done about this, national defence, which even in peacetime will always take priority. However, international standard applicable to air industry can be adopted for the transport aircraft at this moment and for new fighter aircraft coming into existence. Therefore, Aircraft Act, 1934 requires an amendment.

High noise levels are common in industries such as petrochemicals, steel, thermal power stations, etc. Some industrial installations produce such a high intensity of sound that an ordinary human being cannot bear it, even for a few moments, without the help of ear protecting device. Generators cause this much high noise that everyone suffers numbness in his ears, when he enters the power station generator rooms. It has been found that maximum of the operators/farmers are not aware that they are working in health hazardous noisy environment. If asked, they say that the particular equipment emits slight more sound but they do not deem it as noise pollution.

During my survey visit in the North Eastern part of India, I noted that the major source of noise in this part of country is only 'traffic noise'. The noise proves to be non-sensical, when miscreants intentionally cause it by removing silencers from their vehicles. Fitment of horn system in the vehicle is very important for the purpose of road safety, but the indiscriminate use of unauthorized types of horns, producing funny sounds like that of siren, singing, child laughing or weeping, becomes the cause of many road accidents, in addition to the noise nuisance. However, Motor Vehicle Act, 1939 and some state's Vehicles Acts, prohibits such act, but who bothers, if not checked. Sometimes, the court has to issue appropriate and elaborate directions to enforce the provisions of such laws.

Railway industry is also not less noisy and decibels are very high in its yards, generator set rooms and engines. Whereas, Railway Act, 1889 is silent on this account and hence required an amendment accordingly. Indian Railway Budget, each year, has a unique feature of increasing number of trains, route extensions, and the cycles of trains on the same limited tracks, with almost no effort to quieting of the trains and the tracks on which they run with high speed. The Metro Rail plan in Delhi, need to be planned noise resistive, otherwise it would add another fuel to the fire and shall add high number of decibels

2. DIRE NEED OF SUSTAINABLE DEVELOPMENT

In the process of development, through which India is passing is to achieve desired socio-economic development, safeguard of the environment, and maintaining of good living conditions. Development mania and economic gains have forced everyone to become more and more rich, be it at the cost of environment, into which everyone has to breathe to remain alive.

To meet the needs of future depends upon the fact that, how well we balance our social, economic, and environmental objectives, while making today's decisions. Therefore, there is a need to balance all social, economic, and environmental objectives in the short-term, so as to sustain our development in the long-term.[8]

Former Prime Minister of Britain, Margaret Thatcher had observed, "if every government espouses the concept of sustainable economic development, stable prosperity can be achieved throughout the world, provided the environment is nurtured and safeguarded."[9]

It is evident that major challenge is not just finding a site for an industry or a developmental activity, but is to find out a solution for achieving sustainable development. Apart from the need of environmental education, based on sustainable development and spatial planning, there is a need to encourage scientists, industrialists, engineers, designers and the general public, by way of incentives, tax rebates, easy finances, etc. to use eco-friendly machineries and tools of management.

3. CONTROL THROUGH LAW

In independent India, various legal measures have been taken to protect and improve the environment. Besides the constitutional provisions, a survey of these Indian laws reveals that these numerous enactments passed, either by the central or the state legislators, have not been able to check environmental degradation and eco-system imbalances. Courts in India have played a pivotal role and created an environmental jurisprudence, which seek to strike a balance between environmental protection and the sustainable development. Lawmakers, lack sufficient awareness of environmental problems, which restricts formulation of comprehensive legislation on environment.[10]

In most of the developed countries, specific legislations have been made and scientific methods have been invented to control noise pollution. For instance, "Noise Abatement Act, 1960 was the legislation in England to deal with the problem of noise pollution, which has been replaced with 'Control of Pollution Act, 1974."

However, creation of separate department of environment, followed by the formation of a new Ministry of Environment and Forest, and enactment of various laws on environment in India, shows encouraging efforts to protect and improve environment, but still, we are unable to control the menace of environmental noise pollution substantially.[11]

The study of different aspects of the noise pollution in Indian perspective and under legal systems of different countries reveal that the problem of noise in India is in no way lesser grave than that in any industrialized country. But, legislation on noise pollution in India, like other countries, is yet to be enacted. Consequently, the problem is rapidly growing all over the country. It is said that a stitch in time saves nine. Therefore, it is high time to strive and struggle against this most dreaded disease. We should not put off till tomorrow whatever we can do today.[11A] Krishna Iyer, J. rightly said, "The constitution commands us, the law forbids, let us by nature, be patriots. Regulatory legislation to control environmental pollution is a must, since the rule of the law must define the rules of life and life will survive only if the biosphere is safe.[12]

Where the question of noise pollution is concerned, even old weapons can be put to new uses and the law of nuisance is one of them. The action for nuisance is the oldest action controlling the noise pollution[13] such as in *Messers Dutta Mal Chiranji Lal* Vs. *L. Ladli Prasad and Others*, noise and vibrations, by running of a mill, causing inconveniences and serious discomforts to the plaintiff and the residents thereof, was considered to amount private nuisance and hence could not be permitted.[14]

In *Kishorimal Bishambar Dayal* Vs. *State*,[15] the penal action was initiated u/s 290 of IPC for causing the noise and vibration by operating heavy machinery in the residential area. Also the same action was taken u/s 290 IPC, for causing noise by paddy husking machine at night.

Although, the noise causing trivial harms like loud sound of radio, has not been taken as a nuisance by the courts because a person of ordinary temper and sense will hardly complain for such disturbing noises. Therefore, the court refused to give remedy in such cases. In *Ivour Hden's case*, the careful reading of section 95 of IPC during this study has shown that, only that harm is excused, which is not expected to be complained by the person of ordinary prudence.

Examined critically, this decision of the court seems to be erroneous and invites a fresh look, because the playing of radio at a moderate volume may be tolerable but not at a high pitched frequency, which is certainly objectionable by the man of ordinary prudence. Specially, if the affected person is busy with any mental work, such noise is definitely very offending to him.

No doubt, Motor Vehicle Act, 1939 provides certain restrictions on the use of horns and there is a provision for the fitment of silencers on every motor vehicle. But, this Act does not prescribe noise-limits, caused by particular vehicle.

4. LAW ENFORCEMENT

No doubt legislation is one of the major and the most

effective measures of control. Letters of the law become meaningful only when they are enforced in their spirit and letter, which consequently generates public opinion and sensitizes them for obedience. The illustration is not far to seek. The rules of the road regarding drivers of two-wheelers, to wear crash helmet, were in existence for a long time, but were not sincerely enforced so far in Jodhpur city. Only a few months before city police administration became very particular to enforce the said rule in the city of Jodhpur. Now, the citizens have also become aware of the rules and sincerely obeying them. Therefore, sincere enforcement has always fostered sensible public opinion. It proves that law in action sensitized the citizens to obey. However, now the Delhi Government decided to purchase remote sensing devices capable of noting pollution level of a moving vehicle.[15A] Also, the Delhi Government declared that the polluting vehicles which do not confirm to Euro-II norms was to be banned from entering the capital with effect from February 2005. All vehicles, be it an inter-state bus run by a neighbouring state, trucks, call centre cabs, three-wheeler commercial transporters, two-wheelers or personal transport were to be made liable for inspection. But, nothing so seems to be in reality for Delhi as nowhere such inspections are seen.

5. IMPEDIMENTS IN ENFORCEMENT

(a) Overloading of Enforcement Machinery

Overloading of statutory authorities results in non-performance or mal-performance of statutory tasks. For example, it has been observed during survey, that the Boards set-up for implementing the provisions of Water Pollution Act, have also been assigned the task to enforce the provisions of Air Pollution Act, placing no additional resources and expertise. Now, the same overloaded Boards have been assigned with the duty to monitor the noise levels also. The same stands true in case of other enforcement agencies.

(b) Reluctances

In persuasion with the court directives, police administrations has opened separate cell to control noise pollution. But, the cells are slow in enforcement because they do not take noise pollution seriously and do not want to earn the wrath of the people.

(c) Scattered Law

There has been 'proliferation of legislation', on environment, particularly, the series of notifications issued under EPA. Moreover, the law on noise pollution is a scattered law in different statutes dealt by different authorities and failing to bring comprehensive achievement.

(d) Negligence to Law Bodies

When the law deals with highly technical matters, the colonial method of law-making ensures its failure from the moment of its birth. The matter of concern is that no law expert of the Law Commission of India has ever been consulted by any environmental law-making or law reform committee on the issue of drafting the text or amendment of law. Hence, law-making or law reform remains innocent of inputs arising from the operation of the Indian legal system as a whole.[16] If legislation is an important component of planning, and planning is intended to achieve results, then we must abandon the odd belief that the law is merely a technique, not relevant at the stage of policy formulation, which can be pressed into service at the level of converting the settled policy into a binding enactment. The law has its own resilient properties, which if not grasped and grappled with, at the policy-making stage, it will tend to defeat the goal. At the stage of formulation of policies of development, a total neglect of law experts and lawyers results often in enacting a weak law lacking force of enforcement, which fails to raise public awareness to obey.

(e) Quality of the Law

The study reveals that for want of quality in law, even comprehensive, integrated, and up-to-date code is not enough to prevent and control noise pollution but only partially or partly solves the problem. The phrase 'quality of law' refers to many aspects, as under:

> (i) Does the law communicate, the desired message to the addressees?

(ii) Does it clearly define rights, privileges, powers and immunities of various agencies of the government and the individual?

(iii) Is its management of sanctions, both positive and the negative (that is rewards, incentives, tax rebate or punishments), are adequate to attain the purpose of law according to Bentham's pain and pleasure theory and Austine's theory of sanction behind law?

(iv) Is the law catering the society into right direction?

(v) Is the structure of adjudication or settlement of disputes, efficient, fair, and sensitive?

(vi) Does it create desired awareness among public.

These questions are important, not just from the standpoint of sociology of law, but they are quite crucial from the technocratic perspectives of environmental noise management and sustainable development.

6. CONFLICT BETWEEN RIGHT TO ENVIRONMENT AND RIGHT TO ECONOMIC DEVELOPMENT

It is very easy to propagate the noise free environment as an essential human right, but the difficulty arises when this right comes in conflict with the right to economic development. Every one is behind economic liberty, let be it, at the stake of his own health, without accepting sensible limits as for whom, he is attempting to amass wealth, which shall remain unused and un-enjoyable in a poisonous environment, caused by himself in the process of collecting unbound wealth.

It is the quest of economic development only that a person of industrialized countries uses the energy, 15 times more than a person of developing countries. Likewise, there are 405 cars per thousand population in developed nations, whereas this figure is only 5 in developing countries. It shows the intensity of pollutants in the environment of developed countries. In Kyoto Conference, an accord was reached that US will cut 5% in the emissions of green house gases between 2008 to 2012, from the level of 1990. But, US has already rejected this accord. It shows that the industrialized countries are causing more pollution, but are less serious about it.[17]

7. JUDICIAL TRENDS NEEDS DYNAMICITY

Judiciary can also play a vital role in the growth and development of the environmental law and provides the flesh to bare skeleton of the law. It is also to be noted, that in case if the state or citizen, either do not perform their duties or because of the law's silence on the point, continues to deteriorate the environment, then our well matured and conscious judiciary *suo-moto* or otherwise, can contribute a lot in this direction. Although, courts under Art. 51 directed the Government to ask all media to raise public awareness by way of advertisement slides, programs, seminars, etc. The attitude of Judiciary towards noise nuisance is still lukewarm. The courts ordinarily admit the defence of accused for the enjoyment of their legal and fundamental rights. The judges are not fully aware of its health hazards. Courts, usually, take it very lightly. The courts generally did not regard noise as public nuisance, unless it affected the whole locality or individual in specific worth damages. For instance in a case, *Health* Vs. *Mayor of Brighton*,[18] the court refused to grant injunction against a noise causing annoyance and irritation emerging from defendant's power station and observed that the noise did not cause annoyance to any other person, but the incumbent.

The concept of *locus standi* prior to post-emergency era was too narrow to bring forth the diffused rights such as right to noise free environment. The public, officials, and even the judiciary took the water and air pollution on priority than the noise. But, in the post-emergency era of PIL, judicial activism, and the liberal view of concept of *locus standi* have sown new seeds, and have made it easy to protect and improve environment through law courts, to make it worth for peaceful living. It is appreciable that our activist judges of dynamic judiciary have started interpreting the environmental laws into the felt necessities, i.e. in favour of nature and public green good.

(a) Milestone Decisions to be followed

The court himself has been the captive audience of noise pollution and in *M.S. Appa Rao* Vs. *The Government of Tamilnadu and Others*[19] observed:

"In fact, this court has often been the victim of noise

pollution. If we can put it mildly, it would be practically impossible to hear the arguments of the counsels. For example, on the 30th ultimo, which supposed to be a 'Sarvodaya Day' or Martyrs' Day', when the whole nation is supposed to pay homage to its Father, the authorities concerned had permitted public agitation by Bank employees on the public road abutting the High Court compound, who were using loudspeakers and sound amplifiers without any restriction for over five hours continuously, during the court working hours. We were somewhat surprised, if not shocked, that the concerned authorities were not aware of a notification issued under sections 6 and 25 of EPA, 1986, by the Ministry of Environment and Forest, New Delhi in 1989,[19A] prescribing ambient air quality standards in respect of noise with regard to different categories of areas, classified as industrial area, commercial area, residential area and the silence zone.

In another case *Jacob* Vs. *The Supdt. of Police*,[20] it was observed that no one has a right to trespass on the mind or ear of another and commit auricular or visual aggression. Hence, limits must be drawn for liberties, lest they turn into licence and the antithesis of liberty in its true sense.

In US case, *Frisby* Vs. *Schultz*, the court emphasized on the importance of right of privacy and said that individuals are not required to welcome unwanted speech into their own homes and the government may protect the said freedom.

In *Election Commission of India* Vs. *All India Dravida Munetra Kazkhgam and Others*,[21] the court took the cognizance of noise nuisance and upheld the ban, imposed by Election Commission under Art. 324 for the use of loudspeakers, mounted on mobile vehicles for the election campaigns. However, exemption given to the Chief Minister of the state does not seem proper. Because, the noise pollution is equally hazardous to the health and is inconvenient to the public, whether it is caused by the chief minister or by an ordinary citizen.

In a recent case, *Church of God* Vs. *KRK Majestic Welfare Association*, the apex court has clearly ruled, that to pray with loudspeakers is not a fundamental right under Article 25 of the Constitution.[22]

In RE: Noise Pollution, the Supreme Court has observed various aspects, causes and evils of Noise Pollution in India. In this case not only the love to noise free environment has been shown but also the court has judiciously balanced the fundamental rights of a man with his right to healthy environment.[22A]

The court has also removed difficulties of state governments in implementing noise rules, 2000. For instance, the Supreme Court has laid down the guidelines for states to follow regarding the relaxation in use of loudspeakers at some occasions.

(b) Exceptions Be Not Allowed

To quote a few exceptions, wherein courts and citizens are not serious to make environment, noise free and worth-living. Their lack of knowledge about the noise hazards, unawareness and also ignorance of provisions of law and penalty, keeps them effortless in curbing noise pollution. There are more than 200 laws, enacted by state and centre in India, which pertain to environment. But many of them are not known, even to the judges and lawyers, and consequently they fail to understand environment in proper perspective.[23] The ordinary legal remedies, provided by law courts, are absolutely inadequate to meet the growing needs for effective control over noise pollution. Tort remedies under the law of nuisance and outdated municipal laws are significantly insufficient to provide safeguards to protect individual rights, public health and safety against the inroads of noise pollution.

The efforts of executive and judiciary are of little help and cannot break a new ground, unless individual outlook changes by conviction. Hence, unless the individual is fully informed and realizes that unwanted noise is equally serious threat to health as much as the polluted water or air is. The law alone cannot control the noise malady. Individual has to be educated upon that noise is not just an unpleasant irritant to be tolerated and ignored, but is a serious health hazard and one may has to pay price of his blind race for development. The psychology of the individual need be changed. Public pressure could be a very effective catalyst for securing special legal regulation of specific noise producing sources.

8. LAW TO RAISE PUBLIC AWARENESS

We lack awareness, in spite of the fact that we have knowledge about many things in general, and about specific in particular. But, without awareness we hardly undertake any action. Mere acquisition of knowledge is not enough and does not mean that one shall definitely transform such knowledge into action. For illustration, everyone knows that if one is exposed to high noise, his hearing power is most likely to be impaired and his personality becomes deficient. But still, one is hardly serious towards such loss and does not adopt preventive measures. It is not knowledge, but the right education in right direction, which prompts a person to take action.

In all countries world over, environmental education is provided by the state, free of costs. First, to individuals; second, groups; and third, to general public, through mass media of communication. An in-depth study of the literature also reveals, that even the environmentalist are not attaching due emphasis, on awareness against noise pollution. No attention is being paid to impart such education to the children at school level, and thus, 42% of total population remains ignorant, below the age of 15. If environmental education is imparted to this major group of children, it will certainly be result-oriented. An appreciable step, which has been taken by the police of Rajasthan state is worthy of mention, which has taken keen interest in imparting knowledge of traffic rules, by taking periods in schools, which definitely needs extension followed by other states of the country. Today, the availability of books on environment in the educational institutions is the outcome of court's directive to introduce environmental education as a subject to be taught in first ten classes. Not only this, court also directed the central and state governments to get the text books on environment and get them distributed in Educational institutions free of cost.[24]

The Court has warned that, every citizen, every son of the soil of India, i.e. Bharat, whether he is a tiller, blacksmith, goldsmith, cobbler, industrialist, labour, worker, a peasant, farmer or a land-owner, educated or uneducated, male or female, rich or poor or of any caste or religion has to understand the value of clean environment and hence should protect it as part of his duty for his own as well as others' survival. The ecology is a *sine qua non* to the survival of mankind on the pious planet earth and if it is not done, he will dig his own grave which will be a suicidal attempt with almost no rather nil chance of his survival.[25] Law not only imposes the sanctions, according to John Austin, but compels one to come into action as a results of pain pleasure theory of jurisprudence as propounded by Bentham. Traffic noise is controlled in Japan by such nature of the road traffic law and safety standards of vehicles for road transportation. Thus, it is the law which undoubtedly, is capable to raise not only the awareness but also, brings into action, be it the enforcement machinery, government, public, private, or the citizens.

But, there is a general feeling, even among the educated citizens that anti-pollution programme is the headache for governments or the industrialists. In 1983, when the public awareness on noise pollution in India was almost negligible, in Japan, the percentage of complaints against the noise was 32.7% of the total complaints on environment.

However, the case of *M.S. Appa Rao* Vs. *The Government of Tamilnadu and Others* is the blaring example, which shows the awareness of public against the noise pollution. The first Writ Petition of its own kind was, for issuing of a *mandamus*, directing the State Government to impose strict conditions for obtaining licence, for the use of amplifiers and loudspeakers under Secs. 41 and 71-A of Madras City Police Act, 1888 and Sec. 10 of Madras Towns Nuisance Act, 1889. It was to ensure that the licences do not violate the conditions thus imposed, and do not cause noise pollution.

It is also imperative that there should be a genuine public participation in decision-making bodies, concerning to environment. The citizens can play crucial role in the form of people's movement, in order to protect the environment. This social obligation has to be discharged by every citizens and has been emphasized upon by the court on everyone through *Rural Litigation Entitlement Kendra* Vs. *State of U.P.*[26]

9. INTERNATIONAL SCENARIO: EFFORTS OF DIFFERENT COUNTRIES TO BE APPRECIATED

International concern toward the deterioration of environment may be recorded from the fact, that world bodies had to think for compensating Malaysia, but not to allow cutting of forests in any case, which was not destructive to Malaysia only, but also had its impact over the environment of whole cosmos.[27] It proves that the problem of environmental pollution is of no continent, no hemisphere, no race, no system or no individual, but is a collective and joint problem of entire world. Realizing this collective and joint responsibility, UN had to hold a Conference on Human Environment, in June 1972 at Stockholm.

Following the Stockholm Conference, many countries developed a substantial body of environmental law and regulations, dealing with the protection of the environment and the management of natural resources. In many South East Asian Nations, laws and regulations were revised, updated and expanded, to cover areas concerning pollution control. In Thailand, many environmental regulations were included in the Constitution of 1997 to make them more binding, and easier to implement.[28] Recent efforts of the Chinese government, to implement environmental laws and regulations, have culminated in a comprehensive Environmental Protection Law, which focuses mainly on its implementation and enforcement. The law defines accountability, legal responsibility, and imposes sanctions for non-compliance. Growing numbers of environmental professionals are now also employed in both, the state and the private industrial sectors.

Laws and institutions dealing with New Zealand's environment were reduced in number and were ma 'e more coherent. Central government still has primary respons lity of environmental issues in national interest. Trade and investment has been the principal engine of economic growth but they have resulted in serious environmental degradation.

10. ECO-SYMPATHIES OF INDIAN CONSTITUTION

The original Chapter on Directive Principles in the Indian Constitution could indirectly locate the protection of environment in Art. 47, which cast a primary duty upon the state to improve public health along with raising the level of nutrition and standard of living of its people. It is the cardinal principles that a Constitution to be living, must be growing. However, in 1976 the specific provision have been included in the Constitution by

42nd Amendment, i.e. inclusion of Article 48A and Article 51A(g). Article 48 mandates that state shall endeavor to protect and improve the environment and to safeguard the forest and wild life of the country. Whereas, Art. 51(A)(g), imposes a fundamental duty upon every citizen of India to protect and improve the natural environment including forests, lakes, rivers and wild life, and to have compassion for living creatures. It has been well observed in *Kinkri Devi's case*, that these two Articles serve as constitutional pointer to both, the state as well as citizens, who have a constitutional duty, not only to protect the environment but also a step further, 'to improve', preserve and safeguard it in its natural form. But, our Constitution is silent as to what machinery shall be employed to enforce citizens' duty keeping environment natural. In spite of the fact that the state is empowered to invent any legislative or executive procedure or any other device of its own to enforce the duty of citizen, yet the state has not exercised its power.

It can be noted that in our Constitution, two anomalies still continue, which require to be urgently remedied, either through amendments or through judicial activism. The first anomaly is, that if the state fails in its obligatory duty to protect environment, citizen has no remedy against state inaction. The second is, that if the state is violator of environmental laws and causes the environment to deteriorate, then also the citizens has no remedy against the state.

The answer has probably been attempted by the judicial activism of Rajasthan High Court, in *L.K. Koolwal's* case by observing:

> "That Art. 51(A)(g) can ordinarily be called as the duty of citizens, but in fact, it is the 'right' of the citizens to move the court, to see that the state performs its obligatory and primary duties faithfully, in accordance with the law of the land. Omissions or commissions are to be brought to the notice of the court by the citizens."

Without stopping here, the Apex Court has gone further and has observed in Sachidanand's case that the ecological balance shall be maintained by the court, in spite of the fact, that such duty imposed on the government is merely a directive principle of state's policy, under Part IV of the Constitution and held:

"Whenever a problem of ecology is brought before the court, the court is bound to bear in mind Art. 48(A) of the Constitution, which directly deals with the protection and improvement of the environment."

11. FUNDAMENTAL RIGHT TO INCLUDE POLLUTION FREE ENVIRONMENT SPECIFICALLY

The Constitution of India, through Preamble, ensures to secure justice to all its citizens, social, economic, and political. Every one has, therefore, a fundamental right to get social justice. To provide pollution-free environment is also a part of social justice without which, the survival of mankind would be too difficult. Thus, right to health becomes primary to all the fundamental rights *vis-à-vis*, right to equality, freedom; religion becomes dependent upon it. Hence, by a new amendment in Part III, it becomes imperative to incorporate the fundamental right, not only the right to health but also right to healthy environment and in turn right to noiseless environment, calm and peaceful.

12. FREEDOMS UNDER ART. 19 NOT TO CAUSE NOISE POLLUTION

The dynamic Judiciary declared public interest to be on priority, than the individual freedom of making noise. The court said that it is erroneous to bring unrestricted freedom, causing pollution within the ambit of Art. 19. Being custodian of the Constitution, the conscious judiciary had gone up to the extent of closing down the sources of environmental noise, e.g. industries causing pollution in spite of the fact that such entrepreneurs were a strong revenue source for the nation as well as national development. However, in few instances, individual could succeed to satisfy the judiciary, to prefer their individual rights to the public right to health and *Ivour Hyden's* case is one of those in which the High Court excused the act of playing radio on loud voice, being the act of trivial nature.

Again on the contrary, *D. Anant Prabhu* Vs. *The District Collector, Ernakulam and Others,*[29] is the case in which court held:

". . . the right, guaranteed by Art. 19(1)(a) is not merely a right to express and propagate one's views, but includes in it, the right to circulate one's views to others by all such means as are available to the citizens to make known them with their views. Under the circumstances, in our judgment, any legislation or order, which puts a ban on the use of a loudspeaker, which helps the citizens in circulating his views, to as large audience as he can, will be a *prima-facie* infringement of his fundamental right to freedom of speech and expression unless the infringement is justified by clause (2) of Art. 19."

This judicial precedent seems to be erroneous, if not reviewed, it will not only give green signal but will encourage the persons to use loudspeaker let be it indiscriminate. Whereas, in United States also, the US Supreme Court has opined that the restriction on use of loudspeakers was against the right to freedom of speach. But in its later decision in a case, it changed its view and held that reasonable restriction on amplifier does not violate constitutional rights of speech.

13. PRIORITY OF RIGHT TO HEALTHY ENVIRONMENT

Recently appointed, National Committee to Review the Working of the Constitution, in its consultation Paper (on the enlargement of fundamental rights), has proposed the right to a clean and healthy environment. In context of Part III of the Constitution, the main question, which may be raised that, whether it guarantees a fundamental right to a hygienic environment? If so, the next question emerges, where can it be located? Apt answer, to this question has been already answered by Hon'ble Justice Bhagwati, while delivering a historic judgment in Francis *Carolie Mullien* Vs. *Delhi Administration* for the import of the right to life:

"The right to life enshrined in Art. 21 can not be restricted to mere animal existence. It means something more than just physical survival. The right to life includes the 'right to live with human dignity' and all that goes along with it, namely, the bare necessities of life such as adequate nutrition, clothing and shelter over head."

The Supreme Court of Inida is the first Court in the world, to evolve and develop the concept of right to "healthy environment" as a fundamental right. *Bandhua Mukti Morcha* Vs. *Union of India*[30] is the case wherein it was held that any act of endangering the environment, is, therefore, clearly an act of aggression upon the right to life itself. It has been further held, that right to healthy environment is an obligation on state under Arts. 21 and 47 both.[31] It is a matter of satisfaction, that many countries have now followed this path to protect and improve environment under this principle. For example, Supreme Court of South Africa adopted the same principle in its decision dated 27 June, 1996 in a case *Wildlife Society of Southern Africa* Vs. *Minister of Environmental Affairs and Tourism of the Republic of South Africa.* Subsequently, many nations have recognized, in their Constitutions, a right to healthy environment as a corollary duty to defend the environment.

14. RIGHT TO SLEEP: BE AN ATTRIBUTE OF RIGHT TO LIFE

Right to sound and peaceful sleep, right to breathe in free and fresh air, right to drink uncontaminated water, right to reside, work, walk and travel in noise free environment is guaranteed by Art. 21 to all the residents of India. In *Maulana Mufti Md. Syed Noorur Rahaman* Vs. *State of West Bengal*, the court has maintained that the right to leisure, right to remain silent, right to listen, right to rest, right to speak, right not to listen, right to read for examination, are within the ambit of Art. 21. The court, in *State of Himachal Pradesh* Vs. *Umed Ram Sharma*, has gone to the extent of saying, that right to easy access to road in hilly areas, is a fundamental right, covered under Art. 21. Right to life includes right to livelihood too.

15. LOUDSPEAKER NOISE: NO RIGHT TO RELIGION

India, being a secular country, the architects of its Constitution, drafted Art. 25, intending to make India really secular in its true sense by way of giving equal opportunity to each religion, to practice and propagate. But, indiscriminate use of loudspeakers in this behalf, has made the country noisier and is making life miserable. While propagating, the people could neglect the sentiments in their neighbourhood, causing much inconvenience to them. Loudspeakers with their high pitches and loud voices have become the associated part of religious ceremonies, of all religions. Though, the spiritual benefits of kirtan, prayers and mantras, may be good for the praying mind, and emotional heart, yet their loud voice may certainly cause disturbance to a student preparing for the exams, to ailing patients, sleep of the aged people and also those, who are not interested to listen such programme at the moments. Against the victimization by the indiscriminate use of loudspeakers for religious purposes, the High Court of Himachal Pradesh had to comment in *Yoginderlal* Vs. *Municipal Corporation, Shimla*:[32]

> ". . . that though the condition imposed on the use of loudspeakers are laudable indeed, they are mostly being observed in the breach. We may also record that in our court room many times, we have to stand the noise of the loudspeaker used by religious institutions, it appears that some religious institutions are bent upon insisting, the fear of God in the society by using loudspeakers, in such a way that these can be heard over the maximum people of the town. It seems that in their zeal, the religious institutions are following the principles of home delivery services."

However, in recent past some actions, including seizure of the noise-sources, other than the religious ones, have been taken against noise nuisance. But in case of religious noise, no one likes to earn the wrath of this sect, or even the God in turn. It is Indian judiciary, who came forward to protect the people from loudspeaker noise nuisance caused in the name religions. The following few instances are other evident to it.

Calcutta High Court not only banned the use of loudspeakers at all places of worship of all races, but imposed a penalty also and nearly, two dozen, Durgapuja, Kalipuja and Jagadhatripuja Committees of Calcutta, were charged with the contempt of court for violating the noise pollution.

Though, the law was present in the state to deal with such

noise, but no executive could ban such indiscriminate use of loudspeaker by religious sects. It is, undoubtedly, a good beginning, initiated in West Bengal, and is expected that it would gradually be extended to other states in the country.[33]

In case of *Masud Alam* Vs. *Commr. of Police*, it was held that the use of loudspeakers, causing disturbance in the area, can not be justified in the name of religious purposes and the ban on its use for giving 'Azan' was upheld. In this case, it was held that public cannot be made captive audience or listeners by the use of microphones, who are unwilling to bear the sound and/or music or the communication made by the loudspeakers. They are compelled to tolerate it at the cost of their health.

It was extended further and held, that a citizen's right to life includes, right to leisure, right to sleep, right not to hear, right to remain silent, right to read, right to speak with others, right to worship, right to meditation, right to live alone in peace and silence, and right to think any matter. But, the use of microphone certainly squeezes and steals away these rights of citizens. Further, the court viewed that the time has come, when everybody has to think, either to survive or to perish. If the noise pollution is not controlled, the human-being cannot lead a long life and survive in the long-run. One may like high sounds, but he has no right to take away or abridge the right of others. There is no religious freedom involved in this, which may not be subjected to public good.

It is not that the court has confined itself only against religious noise, but also came out against other noises also. For example, court took the cognizance against the noises created by vehicle horns, *Rahib Mukherjee* Vs. *State*[34] and *Nayan Behari Das* Vs. *State of Orissa*,[35] and noise caused by loudspeakers on the occasions of processions in *M.S. Appa Rao* Vs. *The Government of Tamilnadu and Others*.[36] Electioneering noise was taken up in *Election Commission of India* Vs. *All India Dravida Munetra Kazkhgam and Others* and advertisement's noise in *M.S. Appa Rao* Vs. *The Government of Tamilnadu and Others*.[37] Even the court has gone to the extent of raising awareness among the citizens against the noise, through its directions, and has directed the advertising agencies, to give wide publicity to the noise hazards and noise regulations.

There is still a host of decisions, under which the noise has been recognized as a dangerous pollutant to human health and therefore, the public should not be made captive-audience or forced listeners of it, by any sound magnifying devices, even with due prior permission of the authority, basing and arguing on their constitutional rights.

Recently, in a latest case *Church of God in India* Vs. *KKR Majestic Coloney Welfare Association*, the court has observed that the noise pollution in some areas of a city/town, might be exceeding permissible limits prescribed under the rules, but that would not be a ground, for permitting others to increase the same. Therefore, rules prescribing reasonable restrictions, including the rules for the use of loudspeakers and voice amplifiers, framed under the Madras Town Nuisance Act, 1889 and also the Noise Pollution (Regulation and Control) Rules, 2000, requires to be enforced strictly.

16. ROLE PLAYED BY PIL BE ENLARGED

It is PIL concept, which could bring out the various pollutants causing hazards to health and could force the executive and judiciary to look into the state of environmental noise pollution in the country. It would not be amazing or an exaggeration, if these prerogative writs are called by name 'legal Brahamastra' in 'PIL Tarkash' of judiciary. These writs are much contributory to maintaining the judiciary as the custodian of the Constitution and to bridge the gaps, left by executive. Justice Krishna Iyer opined that purpose of PIL concept is to 'wipe out every tear from every eye', and may be that tear on account of environmental noise pollution, a slow agent of unnatural deaths. It is true that PIL could raise consciousness and alertness, but much is yet need to be done, specially in the field of noise pollution.

In fact, it is we, who pollute the environment and it is we, who should protect and improve the same, without inviting any provision of law, or reminding ourselves our own duties. With little conviction, every citizen can do. It is always better to light own candle than to curse darkness and cry in wilderness.

However, taking wing on a request from the Apex court, made in December 2000, it has been reported[38] that the Law

Commission in India will be reviewing the whole range of environmental legislation for the object of consolidation and codification.

Need and call of the hour is that the Law Commissions must pay adequate attention on the malady of noise pollution in the country, consciously suggest and recommend, for a comprehensive code on this kind of pollution, because present noise rules at centre level, i.e. Noise Rules, 2000 are unable to bring down the noise levels in the country and to deal effectively with the noise polluters. Sanctions are to be registered and greater responsibilities are to be imposed on authorities to implement laws. Laws in action have to be legislated expeditiously to check impending harms to the mankind. Encouragement and incentives for promoting better environment, both amongst the rural and urban populace, would be a better substitute to the penal sanctions.

17. POPULATION CONTROL

India's population explosion is one of the main causes of environmental noise problem. The people in this sub-continent from Kashmir to Kanyakumari are struggling and toiling even for their existence. Every birth control measure will definitely be helpful in controlling noise pollution. It is evident and bitter hard, that in India mandatory sterilization method of birth control is not accepted, because the people are either ignorant or religious minded. But, on the pattern of China, the cut in facilities and restrictions on qualifications for higher service posts, or for contesting elections, on account of having the children more than two, may certainly be effective.

18. UNPLANNED URBANIZATION

The old saying that 'India resides in the villages' is being diluted, day-by-day, by the trend of more and more urbanization. The problem of urbanization is linked with this aspect of the problem. The more and more people are moving towards urban areas for economic reasons to seek employment for their existence, which has necessarily added fuel to the fire and have added to the problem of noise pollution and pollution of other kinds in overcrowded cities of the country. The problem is possible to be solved out by rapid development of villages/towns and by providing them those facilities, in want of which the people have to rush to the urban areas.

19. BACK TO BICYCLE-AGE IN JAPAN AND KOREA[39]

The destruction of Japan's infrastructure, during World War-II, forced citizens to employ non-motorized means of transportation. With renewed infrastructure in place, the Japanese were quick to reject bicycling and its post-war reconstruction connotations and took to riding busses, to and fro the railway stations. In course of time, the bus system also became overburdened and riders began to find the system inconvenient, expensive and slow. The increasing aversion against of bus travel and the surging environmental concerns, associated with motorized travel, initiated a shift in public opinion, once again in favour of bicycling and bike ownership. Cycling requires no fuel and the cyclists consume only 32 calories per mile compared to automobiles 1,800 cal/m demand. Cyclists' respiration contributes a scant 2 grams of carbon dioxide per passenger mile, while single-occupancy automobile emits carbon dioxide at the rate of 85 grams per mile. On the road, eight cyclists can occupy the space needed for one automobile and when stopped, twenty bikes can be parked where there is space for just one automobile. One more advantage of cycling, as a mode of transport is the effort towards curbing traffic noise pollution, as this mode of transportation causes almost no noise. From an energy, pollution and density standpoint, the bicycle is more efficient than any other mode of short-trip travel. The travel by cycle is not only in favour of environmental quality but is a measure towards keeping the health in good condition.

Urban planning encourages use of bicycle, by adopting traffic calming techniques to intentionally slow down and discourage automobile use. The consequences of the bicycle-intensive transportation system in Japan is favourable. Over 80% of Japanese households own at least one bike, and the national average is 1.42 bike per household. High non-motorized mode share has lowered Japanese per capita fuel consumption to 10% of Americans.

20. WEAPON'S NOISE BE CALMED

Weapon's noise comes generally from muzzle blast, is produced by propellant gas, bursting out of muzzle with bullet. According to its spectral characteristics and high sound pressure level, muzzle noise causes more severe injury to human body than steady noise. Typical sound pressure levels recorded from one of the armored fighting vehicle, are found to vary from 88 to 112.5 dB,[40] whereas these levels measured from several work places in any military workshop varies from 88 to 107 dB. It is a matter of concern that neither the Army Act, 1959, Nor Air Force Act, 1950 makes any provision for the control of noise caused by the weapons, vehicles, aircrafts or any other means.

A survey carried out in UK has estimated that 14% of the adult population was bothered by neighbourhood noise, compared with 11% from road traffic noise, and 7% bothered by aircraft noise. The sources of neighbourhood noise, in order of number of complaints, was Amplified music; barking of dogs; domestic activities; voices; car repairs; and 10% complaining about other noises.

21. PLANTING TREES

From a tree, which serves for 50 years, according to an estimate by a newspaper, we get:

The oxygen, worth Rs. 5.3 lakh;
The soil fertility, worth Rs. 6.4 lakh;
The soil conservation, worth Rs. 6.4 lakh;
The control of air pollution, including noise, worth Rs. 10.5 lakh; and
Protection to the wild life animals and birds and residence, worth Rs. 33 lakh.

Thus, in addition to fruits and flowers, we are benefited for more than 33 lakh in total from a tree. Hence, there is a great need not only to plant trees but also to maintain them.

But the national goal of greening the country is sleeping so badly that it might as well be junked. Planning Commission mandarines are understood to have veered around to the view that bringing 33% of the country under tree cover in seven years is not achievable and the target itself may need to be dropped. This view came up during the mid-term review of the 10th Plan. The latest estimates conclude that the country's forest and tree cover crosses 23% against national goal of 25% by 2007 and 33% by 2012.[40A]

22. CONSTRUCTIVE SUGGESTIONS

From more than two years in-depth study of noise pollution menace, in its all possible dimensions, directions, and the role of law to control it, and the conclusions arrived at, following few constructive suggestions emerged, are as under:

1. Felt Need of an Integrated and Comprehensive Code

An integrated and comprehensive code on noise pollution, which has already been delayed, is the urgent need of the hour and call of the time, in India. But, before such comprehensive legislation is contemplated, the government should appoint a full-fledged commission, to prepare a comprehensive programme and policy for its consideration. The state governments should also prepare a comprehensive anti-noise programme to be implemented at district and sub-divisional levels. There is a necessity to make the legislators and leaders of social and economic institutions, to think the scientific intricacies of noise pollution as well as the legal complications arising out of anti-noise legislation.

The new code must deal with all kinds of noise nuisance from all kinds of multifarious increasing sources. Human is to err but the err of past must be overcome with next available opportunity. Therefore, all the deficiencies or discrepancies left in the earlier concerned statutes such as Air Act, 1981, EPA, 1986, or Noise Rules, 2000, which have been discussed under the respective heads at appropriate place must be rectified now.

2. Enforcement of Law

In UK, USA and Japan 'theory of compensation' has been adopted in place of 'theory of injunction'. But, the Indian courts are still following the old theory of injunction and hence, noise polluters are violating noise rules and regulations conveniently.

This attitude of the court does not have deterring effect.

3. Evaluations or Scrutiny of Noise Assessment Report before Issue of NOC Clearance

There are several legal formalities to be completed before setting up an industry, as prescribed under the rules lay down by the ministry of industries and labour and many other bodies. Out of these, essential one to be complied is to produce a project report as to what impact in question industry is going to have on the environment in its vicinity, particularly the adverse effects of noise pollution. Although, such assessment report is produced, but unfortunately, neither the report is based upon expert opinion nor there are analysts, to evaluate the validity of such report. The same report goes to Indian Meteorological Department for approval. But again, there also, expert services are not available for right approval regarding noise pollution. As such, it remains a paper formality without practical implementation.

Therefore, it is suggested that expert's services must be made available to properly assess and approve the report, at every step. Although, the noise monitoring power has been assigned to Pollution Control Boards, but with no power to implement them, i.e. to punish the polluters causing noise, unlike in case of water and air pollution. The result is that the polluters who know this fact, hardly care for the authorities of the Board and hence, monitoring power remains a paper tiger.

The suggestions therefore are:

(i) The infrastructure and expert services must be made available with special reference to control industrial noise pollution.

(ii) The Boards must be empowered to punish polluters of industrial noise. Thus the Boards, which are otherwise dormant, shall have to be actively involved in controlling industrial noise.

(iii) Presently, the power to enforce noise standards lies with the District Collectors and Police Commissioners, who are otherwise busy in multifarious administrative activities. The consequence is that the sound pollution continues.

The suggestion, therefore is, that the power of Collectors and Commissioners regarding the traffic noise, be delegated to transport officers, who are the proper persons to administer traffic noise.

4. Concept of Decibel Limit

We have to accept the concept of 'decibel limit' to deal with the problem of noise pollution. Since the offence of noise pollution is subjective, because one's music may be pollution to others. Therefore, all the noise offences should be based on the concept of decibel, which will not only expedite trials in environmental cases, but will save the time and energy of judicial world. It will bring drastic drop in environmental litigations, because available executive remedies will be exhausted first.

The suggestion therefore is, that the court must follow the theory of compensation against noise nuisances by accepting the concept of decibel limit.

4A. The Department of Explosives should in public interest undertake necessary research activity for the purpose and come out with the chemical formulae for each firecracker. The Department shall at the time of giving the license for manufacturing a particular firecracker shall specify the ratio as well as the maximum permissible weight of every chemical used for the purpose.

5. Environmental Courts in all States at all Levels

Although environmental courts are being established in some states, but must be extended in all states at all levels, without further delay.

6. 'Green Interest Litigation' (GIL), New Name for PIL for Environment

All the writ petitions brought for the protection and improvement of the environment, may be addressed as *'Green Interest Litigation'* (GIL), so that court immediately come to know that it is PIL for environment and is to be exclusively dealt with by environmental courts.

7. Creation of Noise Complain Cells

In UK, noise complain cells are created, equipped with

telephone, in each district, police stations, and in big industries itself, such as airports. In New York, police is provided with portable noise level meters with automatic switches, which takes snaps as well as reading of the noise levels, of the vehicle, when it exceeds the noise limits.

The suggestion, therefore is, that the complaint cells like UK and noise level meters like in USA, must be taken use of, in India.

8. Amendment in Constitution

(i) New Article 21(A) should run in essence like this: "No person in India shall be deprived of his right to clean environment and right to sleep."

(ii) Noise pollution should be an exception to Art. 19(1) and may be added specifically to the list of reasonable restrictions under Art. 19 (2), because the defence taken by noise polluters is that to use loudspeakers is the part of their right to speech and expression and also the right to trade and business.

9. Amendment in Industrial Laws

Industrial laws are devoid of specific noise pollution control provisions, one could hardly locate it under Sec. 11 of Factories Act, 1948. Therefore, specific provisions should be incorporated in each industrial law so as to protect the health of persons working in such industries from noise pollution.

There should be a noise monitoring committee appointed in each industry and for this purpose, provision may be incorporated into Factories Act.

Public Liability Act, 1991

Public Liability Act, 1991 is the outcome of Bhopal Tragedy, which deals with the liability, arising from the harm caused only by hazardous substances. On being established, that the noise pollution is so hazardous to the health, that it confiscates one's hearing power and also captures his psycho-power, in absence of which one can hardly do anything, neither for himself nor for the nation. It is, therefore, recommended that noise should also be brought under the category of hazardous substance of the Act and the victims of noise, be provided relief accordingly including the relief from environmental relief fund, which has been established by an amendment to the Act in 1992.

10. Obligation on Industrialists

In order to control industrial noise, the following provisions should be incorporated in the Factories Act, 1948:

    (i) The duty of the factory owners, to undertake 'audible tests' of their workers in factories after every six months. ENT specialists should conduct such tests. For ensuring this, the Government in exercise of their power u/s 87(c) of the Factories Act, should frame appropriate rules.

    (ii) The workers in the factories should not only be provided with earmuffs but also needs its compliance in fact. The written instruction to this effect, alongwith the details of noise health hazards, in Hindi and English both, in addition to local language, if applicable, should be pasted at the conspicuous place and on the notice board.

    (iii) Permissible noise in industrial areas should be maintained strictly, for which enforcement cell should be created in each district.

    (iv) Additionally, SPCBs should be empowered to enforce the noise standards in industrial areas like under air and water Acts.

11. Public Awareness: Laid down in *M.C. Mehta* Vs. *UOI*, and RE: Noise Pollution Warrant Strict and Urgent Enforcement, which are:

(i) The State Governments and Union Territories will require, as a condition of licenses to all cinema halls, touring cinemas and video parlors, that at least two slides/messages provided by the Ministry of Environment, and which deal with environmental issues, will be shown free of cost as part of each show. Failure to comply with this order must be a ground for cancellation of a license.

(ii) The Ministry of Information and Broadcasting will start producing short films, dealing with the environmental pollution. One such film will be shown, as far as practicable, in one show every day by the cinema halls.

(iii) All India Radio and Dooradarshan will take steps to make and broadcast interesting programmes on the environment and pollution evils. The Attorney General has said that five to seven minutes can be devoted to these programs each day on these radio/TV stations.

(iv) The University Grants Commission will take appropriate steps to require universities to prescribe a course on the environment. They should consider making this course as a compulsory subject.

(v) As far as education up to the college level, every State Government and every Education Board is required to take steps to enforce compulsory education on the environment in a graded way. Strict compliance is required for the next academic year.

12. Awareness about Consumer Protection Laws

The low awareness of the consumers regarding Consumer Protection Act and consequent right to sue the noise polluter, is responsible for continuance of noise nuisance, in innumerable fields, e.g. traffic noise caused on account of old and technologically outdated vehicles.

The suggestion, therefore is, that the state, NGOs and public-spirited bodies not only in cities but also in towns and villages should make the consumers aware. Public should have the right to sue even against the Pollution Control Boards for the inaction on their part.

13. Environmental Law Reporter

Ministry of Environment and Forest must publish Environmental Law Reporter, and noise pollution laws, regulations must be made an integrated part of each issue under separate head.

14. International Ombudsman

All nations must seriously enact required new laws and vigorously enforce existing laws in their letter and spirit and create enforcement machinery for this purpose because environmental noise pollution is a problem of no nation, no hemisphere, no continent, but of the whole world. The possibility of establishing the office of an "International Ombudsman", to control noise pollution, cannot be ruled out.

15. Collection of Cess, from Noisy Industries

Rules must be framed and applied on industries causing noise, and cess must be imposed upon them, like those of The Water (Prevention and Control of Pollution) Cess Rules, 1978 framed under Water Act, 1974. The tax may be imposed even upon the activities, causing noises in fields other than industries. The amount collected through such cess must be invested upon developing new technology to bring noise levels down in industries and otherwise, i.e. on researches, monitoring, law administration and regulating this pollution.

16. Incentives/Tax Rebates/Easy Finances

(i) The incentives and easy finances on low interest may be provided to the industries, to employ measures against noise pollution.

(ii) To the industries, which have timely adopted anti-noise techniques and appliances, the rebate in tax may be provided by incorporating an amendment in Income Tax Act, 1961 in tune with water and air pollution.

17. Population Control

Population explosion, world over is responsible for noise pollution in infinite ways. One-third population consumes two-third energy of the world.

Suggestion, as given by great Osho-Rajnish, therefore is, compulsory birth control for 20-30 years must be implemented by the entire world, because mother of all problems in general is population explosion. Harsh measures are to be employed by the Governments of all countries. Compulsory sterilization or abortion is not accepted in India but to declaration disqualified for higher posts, promotions, and withdrawal of facilities, seizure of right to vote, and right to contest any election is most effective weapon.

18. Unplanned Urbanization

Increasing mania of urbanization is proving a major source of noise in cities. Only the development of rural areas can solve this problem. The people can be restrained to urbanize, only if, they are provided with the amenities in towns and villages, for want of which, they are forced to migrate into the urban areas.

19. Airport Noise

A target date must be fixed for implementation of the aircraft engine emission standards and for prohibition of operation of aircraft, which is not noise certified.

A committee of experts should be appointed by Ministry of Aviation to reduce airport noise. Some new noiseless technology must be invented and adopted for aircrafts engines, as in USA, pilot monitoring special screen, fitted in the plane's cockpit to show the quietest route to take-off and landing. This would generally mean using a route that avoids flying over residential areas.

20. Railway Noise

Jodhpur railway has invited the tenders from the agencies to plant and maintain the trees both sides of rail track from Jodhpur to Jaisalmer. In consideration, these agencies have been given the facility to advertise their products through signboards or otherwise at the railway premises.

From the experiment undertaken by Jodhpur city, it is suggested therefore, that trees be planted around all railway tracks in the country.

Sameway, Mumbai Railway adopted a plan to lease out the lands, near both sides of railway tracks, so as to the vegetation grow leading to environmental purity maintenance. This will not only curb the pollution, but also restricts the growth of dirty slum colonies near the tracks close to railway stations. The suggestion, therefore is, that this idea may be implemented throughout the country.

In Japan, to reduce rail noise, some special material is placed on the upper surface of the tracks. The suggestion, therefore is, if financially viable, this technique may be imported and be adopted in India.

21. Road Traffic Noise

(a) Conditions to use only authorized type of horn and that to only in need, must be printed on the driving licence. Proper maintenance of roads no doubt will be helpful to reduce road traffic noise.

(b) There is a need to adopt new technology by which less noise is caused, as has been adopted in a Car vehicle in

Nandakanan National Park, in which the animals can be seen without disturbing them.

(c) Suggestions for users:

(i) Avoid, slamming of vehicle doors;

(ii) Do not rev the engine unnecessary;

(iii) Use only the authorised kind of horns and that too, on road in emergency only;

(iv) Keep the windows close, if you play music in the vehicle;

(v) Keep the silencer in good order;

(vi) Check that brakes are properly adjusted and do not squeal;

(vii) Carryout noisy repair works on vehicles, during day time;

(viii) Maintain regular service of the vehicle for quietness; and

(ix) Apart from the above, the researcher would like to appeal to the user of all kinds of vehicle, that they should not only try to keep their vehicle as quiet as it can be, but also, they should raise public awareness and educate the public in this direction, so as to protect public health from noise pollution.

(d) If can be accepted by the people, there is another remedy available which recommends a shift from individual automobile transportation to mass transportation. Perhaps, this should end the long romance with the automobiles, but there should be a viable alternative in the form of fat, efficient and quiet mass transportation.

(e) Judicial compulsions have proved to be an apt measure to curb traffic noise pollution in Delhi, resulting thereby into fall of pollution level. It is none but judicial activism and decisional compulsions on environmental issues. The Supreme Court's decision to shift from diesel engine vehicles to CNG vehicles, as had been supported by Central Research Institute (CRRI) has immensely helped in curbing pollutions in Delhi. A number of states in the western countries have introduced motor vehicle statutes prescribing mufflers on automobiles, trucks and buses to prevent excessive or unusual noise. New York and Connecticut and in several other countries, positive measures have been taken to restrict the noise of traffic through comprehensive anti-noise legislation, stipulating maximum decibel noise-levels for motor vehicles. For instance, in New York states, vehicles on toll ways, and on public highways, are put into limitations by law, to a decibel count of 88. The police of New York City, has been provided with the portable decibel meters at toll-booths, so as to enforce the law. It is reported that the automobile noise level has been substantially lowered. The state of California has adopted a comprehensive anti-highway-noise legislation, which prohibits noise levels exceeding 82 dB for passenger car and 92 dB for trucks and buses at posted highway speeds.

(f) Restriction on the sale of vehicles, which do not meet with prescribed noise standards.

(g) As an additional measure, California is restricting the sale of new motor vehicles, which exceed the prescribed noise level. A new electronic system is being employed by the State Police of Connecticut, to record the noise level of passing vehicles and to photograph each car or truck exceeding the prescribed decibel level. If the noise emitted from the passing vehicle reaches a certain level, the system trips a Camera, which photographs of a noise-level gauge, in a corner of the photograph fixes of the offending vehicle. In the process, a signal is automatically relayed to the State Police patrol, so that an immediate warning or arrest could be affected.

(h) Through technology, the traffic noise can be controlled in several ways. One of the solutions is to place major thoroughfares in "ditches"—that is, constructing the in-troughs, which are normally 15 to 20 feet below the ordinary land surface. This is particularly necessary where the high-speed roads are extended into the heart of major cities. Some architects, who look into the future, have predicted the use of covered tunnels for all vehicular traffic of cities. Even lining the streets and highways with trees, fences, earth banks, etc. help to insulate and to protect the surrounding area from noise. Construction of peripheral expressing like that of Delhi, may also bring down the pollution in city.

The plan of Rajasthan state police to impart 'traffic rules knowledge' by taking the period in schools warrants countrywide extension.

22. Noise Level as a Criteria of Pollution Testing Certificate

While providing 'Pollution testing certificate', the noise pollution caused by the vehicle must specially be tested as per the prescribed noise standards. Noise free generator sets must be employed in industries, shops, even in marriages, which victimizes the whole colony in the night and disturbs sleep and peace in the vicinity.

23. Farmers

There is a great need to educate farmers about the long-term harmful effects of high noise, produced by the agricultural equipments about which, they are ignored and negligent and say that it is inevitable noise for them.

24. Role of Headman in the Villages

During survey visit to Meghalay State Pollution Control Board, Shillong, the author came across the fact that in north-east states, the headman of the villages or towns is very powerful person and is contributing a lot to reduce the noise pollution, specially of loudspeaker noise.

The suggestion, therefore is, that the headmen of the towns or villages can be inspired to use such influential example.

25. Duties of Manufacturer

It is strongly recommended that, by law, every manufacturer of any appliance, machinery, tools or the like, be imposed with a duty to reflect the decibels of sound, produced by the product and to stamp, write, or paste the same on the face of it, as well as mention it, in its log book.

It will work many ways:

   (i) To declare the decibels of noise produced by the product;

   (ii) Raise public awareness; and

   (iii) It will initiate a fare competition between the manufacturers to produce too silent product for picking up the market.

26. Firecrackers' Noise

Strict implementation of the whip, passed by Supreme Court on the use of crackers at the occasions of festivals such as Deepawali, is to be met with strict execution. No cracker should be manufactured beyond notified intensities of sound.

27. Construction Noise

Two-fold suggestions:

   (i) The builders should be commanded by law to maintain the prescribed noise at the site of constructions.
   (ii) The builders must use sound absorbing material in noise prone areas. The example is Noida Bridge, near Delhi, the construction of which is one of its own kind, with the use of such material. Recently, Ready Mix Concrete (Popularly known as RMX) offers a Pollution free option to the construction industry, which reduces noise during construction.

28. Loudspeaker Noise

No loudspeaker or any other sound magnifying device should be used, without permit or licence from appropriate authority, with prior approval of the SPCBs. The concept of decibel limit is to be observed and maintained at the site. Categorically and specifically it must be printed on the licence duly signed by the licensee. Each state should frame its own policy, on the use of loudspeakers on the pattern of UP and Delhi.

Noise Control at Source

The most obvious solution of noise pollution is to control the very source of noise at its initial level, i.e. machine design, process or operating methods. The problem of noise emissions from the machines has to be tackled at the design and manufacturing stage. Recently designed noiseless vehicle by Instrument Design Development Centre in Indian Institute of Technology Delhi is an example to the manufacturers/designers. Much can be done to reduce the source noise of equipment by making suitable adjustments in the design itself e.g. enclosing the engine pat with proper noise insulating material. Lead impregnated plastic sheets used between sandwiches layers of light-metals can act as a good sound deadening material.

Mechanical noise can be reduced by damping or isolation of the vibration.

Pneumatic noise, caused by sudden in rush or discharge of air, e.g. leaking compressed air through pipelines, ventilation fans, air compressors, pneumatic drills, fans used for air-cooling of motors, etc. Electric motors are quitters than compressed air or internal combustion engines. Electromagnetic vibrations should be avoided as far as possible in all electrical equipments.

Noise Control on Path: By Diversion of Direction

If noise cannot be reduced to the desired level at the source, the following methods can be applied to the path of noise between the source and the receiver:

(i) **Orientation and Location** .
Control may be achieved by moving the source away from the noise sensitive areas.

(ii) **Enclosure**
Housing the noisy machines in isolated buildings or providing a glass cabin for the operator of noisy machine may serve as an acoustic barrier. Thick walls and heavy materials are more effective. A 25 cms thick, brick wall may attenuate noise, by about 45 dB(A). Double glazed windows and double walls separated by an air space can serve as most effective barrier. Recently the Delhi High Court has taken a step to ensure the acoustic enclosures to generators by way of rejecting a petition filed by the generator manufacturers. The court has also directed that this enclosure is to ensure that the maximum permissible sound pressure of a generator is 75 dB.[41]

(iii) **Silencers**
Depending upon the frequency, reactive, absorptive or combination types of silencers can be used to suppress the noise, generated when air, gas or steam flow in pipes or ducts or are exhausted to atmosphere.

(iv) Pipe Lagging

On pies carrying steam or hot fluids lagging can be used as an alternative to enclosure and can achieve attenuations between 10 and 20 dBA, but it is only effective at frequencies above 500 HZ.

(v) Acoustic Screens and Barriers

A masonry wall or earth pile can form a substantial barrier. A steel plate with resilient material can act as a barrier.

(vi) Absorption Treatment

Where there is a high degree of reflection of sound waves (including multiple reflection), the reverberant component can dominate the noise field over a large part of the work area. The introduction of an acoustically absorbent material in the form of wall treatment (the wall covered first with a thick layer of mineral wool and then with a polythene sheet) and/or functional hanging absorbers at ceiling height will reduce the reverberant component up to 10 dBA but will reduce the noise radiated directly by the source.

(vii) Damping

Where large panels are radiating noise, a significant reduction can be achieved by fitting proprietary damping pads, stiffing ribs, or using a double skin construction.

(viii) Green Belt

Creation of green belt in residential and industrial areas can act as an effective noise barrier. It can reduce noise levels to an extent before reaching its receiver.

Noise Control at Receiver's Instance

The receiver is the final part of the sound transmission system. The receiver determines the acoustic objective system. When it is not practical or economical, to reduce noise levels to meet the acoustic objective, 'ear protectors' are used. Ear protectors are capable of reducing the noise level to the ear by 10 to 55 dB, depending on the make and frequency.

Some Suggestions for Political Parties and Social Organizations

Political Parties must:

    (a) include environmental issues as items, on their agenda;

    (b) pay more attention to the concept of "environment and sustainable development;

    (c) take account of environmental requirements and sustainable development on each level of negotiations;

    (d) establish a special committee or working group on environmental issues. Sustainable development can be taken up by all existing committees and working groups, especially in the Committee on Commodities; and

    (e) provide information to other national/international actors, initiate and co-ordinate international actions, and follow up implementation actions, concerning environment.

It is worth mentioning that the concept of development should include the satisfaction of human needs in harmony with the environment and full participation of the people concerned. Development should not only be sustainable and protective to environment, but it must also be humane and produce good quality of life into which everyone breathes and lives. Development, while it presupposes growth, cannot be reduced to mere economic development and the key to preserve nature in culture, a new kind of development humane, sustainable and harmonious with the environment is a condition precedent on global basis.

Sweat music and soneral voice brings joy, cordiality, relaxations, mental peace, and makes life worth living. Normal sound makes day-to-day life affairs easy and communicable. But, undesired noise brings disturbance to peace, mental disorders, and hence makes the life miserable.

NOTES AND REFERENCES

1.   International Status of Jowai, a report prepared by Meghalaya State Pollution Control Board, 'Arden' Lumpyngngad, Shillong in December 2000.

1A. R.K. Sapru, *Environment Management in India-I*, p. 59.

2. *The Indian Express*, dated 1 April, 2000.

3. D.D. Ojha, *Noise Pollution*, p. 70 (Hindi).

4. *Times of India*, 1 May, 2002.

5. I. Mohan, *Environmental Pollution and Management*, p. 40.

6. *Dainik Bhaskar*, July 27, 2000.

7. N.S. Kamboj, *Control of Noise Pollution*, p. 19.

8. dep@worldbank.org.

9. Former PM Margaret Thatcher's Speech to the Royal Society on Sept. 27, 1988.

10. The Ministry invited the Indian Law Institute for the Comment on the proposed legislation. The same were discussed in the Ministry in a meeting of environmental experts from various parts of India including Indian Law Institute. (See *Journal of the ILI*, Vol. 43, July-September, 2001, p. 386).

11. *Supra* 1A, p. 59.

11A. R.K. Sapru, *Environment Management in India-I*, p. 103.

12. R.P. Anand, Rahamtulla Khan, M.S. Bhatt, *Law, Science and Environment*, p. 135.

13. *Ibid.*

14. AIR 1960 All 632.

15. AIR 1958 Punjab 11.

15A. *TOI*, 4-8-05.

16. *Supra* 12, p. 159.

17. *Rajasthan Patrika*, 3 July, 2002.

18. (1998) 98 LT 718: 24 TLR 414.

19. 1995 AIHC 4168.

19A. See G.S.R. 106(E) dated 26 December, 1989.

20. AIR 1993 Kerala 1.

21. Civil Appeal of 1994 (Arising out of SLP (C) No. 9059 of 1994), decided on May 12, 1994.

22. *Rajasthan Patrika*, August 31, 2000.

22A. RE: Noise Pollution, 2005(5) SCALE.

23. *Sunday Times of India*, New Delhi, January 13, 2002.

24. Chetan Singh Mehta; *Environmental Protection and the Law*, p. 90.

25. *Ibid.*, p.103.

26. A.I.R. 1985 SC 652.

27 G.S. Nagi; Noise Pollution; for details see Lankawi declaration adopted by Common Wealth heads of Nations (16 point charter on *Human Environment*, p. 11).

28. Government of Thailand 1997.

29. AIR 1975 Kerala 117.

30. (1984) 3 SCC 161: 1984 SCC (L&S) 389.

31. *State of Punjab* Vs. *Ramlubhaya Bagga* (1998) 4 SCC.

32. AIR 1984 (NOC) 137 HP.

33. http://www.islamicvoice.com/may97/#Top.

34. AIR 1985 Cal 222.

35. AIR 1998 Orissa 39.

36. 1995 AIHC 4168.

37. *Ibid.*

38. See 'Environment Law to be Reviewed', Chandrika Mago, *Times of India*, dated 23rd March, 2002.

39. Replogle, Michael, 1992, *ITE Journal*. (Dec.) http://www.colby.edu/personal/thtieten/cases.htl.

40. G.S. Nagi, *Noise Pollution*, p. 82.

40A. Green Goal just a Pipe dream; *Times of India*, April 4, 2005.

41. High Court Tightens screws on generator manufacturers, *Times of India*, April 8, 2004.

APPENDIX "A"

MINISTRY OF ENVIRONMENT AND FORESTS
NOTIFICATION
New Delhi, the 14 February, 2000

S.O. 123(E).—Whereas the increasing ambient noise levels in public places from various sources, *inter-alia*, industrial activity, construction activity, generator sets, loudspeakers, public address systems, music systems, vehicular horns and other mechanical devices have deleterious effects on human health and the psychological well-being of the people; it is considered necessary to regulate and control noise producing and generating sources with the objective of maintaining the ambient air quality standards in respect of noise;

Whereas a draft of Noise Pollution (Control and Regulation) Rules, 1999 was published under the notification of the Government of India in the Ministry of Environment and Forests vide number S.O. 528(E) dated the 28 June, 1999 inviting objections and suggestions from all the persons likely to be affected thereby, before the expiry of the period of sixty days from the date on which the copies of the Gazette containing the said notification are made available to the public-,

And whereas copies of the said Gazette were made available, to the public on the I" day of July, 1999.

And whereas the objections and suggestions received from the public in respect of the said draft rules have been duly considered by the Central Government—,

Now, therefore, in exercise of the powers conferred by clause (ii) of sub-section (2) of section 3, sub-section (1) and clause (b)

of sub-section (2) of section 6 and section 25 of the Environment (Protection) Act, 1986 (29 of 1986) read with Rule 5 of the Environment (Protection) Rules, 1986, the Central Government hereby makes the following rules for the regulation and control of noise producing and generating sources, namely:

THE NOISE POLLUTION (REGULATION AND CONTROL) RULES, 2000

1. Short-title and commencement.—(1) These rules may be called the Noise Pollution (Regulation and Control) Rules, 2000.

(2) They shall come into force on the date of their publication in the Official Gazette.

2. Definitions.—In these rules, unless the context otherwise requires,

  (a) "Act" means the Environment (Protection) Act, 1986 (29 of 1986);

  (b) "area/zone" means all areas which fall in either of the four categories given in the Schedule annexed to these rules;

  (c) "authority" means any authority or officer authorised by the Central Government, or as the case may be, the State Government in accordance with the laws in force and includes a District Magistrate, Police Commissioner, or any other officer designated for the maintenance of the ambient air quality standards in respect of noise under any law for the time being in force;

  (d) "person" in relation to any factory or premises means a person or occupier or his agent, who has control over the affairs of the factory or premises; and

  (e) "State Government" in relation to a Union territory means the Administrator thereof appointed under Article 239 of the Constitution.

3. Ambient air quality standards in respect of noise for different areas/zones.—(1) The ambient air quality standards in respect of noise for different areas/zones shall be such as specified in the Schedule annexed to these rules.

(2) The State Government may categorize the areas into industrial, commercial, residential or silence areas/zones for the purpose of implementation of noise standards for different areas.

(3) The State Government shall take measures for abatement of noise including noise emanating from vehicular movements and ensure that the existing noise levels do not exceed the ambient air quality standards specified under these rules.

(4) All development authorities, local bodies and other concerned authorities while planning developmental activity or carrying out functions relating to town and country planning shall take into consideration all aspects of noise pollution as a parameter of quality of life to avoid noise menace and to achieve the objective of maintaining the ambient air quality standards in respect of noise.

(5) An area comprising not less than 100 metres around hospitals, educational institutions and courts may be declared as silence area/zone for the purpose of these rules.

4. Responsibility as to enforcement of noise pollution control measures.—(1) The noise levels in any area/zone shall not exceed the ambient air quality standards in respect of noise as specified in the Schedule.

(2) The authority shall be responsible for the enforcement of noise pollution control measures and the due compliance of the ambient air quality standards in respect of noise.

5. Restrictions on the use of loudspeakers/public address system.—(1) A loudspeaker or a public address system shall not be used except after obtaining written permission from the authority.

(2) A loudspeaker or a public address system shall not be used at night (between 10.00 p.m. to 6.00 a.m.) except in closed premises for communication within, e.g. auditoria, conference rooms, community halls and banquet halls.

6. Consequences of any violation in silence zone/area.— Whoever, in any place covered under the silence zone/area commits any of the following offence, he shall be liable for penalty under the provisions of the Act:

- (i) whoever, plays any music or uses any sound amplifiers,

(ii) whoever, beats a drum or tom-tom or blows a horn either musical or pressure, or trumpet or beats or sounds any instrument, or

(iii) whoever, exhibits any mimetic, musical or other performances of a nature to 44raq crowds.

7. Complaints to be made to the authority.—(1) A person may, if the noise level exceeds the ambient noise standards by 10 dB(A) or more given in the corresponding columns against any area/zone, make a complaint to the authority.

(2) The authority shall act on the complaint and take action against the violator in accordance with the provisions of these rules and any other law in force.

8. Power to prohibit, etc. continuance of music sound or noise.—(1) If the authority is satisfied from the report of an officer-in-charge of a police station or other information received by him that it is necessary to do so in order to prevent annoyance, disturbance, discomfort or injury or risk of annoyance, disturbance, discomfort or injury to the public or to any person who dwell or occupy property on the vicinity, he may, by a written order issue such directions as he may consider necessary to any person for preventing, prohibiting, controlling or regulating:

(a) the incidence or continuance in or upon any premises of—

(i) any vocal or instrumental music,

(ii) sounds caused by playing, beating, clashing, blowing or use in any manner whatsoever of any instrument including loudspeakers, public address systems, appliance or apparatus or contrivance which is capable of producing or re-producing sound, or

(b) the carrying on in or upon, any premises of any trade, avocation or operation or process resulting in or attended with noise.

(2) The authority empowered under sub-rule (1) may, either on its own motion, or on the application of any person aggrieved by an order made under sub-rule (1), either rescind, modify or alter any such order:

Provided that before any such application is disposed of, the said authority shall afford to the applicant an opportunity of appearing before it either in person or by a person representing him and showing cause against the order and shall, if it rejects any such application either wholly or in part, record its reasons for such rejection.

SCHEDULE
[See Rule 3(l) and 4(l)]

Ambient Air Quality Standards in Respect of Noise

Area Code	Category of Area/Zone	Limits in dB(A) Leq *	
		Day Time	Night Time
(A)	Industrial Area	75	70
(B)	Commercial Area	65	55
(C)	Residential Area	55	45
(D)	Silence Zone	50	40

Notes:

1. Day time shall mean from 6.00 a.m. to 10.00 p.m.
2. Night time shall mean from 10.00 p.m. to 6.00 a.m.
3. Silence zone is defined as an area comprising not less than 100 metres around hospitals, educational institutions and courts. The silence zones are zones which are declared as such by the competent authority.
4. Mixed categories of areas may be declared as one of the four above mentioned categories by the competent authority.
* dB(A) Leq denotes the time weighted average of the level of sound in decibels on scale A which is relatable to human hearing.
A "decibel" is a unit in which noise is measured.
"A", in dB(A) Leq, denotes the frequency weighting in the measurement of noise and corresponds to frequency response characteristics of the human ear.
Leq: It is an energy mean of the noise level, over a specified period.

The Union Territory of Delhi Loudspeakers (Licensing and Controlling) Regulations, 1980

Whereas the Commissioner of Police considers it expedient that regulations should be framed for licensing and controlling loudspeakers in the Union Territory of Delhi.

And whereas the Commissioner of Police is satisfied that circumstances exist which render it necessary that such regulation should be brought into force at once.

Now, therefore, the Commissioner of Police with the previous sanction of the Administrator of Union Territory of Delhi and in exercise of powers conferred by sub-clause (iii) of clause (s) of Section 28(1) read with sub-sections (2) and (3) of section 28 of the Delhi Police Act, 1978, is pleased to make the following regulations, namely:

1. **Short title, extent and application.**—These regulations may be called the Union Territory of Delhi Loudspeaker (Licensing and Controlling) Regulations, 1980.

(a) They shall extend to the Union Territory of Delhi.

(b) These regulations shall come into force from the date of their publication in Delhi Gazette.

2. **Definitions.**—In these regulations unless the context requires otherwise—

(a) "Commissioner" means the Commissioner of Police, Union Territory of Delhi.

(b) "Licence" means a Licence granted under these regulations for using the loudspeaker in the Union territory of Delhi.

(c) "Licensee" means a person who has been granted a licence under these regulations.

(d) "Licensing Authority" means the Commissioner of Police or any other officer as may be authorised by him.

3. No person shall use, operate or permit the use or operation of a loudspeaker in any public place or within distance of 200 meters from any public place or in any place of public entertainment, except under and in accordance with the conditions of license granted by the Commissioner of Police, Delhi, or by any officer authorised by him in that behalf.

4. No Loudspeaker shall be used or operated or permitted to be used or operated from a moving vehicle for any purpose except with the permission of the Commissioner of Police of Delhi, or any other officer so authorised.

5. No Loudspeaker shall be installed or operated from a position which overlooks a public road, except with the previous permission of the Commissioner of Police, Delhi or any other officer so authorised.

6. (i) No Licence for the use of Loudspeaker from stationary vehicle will be granted unless :

(a) a list of public places where the vehicle carrying a Loudspeaker is intended to be stationed alongwith the date and time of its use is furnished to the Licensing Authority along with the application for the licence, and

(b) the Licensing Authority is satisfied that no obstruction is likely to be caused to traffic by the use of Loudspeaker from the vehicle.

(ii) The Licence under sub-section (1) shall always be subject to the condition that if in order to remove congestion on roads, maintain order or prevent commission of a nuisance, any Police Officer thinks it necessary that the vehicle from which a

Loudspeaker is used should be shifted to some other place, he shall have the right to direct the Licensee to shift the vehicle and ensure its compliance.

7. No Loudspeaker shall be used or operated or permitted to be used or operated by any person holding licence in such manner as to disturb or cause annoyance to any other person residing in or carrying on business in any building or premises adjoining the public place or place of public entertainment.

8. Any Police Officer above the rank of Constable having jurisdiction in the area shall have free access to the place of public entertainment, where a Loudspeaker is being used, to satisfy himself that the conditions of its licence are not violated.

9. The Commissioner of Police, Delhi, or any officer authorised under regulation 3, may cancel the license issued under regulation 3 if the holder of such licence contravenes any of the above regulations or the conditions subject to which the licence is issued.

10. The foregoing regulations shall not be deemed to prevent the Commissioner of Police, Delhi, or subject to his orders any Police Officer from giving, as occasion may require, any special direction or order under section 29 or from issuing any notification under sub-section (1) of section 30 or any order under sub-section (1) of section 32 of the Delhi Police Act, 1978.

11. Notwithstanding anything contained in these regulations or in the provisions of any licence thereunder, the Commissioner of Police, Delhi, or any other officer authorised by him may, by order prohibit the use by the licensee of any or all Loudspeakers in any place for such period as he may deem fit, in order to prevent obstruction, inconvenience, annoyance, risk, danger or danger to the residents or passengers in the vicinity.

12. Necessary register regarding grant of permission must be maintained with the following columns and staff detailed for patrolling be advised to keep necessary watch accordingly to avoid misuse of such permission.

Sl. No.	Date	Times of permission accorded	Name/address of the owners of Loudspeaker

13. While granting permission to use Loudspeaker, a condition shall be imposed that the Loudspeaker will be played at a minimum volume audible to the persons for whom it is meant, i.e., immediate congregation.

The Air (Prevention and Control of Pollution) Act, 1981

No. 14 of 1981

[29th March, 1981]

An Act to provide for the prevention, control and abatement of air pollution, for the establishment, with a view to carrying out the aforesaid purposes, of Boards, for conferring on and assigning to such Boards powers and functions relating thereto and for matters connected therewith.

WHEREAS decisions were taken at the United Nations Conference of the Human Environment held in Stockholm in June, 1972, in which India participated, to take appropriate steps for the preservation of the natural resources of the earth which, among other things, include the preservation of the quality of air and control of air pollution;

AND WHEREAS it is considered necessary to implement the decisions aforesaid in so far as they relate to the preservation of the quality of air and control of air pollution;

BE it enacted by Parliament in the Thirty-second Year of the Republic of India as follows:—

CHAPTER I

PRELIMINARY

1. Short title, extend and commencement.—(1) This Act may be called the Air (Prevention and Control of Pollution) Act, 1981.

(2) It extents to the whole of India.

(3) It shall come into force on such date 16th May 1981, vide

Notification No. G.S.R. 351(E), dated 15-5-1981, Gazette of India, Extraordinary, Pt. II, Sec. 3(I), p. 944 as the Central Government May, by notification in the Official Gazette, appoint.

2. **Definitions.**—In this Act, unless the context otherwise requires,—

(a) "air pollutant" means any solid, liquid or gaseous substance present in the atmosphere in such concentration as may be or tend to be injurious to human beings or other living creatures or plants or property or environment.

(b) "air pollution" means the presence in the atmosphere of any air pollutant;

(c) "Approved appliance" means any equipment or gadget used for the burning of any combustible material or for generating or consuming any fume, gas or particulate matter and approved by the State Board for the purposes of this Act;

(d) "Approved fuel" means any fuel approved by the State Board for the purposes of this Act;

(e) "Automobile " means any vehicle powered either by internal combustion engine or by any method of generating power to drive such vehicle by burning fuel;

(f) "Board" means the Central Board or a State Board;

(g) "Central Board" means the Central Board for the Prevention and Control of Water Pollution constituted under section 3 of the water (prevention and Control of Pollution) Act, 1974; (6 of 1974.)

(h) "chimney" includes any structure with an opening or outlet from or through which any air pollutant may be emitted;

(i) "control equipment" means any apparatus, device, equipment or system to control the quality and manner of emission of any air pollutant and includes any device used for securing the efficient operation of any industrial plant;

(j) "emission" means any solid or liquid or gaseous substance coming out of any chimney, duct or flue or any other outlet;

(k) "industrial plant" means any plant used for any industrial or trade purposes and emitting any air pollutant into the atmosphere;

(l) "member" means a member of the Central Board or a State Board, as the case may be, and includes the chairman thereof;

(m) "occupier", in relation to any factory or premises, means the persons who has control over the affairs of the factory or the premises and where the said affairs are entrusted to a managing agent, such agent shall be deemed to be the occupier of the factory or the premises;

(n) "prescribed" means prescribed by rules made under this Act by the Central Government or, as the case may be, the State Government;

(o) "State Board" means,—

(i) in relation to a State in which the Water (Prevention and Control of Pollution) Act, 1974, (6 of 1974) is in force and the State Government has constituted for that State a State Board for the Prevention and Control of Water Pollution under section 4 of that Act, the said State Board; and

(ii) in relation to any other State, the State Board for the Prevention and Control of Air Pollution constituted by the State Government under section 5 of this Act.

CHAPTER II
CENTRAL AND STATE BOARDS FOR THE PREVENTION AND CONTROL OF AIR POLLUTION

3. The Central Board for the Prevention and Control of Air Pollution.—The Central Board for the Prevention and Control of Water Pollution constituted under section 3 of the Water (Prevention and Control of Pollution) Act, 1974, (6 of 1974) shall, without prejudice to the exercise and performance of its powers and functions under that Act, exercise the powers and performs the functions of the Central Board for the Prevention and Control of Air Pollution under this Act.

4. State Boards for the Prevention and Control of Water Pollution to be State Boards for the Prevention and Control of Air Pollution.—In any State in which the Water (Prevention and

Control of Pollution) Act, 1974, (6 of 1974) is in force and the State Government has constituted for that State a State Board for the Prevention and Control of Water Pollution under section 4 of that Act, such State Board shall be deemed to be the State Board for the Prevention and Control of Air Pollution constituted under section 5 of this Act and accordingly that State Board for the Prevention and Control of Water Pollution shall, without prejudice to the exercise and performance of its powers and functions under that Act, exercise the powers and perform the functions of the State Board for the Prevention and Control of Air Pollution under this Act.

5. Constitution of State Boards.—(1) In any State in which the Water (prevention and Control of Pollution) Act, 1974, (6 of 1974) is not in force, or that Act is in force but the State Government has not constituted a State Board for the Prevention and Control of Water Pollution under that Act, the State Government shall, with effect from such date as it may, by notification in the Official Gazette, appoint, constitute a State Board for the Prevention and Control of Air Pollution under such name as may specified in the notification, to exercise the powers conferred on, and perform the functions assigned to, that Board under this Act.

(2) A State Board constituted under this Act shall consist of the following members, namely:—

(a) a Chairman, being a person having special knowledge or practical experience in respect of matters relating to environmental protection, to be nominated by the State Government:

Provided that the Chairman may be either whole time or part-time as the State Government may think fit;

(b) Such number of officials, not exceeding five, as the State Government may think fit, to be nominated by the State Government to represent that Government;

(c) Such number of persons, not exceeding five, as the State Government may think fit, to be nominated by the State Government from amongst the members of the local authorities functioning within the State.

(d) Such number of non-officials, not exceeding three, as the State Government may think fit, to be nominated by the State Government to represent the interests of agriculture, fishery or industry or trade or labour or any other interests, which, in the opinion of that Government, ought to be represented;

(e) Two persons to represent the companies or corporations owned, controlled or managed by the State Government, to be nominated by that Government;

(f) a full-time member-secretary having practical experience in respect of matters relating to environmental protection and having administrative experience, to be appointed by the State Government: Provided that the State Government shall ensure that not less than two of the members are persons having special knowledge or practical experience in respect of matters relating to the improvement of the quality of air or the prevention, control or abatement of air pollution.

(3) Every State Board constituted under this Act shall be a body corporate with the name specified by the State Government in the notification issued under sub-section (1), having perpetual succession and a common seal with power, subject to the provisions of this Act, to acquire and dispose of property and to contract, and may by the said name sue or be used.

6. Central Board to exercise the powers and perform the functions of a State Board in the Union Territories.—No State Board shall be constituted for a Union territory and in relation to a Union territory, the Central Board shall exercise the powers and perform the functions of a State Board under this Act for that Union territory: Provided that in relation to any Union territory the Central Board may delegate all or any of its powers and functions under this section to such person or body of persons as the Central Government may specify.

7. Terms and conditions of service of member.—(1) Save as otherwise provided by or under this Act, a member of a State Board constituted under this Act, other than the member secretary, shall hold office for a term of three years from the date on which his nomination is notified in the Official Gazette:

Provided that a member shall, notwithstanding the expiration of his term, continue to hold office until his successor enters upon his office.

(2) The term of office of a member of a State Board constituted under this Act and nominated under clause (b) or clause (e) of sub-section (2) of section 5 shall come to an end as soon as he ceases to hold the office under the State Government or, as the case may be, the company or corporation owned, controlled or managed by the State Government, by virtue of which he was nominated.

(3) A member of a State Board constituted under this Act, other than the member-secretary, may at any time resign his office by writing under his hand addressed—

(a) in the case of the Chairman, to the State Government; and

(b) in any other case, to the Chairman of the State Board, and the seat of the Chairman or such other member shall thereupon become vacant.

(4) A member of a State Board constituted under this Act, other than the member-secretary, shall be deemed to have vacated his seat, if he is absent without reason, sufficient in the opinion of the State Board from three consecutive meetings of the State Board or where he is nominated under clause (c) of sub-section (2) of section 5, he ceases to be a member of the local authority and such vacation of seat shall, in either case, take effect from such date as the State Government may, by notification in the Official Gazette, specify.

(5) A casual vacancy in a State Board constituted under this Act shall be filled by a fresh nomination and the person nominated to fill the vacancy shall hold office only for the remainder of the term for which the member whose place he takes was nominated.

(6) A member of a State Board constituted under this Act shall be eligible for re-nomination but not for more than two terms.

(7) The other terms and conditions of service of the Chairman and other members (except the member-secretary) of a State Board constituted under this Act shall be such as may be prescribed.

8. **Disqualifications.**—(1) No person shall be a member of a State Board constituted under this Act, who—

(a) is, or at any time has been, adjudged insolvent or

(b) is of unsound mind and has been so declared by a competent court, or

(c) is, or has been, convicted of an offence which, in the opinion of the State Government, involves moral turpitude, or

(d) is, or at any time has been, convicted of an offence under this Act, or

(e) has directly or indirectly by himself or by any partner, any share or interest in any firm or company carrying on the business of manufacture, sale, or hire of machinery, industrial plant, control equipment or any other apparatus for the improvement of the quality of air or for the prevention, control of abatement of air pollution, or

(f) is a director or a secretary, manager or other salaried officer or employee of any company or firm having any contract with the Board, or with the Government constituting the Board or with a local authority in the State, or with a company or corporation owned, controlled or managed by the Government, for the carrying out of programs for the improvement of the quality of air or for the prevention, control or abatement of air pollution, or

(g) has so abused, in the opinion of the State Government, his position as a member, as to render his continuance or the State Board detrimental to the interests of the general public.

(2) The State Government shall, by order in writing, remove any Member who is, or has become, subject to any disqualification mentioned In sub-section (1):

Provided that no order of removal shall be made by the State Government under this section unless the member concerned has been Given a reasonable opportunity of showing cause against the same.

(3) Notwithstanding anything contained in sub-section (1) or sub-section (6) Of section 7, a member who has been removed under this Section shall not be eligible to continue to hold office until his successor Enters upon his office, or, as the case may be, for re-nomination as a member.

9. Constitution of by members.—If a member of a State Board constituted under this Act becomes Subject to any of the disqualification's specified in section 8, his seat Shall become vacant.

10. Meetings of Board.—(1) For the purposes of this Act, a Board shall meet at least one in every three months and shall observe such rules of procedure in regard to the transaction of business at its meetings as may be prescribed:

Provided that if, in the opinion of the Chairman, any business of an Urgent nature is to be transacted, he may convene a meeting of the Board at such time as he thinks fit for the aforesaid purpose.

(2) Copies of the minutes of the meetings under sub-section (1) shall be forwarded to the Central Board and to the State Government Concerned.

11. Constitution of committees.—(1) A Board may constitute as many committees consisting wholly of members or partly of members and partly of other persons and for such purpose or purposes as it may think fit.

(2) A committee constituted under this section shall meet as such time and at such place, and shall observe such rules of procedure in regard to the transaction of business at its meetings, as may be prescribed.

(3) The members of a committee other than the members of the Board shall be paid such fees and allowances, for attending its meetings and for attending to any other work of the Board as may be prescribed.

12. Temporary association of persons with Board for Particular purpose.—(1) A Board may associate with itself in such manner, and for such purposes, as may be prescribed, any person whose assistance or advice it may desire to obtain in performing any of its functions under this Act.

(2) A person associated with the Board under sub-section (1) for any purpose shall have a right to take part in the discussions of the Board relevant to that purpose, but shall not have a right to vote at a meeting of the Board an d shall not be ₁ member of the Board for any other purpose.

(3) A person associated with a Board under sub-section (1) all be entitled to receive such fees and allowances as may be ₂scribed.

13. Vacancy in Board not to invalidate acts or proceedings.—No act or proceeding of a Board or any committee thereof shall Be called in question on the ground merely of the existence of any Vacancy in, or any defect in the constitution of, the Board or such committee, as the case may be.

14. Member-secretary and officers and other employees of State Boards.—(1) The terms and conditions of service of the member-secretary of a State Board constituted under this Act shall be such as may be Prescribed.

(2) The member-secretary of a State Board, whether constituted Under this Act or not, shall exercise such powers and perform such duties as may be prescribed.

(3) Subject to such rules as may be made by the State Government in this behalf, a State Board, whether constituted under this Act or not, may appoint such officers and other employees as it considers necessary for the efficient performance of its functions under this Act.

(4) The method of appointment, the conditions of service and the scales of pay of the officers (other than the member-secretary) and other employees of a State Board appointed under sub-section (3) shall be such as may be determined by regulations made by the State Board—under this Act.

(5) Subject to such conditions as may be prescribed, a State Board constituted under this Act may from time to time appoint any qualified person to be a consultant to the Board and pay him such salary and allowances or fees, as it thinks fit.

15. Delegation of powers.—A State Board may, by general or special order, delegate to the Chairman or the member-secretary or any other officer of the Board subject to such conditions and limitations, if any, as may be specified in the order, such of its powers and functions under this Act as it may deem necessary.

CHAPTER III

POWERS AND FUNCTIONS OF BOARDS

16. Functions of Central Board.—(1) Subject to the provisions of this Act, and without prejudice to the performance of its functions under the Water (Prevention and Control of Pollution) Act, 1974, (6 of 1974) the main functions of the Central

Board shall be to improve the quality of air and to prevent, control or abate air pollution in the country.

(2) In particular and without prejudice to the generality of the foregoing functions, the Central Board may—

(a) advise the Central Government on any matter concerning the improvement of the quality of air and the prevention, control or abatement of air pollution;

(b) plan and cause to be executed a nation-wide programme for the prevention, control or abatement of air pollution.

(c) co-ordinate the activity of the State Boards and resolve disputes among there.

(d) Provide technical assistance and guidance to the State Boards, carry out and sponsor investigations and research relating to problems of air pollution and prevention, control or abatement of air pollution;

(e) Plan and organise the training of persons engaged or to be engaged in programmes for the prevention, control or abatement of air pollution on such terms and conditions as the Central Board may specify;

(f) Organise through mass media a comprehensive programme regarding the prevention, control or abatement of air pollution;

(g) Collect, compile and publish technical and statistical data relating to air pollution and the measures devised for its effective prevention, control or abatement and prepare manuals, codes or guides relating to prevention, control or abatement of air pollution;

(h) Lay down standards for the quality of air;

(i) collect and disseminate information in respect of matters relating to air pollution;

(j) perform such other functions as may be prescribed.

(3) The Central Board may establish or recognise a laboratory or laboratories to enable the Central Board to perform its functions under this section efficiently.

(4) The Central Board may—

(a) delegate any of its functions under this Act generally or specially to any of the committees appointed by it;

(b) do such other things and perform such other acts, as it

may think necessary for the proper discharge of its functions and generally for the purpose of carrying into effect the purposes of this Act.

17. Functions of State Boards.—(1) Subject to the provisions of this Act, and without prejudice to the performance of its functions, if any, under the Water (Prevention and Control of Pollution) Act, 1974, (6 of 1974) the functions of a State Board shall be—

(a) to plan a comprehensive programme for the prevention, control or abatement of air pollution and to secure the execution thereof;

(b) to advise the State Government on any matter concerning the prevention, control or abatement of air pollution;

(c) to collect and disseminate information relating to air pollution;

(d) to collaborate with the central Board in organising the training of persons engaged or to be engaged or to be engaged in programmes relating to prevention, control or abatement of air pollution and to organise mass-education programme relating thereto;

(e) to inspect, at all reasonable times, any control equipment industrial plant or manufacturing process and to give, by order, such directions to such persons as it may consider necessary to take steps for the prevention, control or abatement of air pollution;

(f) to inspect air pollution control areas at such intervals as it may think necessary, assess the quality of air therein and take steps for the prevention, control or abatement of air pollution in such areas;

(g) to lay down, in consolations with the Central Board and having regard to the standards for the quality of air laid down by the Central Board, standards for emission of air pollutants into the atmosphere from industrial plants and automobiles or for the discharge of any air pollutant into the atmosphere from any other source whatsoever not being a ship or an aircraft;

Provided that different standards for emission may be laid down under this clause for different industrial plants having regard to the quantity and composition of emission of air pollutants into the atmosphere from such industrial plants;

(h) to advise the State Government with respect to the suitability of any premises or location for carrying on any industry which is likely to cause air pollution;

(i) to perform such other functions as may be prescribed or as may, from time to time, be entrusted to it by the Central Board or the State Government;

(j) to do such other things and to perform such other acts as it may think necessary for the proper discharge of its functions and generally for the purpose of carrying into effect the purposes of this Act.

(2) A State Board may establish or recognise a laboratory or laboratories to enable the State Board to perform its functions under this section efficiently.

18. Power to give directions.—In the performance of its functions under this Act—

(a) the Central Board shall be bound by such directions in writing as the Central Government may give to it; and

(b) every State Board shall be bound by such directions in writing as the Central Board or the State Government may give to it;

Provided that where a direction given by the State Government is inconsistent with the direction given by the Central Board, the matter shall be referred to the Central Government for its decision.

CHAPTER IV
PREVENTION AND CONTROL OF AIR POLLUTION

19. Power to declare air pollution control areas.—(1) The State Government may, after consultation with the State Board, by notification in the Official Gazette, declare in such manner as may be prescribed, any area or areas within the State as air pollution control area or areas for the purposes of this Act.

(2) The State Government may, after consolation with the State Board, by notification in the Official Gazette,—

(a) alter any air pollution control area whether by way of extension or reduction;

(b) declare a new air pollution control area in which may be merged one or more existing air pollution control areas or any part or parts thereof.

(3) If the State Government, after consultation with the State Board, is of opinion that the use of any fuel, other than an approved fuel, in any air pollution control area or part thereof, may cause or is likely to cause air pollution, it may, by notification in the Official Gazette, prohibit the use of such fuel in such area or part thereof with effect from such date (being not less than three months from the date of publication of the notification) as may be specified in the notification.

(4) The State Government may, after consultation with the State Board, by notification in the Official Gazette, direct that with effect from such date as may be specified therein, no appliance, other than an approved appliance, shall be used in the premises situated in an air pollution control area:

Provided that different dates may be specified for different parts of an air pollution control area or for the use of different appliances.

(5) If the State Government, after consultation with the State Board, is of opinion that the burning of any material (not being fuel) in any air pollution control area of part thereof may cause or is likely to cause air pollution, it may, by notification in the Official Gazette, prohibit the burning of such material in such area or part thereof

20. Power give instructions for ensuring standards for emission form automobiles.—With a view to ensuring that the standards for emission of air pollutants form automobiles laid down by the State Board under clause (g) of sub-section (1) of section 17 are complied with, the State Government shall, in consultation with the State Board, give such instructions as may be deemed necessary to the concerned authority in charge of registration of motor vehicles under the Motor Vehicles Act, 1939, (4 of 1939) and such authority shall, notwithstanding anything contained in that Act or the rules made thereunder be bold to comply with such instructions.

21. Restrictions on use of certain industrial plants.—(1) Subject to the provisions of this section, no person shall, without the previous consent of the State Board, operate any industrial plant for the purpose of any industry specified in the Schedule in an air pollution control area.

(2) An application for consent of the State Board under subsection (1) shall be accompanied by such fees as may be prescribed and shall be made in the prescribed form and shall contain the particulars of the industrial plant and such other particulars as may be prescribed:

> Provided that where any person, immediately before the declaration of any area as an air pollution control area, operation in such area any industrial plant for the purpose of any industry specified in the Schedule such person shall make the application under this sub-section within such period (being not less than three months form the date of such declaration) as may be prescribed and where such person makes such application, he shall be deemed to be operating such industrial plant with the consent of the State Board until the consent applied for has been refused.

(3) The State Board may make such inquiry as it may deem fit in respect of the application for consent referred to in subsection (1) and in making any such inquiry, shall follow such procedure as may be prescribed.

(4) Within a period of four months after the receipt of the application for consent referred to in sub-section (1), the State Board shall, by order in writing, either grant or refuse, for reasons to be recorded in the order, the consent applied for.

(5) Every person to whom consent has been granted by the State. Board under sub-section (4), shall comply with the following conditions, namely:—

> (i) the control equipment of such specification as the State Board may approve in this behalf shall be installed and operated in the premises where the industry is carried on or proposed to be carried on;
>
> (ii) the existing control equipment, if any, shall be altered or replaced in accordance with the directions of the State Board;
>
> (iii) the control equipment referred to in clause (I) or clause (ii) shall be kept at all times in good running condition;
>
> (iv) chimney, wherever necessary, of such specification as the State Board may approve in this behalf shall be

erected or re-erected in such premises;

(v) such other conditions as the State Board may specify in this behalf; and

(vi) the conditions referred to in clauses (i), (ii) and (iv) shall be complied with within such period as the State Board may specify in this behalf:

Provided that in the case of a person operating any industrial plant for the purpose of any industry specified in the Schedule in an air pollution control area immediately before the date of declaration of such area as an air pollution control area, the period so specified shall not be less than six months:

Provided further that—

(a) after the installation of any control equipment in accordance with the specifications under clause (i), or

(b) after the alteration or replacement of any control equipment in accordance with the directions of the State Board underclause (ii), or

(c) after erection or re-erection of any chimney under clause (iv),

no control equipment or chimney shall be altered or replaced or, as the case may be, erected or re-erected except with the previous approval of the State Board.

(6) If due to any technological improvement or otherwise the State Board is of opinion that all or any of the conditions referred to in sub-section (5) require or requires variation (including the change of any control equipment, either in whole or in part), the State Board shall, after giving the person to whom consent has been granted an opportunity of being heard, vary all or any of such conditions as so varied.

(7) Where a person to whom consent has been granted by the State Board under sub-section (4) transfers his interests in the industry to any other person, such consent shall be deemed to have been granted to such other person and he shall be bound to comply with all the conditions subject to which it was granted as if the consent was granted to him originally.

22. Persons carrying on industry, etc., not to allow emission of air pollutants in excess of the standards laid down

by State Board.—No person carrying on any industry specified in the Schedule or operating any industrial plant, in any air pollution control area shall discharge or cause or permit to be discharged the emission of any air pollutant in excess of the standards laid down by the State Board under clause (g) of sub-section (1) of section 17.

23. Furnishing of information to State Board and other agencies in certain cases.—(1) Where in any air pollution control area the emission of any air pollutant into the atmosphere in excess of the standards laid down by the State Board occurs or is apprehended to occur due to accident or other unforeseen act or event, the person in charge of the premises from where such emission occurs or is apprehended to occur shall forthwith intimate the fact of such occurrence or the apprehension of such occurrence to the State Board and to such authorities or agencies as may be prescribed.

(2) On receipt of information with respect to the fact or the apprehension of any occurrence of the nature referred to in sub-section (1), whether through intimation under that sub-section or otherwise, the State Board and the authorities or agencies shall, as early as practicable, Cause such remedial measures to be taken as are necessary to mitigate the emission of such air pollutants.

(3) Expenses, if any, incurred by the State Board, authority or agency with respect to the remedial measures referred to in sub-section (2) together with interest (at such reasonable rate, as the State Government may, by order, fix) from the date when a demand for the expenses is made until it is paid, may be recovered by that Board, authority or agency from the person concerned, as arrears of land revenue, or of public demand.

24. Power of entry and inspection.—(1) Subject to the provisions of this section, any person empowered by a State Board in this behalf shall have a right to enter, at all reasonable times with such assistance as he considers necessary, any place—

(a) for the purpose of performing any of the functions of the State Board entrusted to him;

(b) for the purpose of determining whether and if so in what manner, any such functions are to be performed or whether any provisions of this Act or the rules made thereunder or any notice, order, direction or authorisation served, made, given or granted under this

Act is being or has been complied with;

(c) for the purpose of examining and testing any control equipment, industrial plant, record, register, document or any other material object or for conducting a search of any place in which he has reason to believe that an offence under this Act or the rules made thereunder has been or is being or is about to be committed to do so without and for seizing any such control equipment, industrial plant, record, register, document or other material object if he has reasons to believe that it may furnish evidence of the commission of an offence punishable under this Act or the rules made thereunder.

(2) Every person carrying on any industry specified in the Schedule and every person operating any control equipment or any industrial plant, in an air pollution control area shall be bound to render all assistance to the person empowered by the State Board under sub-section (1) for carrying out the functions under that sub-section and if he fails to do so without any reasonable cause or excuse, he shall be guilty of an offence under this act.

(3) If any person will fully delays or obstructs any person empowered by the State Board under sub-section (1) in the discharge of his duties, he shall be guilty of an offence under this Act.

(4) The provisions of the Code of Criminal Procedure, 1973, or, in relation to the State of Jam and Kashmir, or any area in which that Code is not in force, the provisions of any corresponding law in force in that State or area, shall, so far as may be, apply to any search or seizure under this section as they apply to any search or seizure made under the authority of a warrant issued under section 94 of the said Code or, as the case may be, under the corresponding provisions of the said law. (2 of 1974).

25. Power to obtain information.—For the purposes of carrying out the functions entrusted to it, the State Board or any officer empowered by it in that behalf may call for any information (including information regarding the types of air pollutants emitted into the atmosphere and the level of the emission of such air pollutants) from the occupier or any other person carrying on any industry or operating any control equipment or industrial plant and for the purpose of verifying the correctness of such information, the State Board or such officer shall have the right to inspect the premises where such industry, control equipment or industrial plant is being carried on or operated.

26. Power to take samples of air or emission and procedure to be followed in connection there with.—(1) A State Board or any officer empowered by it in this behalf shall have power to take, for the purpose of analysis, samples of air or emission from any chimney, flue or duct or any other outlet in such manner as may be prescribed.

(2) The result of any analysis of a sample of emission taken under sub-section (1) shall not be admissible in evidence in any legal proceeding unless the provisions of sub-sections (3) and (4) are complied with.

(3) Subject to the provisions of sub-section (4), when a sample of emission is taken for analysis under sub-section (1), the person taking the sample shall—

(a) serve on the occupier or his agent, a notice, then and there, in such form as may be prescribed, of his intention to have it so analysed;

(b) in the presence of the occupier or his agent, collect a sample of emission for analysis;

(c) cause the sample to be placed in a container or containers which shall be marked and sealed and shall also be signed both by the person taking the sample and the occupier or his agent;

(d) send, without delay, the container or containers to the laboratory established or recognised by the State Board under section 17 or, if a request in that behalf is made by the occupier or his agent when the notice is served on him under clause (a), to the laboratory established or specified under sub-section (1) of section 28.

(4) When a sample of emission is taken for analysis under sub-section (1) and the person taking the sample serves on the occupier or his agent, a notice under clause (a) of sub-section (3), then,—

(a) in a case where the occupier or his agent will fully absents himself, the person taking the sample shall collect the sample of emission for analysis to be placed in a container or containers which shall be marked and sealed and shall also be singed by the person taking the sample, and

(b) in a case where the occupier or his agent is present at the time of taking the sample but refuses to singe the marked and sealed container or containers of the sample of emission as required under clause (c) of sub-section (3), the marked and sealed container or containers shall be signed by the person taking the sample, and the container or containers shall be sent without delay by the person taking the sample for analysis to the laboratory established or specified under sub-section (1) of section 28 and such person shall inform the Government analyst appointed under sub-section (1) of section 29, in writing, about the will ful absence of the occupier or his agent, or, as the case may be, his refusal to sign the container or containers.

27. Reports of the result of analysis on samples taken under section 26.—(1) Where a sample of emission has been sent for analysis to the laboratory established or recognised by the State Board, the Board analyst appointed under sub-section (2) of section 29 shall analyse the sample and submit a report in the prescribed form of such analysis in triplicate to the State Board.

(2) On receipt of the report under sub-section (1), one copy of the report shall be sent by the State Board to the occupier or his agent referred to in section 26, another copy shall be preserved for production before the court in case any legal proceedings are taken against him and the other copy shall be the State Board.

(3) Where a sample has been sent for analysis under clause (d) of sub-section (3) or sub-section (4) of section 26 to any laboratory mentioned therein, the Government analyst referred to in the said sub-section (4) shall analyse the sample and submit a report in the prescribed form of the result of the analysis in triplicate to the State Board which shall comply with the provisions of sub-section (2).

(4) Any cost incurred in getting any sample analysed at the request of the occupier or his agent as provided in clause (d) of

sub-section (3) of section 26 or when he will fully absents himself or refuses to sign the marked and sealed container or containers of sample of emission under sub-section (4) of that section, shall be payable by such occupier or his agent and in case of default the same shall be recoverable from him as arrears of land revenue or of public demand.

28. State Air Laboratory.—(1) The State Government may, by notification in the Official Gazette,—

   (a) establish one or more State Air Laboratories; or
   (b) specify one or more laboratories or institutes as State Air Laboratories to carry out the functions entrusted to the State Air Laboratory under this Act.

(2) The State Government may, after consultation with the State Board, make rules prescribing—

   (a) the functions of the State Air Laboratory;
   (b) the procedure for the submission to the said Laboratory of samples of air or emission for analysis or tests, the form of the Laboratory's report thereon and the fees payable in respect of such report;
   (c) such other matters as may be necessary or expedient to enable that Laboratory to carry out its functions.

29. Analysts.—(1) The State Government may, by notification in the Official Gazette, appoint such persons as it thinks fit and having the prescribed qualifications to be Government analysts for the purpose of analysis of samples of air or emission sent for analysis to any laboratory established or specified under sub-section (1) of section 28.

(2) Without prejudice to the provisions of section 14, the State Board may, by notification in the Official Gazette, and with the approval of the State Government, appoint such persons as it thinks fit and having the prescribed qualifications to be Board analysts for the purpose of analysis of samples of air or emission sent for analysis to any laboratory established or recognised under section 17.

30. Reports of analysts.—Any document purporting to be a report signed by a Government analyst or, as the case may be a State Board analyst may be used as evidence of the facts stated therein in any proceeding under this Act.

31. Appeals.—(1) Any person aggrieved by an order made by the State Board under this Act may within thirty days from the date on which the order is communicated to him, prefer an appeal to such authority (hereinafter referred to as the Appellate Authority) as the State Government may think fit to constitute.

Provided that the Appellate Authority may entertain the appeal after the expiry of the said period of thirty days if such authority is satisfied that the appellant was prevented by sufficient cause form filing the appeal in time.

(2) The Appellate Authority shall consist of a single person or three persons as the State Government may think fit to be appointed by the State Government.

(3) The form and the manner in which an appeal may be preferred under sub-section (1), the fees payable for such appeal and the procedure to be followed by the Appellate Authority shall be such as may be prescribed.

(4) On receipt of an appeal preferred under sub-section (1), the Appellate Authority shall, after giving the appellant and the State Board an opportunity of being heard, dispose of the appeal as expeditiously as possible.

CHAPTER V
FUND, ACCOUNTS AND AUDIT

32. Contributions by Central Government.—The Central Government may, after due appropriation made by Parliament by law in this behalf, make in each financial year such contributions to the State Boards as it may think necessary to enable the State Boards to perform their functions under this Act:

Provided that nothing in this section shall apply to any State Board for the Prevention and Control of Water Pollution constituted under section 4 of the Water (Prevention and Control of Pollution) Act, 1974, (6 of 1974) which is empowered by that Act to expend money from its fund thereunder also for performing its functions, under any law for the time being in force relating to the prevention, control or abatement of air pollution.

33. Fund of Board.—(1) Every State Board shall have its own fund for the purposes of this Act and all sums which may, from time to time, be paid to it by the Central Government and all other receipts (by way of contributions, it any, form the State

Government, fees, gifts, grants, donations, benefactions or otherwise) of that Board shall be carried to the fund of the Board and all payments by the Board shall be made therefrom.

(2) Every State Board may expend such sums as it thinks fit for performing its functions under this Act and such sums shall be treated as expenditure payable out of the fund of that Board.

(3) Nothing in this section shall apply to any State Board for the Prevention and Control of Water Pollution constituted under section 4 of the Water (Prevention and Control of Pollution) Act, 1974, (6 of 1974) which is empowered by that Act to expend money form its fund thereunder also for performing its functions, under any law for the time being in force relating to the prevention, control or abatement of air pollution.

34. Budget.—The Central Board or, as the case may be, the State Board shall, during each financial year, prepare, in such form and at such time as may be prescribed, a budget in respect of the financial year next ensuing showing the estimated receipt and expenditure under this Act, and copies thereof shall be forwarded to the Central Government or, as the case may be, the State government.

35. Annual report.—(1) The Central Board shall, during each financial year, prepare, in such form and at such time as may be prescribed, an annual report giving full account of its activities under this Act during the previous financial year and copies thereof shall be forwarded to the Central Government and that Government shall cause every such report to be laid before both House of Parliament within six months of the date of which it is received by that Government.

(2) Every State Board shall, during each financial year, prepare, in such form and at such time as may be prescribed, an annual report giving full account of its activities under this Act during the previous financial year and copies thereof shall be forwarded to the State Government and that government shall cause every such report to be laid before the State Legislature within a period of nine months of the date on which it is received by that Government.

36. Accounts and audit.—(1) Every Board shall, in relation to its functions under this Act, maintain proper accounts and other relevant records and prepare an annual statement of accounts in such form as may be prescribed by the Central Government or, as the case may be, the State Government.

(2) The accounts of the Board shall be audited by an auditor duly qualified to act as an auditor of companies under section 225 of the Companies Act, 1956 (1 of 1956).

(3) The said auditor shall be appointed by the Central government or, as the case may be, the State Government on the advice of the Comptroller and Auditor-General of India.

(4) Every auditor appointed to audit the accounts of the Board under this Act shall have the right to demand the production of books, accounts, connected vouchers and other documents and papers and to inspect any of the offices of the Board.

(5) Every such auditor shall send a copy of his report together with an audited copy of the accounts to the Central Government or, as the case may be the State Government.

(6) The Central Government shall, as soon as may be after the receipt of the audit report under sub-section (5), cause the same to be laid before both House of Parliament.

(7) The State government shall, as soon as may be after the receipt of the audit report under sub-section (5), cause the same to be laid before the State Legislature.

CHAPTER VI
PENALTIES AND PROCEDURE

37. Failure to comply with the provisions of section 21(5) or section 22 or with orders or directions issued under the Act.—(1) Whoever fails to comply with the provisions of sub-section (5) of section 21 or section 22 or with any order or direction given under this Act shall, in respect of each such failure, be punishable with imprisonment for a term which may extend to three months or with fine which may extend to ten thousand rupees, or with both, and in case the failure continues, with an additional fine which may extend to one hundred rupees for every day during which such failure continues after the conviction for the first such failure.

(2) If the failure referred to in sub-section (1) continues beyond a period of one year after the date of conviction, the offender shall be punishable with imprisonment for a term which may extend to six months.

38. Penalties for certain acts.—Whoever—

(a) destroys, pulls down, removes, injures or defaces any pillar, post or stake fixed in the ground or any notice or other matter put up, inscribed or placed, by or under the authority of the Board, or

(b) obstructs any person acting under the orders or directions of the Board from exercising his powers and performing his functions under this Act, or

(c) damages any works or property belonging to the Board, or

(d) fails to furnish to the Board or any officer or other employee of the Board any information required by the Board or such officer or other employee for the purpose of this Act, or

(e) fails to intimate the occurrence of the emission of air pollutants into the atmosphere in excess of the standards laid down by the State Board or the apprehension of such occurrence, to the State Board and other prescribed authorities or agencies as required under sub-section (1) of section 23, or

(f) in giving any information which he is required to give under this Act, makes a statement which is false in any material particular, or

(g) for the purpose of obtaining any consent under section 21, makes a statement which is false in any material particular,

shall be punishable with imprisonment for a term which may extend to three months or with fine which may extend to five hundred rupees or with both.

39. Penalty for contravention of certain provision of the Act.—Whoever contravenes any of the provisions of this Act, for which no penalty has been elsewhere provided in this Act, shall be punishable with fine which may extend to five thousand rupees, and in the case of continuing contravention, with an additional fine which may extend to one hundred rupees for every day during which such contravention continues after conviction for the first such contravention.

40. Offences by companies.—(1) Where an offence under

this Act has been committed by a company, every person who, at the time the offence was committed, was directly in charge of and was responsible to, the company for the conduct of the business of the company, as well as the company, shall be deemed to be guilty of the offence and shall be liable to be proceeded against and punished accordingly

Provided that nothing contained in this sub-section shall render any such person liable to any punishment provided in this Act, if he proves that the offence was committed without his knowledge or that he exercised all due diligence to prevent the commission of such offence.

(2) Notwithstanding anything contained in sub-section (1), where an offence under this Act has been committed by a company and it is proved that the offence has been committed with the consent or connivance of, or is attributable to any neglect on the part of, any director, manager, secretary or other officer of the company, such director, manager, secretary or other officer shall also be deemed to be guilty of that offence and shall be liable to be proceeded against and punished accordingly.

Explanation.—For the purposes of this section,—

(a) "company" means any body corporate, and includes a firm or other association of individuals; and

(b) "director", in relation to a firm, means a partner in the firm.

41. Offences by Governments Departments.—(1) Where an offence under this Act has been committed by any Department of Government, the Head of the Department shall be deemed to be guilty of the offence and shall be liable to be proceeded against and punished accordingly:

Provided that nothing contained in this section shall render such Head of the Department liable to any punishment if he proves that the offence was committed without his knowledge or that he exercised all due diligence to prevent the commission of such offence.

(2) Notwithstanding anything contained in sub-section (1), where an offence under this Act has been committed by a Department of Government and it is proved that the offence has been committed with the consent or connivance of, or is

attributable to any neglect on the part of, any officer, other than the Head of the Department, such officer shall also be deemed to be guilty of that offence and shall be liable to be proceeded against and punished accordingly.

42. Protection of action taken in good faith.—No suit, prosecution or other legal proceeding shall lie against the Government or any officer of the Government or any member or any officer or other employee of the Board in respect of anything which is done or intended to be done in good faith in pursuance of this Act or the rules made thereunder.

43. Cognizance of offences.—No court shall take cognizance of any offence under this Act except on a complaint made by, or with the previous sanction in writing of, the State Board, and no court inferior to that of a Metropolitan Magistrate or a Judicial Magistrate of the first class shall try any offence punishable under this Act.

44. Members, officers and employees of Board to be public servants.—All the members and all officers and other employees of a Board when acting or purporting to act in pursuance of any of the provisions of this Act or the rules made thereunder shall be deemed to be public servants within the meaning of section 21 of the Indian Penal Code. (45 of 1860)

45. Reports and returns.—The Central Board shall, in relation to its functions under this Act, furnish to the Central Government, and a State Board shall, in relation to its functions under this Act, furnish to the State Government and to the Central Board such reports, returns, statistics, accounts and other information as that Government, or, as the case may be, the Central Board may, from time to time, require.

46. Bar of jurisdiction.—No civil court shall have jurisdiction to entertain any suit or proceeding in respect of any matter which an Appellate Authority constituted under this Act is empowered by or under this Act to determine, and no injunction shall be granted by any court or other authority in respect of any action taken or to be taken in pursuance of any power conferred by or under this Act.

CHAPTER VII
MISCELLANEOUS

47. Power of State Government to supersede State Board.—(1) If any time the State Government is of opinion—

(a) that a State Board constituted under this Act has persistently made default in the performance of the functions imposed on it by or under this Act, or

(b) that circumstances exits which render it necessary in the public interest so to do,

the State Government may, by notification in the Official Gazette, supersede the State Board for such period, not exceeding six months, as may be specified in the notification:

Provided that before issuing a notification under this sub-section for the reasons mentioned in clause (a), the State Government shall give a reasonable opportunity to the State Board to show cause why it should not be superseded and shall consider the explanations and objections, if any, of the State Board,

(2) Upon the publication of a notification under sub-section (1) superseding the State Board,—

(a) all the members shall, as form the date of suppression, vacate their offices as such;

(b) all the powers, functions and duties which may, by or under this Act, be exercised, performed or discharged by the State Board shall, until the State Board is reconstituted under sub-section (3), be exercised, performed or discharged by such person or persons as the State Government may direct;

(c) all property owned or controlled by the State Board shall, until the Board is reconstituted under sub-section (3), vest in the State government.

(3) On the expiration of the period of suppression specified in the notification issued under sub-section (1), the State Government may —

(a) extend the period of suppression for such further term, not exceeding six months, as it may consider necessary; or

(b) reconstitute the State Board by a fresh nomination or appointment, as the case may be, and in such case any person who vacated his office under clause (a) of sub-section (2) shall also be eligible for nomination or appointment:

Provided that the State government may at any time before the expiration of the period of suppression, whether originally specified under sub-section (1) or as extended under this sub-section, take action under clause (b) of this sub-section.

48. Special provision in the case of suppression of the Central Board or the State Boards constituted under the Water (Prevention and Control of Pollution) Act, 1974.—Where the Central Board or any State Board constituted under the Water (Prevention and Control of Pollution) Act, 1974, (6 of 1974) is superseded by the Central Government or the State Government, as the case may be, under that Act, all the powers, functions and duties of the Central Board or such State Board under this Act shall be exercised, performed or discharged during the period of such suppression by the person or persons, exercising, performing or discharging the powers, functions and duties of the Central Board or such State Board under the Water (Prevention and Control of Pollution) Act, 1974, during such period.

49. Dissolution of State Boards constituted under the Act.—(1) As and when the Water (Prevention and Control of Pollution) Act, 1974, (6 of 1974) comes into force in any State and the State government constitutes a State Board for the Prevention and Control of Water Pollution under that Act, the State Board constituted by the State Government under this Act shall stand dissolved and the Board first-mentioned shall exercise the powers and perform the functions of the Board second mentioned in that State.

(2) On the dissolution of the State Board constituted under this Act,—

(a) all the members shall vacate their offices as such;

(b) all moneys and other property of whatever kind (including the fund of the State Board) owned by, or vested in, the State Board, immediately before such dissolution, shall stand transferred to and vest in the State Board for the Prevention and Control of Water Pollution.

(c) every officer and other employee serving under the State Board immediately before such dissolution shall be transferred to and become an office or other employee of the State Board for the Prevention and Control of Water Pollution and hold office by the same tenure and at the same remuneration and on the same terms and conditions of service as he would have held the same if the State Board constituted under this Act had not been dissolved and shall continue to do so unless and until such tenure, remuneration and terms and conditions of service are duly altered by the State Board for the Prevention and Control of Water Pollution.

Provided that the tenure, remuneration and terms and conditions of service of any such officer or other employee shall not be altered to his disadvantage without the previous sanction of the State Government;

(d) all liabilities and obligations of the State Board of whatever kind, immediately before such dissolution, shall be deemed to be the liabilities or obligations, as the case may be, of the State Board for the Prevention and Control of Water Pollution and any proceeding or cause of action, pending or existing immediately before such dissolution by or against the State Board constituted under this Act in relation to such liability or obligation may be continued and enforced by or against the State Board for the Prevention and Control of Water Pollution.

50. Power to amend the Schedule.—(1) The Central Government may, of its own motion or on the recommendation of a Board, by notification in the Official Gazette, add to, or omit form, the Schedule any industry or alter the description of any industry and thereupon the Schedule shall be deemed to be amended accordingly.

(2) Every notification made under sub-section (1) shall be laid, as soon as may be after it is made, before each House of Parliament.

51. Maintenance of register.—(1) Every State Board shall maintain a register containing particulars of the persons to whom consent has been granted under section 21, the standards for emission laid down by it in relation to each such consent and such other particulars as may be prescribed.

(2) The register maintained under sub-section (1) shall be open to inspection at all reasonable hours by any person interested in or affected by such standards for emission or by any other person authorised by such person in this behalf.

52. Effect of other laws.—Save as otherwise provided by or under the Atomic Energy Act, 1962, (33 of 1962). in relation to radioactive air pollution the provisions of this Act shall have effect notwithstanding anything inconsistent therewith contained in any enactment other than this Act.

53. Power of Central Government to make rules.—(1) The Central Government may, in consultation with the Central Board, by notification in the Official Gazette, make rules in respect of the following matters, namely:—

(a) the intervals and the time and place at which meetings of the Central Board or any committee thereof shall be held and he procedure to be followed at such meetings, including the quorum necessary for the transaction of business thereat, under sub-section (1) of section 10 and under sub-section (2) of section 11;

(b) the fees and allowances to be paid to the members of a committee of the Central Board, not being members of the Board, under sub-section (3) of section 11;

(c) the manner in which and the purposes for which persons may be associated with the Central Board under sub-section (1) of section 12.

(d) the fees and allowances to be paid under sub-section (3) of section 12 to persons associated with the central board under sub-section (1) of section 12;

(e) the functions to be performed by the Central Board under clause (j) of sub-section (2) of section 16;

(f) the form in which and the time within which the budget and the annual report of the Central Board may be prepared and forwarded to the Central Government under sections 34 and 35;

(g) the form in which the accounts of the Central Board may be maintained under sub-section (1) of section 36.

(2) Every rule made by the Central Government under this Act shall be laid, as soon as may be after its is made, before each House of Parliament, while it is in session, for a total period of thirty days which may be comprised in one session or in two or more successive sessions, and if, before the expiry of the session immediately following the session or the successive sessions aforesaid, both Houses agree in making any modification in the rule or both Houses agree that the rule should not be made, the rule shall thereafter have effect only in such modified form or be of no effect, as the case may be; so, however, that any such modification or annulment shall be without prejudice to the validity of anything previously done under that rule.

54. Power of State Government to make rules.—(1) Subject to the provisions of sub-section (3), the State Government may, by notification in the Official Gazette, make rules to carry out the purposes of this Act in respect of matters not falling within the purview of section 53.

(2) In particular, and without prejudice to the generality of the foregoing power, such rules may provide for all or any of the following matters, namely:—

(a) the terms and conditions of service of the Chairman and other members (other than the member-secretary) of the state Board constituted under this Act under sub-section (7) of section 7:

(b) the intervals and the time and place at which meetings of the State Board or any committee thereof shall be held and the procedure to be followed at such meetings, including the quorum necessary for the transaction of business thereat, under sub-section (1) of section 10 and under sub-section (2) of section 11;

(c) the fees and allowances to be paid to the members of a committee of the State Board, not being members of the Board under sub-section (3) of section 11;

(d) the manner in which and the purposes for which persons may be associated with the State Board under sub-section (1) of section 12;

(e) the fees and allowances to be paid under sub-section

(3) of section 12 to persons associated with the State Board under sub-section (1) of section 12;

(f) the terms and conditions of service of the member - secretary of a State Board constituted under this Act under sub-section (1) of section 14;

(g) the powers and duties to be exercised and discharged by the member-secretary of a State Board under sub-section (2) of section 14;

(h) the conditions subject to which a State Board may appoint such officers and other employees as it considers necessary for the efficient performance of its functions under sub-section (3) of section 14;

(i) the conditions subject to which a State Board may appoint a consultant under sub-section (5) of section 14;

(j) the functions to be performed by the State Board under clause (I) of sub-section (1) of section 17;

(k) the manner in which any area or areas may be declared as air pollution control area or areas under sub-section (1) of section 19;

(l) the form of application for the consent of the State Board, the fees payable-therefor, the period within which such application shall be made and the particulars it may contain, under sub-section (2) of section 21;

(m) the procedure to be followed in respect of an inquiry under sub-section (3) of section 21;

(n) the authorities or agencies to whom information under sub-section (1) of section 23 shall be furnished.

(o) the manner in which samples of air or emission may be taken under sub-section (1) of section 26;

(p) the form of the notice referred to in sub-section (3) of section 26;

(q) the form of the report of the Government analyst under sub-section 27;

(r) the form of the report of the Government analyst under sub-section (3) of section 27;

(s) the functions of the State Air Laboratory, the procedure for the submission to the said Laboratory of samples of air or emission for analysis or tests, the form of

Laboratory's report thereon, the fees payable in respect of such report and other matters as may be necessary or expedient to enable that Laboratory to carry out its functions, under sub-section (2) of section 28;

(t) the qualifications required for State Board analysts under sub-section (1) of section 29;

(u) the qualifications required for State Board analysts under sub-section (2) of section 29;

(v) the form and the manner in which appeals may be preferred, the fees payable in respect of such appeals and the procedure to be followed by the Appellate Authority in disposing of the appeals under sub-section (3) of section 31;

(w) the form in which and the time within which the budget and annual report of State Board may be prepared and forwarded to the State Government under sections 34 and 35;

(x) the form in which the accounts of State Board may be maintained under sub-section (1) of section 36;

(y) the particulars which the register maintained under section 51 may contain;

(z) any other matter which has to be, or may be, prescribed.

(3) After the first constitution of the State Board, no rule with respect to any of the matters referred to in sub-section (2) [other than those referred to in clause (a) thereof], shall be made, varied, amended or repealed without consulting that Board.

THE SCHEDULE
(See Sections 21,22,24 and 50)

1. Asbestos and asbestos products industries.
2. Cement and cement products industries.
3. Ceramic and ceramic products industries.
4. Chemical and allied industries.
5. Coal and lignite based chemical industries.
6. Engineering industries.
7. Ferrous metallurgical industries.

8. Fertilizer industries.
9. Foundries.
10. Food and agricultural products industries.
11. Mining industry.
12. Non-ferrous metallurgical industries.
13. Ores/mineral processing industries including benefaction, pelletization, etc.
14. Power (coal, petroleum and their products) generating plants and boiler plants.
15. Paper and pulp (including paper products) industries.
16. Textile processing industry (made wholly or in part of cotton).
17. Petroleum refineries.
18. Petroleum products and petro-chemical industries.
19. Plants for recovery from and disposal of wastes.
20. Incinerators.

APPENDIX "D"

The Environment (Protection) Act, 1986

No. 29 of 1986

[23rd May, 1986]

An Act to Provide for the Protection and Improvement of Environment and for Matters Connected therewith.

WHEREAS decisions were taken at the United Nations Conference on the Human Environment held at Stockholm in June, 1972, in which India participated, to take appropriate steps for the protection and improvement of human environment;

AND WHEREAS it is considered necessary further to implement the decisions aforesaid in so far as they relate to the protection and improvement of environment and the prevention of hazards to human beings, other living creatures, plants and property;

BE it enacted by Parliament in the Thirty-seventh Year of the Republic of India as follows:—

CHAPTER I
PRELIMINARY

1. Short title, extent and commencement.—(1) This Act may be called the Environment (Protection) Act, 1986.

(2) It extends to the whole of India.

(3) It shall come into force on such date *[19-11-1986: vide Notification No. G.S.R. 1198(E), dated 12-11-1986, Gazette of India, 1986, Extra-ordinary, Part II, Section 3(i).]* as the Central Government may, be notification in the Official Gazette, appoint and different dates may be appointed for different provisions of

this Act and for different areas.

2. **Definitions.**—In this Act, unless the context otherwise requires,—

(a) "environment" includes water, air and land and the inter-relationship which exists among and between water, air and land, and human beings, other living creatures, plants, micro-organism and property;

(b) "environmental pollutant" means any solid, liquid or gaseous substance present in such concentration as may be, or tend to be, injurious to environment;

(c) "environment pollution" means the presence in the environment of any environment pollutant;

(d) "handling", in relation to any substance, means the manufacture, processing, treatment, package, storage, transportation, use, collection, destruction, conversion, offering for sale, transfer or the like of such substance;

(e) "hazardous substance" means any substance or preparation which, by reason of its chemical or physico-chemical properties or handling, is liable to cause harm to human beings, other living creatures, plants, micro-organism, property or the environment;

(f) "occupier", in relation to any factory or premises, means a person who has control over the affairs of the factory or the premises and includes, in relation to any substance, the person in possession of the substance;

(g) "prescribed" means prescribed by rules made under this Act.

CHAPTER II
GENERAL POWERS OF THE CENTRAL GOVERNMENT

3. **Power of Central Government to take measures to protect and improve environment.**—(1) Subject to the provisions of this Act, the Central Government shall have the power to take all such measures as it deems necessary or expedient for the purpose of protecting and improving the quality of the environment and preventing, controlling and abating environment pollution.

(2) In particular, and without prejudice to the generality of the provisions of sub-section (1), such measures may include

measures with respect to all or any of the following matters, namely:—

(i) co-ordination of actions by the State Governments, officers and other authorities—

(a) under this Act, or the rules made thereunder; or

(b) under any other law for the time being in force which is relatable to the objects of this Act;

(ii) planning and execution of a nation-wide programme for the prevention, control and abatement of environmental pollution;

(iii) laying down standards for the quality of environment its various aspects;

(iv) laying down standards for emission or discharge of environmental pollutants form various sources whatsoever:

Provided that different standards for emission or discharge may be laid down under this clause from different sources having regard to the quality or composition of the emission or discharge of environmental pollutants from such sources;

(v) restriction of areas in which any industries, operations or processes or class of industries, operations or processes shall not be carried out or shall be carried out subject to certain safeguards;

(vi) laying down procedures and safeguards for the prevention of accidents which may cause environmental pollution and remedial measures for such accidents;

(vii) laying down procedures and safeguards for the handling of hazardous substances;

(viii) examination of such manufacturing processes, materials and substances as are likely to cause environmental pollution;

(ix) carrying out and sponsoring investigations and research relating to problems of environmental pollution;

(x) inspection of any premises, plant, equipment, machinery, manufacturing or other processes, materials or substances and giving, by order, of such directions to such authorities, officers of persons as it may consider necessary to take steps for the prevention, control and abatement of environmental pollution;

(xi) establishment or recognition of environmental laboratories and institutes to carry out the functions entrusted to such environmental laboratories and institutes under this Act;

(xii) collection and dissemination of information in respect of matters relating to environmental pollution;

(xiii) preparation of manuals, codes or guides relating to the prevention, control and abatement of environmental pollution;

(xiv) such other matters as the Central Government deems necessary or expedient for the purpose of securing the effective implementation of the provisions of this Act.

(3) The Central Government may, if it considers it necessary or expedient so to do for the purposes of this Act, by order, published in the Official Gazette, constitute an authority or authorities by such name or names as may be specified in the order for the purpose of exercising and performing such of the powers and functions (including the power to issue directions under section (5) of the Central Government under this Act and for taking measures with respect to such of the matters referred to in sub-section (2) as may be mentioned in the order and subject to the supervision and control of the Central Government and the provisions of such order, such authority or authorities may exercise the powers or perform the functions or take the measures so mentioned in the order as if such authority or authorities had been empowered by this Act to exercise those powers or perform those functions or take such measures.

4. Appointment of officers and their powers and functions.—(1) Without prejudice to the provisions of sub-section (3) of section 3, the Central Government may appoint officers with such designations as it thinks fit for the purposes of this Act and may entrust to them such of the powers and functions under this Act as it may deem fit.

(2) The officers appointed under sub-section (1) shall be subject to the general control and direction of the Central Government or, if so directed by that Government, also of the authority or authorities, if any, constituted under sub-section (3)

of section 3 or of any other authority or officer.

5. Power to give directions.—Notwithstanding anything contained in any other law but subject to the provisions of this Act, the Central Government may, in the exercise of its powers and performance of its functions under this Act, issue directions in writing to any person, officer or any authority and such person, officer or authority shall be bound to comply with such directions.

Explanation.—For the avoidance of doubts, it is hereby declared that the power to issue directions under this section includes the power to direct—

    (a) the closure, prohibition or regulation of any industry, operation or process; or

    (b) stoppage or regulation of the supply of electricity or water or any other service.

6. Rules to regulate environmental pollution.—(1) The Central Government may, by notification in the Official Gazette, make rules in respect of all or any of the matters referred to in section 3.

(2) In particular, and without prejudice to the generality of the foregoing power, such rules may provide for all or any of the following matters, namely:—

    (a) the standards of quality of air, water or soil for various areas and purposes;

    (b) the maximum allowable limits of concentration of various environmental pollutants (including noise) for different areas;

    (c) the procedures and safeguards for the handling of hazardous substances;

    (d) the prohibition and restrictions on the handling of hazardous substances in different areas;

    (e) the prohibition and restrictions on the location of industries and the carrying on of processes and operations in different areas;

    (f) the procedures and safeguards for the prevention of accidents which may cause environmental pollution and for providing for remedial measures for such accidents.

CHAPTER III

PREVENTION, CONTROL AND ABATEMENT OF ENVIRONMENTAL POLLUTION

7. Persons carrying on industry, operation, etc., not to allow emission or discharge of environmental pollutants in excess of the standards.—No person carrying on any industry, operation or process shall discharge or emit or permit to be discharged or emitted any environmental pollutant in excess of such standards as may be prescribed.

8. Persons handling hazardous substances to comply with procedural safeguards.—No person shall handle or cause to be handled any hazardous substance except in accordance with such procedure and after complying with such safeguards as may be prescribed.

9. Furnishing of information to authorities and agencies in certain cases.—(1) Where the discharge of any environmental pollutant in excess of the prescribed standards occurs or is apprehended to occur due to any accident or other unforeseen act or event, the person responsible for such discharge and the person in charge of the place at which such discharge occurs or is apprehended to occur shall be bound to prevent or mitigate the environmental pollution caused as a result of such discharge and shall also forthwith—

(a) intimate the fact of such occurrence or apprehension of such occurrence; and

(b) be bound, if called upon, to render all assistance, to such authorities or agencies as may be prescribed.

(2) On receipt of information with respect to the fact or apprehension of any occurrence of the nature referred to in sub-section (1), whether through intimation under that sub-section or otherwise, the authorities or agencies referred to in sub-section (1) shall, as early as practicable, cause such remedial measures to be taken as are necessary to prevent or mitigate the environmental pollution.

(3) The expenses, if any, incurred by any authority or agency with respect to the remedial measures referred to in sub-section (2), together with interest (at such reasonable rate as the Government may, by order, fix) from the date when a demand

for the expenses is made until it is paid, may be recovered by such authority or agency from the person concerned as arrears of land revenue or of public demand.

10. Powers of entry and inspection.—(1) Subject to the provisions of this section, any person empowered by the Central Government in this behalf shall have a right to enter, at all reasonable times with such assistance as he considers necessary, any place—

(a) for the purpose of performing any of the functions of the Central Government entrusted to him;

(b) for the purpose of determining whether and if so in what manner, any such functions are to be performed or whether any provisions of this Act or the rules made thereunder or any notice, order, direction or authorisation served, made, given or granted under this Act is being or has been complied with;

(c) for the purpose of examining and testing any equipment, industrial plant, record, register, document or any other material object or for conducting a search of any building in which he has reason to believe that an offence under this Act or the rules made thereunder has been or is being or is about to be committed and for seizing any such equipment industrial plant, record, register, document or other material object if he has reasons to believe that it may furnish evidence of the commission of an offence punishable under this Act or the rules made thereunder or that such seizure is necessary to prevent or mitigate environment pollution.

(2) Every person carrying on any industry, operation or process or handling any hazardous substance shall be bound to render all assistance to the person empowered by the Central Government under sub-section (1) for carrying out the functions under that sub-section and if he fails to do so without any reasonable cause or excuse, he shall be guilty of an offence under this Act.

(3) If any person wilfully delays or obstructs any person empowered by the Central Government under sub-section (1) in the performance of his functions, he shall be guilty of an offence under this Act.

(4) The provisions of the Code of Criminal Procedure, 1973 (2 of 1974), or in relation to the State of Jammu and Kashmir, or any area in which that Code is not in force, the provisions of any corresponding law in force in that State or area shall, so far as may be, apply to any search or seizure under this section as they apply to any search or seizure made under the authority of a warrant issued under section 94 of the said Code or, as the case may be, under he corresponding provision of the said law.

11. Power to take sample and procedure to be followed in connection therewith.—(1) The Central Government or any officer empowered by it in this behalf, shall have power to take, for the purpose of analysis, samples of air, water, soil or other substance from any factory, premises or other place in such manner as may be prescribed.

(2) The result of any analysis of a sample taken under sub-section (1) shall not be admissible in evidence in any legal proceeding unless the provisions of sub-sections (3) and (4) are complied with:

(3) Subject to the provisions of sub-section (4), the person taking the sample under sub-section (1) shall—

(a) serve on the occupier or his agent or person in charge of the place, a notice, then and there, in such form as may be prescribed, of his intention to have it so analysed;

(b) in the presence of the occupier or his agent or person, collect a sample for analysis;

(c) cause the sample to be placed in a container or containers which shall be marked and sealed and shall also be signed both by the person taking the sample and the occupier or his agent or person;

(d) send without delay, the container or the containers to the laboratory established or recognised by the Central Government under section 12.

(4) When a sample is taken for analysis under sub-section (1) and the person taking the sample serves on the occupier or his agent or person, a notice under clause (a) of sub-section (3), then—

(a) in a case where the occupier, his agent or person wilfully absents himself, the person taking the sample shall collect the sample for analysis to be placed in a container or containers which shall be marked and sealed and shall also be signed by the person taking the sample, and

(b) in a case where the occupier or his agent or person present at the time of taking the sample refuses to sign the marked and sealed container or containers of the sample as required under clause (c) of sub-section (3), the marked and sealed container or containers shall be signed by the person taking the samples, and the container or containers shall be sent without delay by the person taking the sample for analysis to the laboratory established or recognised under section 12 and such person shall inform the Government Analyst appointed or recognised under section 13 in writing, about the wilful absence of the occupier or his agent or person, or, as the case may be, his refusal to sign the container or containers.

12. Environmental laboratories.—(1) The Central Government may, be notification in the Official Gazette,—

(a) establish one or more environmental laboratories;

(b) recognise one or more laboratories or institutes as environmental laboratories to carry out the functions entrusted to an environmental laboratory under this Act.

(2) The Central Government may, by notification in the Official Gazette, make rules specifying—

(a) the functions of the environmental laboratory;

(b) the procedure for the submission to the said laboratory of samples of air, water, soil or other substance for analysis or tests, the form of the laboratory report thereon and the fees payable for such report;

(c) such other matters as may be necessary or expedient to enable that laboratory to carry out its functions.

13. Government Analysts.—The Central Government may, by notification in the Official Gazette, appoint or recognise such persons as it thinks fit and having the prescribed qualifications to be Government Analysts for the purpose of analysis of samples of air, water, soil or other substance sent for analysis to any environmental laboratory established or recognised under sub-section (1) of section 12.

14. Reports of Government Analysts.—Any document purporting to be a report signed by a Government Analyst may be used as evidence of the facts stated therein in any proceeding under this Act.

15. Penalty for contravention of the provisions of the Act and the rules, orders and directions.—(1) Whoever fails to comply with or contravenes any of the provisions of this Act, or the rules made or orders or directions issued thereunder, shall, in respect of each such failure or contravention, be punishable with imprisonment for a term which may extend to five years or with fine which may extend to one lakh rupees, or with both, and in case the failure or contravention continues, with additional fine which may extend to five thousand rupees for every day during which such failure or contravention continues after the conviction for the first such failure or contravention.

(2) If the failure or contravention referred to in sub-section (1) continues beyond a period of one year after the date of conviction, the offender shall be punishable with imprisonment for a term which may extend to seven years.

16. Offences by companies.—(1) Where any offence under this Act has been committed by a company, every person who, at the time the offence was committed, was directly in charge of, and was responsible to, the company for the conduct of the business of the company, as well as the company, shall be deemed to be guilty of the offence and shall be liable to be proceeded against and punished accordingly:

Provided that nothing contained in this sub-section shall render any such person liable to any punishment provided in this Act, if he proves that the offence was committed without his knowledge or that he exercised all due diligence to prevent the commission of such offence.

(2) Notwithstanding anything contained in sub-section (1), where an offence under this Act has been committed by a company and it is proved that the offence has been committed with the consent or connivance of, or is attributable to any neglect on the part of, any director, manager, secretary or other

officer of the company, such director, manager, secretary or other officer shall also be deemed to be guilty of that offence and shall be liable to be proceeded against and punished accordingly.

Explanation.—For the purposes of this section,—

(a) "company" means any body corporate, and includes a firm or other association of individuals; and

(b) "director", in relation to a firm, means a partner in the firm.

17. Offences by Government Departments.—(1) Where an offence under this Act has been committed by any Department of Government, the Head of the Department shall be deemed to be guilty of the offence and shall be liable to be proceeded against and punished accordingly:

Provided that nothing contained in this section shall render such Head of the Department liable to any punishment if he proves that the offence was committed without his knowledge or that he exercised all due diligence to prevent the commission of such offence.

(2) Notwithstanding anything contained in sub-section (1), where and offence under this Act has been committed by a Department of Government and it is proved that the offence has been committed with the consent or connivance of, or is attributable to any neglect on the part of, any officer, other than the Head of the Department, such officer shall also be deemed to be guilty of that offence and shall be liable to be proceeded against and punished accordingly.

CHAPTER IV
MISCELLANEOUS

18. Protection of action taken in good faith.—No suit, prosecution or other legal proceeding shall lie against the Government or any officer or other employee of the Government or any authority constituted under this Act or any member, officer or other employee of such authority in respect of anything which is done or intended to be done in good faith in pursuance of this Act or the rules made or orders or directions issued thereunder.

19. Cognizance of offences.—No court shall take

cognizance of any offence under this Act except on a complaint made by—

(a) the Central Government or any authority or officer authorised in this behalf by the Government; or

(b) any person who has given notice of not less than sixty days, in the manner prescribed, of the alleged offence and of his intention to make a complaint, to the Central Government or the authority or officer authorised as aforesaid.

20. Information, reports or returns.—The Central Government may, in relation to its functions under this Act, from time to time, require any person, officer, State Government or other authority to furnish to it or any prescribed authority or officer any reports, returns, statistics, accounts and other information and such person, officer, State Government or other authority shall be bound to do so.

21. Members, officers and employees of the authority constituted under section 3 to be public servants.—All the members of the authority, constituted, if any, under section 3 and all officers and other employees of such authority when acting or purporting to act in pursuance of any provisions of this Act or the rules made or orders or directions issued thereunder shall be deemed to be public servants within the meaning of section 21 of the Indian Penal Code (45 of 1860).

22. Bar of jurisdiction.—No civil court shall have jurisdiction to entertain any suit or proceeding in respect of anything done, action taken or order or direction issued by the Central Government or any other authority or officer in pursuance of any power conferred by or in relation to its or his functions under this Act.

23. Power to delegate.—Without prejudice to the provisions of sub-section (3) of section 3, the Central Government may, by notification in the Official Gazette, delegate, subject to such conditions and limitations as may be specified in the notification, such of its powers and functions under this Act [except the power to constitute an authority under sub-section (3) of section 3 and to make rules under section 25] as it may deem necessary or expedient, to any officer, State Government or other authority.

24. Effect of other laws.—(1) Subject to the provisions of sub-section (2), the provisions of this Act and the rules or orders made therein shall have effect notwithstanding anything inconsistent therewith contained in any enactment other than this Act.

(2) Where any act or omission constitutes an offence punishable under this Act and also under any other Act then the offender found guilty of such offence shall be liable to be punished under the other Act and not under this Act.

25. Power to make rules.—(1) The Central Government may, by notification in the Official Gazette, make rules for carrying out the purposes of this Act.

(2) In particular, and without prejudice to the generality of the foregoing power, such rules may provide for all or any of the following matters, namely—

(a) the standards in excess of which environmental pollutants shall not be discharged or emitted under section 7;

(b) the procedure in accordance with and the safeguards in compliance with which hazardous substances shall be handled or cause to be handled under section 8;

(c) the authorities or agencies to which intimation of the fact of occurrence or apprehension of occurrence of the discharge of any environmental pollutant in excess of the prescribed standards shall be given and to whom all assistance shall be bound to be rendered under sub-section (1) of section 9;

(d) the manner in which samples of air, water, soil or other substance for the purpose of analysis shall be taken under sub-section (1) of section 11;

(e) the form in which notice of intention to have a sample analysed shall be served under clause (a) of sub-section (3) of section 11;

(f) the functions of the environmental laboratories, the procedure for the submission to such laboratories of samples of air, water, soil and other substances for analysis or test; the form of laboratory report; the fees payable for such report and other matters to enable such laboratories to carry out their functions under sub-section (2) of section 12;

(g) the qualifications of Government Analyst appointed or recognised for the purpose of analysis of samples of air, water, soil or other substances under section 13;

(h) the manner in which notice of the offence and of the intention to make a complaint to the Central Government shall be given under clause (b) of section 19;

(i) the authority or officer to whom any reports, returns, statistics, accounts and other information shall be furnished under section 20;

(j) any other matter which is required to be, or may be, prescribed.

26. Rules made under this Act to be laid before Parliament. —Every rule made under this Act shall be laid, as soon as may be after it is made, before each House of Parliament, while it is in session, for a total period of thirty days which may be comprised in one session or in two or more successive sessions, and if, before the expiry of the session immediately following the session or the successive sessions aforesaid, both houses agree in making any modification in the rule or both Houses agree that the rule should not be made, the rule shall, thereafter have effect only in such modified form or be of no effect, as the case may be; so however, that any such modification or annulment shall be without prejudice to the validity of anything previously done under that rule.

The Water (Prevention and Control of Pollution) Act, 1974

No. 6 of 1974

[23rd March, 1974]

An Act to provide for the prevention and control of water pollution and the maintaining or restoring of wholesomeness of water, for the establishment, with a view to carrying out the purposes aforesaid, of Boards for the prevention and control of water Pollution, for conferring on and assigning to such Boards Powers and functions relating thereto and for matters connected therewith.

WHEREAS it is expedient to provide for the prevention and control of water pollution and the maintaining or restoring of wholesomeness of water, for the establishment, with a view to carrying out the purposes aforesaid, of Board for the prevention and control of water pollution and for conferring on and assigning to such Boards powers and functions relating thereto;

AND WHEREAS Parliament has no power to make laws for the States with respect to any of the matters aforesaid except as provided in articles 249 and 250 of the Constitution;

AND WHEREAS in pursuance of clause (1) of article 252 of the Constitution resolutions have been passed by all the Houses of the Legislatures of the States of Assam, Bihar, Gujarat, Haryana, Himachal Pradesh, Jammu and Kashmir, Karnataka, Kerala, Madhya Pradesh, Rajasthan, Tripura and West Bengal to the effect that the matters aforesaid should be regulated in those States by Parliament by law;

Be it enacted by Parliament in the Twenty-fifth Year of the Republic of India as follows:—

CHAPTER I
PRELIMINARY

1. Short title, application and commencement.—(1) This Act may be called the Water (prevention and Control of Pollution) Act, 1974.

(2) It applies in the first instance to the whole of the States of Assam, Bihar, Gujarat, Haryana, Himachal Pradesh, Jammu and Kashmir, Karnataka, Kerala, Madhya Pradesh, Rajasthan, Tripura and West Bengal and the Union Territories; and it shall apply to such other State which adopts this Act by resolution passed in that behalf under clause (1) of article 252 of the Constitution.

(3) It shall come into force, at once in the States of Assam, Bihar, Gujarat, Haryana, Himachal Pradesh, Jammu and Kashmir, Karnataka, Kerala, Madhya Pradesh, Rajasthan, Tripura and West Bengal and it the Union Territories, and in any other State which adopts this Act under clause (1) of article 252 of the Constitution on the date of such adoption and any reference in this Act to the commencement of this Act shall, in relation to any State or Union territory, mean the date on which this Act comes into force in such State or Union territory.

2. Definitions.—In this Act, unless the context otherwise requires,—

(a) "Board" means the Central Board or a State Board;
(b) "Central Board" means the Central Board for the Prevention and Control of Water Pollution constituted under section 3;
(c) "member" means a member of a Board and includes the chairman thereof;
(d) "occupier" in relation to any factory or premises means the person who has control over the affairs of the factory or the premises and where the said affairs are entrusted to a managing agent, such agent shall be deemed to be the occupier of the factory or the premises;

(e) "pollution" means such contamination of water or such alteration of the physical, chemical or biological properties of water or such discharge of any sewage or trade effluent or of any other liquid, gaseous or solid substance into water (whether directly or indirectly) as may, or is likely to, create a nuisance   or render such water harmful or injurious to public health or safety, or to domestic, commercial, industrial, agricultural or other legitimate uses, or to the life and health of animals or plants or of acquatic organisms;

(f) "prescribed" means prescribed by rules made under this Act by the Central Government or, as the case may be, the State Government;

(g) "sewage effluent" means effluent from any sewerage system or sewage disposal works and includes sludge from open drains;

(h) "State Board" means a State Board for the Prevention and Control of Water Pollution constituted under section 4;

(i) "State Government" in relation to a Union territory means the Administrator thereof appointed under article 239 of the Constitution;

(j) "stream" includes—

  (i) river;
  (ii) water course (whether flowing or for the time being dry);
  (iii) inland water (whether natural or artificial);
  (iv) sub-terranean waters;
  (v) sea or tidal waters to such extent or, as the case maybe, to such point as the State Government may, by notification in the Official Gazette, specify in this behalf;

(k) "trade effluent" includes any liquid, gaseous or solid substance which is discharged from any premises used for carrying on any trade or industry, other than domestic sewage.

CHAPTER II

THE CENTRAL AND STATE BOARDS FOR PREVENTION TO
CONTROL OF WATER POLLUTION

3. Constitution of Central Boards.—(1) The Central Government shall, with effect from such date (being a date not later than six months of the commencement of this Act in the States of Assam, Bihar, Gujarat, Haryana, Himachal Pradesh, Jammu and Kashmir, Karnataka, Kerala, Madhya Pradesh, Rajasthan, Tripura and West Bengal and in the Union territories) as it may, by notification in the Official Gazette, appoint, constitute a Central Board to be called the Central Board for the Prevention and Control of Water Pollution to exercise the powers conferred on and perform the functions assigned to that Board under this Act.

(2) The Central Board shall consist of the following members, namely:—

(a) a full-time chairman, being a person having special knowledge or practical experience in respect of maters relating to the use and conservation of water resources or the prevention and control of water pollution or a person having knowledge and experience in administering institutions dealing with the matters aforesaid, to be nominated by the Central Government;

(b) five officials to be nominated by the Central Government to represent that Government;

(c) such number of persons, not exceeding five, to be nominated by the Central Government, from amongst the members of the State Boards, of whom not exceeding two shall be from those referred to in clause (c) of sub-section (2) of section 4;

(d) three non-officials to be nominated by the Central Government, to represent the interests of agriculture, fishery or industry or trade or any other interest which, in the opinion of the Central Government, ought to be represented;

(e) two persons to represent the companies or corporations owned, controlled or managed by the Central Government, to be nominated by that Government;

(f) a full-time member-secretary qualified in public health

engineering and having administrative experience, to be appointed by the Central Government.

(3) The Central Board shall be a body corporate with the name aforesaid having perpetual succession and a common seal with power, subject to the provisions of this Act, to acquire, hold and dispose of property and to contract, and may by the aforesaid name, sue or be sued.

4. Constitution of State Board.—(1) The State Government shall with effect from such date (being a date not later than six months of the commencement of this Act in the State) as it may, by notification in the Official Gazette appoint constitute a State Board, under such name as may be specified in the notification, to exercise the powers conferred on and perform the function assigned to that Board under this Act.

(2) A State Board shall consist of the following members, namely:—

(a) a full-time chairman, being a person having special knowledge or practical experience in respect of matters relating to the use and conservation of water resources or the prevention and control of water pollution or a person having knowledge and experience in administering institutions dealing with the matters aforesaid, to be nominated by the State Government;

(b) five officials to be nominated by the State Government to represent that Government;

(c) five persons to be nominated by the State Government from amongst the members of the local authorities functioning within the State;

(d) three non-officials to be nominated by the State Government to represent the interests of agriculture, fishery or industry or trade or any other interest which, in the opinion of the State Government, ought to be represented;

(e) two persons to represent the companies or corporations owned, controlled or managed by the State Government, to be nominated by that Government;

(f) a full-time member-secretary qualified in public health engineering and having administrative experience, to be appointed by the State Government.

(3) Every State Board shall be a body corporate with the name specified by the State Government in the notification under sub-section (1), having perpetual succession and a common seal with power, subject to the provisions of this Act, to acquire, hold and dispose of property and to contract, and may, by the said name, sue or be sued.

(4) Notwithstanding anything contained in this section, no State Board shall be constituted for a Union territory and in relation to a Union territory, the Central Board shall exercise the powers and perform the functions of a State Board for that Union territory:

> Provided that in relation to any Union territory the Central Board may delegate all or any of its powers and functions under this sub-section to such person or body of persons as the Central Government may specify.

5. Terms and conditions of service of members.—(1) Save as otherwise provided by or under this Act, a member of a Board, other than a member-secretary, shall hold office for a term of three years from the date of his nomination:

> Provided that a member shall, notwithstanding the expiration of his term, continue to hold office until his successor enters upon his office.

(2) The term of office of a member of a Board nominated under clause (b) of sub-section (2) of section 3 or clause (b) of sub-section (2) of section 4 shall come to an end as soon as he ceases to hold the office under the Central Government or, as the case may be, the State Government, by virtue of which he was nominated.

(3) The Central Government or, as the case maybe, the State Government may, if it thinks fit, remove any member of a Board before the expiry of his term of office, after giving him a reasonable opportunity of showing cause against the same.

(4) A member of a Board, other than the member-secretary, may at any tie resign his office by writing under his hand addressed—

> (a) in the case of the chairman to the Central Government or, as the case may be, the State Government; and
> (b) in any other case, to the chairman of the Board;

and the seat of the chairman or such other member shall thereupon become vacant.

(5) A member of a Board, other than the member-secretary, shall be deemed to have vacated his seat if he is absent without reason, sufficient in the opinion of the Board, from three consecutive meetings of the Board, or where he is nominated under clause (c) of sub-section (2) of section 3 or under clause (c) of sub-section (2) of section 4, if he ceases to be a member of the State Board, or as the case may be, of the local authority.

(6) A casual vacancy in a Board shall be filled by a fresh nomination and the person nominated to fill the vacancy shall hold office only for the remainder of the term for which the member in whose place he was nominated.

(7) A member of a Board shall not be eligible for renomination for more than two terms.

(8) The other terms and conditions of service of a member of a Board, other than the chairman and member-secretary, shall be such as maybe prescribed.

(9) The other terms and conditions of service of the chairman shall be such as may be prescribed.

6. Disqualifications.—(1) No person shall be a member of a Board, who—

(a) is, or at any time has been adjudged insolvent or has suspended payment of his debts or has compound with his creditors, or

(b) is of unsound mind and stands so declared by a competent court, or

(c) is, or has been, convicted of an offence which, in the opinion of the Central Government or, as the case may be, of the State Government, involves moral turpitude, or

(d) is, or at any time has been, convicted of an offence under this Act, or

(e) has directly or indirectly by himself or by any partner, any share or interest in any firm or company carrying on the business of manufacture, sale or hire of machinery, plant, equipment, apparatus or fittings for the treatment of a sewage or trade effluents, or

(f) is a director or a secretary, manager or other salaried officer or employee of any company or firm having any contract with the Board, or with the Government constituting the Board, or with a local authority in the State, or with a company or corporation owned, controlled or managed by the Government, for the carrying out of sewerage schemes or for the installation of plants for the treatment of sewage or trade effluents, or

(g) has so abused, in the opinion of the Central Government or as the case may be, of the State Government, his position as a member, as to render his continuance on the Board detrimental to the interest of the general public.

(2) No order of removal shall be made by the Central Government for the State Government, as the case maybe, under this section unless the member concerned has been given a reasonable opportunity of showing cause against the same.

(3) Notwithstanding anything contained in sub-sections (1) and (7) of section 5, a member who has been removed under this section shall not be eligible for renomination as a member.

7. Vacation of seats by members.—If a member of a Board becomes subject to any of the disqualification specified in section 6, his seat shall become vacant.

8. Meetings of Board.—A Board shall meet at least once in every three months and shall observe such rules of procedure in regard to the transaction of business at its meetings as maybe prescribed:

Provided that if, in the opinion of the chairman, any business of an urgent nature is to be transacted, he may convene a meeting of the Board at such time as he thinks fit for the aforesaid purpose.

9. Constitution of committees.—(1) A Board may constitute as many committees consisting wholly of members or wholly of their persons or partly of members and partly of other persons, and for such purpose or purposes as it may think fit.

(2) A committee constituted under this section shall meet at such time and at such place, and shall observe such rules of procedure in regard to the transaction of business at its meetings, as may be prescribed.

(3) The members of a committee (other than the members

of the Board) shall be paid such fees and allowances, for attending its meetings and for attending to any other work of the Board as may be prescribed.

10. Temporary association of persons with Board for particular purposes.—(1) A Board may associate with itself in such manner, and for such purposes, as may be prescribed any person whose assistance or advice it may desire to obtain in performing any of its functions under this Act.

(2) A person associated with the Board under sub-section (1) for any purpose shall have a right to take part in the discussions of the Board relevant to that purpose, but shall not have a right to vote at a meeting of the Board, and shall not be member for any other purpose.

11. Vacancy in Board not to invalidate acts or proceedings.—No act or proceeding of a Board or any committee thereof shall be called in question on the ground merely of the existence of any vacancy in, or any defect in the constitution of, the Board or such committee, as the case may be.

12. Member-secretary and officers and other employees of Board.—(1) The terms and conditions of service of the member-secretary shall be such as may be prescribed.

(2) The member-secretary shall exercise such powers and perform such duties as may be prescribed or as may, from time to time, be delegated to him by the Board or its chairman.

(3) Subject to such rules as may be made by the Central Government or, as the case may be, the State Government in this behalf, a Board may appoint such officers and employees as it considers necessary for the efficient performance of its functions and the rules so made may provide for the salaries and allowances and other terms and conditions of service of such officers and employees.

(4) Subject to such conditions as may be prescribed, a Board may from time to time appoint any qualified person to be a consulting engineer to the Board and pay him such salaries and allowances and subject him to such other terms and conditions of service as it thinks fit.

CHAPTER III

JOINT BOARDS

13.Constitution of Joint Board.—(1) Notwithstanding anything contained in this Act, an agreement may be entered into—

(a) by two or more Governments of contiguous States, or

(b) by the Central Government (in respect of one or more Union territories) and one or more Governments of States contiguous to such Union territory or Union territories,

to be force for such period and to be subject to renewal for such further period, if any, as maybe specified in the agreement to provide for the constitution of a Joint Board,—

(i) in a case referred to in clause (a), for all the participating States, and

(ii) in a case referred to in clause (b), for the participating Union territory or Union territories and the State or States.

(2) An agreement under this section may—

(a) provide, in a case referred to in clause (a) of sub-section (1), for the apportionment between the participating States and in a case referred to in clause (b) of that sub-section, for the apportionment between the Central Government and the participating State Government or State Governments, of the expenditure in connection with the Joint Board;

(b) determine, in a case referred to in clause (a) of sub-section (1), which of the participating State Governments and in a case referred to in clause (b) of that sub-section, whether the Central Government or the participating State Government (if there are more than one participating State, also which of the participating State Governments) shall exercise and perform the several powers and functions of the State Government under this Act and the references in this Act to the State Government shall be construed accordingly;

(c) provide for consultation, in a case referred to in clause (a) of sub-section (1), between the participating State Governments and in a case referred to in clause (b) of that sub-section, between the Central Government and the participating State Government or State Government either generally or with reference to particular maters arising under this Act;

(d) make such incidental and ancillary provisions, not inconsistent with this Act, as maybe deemed necessary or expedient for giving effect to the agreement.

(3) An agreement under this section shall be published, in a case referred to in clause (a) of sub-section (1), in the Official Gazette of the participating States and in a case referred to in clause (b) of that sub-section, in the Official Gazette of the participating Union territory or Union territories and the participating State or States.

14. Composition of Joint Boards.—(1) A Joint Board constituted in pursuance of an agreement entered into under clause (a) of sub-section (1) of section 13 shall consist of the following members, namely;—

(a) a full-time chairman, being a person having special knowledge or practical experience in respect of matters relating to the use and conservation of water resources or the prevention and control of water pollution or a person having knowledge and experience in administering institutions dealing with the matters aforesaid, to be nominated by the Central Government;

(b) two officials from each of the participating States to be nominated by the concerned participating State Government to represent that Government;

(c) one person to be nominated by each of the participating State Governments from amongst them members of the local authorities functioning within the State concerned;

(d) one non-official to be nominated by each of the participating State Governments to represent the interests of agriculture, fishery or industry or trade in the State concerned or any other interest which, in the opinion of the participating State Government, is to be represented;

(e) two persons to be nominated by the Central Government to represent the companies or corporations owned, controlled or managed by the participating State Governments;

(f) a full-time member-secretary qualified in public health engineering and having administrative experience, to be appointed by the Central Government.

(2) A Joint Board constituted in pursuance of an agreement entered into under clause (b) of sub-section (i) of section 13 shall consist of the following members, namely:—

(a) a full-time chairman, being a person having special knowledge or practical experience in respect of matters relating to the use and conservation of water resources or the prevention and control of water pollution or a person having knowledge and experience in administering institutions dealing with the matters aforesaid, to be nominated by the Central Government;

(b) two officials to be nominated by the Central Government from the participating Union territory or each of the participating Union territories, as the case may be, and two officials to be nominated, from the participating State or each of the participating States, as the case maybe, by the concerned participating State Government;

(c) one person to be nominated by the Central Government from amongst the members of the local authorities functioning within the participating Union territory or each of the participating Union territories, as the case maybe, and one person to be nominated, form amongst the members of the local authorities functioning within the participating State or each of the participating States, as the case may be, by the concerned participating State Government;

(d) one non-official to be nominated by the Central Government and one person to be nominated by the participating State Government or State Governments to represent the interests of agriculture, fishery or industry or trade in the Union territory or in each of the Union territories or the State or in each of the States,

as the case maybe, or any other interest which in the
opinion of the Central Government or, as the case may
be, of the State Government is to be represented;

(e) two persons to be nominated by the Central
Government to represent the companies or corporations
owned, controlled or managed by the Central
Government and situate in the participating Union
territory or territories and two persons to be nominated
by the Central Government to represent the companies
or corporations owned, controlled or managed by the
participating State Governments;

(f) a full-time member-secretary qualified in public health
engineering and having administrative experience, to
be appointed by the Central Government.

(3) When a Joint Board is constituted in pursuance of an
agreement under clause (b) of section (1) of section 13, the
provisions of sub-section (4) of section 4 shall cease to apply in
relation to the Union territory for which the Joint Board is
constituted.

(4) Subject to the provisions of sub-section (3), the provisions
of sub-section (3) of section 4 and sections 5 to 12 (inclusive) shall
apply in relation to the Joint Board and its member-secretary as
they apply in relation to a State Board and its member-secretary.

(5) Any reference in this Act to the State Board shall, unless
the context otherwise requires, be construed as including a Joint
Board.

15. Special provision relating to giving of directions.—
Notwithstanding anything contained I this Act where any Joint
Board is constituted under section 13,—

(a) the Government of the State for which the Joint Board
is constituted shall be competent to give any direction
under this Act only in cases where such direction
relates to a matte within the exclusive territorial
jurisdiction of the State;

(b) the Central Government alone shall be competent to
give any direction under this Act where such direction
relates to a mater within the territorial jurisdiction of
two or more States or pertaining to a Union territo ·

CHAPTER IV
POWER AND FUNCTIONS OF BOARDS

16. Functions of Central Board.—(1) Subject to the provisions of this Act, the main function of the Central Board shall be to promote cleanliness of streams and wells in different areas of the States.

(2) In particular and without prejudice to the generality of the foregoing function, the Central Board may perform all or any of the following functions namely:—

    (a) advise the Central Government on any matter concerning the prevention and control of water pollution;

    (b) co-ordinate the activities of the State Boards and resolves disputes among them;

    (c) provide technical assistance and guidance to the State Boards, carry out and sponsor investigations and research relating to problems of water pollution and prevention, control or abatement of water pollution;

    (d) plan and organise the training of persons engaged or to be engaged in programmes for the prevention, control or abatement of water pollution on such terms and conditions as the Central Board any specify;

    (f) collect, compile and publish technical and statistical data relating to water pollution and the measures devised for its effective prevention and control and prepare manuals, codes or guides relating to treatment and disposal of sewage and trade effluents and disseminate information connected therewith;

    (g) lay down, modify or annul, in consultation with the State Government concerned, the standards for a stream or well:

    Provided that different standards may be laid down for the same stream or well or for different streams or wells, having regard to the quality of water, flow characteristics of the streams or well and the nature of the use of the water in such stream or well or streams or wells;

    (h) plan and cause to be executed a nation-wide

programme for the prevention, control or abatement of water pollution;

(i) perform such other functions as may be prescribed.

(3) The Board may establish or recognise a laboratory or laboratories to enable the Board to perform its functions under this section efficiently including the analysis of samples of water from any stream or well or of samples of any sewage or trade effluents.

17. Functions of State Board.—(1) Subject to the provisions of this Act, the functions of a State Board shall be—

(a) to plan a comprehensive programme for the prevention, control or abatement of pollution of streams and wells in the State and to secure the execution thereof;

(b) to advise the State Government on any matter concerning the prevention, control or abatement of water pollution;

(c) to collect and disseminate information relating to water pollution and the prevention, control or abatement thereof;

(d) to encourage, conduct and participate in investigations and research relating to problems of water pollution and prevention, control or abatement of water pollution;

(e) to collaborate with the Central Board in organising the training of persons engaged or to be engaged in programmes relating to prevention, control or abatement of water pollution and to organise mass education programmes relating thereto;

(f) to inspect sewage or trade effluents, works and plants for the treatment of sewage and trade effluents and to review plans, specification or other data relating to plants set up for the treatment of water, works for the purification thereof and the system for the disposal of sewage or trade effluents or in connection with the grant of any consent as required by this Act;

(g) to lay down, modify or annul effluent standards for the sewage and trade effluents and for the quality of receiving waters (not being water in an inter-State stream) resulting from the discharge of effluents and to classify waters of the State;

(h) to evolve economical and reliable methods of treatment of sewage and trade effluents, having regard to the peculiar conditions of soils, climate and water resources of different regions and more especially the prevailing flow characteristics of water in streams and wells which render it impossible to attain even the minimum degree of dilution;

(i) to evolve methods of utilisation of sewage and suitable trade effluents in agriculture;

(j) to evolve efficient methods of disposal of sewage and trade effluents on land, as are necessary on account of the predominant conditions of scant stream flows that do not provide for major part of the year the minimum degree of dilution;

(k) to lay down standards of treatment of sewage and trade effluents to be discharged into any particular stream taking into account the minimum fair weather dilution available in that stream and the tolerance limits of pollution permissible in the water of the stream, after the discharge of such effluents;

(l) to make, vary or revoke any order—

  (i) for the prevention, control or abatement of discharges of waste into streams or wells;

  (ii) requiring any person concerned to construct new systems for the disposal of sewage and trade effluents or to modify, alter or extend any such existing system or to adopt such remedial measures as are necessary to prevent, control or abate water pollution;

(m) to lay down effluent standards to be complied with by persons while causing discharge of sewage or sludge or both and to lay down, modify or annul effluent standards for the sewage and trade effluents;

(n) to advise the State Government with respect to the location of any industry the carrying on of which is likely to pollute a stream or well;

(o) to perform such other functions as may be prescribed or as may, from time to time, be entrusted to it by the Central Board or the State Government.

(2) The Board may establish or recognise a laboratory or laboratories to enable the Board to perform its functions under this section efficiently, including the analysis of samples of water from any stream or well or of samples of any sewage or trade effluents.

18. Powers to give directions.—In the performance of its functions under this Act—

(a) the Central Board shall be bound by such directions in writing as the Central Government may give to it; and

(b) every State Board shall be bound by such directions in writing as the Central Board or the State Government may give to it:

Provided that where a direction given by the State Government is inconsistent with the direction given by the Central Board, the matter shall be referred to the Central Government for its decision.

CHAPTER V
PREVENTION AND CONTROL OF WATER POLLUTION

19. Power of State Government to restrict the application of the Act to certain areas.—(1) Notwithstanding anything contained in this Act, if the State Government, after consultation with, or on the recommendation of, the State Board, is of opinion that the provisions of this Act need not apply to the entire State, it may, by notification in the official Gazette, restrict the application of this Act to such area or areas as may be declared therein as water pollution, prevention and control are or areas and thereupon the provisions of this Act shall apply only to such area or areas.

(2) Each water pollution, prevention and control area may be declared either by reference to a map or by reference to the line of any watershed or the boundary of any district or partly by one method and partly by another.

(3) The State Government may, by notification in the Official Gazette,—

(a) alter any water pollution, prevention and control area whether by way of extension or reduction; or

(b) define a new water pollution, prevention and control area in which may be merged one or more water pollution, prevention and control areas, or any part or parts thereof.

20. Power to obtain information.—(1) For the purpose of enabling a State Board to perform the functions conferred on it by or under this Act, the State Board or any officer empowered by it in that behalf, may make surveys of any area and gauge and keep records of the flow or volume and other characteristics of any stream or well in such area, and may take steps for the measurement and recording of the rainfall in such area or any part thereof and for the installation and maintenance for those purposes of gauges or other apparatus and works connected therewith, and carry out stream surveys and may take such other steps as may be necessary in order to obtain any information required for the purposes aforesaid.

(2) A State Board may give directions requiring any person who in its opinion is abstracting water from any such stream or well in the are in quantities which are substantial in relation to the flow or volume of that stream or well or is discharging sewage or trade effluent into any such stream or well, to give such information as to the abstraction or the discharge at such times and in such form as may be specified in the directions.

(3) Without prejudice to the provisions of sub-section (2), a State Board may, with a view to preventing or controlling pollution of water, give directions requiring any person in charge of any establishment where any industry or trade is carried on, to furnish to it information regarding the construction, installation or operation of such establishment or of any disposal system or of any extension or addition thereto in such establishment and such other particulars as may be prescribed.

21. Power to take samples of effluents and procedure to be followed in connection therewith.—(1) A State Board or any officer empowered by it in this behalf shall have power to take for the purpose of analysis samples of water from any stream or well or samples of any sewage or trade effluent which is passing from any plant or vessel or from or over any place into any such stream or well.

(2) The result of any analysis of a sample of any sewage or

trade effluent taken under sub-section (1) shall not be admissible in evidence in any legal proceeding unless the provisions of sub-sections (3), (4) and (5) are complied with.

(3) Subject to the provisions of sub-sections (4) and (5), when a sample (composite or otherwise as may be warranted by the process used) of any sewage or trade effluent is taken for analysis under sub-section (1), the person taking the sample shall—

(a) serve on the person in charge of, or having control over, the plant or vessel or in occupation of the place (which person is hereinafter referred to as the occupier) or any agent of such occupier, a notice, then and there in such form as may be prescribed of his intention to have it so analysed;

(b) in the presence of the occupier or his agent, divide the sample into two parts;

(c) cause each part to be placed in a container which shall be marked and sealed and shall also be signed both by the person taking the sample and the occupier or his agent;

(d) send one container forthwith,—

(i) in a case where such sample is taken from any area situated in a Union territory, to the laboratory established or recognised by the Central Board under section 16; and

(ii) in any other case, to the laboratory established or recognised by the State Board under section 17;

(e) on the request of the occupier or his agent, send the second container,—

(i) in a case where such sample is taken from any area situated in a Union territory, to the laboratory established or specified under sub-section (1) of section 51; and

(ii) in any other case, to the laboratory established or specified under sub-section (1) of section 52.

(4) When a sample of any sewage or trade effluent is taken for analysis under sub-section (1) and the person taking the sample serves on the occupier or his agent, a notice under clause (a) of sub-section (3) and the occupier or his agent wilfully

absents himself, the,, the sample so taken shall be placed in a container which shall be marked and sealed and shall also be signed by the person taking the sample and the same shall be sent forthwith by such person for analysis to the laboratory referred to in sub-clause (I) or sub-clause (ii), as the case may be, of clause (e) of sub section (3) and such personal shall inform the Government analyst appointed under sub-section (1) or sub-section (2), as the case may be, of section 53, in writing about the wilful absence of the occupier or his agent.

(5) When a sample of any sewage or trade effluent is taken for analysis under sub-section (1) and the person taking the sample serves on the occupier or his agent a notice under clause (a) of sub-section (3) and the occupier or his agent who is present at the tie of taking the sample does not make a request for dividing the sample into two parts as provided in clause (b) of sub-section (3), then, the sample so taken shall be placed in a container which shall be marked and sealed and shall also be signed by the person taking the sample and the same shall be sent forthwith by such person for analysis to the laboratory referred to in sub-clause (i) or sub-clause (ii), as the case may be, of clause (d) of sub-section (3).

22. **Reports of the result of analysis on samples taken under section 21.**—(1) Where a sample of any sewage or trade effluent has been sent for analysis to the laboratory established or recognised by the Central Board or, as the case may be, the State Board, the concerned Board analyst appointed under sub-section (3) of section 53 shall analyse the sample and submit a report in the prescribed form of the result of such analysis in triplicate to the Central Board or the State Board, as the case may be.

(2) On receipt of the report under sub-section (1), one copy of the report shall be sent by the Central Board or the State Board, as the Case may be, to the occupier or his agent referred to in section 21, another copy shall be preserved for production before the court in case any legal proceedings are taken against him and the other copy shall be kept by the concerned Board.

(3) Where a sample has been sent for analysis under clause (3) of sub-section (3) or sub-section (4) of section 21 to any laboratory mentioned therein, the Government analyst referred to in that sub-section shall analyse the sample and submit a

report in the prescribed form of the result of the analysis in triplicate to the Central Board or, as the case may be, the State Board which shall comply with the provisions of sub-section (2).

(4) If there is any inconsistency or discrepancy between, or variation in the results of, the analysis carried out by the laboratory established or recognised by the Central Board or the State Board, as the case may be, and that of the laboratory established or specified under section 51 or section 52, as the case may be, the report of the latter shall prevail.

(5) Any cost incurred in getting any sample analysed at the request of the occupier or his agent shall be payable by such occupier or his agent and in case of default the same shall be recoverable from his as arrears of land revenue or of public demand.

23. **Power of entry and inspection.**—(1) Subject to the provisions of this section, any person empowered by a State Board in this behalf shall have a right at any time to enter, with such assistance as he considers necessary, anyplace—

(a) for the purpose of performing any of the functions of the Board entrusted to him;

(b) for the purpose of determining whether and if so in what manner, any such functions are to be performed or whether any provisions of this Act or the rules made thereunder of any notice, order, direction or authorisation served, made, given, or granted under this Act is being or has been complied with;

(c) for the purpose of examining any plant, record, register, document or any other material object or for conducting a search of any place in which he has reason to believe that an offence under this Act or the rules made thereunder has been or is being or is about to be committed and for seizing any such plant, record, register, document or other material object, if he has reason to believe that it may furnish evidence of the commission of an offence punishable under this Act or the rules made thereunder:

Provided that the right to enter under this sub-section for the inspection of a well shall be exercised only at reasonable hours in a case where such well is situated in any premises used for residential purposes and the water thereof is used exclusively for domestic purposes.

(2) The provisions of the Code of Criminal Procedure, 1898, (5 of 1898) or, in relation to the State of Jammu and Kashmir, the provisions of any corresponding law in force in that State, shall, so far as may be, apply to any search or seizure under this section as they apply to any search or seizure made under the authority of a warrant issued under section 98 of the said Code, or, as the case may be, under the corresponding provisions of the said law.

Explanation.—For the purposes of this section, "place" includes vessel.

24. Prohibition on use of stream or well for disposal of polluting matter, etc..—(1) Subject to the provisions of this section,—

(a) no person shall knowingly cause or permit any poisonous, noxious or polluting mater determined in accordance with such standards as may be laid down by the State Board to enter (whether directly or indirectly) into any stream or well; or

(b) no person shall knowingly cause or permit to enter into any stream any other matter which may tend, either directly or in combination with similar matters, to impede the proper flow of the water of the stream in a manner leading or likely to lead to a substantial aggravation of pollution due to other causes or of its consequences.

(2) A person shall not be guilty of an offence under sub-section (1), by reason only of having done or caused to be done any of the following acts, namely:—

(a) constructing, improving or maintaining in or across or on the bank or bed of any stream any building, bridge, weir, dam, sluice, dock, pier, drain or sewer or other permanent works which he has a right to construct improve or maintain;

(b) depositing any materials on the bank or in the bed of any stream for the purpose of reclaiming land or for supporting, repairing or protecting the bank or bed of

such stream provided such materials are not capable
of polluting such stream;

(c) putting into any stream any sand or gravel or other
natural deposit which has flowed from or been
deposited by the current or such stream;

(d) causing or permitting, with the consent of the State
Board, the deposit accumulated in a well, pond or
reservoir to enter into any stream.

(3) The State Government may, after consultation with, or
on the recommendation of, the State Board, exempt, by
notification in the Official Gazette, any person form the operation
of sub-section (1) subject to such conditions, if any, as may be
specified in the notification and any condition so specified may
be a like notification be altered, varied or amended.

25. **Restrictions on new outlets and new discharges.**—(1)
Subject to the provisions of this section no person shall, without
the previous consent of the State Board, bring into use any new
or altered outlet for the discharge of sewage or trade effluent
into a stream or well or begin to make any new discharge of
sewage or trade effluent into a stream or well.

(2) An application for consent of the State Board under sub-
section (1) shall be made in the prescribed form and shall contain
particulars regarding the proposed construction, installation or
operation of the industrial or commercial establishment or of any
treatment and disposal system or of any extension or addition
thereto and such other particulars as may be prescribed.

(3) The State Board may make such inquiry as it may deem
fit in respect of the application for consent referred to in sub-
section (1) and in making any such inquiry shall follow such
procedure as may be prescribed.

(4) The State Board may grant its consent referred to in sub-
section (1), subject to such conditions as it may impose, being—

(a) in the case of a new or altered outlet, conditions as to
the point of discharge into the stream or well or the
construction of the outlet, or as to the use of that outlet
or any other outlet for sewage or trade effluent from
the same land or premises; and

(b) in the case of a new discharge, conditions as to the
nature and composition, temperature, volume or rate

of discharge of the effluent from the land or premises
from which the new discharge is to be made,

and any such conditions imposed shall be binding on any person
using the outlet, or discharging the effluent from the land or
premises aforesaid.

(5) Where, without the consent of the State Board, a new or
altered outlet is brought into use for the discharge of sewage or
trade effluent into a stream or well or a new discharge of sewage
or trade effluent is made, the State Board may serve on the
person using the outlet or making the discharge, as the case may
be, a notice imposing any such conditions as it might have
imposed on an application for its consent in respect to such outlet
or discharge.

(6) Every State Board shall maintain a register containing
such particulars of the conditions imposed under this section in
relation to outlets or in relations to effluent from land or premises
in its jurisdiction and as are for the time being in force (other
than the conditions to be satisfied before an outlet is brought
into use or a new discharge is made) and so much of the register
as relates to any outlet, or to any effluent from such land or
premises shall be open to inspection at all reasonable hours by
any person interested in, or affected by, the outlet, or in the land
or premises, as the case may be, or by any person authorised
by him in this behalf and the conditions so contained in such
register shall be conclusive proof that the consent was granted
subject to such conditions.

(7) The consent referred to in sub-section (1) shall, unless
given or refused earlier, be deemed to have been given
unconditionally on the expiry of a period of four months of the
making of an application in this behalf complete in all respects
to the State Board.

(8) For the purposes of his section and section 27 and 30,—

(a) the expression new or altered outlet" means any outlet
which is wholly or partly constructed on or after the
commencement of this Act or which (whether so
constructed or not) is substantially altered after such
commencement;

(b) the expression "new discharge" means a discharge
which is not, as respects the nature and composition,

temperature, volume, and rate of discharge of the effluent substantially a continuation of a discharge made within the preceding twelve months (whether by the same or a different outlet), so however that a discharge which is in other respects a continuation of previous discharge made as aforesaid shall not be deemed to be a new discharge by reason of any reduction of the temperature or volume or rate of discharge of the effluent as compared with the previous discharge.

26. Provision regarding existing discharge of sewage or trade effluent.—Where immediately before the commencement of this Act any person was discharging any sewage or trade effluent into a stream or well, the provisions of section 25 shall, so far as may be, apply in relation to such person as they apply in relation to the person referred to in that section subject to the modification that the application for consent to be made under sub-section (2) of that section shall be made within a period of three months of the constitution of the State Board.

27. Refusal or withdrawal of consent by State Board.—(1) A State Board shall not grant its consent to the bringing into use of a new or altered outlet unless the outlet is so constructed as to comply with any conditions imposed by the Board to enable it to exercise its right to take samples of the effluent.

(2) A State Board may from time to time review any condition imposed under section 25 (other than a condition to be satisfied before an outlet is brought into use or a new discharge is made), or under section 26 and may serve on the person using the outlet or making the discharge, as the case may be, a notice, making any reasonable variation of or revoking any such condition.

(3) Any condition imposed under section 25 or section 26 shall be subject to any variation made under sub-section (2) and shall continue in force until revoked under that sub-section.

28. Appeals.—(1) Any person aggrieved by an order made by the State Board under section 25, section 26 or section 27 may, within thirty days from the date on which the order is communicated to him, prefer an appeal to such authority (hereinafter referred to as the appellate authority) as the State

Government may think fit to constitute:

Provided that the appellate authority may entertain the appeal after the expiry of the said period of thirty days if such authority is satisfied that the appellant was prevented by sufficient cause from filing the appeal in time.

(2) An appellate authority shall consist of three persons.

(3) The form and manner in which an appeal may be preferred under sub-section (1), the fees payable for such appeal and the procedure to be followed by the appellate authority shall be such as may be prescribed.

(4) On receipt of an appeal preferred under sub-section (1), the appellate authority shall, after giving the appellant and the State Board an opportunity of being heard, dispose of the appeal as expeditiously as possible.

(5) If the appellate authority determines that any condition imposed, or the variation of any condition, as the case may be, was unreasonable, the,—

(b) where the appeal is in respect of the reasonableness of any condition imposed, such authority may direct either that the condition shall be treated as annulled or that there shall be treated as continuing in force unvaried or that it shall be varied in such manner as appears to it to be reasonable.

29. Revision.—(1) The State Government may at any time either of its own motion or on an application made to it in this behalf, call for the records of any case where an order has been made by the State Board under section 25, section 26 or section 27 for the purpose of satisfying itself as to the legality or propriety of any such order and may pass such order in relation thereto as it may think fit:

Provided that the State Government shall not pass any order under this sub-section without affording the State Board and the person who may be affected by such order a reasonable opportunity of being heard in the matter.

(2) The State Government shall not revise any order made under section 25, section 26 or section 27 where an appeal against that order lies to the appellate authority, but has not been preferred or where an appeal has been preferred such appeal is

pending before the appellate authority.

30. Power of State Board to carry out certain works.—(1) Where under this Act any conditions have been imposed on any person for bringing into use any new or altered outlet for the discharge of sewage or trade effluent into a stream or well or for making any new discharge of sewage or trade effluent into a stream or well or on any person who, immediately before the commencement of this Act, was discharging any sewage or trade effluent in a stream or well and such conditions require such person to execute any work in connection therewith and such work has not been executed within such time as may be specified in this behalf, the State Board may serve on the person concerned a notice requiring him within such time (not being less than thirty days) as may be specified in the notice to execute the work specified therein.

(2) If the person concerned fails to execute the work as required in the notice referred to in sub-section (1), then, after the expiration of the time specified in the said notice, the State Board may itself execute or cause to be executed such work.

(3) All expenses incurred by the State Board for the execution of the aforesaid work, together with interest, at such rate as the State Government may, by order, fix, from the date when a demand for the expenses is made until it is paid, maybe recovered by that Board from the person concerned, as arrears of land revenue, or of public demand.

31. Furnishing of information to State Board and other agencies in certain cases.—(1) If at any place where any industry or trade is being carried on, due to accident or other unforeseen act or event, any poisonous, noxious or polluting matter is being discharged or is likely to be discharged into a stream or well and, as a result of such discharge, the water in such stream or well is being polluted, or is likely to be polluted, then, the person in charge of such place shall forthwith intimate the occurrence of such accident, act or event to the State Board and to such other authorities or agencies as may be prescribed.

(2) Where any local authority operates any sewerage system or sewage works, the provisions of sub-section (1) shall apply to such local authority as they apply in relation to the person in charge of the place where any industry or trade is being carried on.

32. Emergency measures in case of pollution of stream or well.—(1) Where it appears to the State Board that any poisonous, noxious or polluting matter is present in any stream or well or has entered into that stream or well due to any accident or other unforeseen act or event, and if the Board is of opinion that it is necessary or expedient to take immediate action, it may for reasons to be recorded in writing, carry out such operations as it may consider necessary for all or any of the following purposes, that is to say,—

(a) removing that matter from the stream or well and disposing it of in such manner as the Board considers appropriate;

(b) remedying or mitigating any pollution caused by its presence in the stream or well;

(c) issuing orders immediately restraining or prohibiting the person concerned from discharging any poisonous, noxious or polluting matter into the stream or well, or from making in sanitary use of the stream or well.

(2) The power conferred by sub-section (1) does not include the power to construct any works other than works of a temporary character which are removed on or before the completion of the operations.

33. Power of Board to make application to courts for restraining apprehended pollution of water in streams or wells.—(1) Where it is apprehended by a Board that the water in any stream or well is likely to be polluted by reason of the disposal of any matter therein or of any likely disposal of any matter therein, or otherwise, the Board may make an application to a court, not inferior to that of a Presidency Magistrate or a Magistrate of the first class, for restraining the person who is likely to cause such pollution from so causing.

(2) On receipt of an application under sub-section (1) the court may make such order as it deems fit.

(3) Where under sub-section (2) the court makes an order restraining any person from polluting the water in any stream or well, it may in that order—

(i) direct the person who is likely to cause or has caused the pollution of the water in the stream or well, to desist from taking such action as is likely to cause pollution or, as the case maybe, to remove from such stream or well, such matter, and

(ii) authorise the Board, if the direction under clause (i) (being a direction for the removal of any matter from such stream or well) is not complied with by the person to whom such direction is issued, to undertake the removal and disposal of the matter in such manner as may be specified by the Court.

(4) All expenses incurred by the Board in removing any matter in pursuance of the authorisation under clause (ii) of sub-section (3) or in the disposal of any such matter may be defrayed out of any money obtained by the Board from such disposal and any balance outstanding shall be recoverable from the person concerned as arrears of land revenue or of public demand.

Chapter VI
FUNDS, ACCOUNTS AND AUDIT

34. Contributions by Central Government.—The Central Government may, after due appropriation made by parliament by law in this behalf, make in each financial year such contributions to the Central Board as it may think necessary to enable the Board to perform its function under this Act.

35. Contributions by State Government.—The State Government may, after due appropriation made by the Legislature of the State by law in this behalf, make in each financial year such contributions to the State Board as it may think necessary to enable that Board to perform its functions under this Act.

36. Fund of Central Board.—(1) The Central Board shall have its own fund, and all sums which may from time to time, be paid to it by the Central Government and all other receipts (by way of gifts, grants, donations, benefactions or otherwise) of that Board shall be carried to the fund of the Board and all payments by the Board shall be made therefrom.

(2) The Central Board may expend such sums as it thinks fit for performing its functions under this Act, and such sums shall be treated as expenditure payable out of the fund of that Board.

37. Fund of State Board.—(1) The State Board shall have its own fund, and the sums which may, from time to time, be paid to it by the State Government and all other receipts (by way of gifts, grants, donations, benefactions or otherwise) of that Board shall be carried to the fund of the Board and all payments by the Board shall be made therefrom.

(2) The State Board may expend such sums as it thinks fit for performing its functions under this Act, and such sums shall be treated as expenditure payable out of the fund of that Board.

38. Budget.—The Central Board or, as the case maybe, the State Board shall, during each financial year, prepare, in such form and at such time as maybe prescribed, a budget in respect of the financial year next ensuing showing the estimated receipt and expenditure, and copies thereof shall be forwarded to the Central Government or, as the case may be, the State Government.

39. Annual Report.—(1) The Central Board shall during each financial year, prepare, in such form and at such time as may be prescribed, an annual report giving a true and full account of its activities during the previous financial year and copies thereof shall be forwarded to the Central Government and that Government shall cause every such report to be laid before both Houses of Parliament within six months of the date on which it is received by that Government.

(2) The State Board shall, during each financial year, prepare, in such form and at such time as maybe prescribed, an annual report giving a true and full account of its activities during the previous financial year and copies thereof shall be forwarded to the State Government and that Government shall cause every such report to be laid before the State Legislature within a period of six months of the date on which it is received by that Government.

40. Accounts and audit.—(1) Every Board shall maintain proper accounts and other relevant records and prepare an annual statement of accounts in such form as may be prescribed by the Central Government or, as the case may be, the State Government.

(2) The accounts of the Board shall be audited by an auditor duly qualified to act as an auditor of companies under section 226 of the Companies Act, 1956. (1 of 1956)

(3) The said auditor shall be appointed by the Central Government or, as the case may be, the State Government on the advice of the Comptroller and Auditor General of India.

(4) Every auditor appointed to audit the accounts of the Board under this Act shall have the right to demand the production of books, accounts, connected vouchers and other documents and papers and to inspect any of the offices of the Board.

(5) Every such auditor shall send a copy of his report together with an audited copy of the accounts to the Central Government or, as the case may be, the State Government.

(6) The Central Government shall, as soon as may be after the receipt of the audit report under sub-section (5), cause the same to be laid before both Houses of Parliament.

(7) The State Government shall, as soon as may be after the receipt of the audit report under sub-section (5), cause the same to be laid before the State Legislature.

CHAPTER VII
PENALTIES AND PROCEDURE

41. Failure to company with directions under sub-section (2) or sub-section (3) of section 20 or orders issued under clause (c) of sub-section (1) of section 32.—(1) Whoever fails to comply with any direction given under sub-section (2) or sub-section (3) of section 20 within such time as may be specified in the direction or fails to comply with any orders issued under clause © of sub-section (1) of section 32 shall, on conviction, be punishable with imprisonment for a term which may extend to three months or with fine which may extend to five thousand rupees or with both and in case the failure continues, with an additional fine which may extend to one thousand rupees for every day during which such failure continues after the conviction for the first such failure.

(2) Whoever fails to comply with any direction issued by a court under sub-section (2) of section 33 shall, on conviction, be punishable with imprisonment for a term which may extend to three months or with fine which may extend to five thousand rupees or with both and in case the failure continues, with an additional fine which may extend to one thousand rupees for

everyday during which such failure continues after the conviction for the first such failure.

42. Penalty for certain acts.—(1) Whoever—

(a) destroys, pulls down, removes, injures or defaces any pillar, post or stake fixed in the ground or any notice or other matter put up, inscribed or placed, by or under the authority of the Board, or

(b) obstructs any person acting under the orders or directions of the Board from exercising his powers and performing his functions under this Act, or

(c) damages any works or property belonging to the Board, or

(d) fails to furnish to any officer or other employee of the Board any information required by him for the purpose of this Act, or

(e) fails to intimate the occurrence of any accident or other unforeseen act or event under section 31 to the Board and other authorities or agencies as required by that section, or

(f) in giving any information which he is required to give under this Act, knowingly or wilfully makes a statement which is false in any material particular, or

(g) for the purpose of obtaining any consent under section 25 or section 26, knowingly or wilfully makes a statement which is false in any material particular,

shall be punishable with imprisonment for a term which may extend to three months or with fine which may extend to one thousand rupees or with both.

(2) Where for the grant of a consent in pursuance of the provisions of section 25 or section 26 the use of a meter or gauge or other measure or monitoring device is required and such device is used for the purposes of those provisions, any person who knowingly or wilfully alters or interferes with that device so as to prevent it from monitoring or measuring correctly shall be punishable with imprisonment for a term which may extend to three months or with fine which may extend to one thousand rupees or with both.

43. Penalty for contravention of provisions of section 24.— Whoever contravenes the provisions of section 24 shall be punishable with imprisonment for a term which shall not be less than six months but which may extend to six years and with fine.

44. Penalty for contravention of section 25 or section 26.— Whoever contravenes the provisions of section 25 or section 26 shall be punishable with imprisonment for a term which shall not be less than six months but which may extend to six years and with fine.

45. Enhanced penalty after previous conviction.—If any person who has been convicted of any offence under section 24 or section 25 or section 26 is again found guilty of an offence involving a contravention of the same provision, he shall, on the second and on every subsequent conviction, be punishable with imprisonment for a term which shall not be less than one year but which may extend to seven years and with fine:

Provided that for the purpose of this section no cognisance shall be taken of any conviction made more than two years before the commission of the offence which is being punished.

46. Publication of names of offenders.—If any person convicted of an offence under this Act commits a like offence afterwards it shall be lawful for the court before which the second or subsequent conviction takes place to cause the offender's name and place of residence, the offence and the penalty imposed to be published at the offender's expense in such newspapers or in such other manner as the court may direct and the expenses of such publication shall be deemed to be part of the cost attending the conviction and shall be recoverable in the same manner as a fine.

47. Offences by companies.—(1) Where an offence under this Act has been committed by a company, every person who at the time the offence was committed was in charge of, and was responsible to the company for the conduct of, the business of the company, as well as the company, shall be deemed to be guilty of the offence and shall be liable to be proceeded against and punished accordingly:

Provided that nothing contained in this sub-section shall render any such person liable to any punishment provided in this Act if he proves that the offence was committed without his knowledge or that he exercised all due diligence to prevent the commission of such offence.

(2) Notwithstanding anything contained in sub-section (1), where an offence under this Act has been committed by a company and it is proved that the offence has been committed with the consent or connivance of, or is attributable to any neglect on the pat of, any director, manager, secretary or other officer of the company, such director, manager, secretary or other officer shall also be deemed to be guilty of that offence and shall be liable to be proceeded against and punished accordingly.

Explanation.—For the purposes of this section,—

   (a) "company" means anybody corporate, and includes a firm or other association of individuals; and
   (b) "director" in relation to a firm means a partner in the firm,

48. Offences by Government Departments.—Where an offence under this Act has been committed by any Department of Government, the Head of the Department shall be deemed to be guilty of the offence and shall be liable to be proceeded against and punished accordingly:

Provided that nothing contained in this section shall render such Head of the Department liable to any punishment if he proves that the offence was committed without his knowledge or that he exercised all due diligence to prevent the commission of such offence.

49. Cognizance of offences.—(1) No court shall take cognizance of any offence under this Act except on a complaint made by, or with the previous sanction in writing of the State Board, and no court inferior to that of a Presidency Magistrate or a Magistrate of the first class shall try any offence punishable under this Act.

(2) Notwithstanding anything contained in section 32 of the Code of Criminal Procedure, 1898, it shall be lawful for any Magistrate of the first class or for any Presidency Magistrate to pass a sentence of imprisonment for a term exceeding two years or of fine exceeding two thousand rupees on any person convicted of an offence punishable under this Acts.

50. Members, officers and servants of Board to be public servants.—All members, officers and servants of a Board when acting or purporting to act in pursuance of any of the provisions of this Act and the rules made thereunder shall be deemed to be public servants within the meaning of section 21 of the Indian Penal Code.

CHAPTER VII
MISCELLANEOUS

51. Central water laboratory.—(1) The Central Government may, by notification in the official Gazette,—

(a) establish a Central Water Laboratory; or

(b) specify any laboratory or institute as a Central Water Laboratory, to carry out the functions entrusted to the Central Water Laboratory under this Act.

(2) The Central Government may, after consultation with the Central Board, make rules prescribing—

(a) the functions of the Central Water Laboratory;

(b) the procedure for submission to the said laboratory of samples of water or of sewage or trade effluent for analysis or tests, the form of the laboratory's report thereunder and the fees payable in respect of such report;

(c) such other matters as may be necessary or expedient to enable that laboratory to carry out its functions.

52. (1) The State Government may, by notification in the official Gazette,—

(a) establish a State Water Laboratory; or

(b) specify any laboratory or institute as a State Water Laboratory, to carry out the function entrusted to the State Water Laboratory under this Act.

(2) The State Government may, after consultation with the State Board, make rules prescribing—

(a) the function of the State Water Laboratory;

(b) the procedure for the submission to the said laboratory of samples of water or of sewage or trade effluent for analysis or tests, the form of the laboratory's report thereon and the fees payable in respect of such report;

(c) such other matters as may be necessary or expedient to enable that laboratory to carry out its functions.

53. (1) The Central Government may, by notification in the official Gazette, appoint such persons as it thinks fit and having the prescribed qualification to be Government analysts for the purpose of analysis of samples of water or of sewage or trade effluent sent for analysis to any laboratory established or specified under sun-section (1) of section 51.

(2) The State Government may, by notification in the Official Gazette, appoint such persons as it thinks fit and having the prescribed qualification to be Government analysts for the purpose of analysis of samples of water or of sewage or trade effluent sent for analysis to any laboratory established or specified under sub-section (1) of 52.

(3) Without prejudice to the provisions of sub-section (3) of section 12, the Central Board or, as the case may be, the State Board may, by notification in the official Gazette, and with the approval of the Central Government or the State Government, as the case may be, appoint such persons as it thinks fit and having the prescribed qualification to be Board analysts for the purpose of analysis of samples of water or of sewage or trade effluent sent for analysis to any laboratory established or recognised under section 16, or, as the case may be, under section 17.

54. Reports of analysts.—Any document purporting to be a report signed by a Government analyst or, as the case may be, a Board analyst may be used as evidence of the facts stated therein in any proceeding under this Act.

55. Local authorities to assist.—All local authorities shall render such help and assistance and furnish such information to the Board as it may require for the discharge of its functions, and shall make available to the Board for inspection and examination such records, maps, plans and other documents as may be necessary for the discharge of its functions.

56. Compulsory acquisition of land for the State Board.— Any land required by a State Board for the efficient performance of its functions under this Act shall be deemed to be needed for a public purpose and such land shall be acquired for the State Board under the provisions of the Land Acquisition Act, 1894, (1 of 1894) or under any other corresponding law for the time being in force.

57. Returns and reports.—The Central Board shall furnish to the Central Government, and a State Board shall furnish to the State Government and to the Central Government Board such reports, returns, statistics, accounts and other information with respect to its fund or activities as that Government, or, as the case may be, the Central Board may, from time to time, require.

58. **Bar of jurisdiction.**—No civil court shall have jurisdiction to entertain any suit or proceeding in respect of any matter which an appellate authority constituted under this Act is empowered by or under this Act to determine, and no injunction shall be granted by any court or other authority in respect of any action taken or to be taken in pursuance of any power conferred by or under this Act.

59. **Protection of action taken in good faith.**—No suit or other legal proceedings shall lie against the Government or any officer of Government or any member or officer of a Board in respect of anything which is in good faith done or intended to be done in pursuance of this Act or the rules made thereunder.

60. **Over-riding effect.**—The provisions of this Act shall have effect notwithstanding anything inconsistent therewith contained in any enactment other than this Act.

61. **Power of Central Government to supersede the Central Board and Joint Boards.**—(1) If at any time the Central Government is of opinion—

(a) that the Central Board or any Joint Board has persistently made default in the performance of the functions imposed on it by or under this Act; or

(b) that circumstances exist which render it necessary in the public interest so to do,

the Central Government may, by notification in the Official Gazette, supersede the Central Board or such Joint Board, as the case may be, for such period, not exceeding one year, as may be specified in the notification:

Provided that before issuing a notification under this sub-section for the reasons mentioned in clause (a), the Central Government shall give a reasonable opportunity to the Central Board or such Joint Board, as the case may be, to show cause why it should not be supersede and shall consider the explanations and objections, if any, of the Central Board or such Joint Board, as the case may be.

(2) Upon the publication of a notification under sub-section (1) superseding the Central Board or any Joint Board,—

    (a) all the members shall, as from the date of supersession vacate their offices as such;

    (b) all the powers, functions and duties which may, by or under this Act, be exercised, performed or discharged by the Central Board or such Joint Board shall, until the Central Board or the Joint Board, as the case may be, is reconstituted under sub-section (3) be exercised, performed or discharged by such person or persons as the Central Government.

    (c) all the property owned or controlled by the Central Board or such Joint Board shall, until the Central Board or the Joint Board, as the case may be, is reconstituted under sub-section (3) vest in the Central Government.

(3) On the expiration of the period of supersession specified in the notification issued under sub-section (1), the Central Government may—

    (a) extend the period of supersession for such further term, not exceeding six months, as it may consider necessary; or

    (b) reconstitute the Central Board or the Joint Board, as the case may be, by fresh nomination or appointment, as the case may be, and in such case any person who vacated his office under clause (a) of sub-section 2 shall not be deemed disqualified for nomination or appointment:

    Provide the Central Government may at any time before the expiration of the period of supersession, whether originally specified under sub-section (1) or as extended under this sub-section, take action under clause (b) of this sub-section.

62. Power of the State Government to supersede the State Board.—(1) If at any time the State Government is of opinion:

    (a) that the State Board has persistently made default in the performance of functions imposed on it by or under this Act; or

    (b) that circumstances exist which render it necessary in

the public interest so to do.

The State Government may, notification in the Official Gazette, supersede the State Board for such period, not exceeding one year, as may be specified in the notification:

Provided that before issuing a notification under this sub-section for the reasons mentioned in clause (a), the State Government shall give a reasonable opportunity to the State Board to show cause why it should not be superseded and shall consider the explanations and objections, if any, of the State Board.

(2) Upon the publication of a notification under sub-section (1) superseding the State Board, the provisions of sub-sections (2) and (3) of section 61 shall apply in relation to the supersession of the State Board as they apply in relation to the supersession of the Central Board or a Joint Board by the Central Government.

63. Power of Central Government to make rules.—(1) The Central Government may, simultaneously with the constitution of the Central Board, make rules in respect of the matters specified in sub-section (2):

Provided that when the Central Board has been constituted, no such rule shall be made, varied, amended or repealed without consulting the Board.

(2) In particular, and without prejudice to the generality of the foregoing power, such rules may provide for all or any of the following matters, namely:—

(a) the terms and conditions of service of the members (other than the chairman and member-secretary) of the Central Board under sub-section (8) of section 5;

(b) the intervals and the time and place at which meetings of the Central Board or of any committee thereof constituted under this Act, shall be held and the procedure to be followed at such meetings, including the quorum necessary for the transaction of the business under section 8, and under sub-section (2) of section 9;

(c) the fees and allowances to be paid to such members of a committee of the Central Board as are not members of the Board under sub-section (3) of section 9;

(d) the manner in which and the purposes for which persons may be associated with a Board under subsection (1) of section 10;

(e) the terms and conditions of service of the chairman and the member-secretary of the Central Board under subsection (9) of section 5 and under sub-section (1) of section 12;

(f) conditions subject to which a person may be appointed as a consulting engineer to the Central Board under sub-section (4) of section 4.

(g) the powers and duties to be exercised and performed by the chairman and the member-secretary of the Central Board.

(h) the prohibition or regulation of bathing in any stream or well or the washing or cleaning therein of things of any class or description, or the putting of litter or other objectionable matter, whether poisonous, noxious or polluting or not into any stream or well;

(i) the prohibition or regulation of the keeping or use, on any stream, of vessels provided with sanitary appliances form which polluting matter passes into the stream;

(j) the form of the report of the Central Board analyst under sub-section (1) of section 22;

(k) the form of the report of the Government analyst under sub-section (3) of section 22;

(l) the form in which, and the time within which, the budget and annul report of the Central Board may be prepared and forwarded to the Central Government under sections 38 and 39;

(m) the form in which the accounts of the Central Board may be maintained under section 40;

(n) any other matter relating to the Central Board, including the powers and functions of that Board in relation to Union territories;

(o) any other matter which has to be, or may be, prescribed.

(3) Every rule made by the Central Government under this Act shall be laid, as soon as may be after it is made, before each House of Parliament while it is in session for a total period of

thirty days which may be comprised in one session or in two or more successive sessions, and if, before the expiry of the session in which it is so laid or the successive sessions aforesaid, both Houses agree in making any modification in the rule or both Houses agree that the rule should not be made, the rule shall thereafter have effect only in such modified form or be of no effect, as the case may be; so. However. That any such modification or annulment shall be without prejudice to the validity of anything previously done under that rule.

64. Power of State Government to make rules.—(1) The State Government may, simultaneously with the constitution of the State Board, make rules to carry out the purposes of this Act in respect of matters not falling within the purview of section 63:

> Provided that when, the State Board has been constituted, no such rule shall be made, varied, amended or repealed without consulting that Board.

(2) In particular, and without prejudice to the generality of the foregoing power, such rules may provide for all of the following matters, namely:—

- (a) the terms and conditions of service of the members (other than the chairman and the member-secretary) of the State Board under sub-section (8) of section 5.
- (b) the time and place of meetings of the State Board or of any committee of that Board constituted under this Act and the procedure to be followed at such meeting, including the quorum necessary for the transaction of business under section 8 and under sub-section (2) of section 9;
- (c) the fees and allowances to be paid to such members of a committee of the State Board as are not members of the Board under sub-section (3) of section 9;
- (d) the manner in which and the purposes for which persons may be associated with the State Board under sub-section (1) of section 10;
- (e) the terms and conditions of service of the chairman and the member-secretary of the State Board under sub-section (9) of section 5 and sub-section (1) of section 12;

(f) the conditions subject to which a person may be appointed as a consulting engineer to the State Board under sub-section (4) of section 12;

(g) the powers and duties to be exercised and discharged by the chairman and the member-secretary of the State Board;

(h) the form of the notice referred to in section 21;

(i) the form of the report of the State Board analyst under sub-section (1) of section 22;

(j) the form of the report of the Government analyst under sub-section (3) of section 22;

(k) the form of application for the consent of the State Board under sub-section (2) of section 25, and the particulars it may contain;

(l) the manner in which inquiry under sub-section (3) of section 25 may be made in respect of an application for obtaining consent of the State Board and the matters to be taken into account in granting or refusing such consent;

(m) the form and manner in which appeals may be filed, the fees payable in respect of such appeals and the procedure to be followed by the appellate authority in disposing of the appeals under sub-section (3) of section 23;

(n) the form in which, and the time within which, the budget and annual report of the State Board may be prepared and forwarded to the State Government under sections 38 and 39;

(o) the form in which the accounts off the State Board may be maintained under sub-section (1) of section 40;

(p) any other matter which has to be, or may be, prescribed.

Table of Cases

Bibliography

A. Books

A.B. Saxena, *Environmental Education.*

A.N. Mathur, N.S. Rathore and V.K. Vijay, *Environmental Education* (Hindi).

Ashutosh Gautam, *Aquatic Environment.*

C.P. Singh, *Environmental Law* (Hindi).

Chetan Singh Mehta, *Environmental Protection and the Law.*

D.D. Ojha, *Noise Pollution* (Hindi).

Debi Prasad Tripathi, *Noise Pollution.*

Dilip Kumar Markandey and Nilima Rajved, *Introductory Environment Pollution and Control.*

Dilip R. Ahuja, *Global Environment Review.*

G.K. Negi, M.K. Dhillon, G.S. Dhaliwal, *Noise Pollution.*

G.S. Karkara, *Environmental Law.*

H.G. Gibbs and T.H. Richards, *Stress, Vibrations and Noise Analysis in Vehicles.*

Human Rights—A Source book of NCERT.

I. Mohan, *Environmental Issues and Programmes.*

——, *Environmental Pollution and Management.*

——, *New World Environment Series—Environmental Issues and Programmes.*

J.J. Ram Upadhyay, *Environmental Law* (Hindi).

Jaiprakash, S.K. Shrivastava, *Environmental Problems, Policies and Strategies.*

Jales K., *Perception of Aircraft Noise in India.*

K. Wark and C. Warner, *Air Pollution and Origin/Control.*

Kanhaya Lal Sharma, *Reconstitution of the Constitution of India.*

L.N. Vyas, *Environmental Issues and Researches in India.*

M. Kovas, *Pollution and Conservation.*

Mahesh Mathur, *Legal Control of Environmental Pollution.*

N.N. Mathur, M.S. Rathore, and B.K. Vijay, *Environmental Awareness.*

N.N. Mathur, N.S. Rathore and V.K. Vijay, *Environmental Pollution* (Hindi).

N.S. Kamboj, *Control of Noise Pollution.*

Naorem Sanajaoba, *Law and Society: Strategy for Policy Choice.*

O. Dreyer, B. Los, V. Los, *Ecology and Development.*

O.N. Pandy, *Indian Medical Gazette.*

P. Sasi Bhushana Rao, P. Mohana Rao, *Environment Management and Audit.*

P.S. Jaswal, Nistha Jaswal, *Environmental Law.*

P.S. Narayana, *Public Interest Litigations.*

Paras Diwan, *Environment Protection.*

Pramod Singh, Smt. Chugh, *Environment Pollution and Management.*

R. Kumar, S.B. Nangia, *Environmental Pollution and Health.*

R.I. Wood, *Noise Control in Mechanical Services.*

R.K. Jain, L.V. Arban and G.S. Stacy, *Environmental Impacts Analysis*, Ed. II, New York.

R.K. Sapru, *Environment Mangement in India*, Vols. I & II.

R.L. Rathi, *Modern Environmental Laws.*

R.M. Lodha, *Environmental Essays.*

R.P. Anand, Rahamatullah Khan and S. Bhatt, *Law, Science and Environment.*

Ramlal Gupta, *A Guide to Police Laws in India.*

Ramprakash, *Man, Science and Environment.*

Ratan Lal and Dheeraj Lal, *The Indian Penal Code.*

———, *Criminal Procedure Code.*

———, *The Law of Torts.*

Robert B. Platt and Johan, F. Griffiphs, *Environmental Measurement and Interpretation.*

S. Lal, *Environment Pollution and Control.*

S.K. Aggarwal, *Environmental Awareness.*

S.S. Dara, *A Text of Environmental Chemistry and Pollution Control.*

Sampat Jain, *Public Interest Litigation.*

The Industrial Environment—its Evaluation and Control, U.S. Deptt. of Health and Welfare, Public Health Service Centre for Diseases, p. 312

The Pollution Crisis, Official Documents, Edward H. Robin, Law University, California.

Timmy Katiyar, M. Starke, *Environmental Pollution*.

V.D. Mahajan, *Jurisprudence and Legal Theory*.

V.N. Shukla, *Constitution of India*.

V.S. Katiyar, *Depleting Resources and Sustainable Development*.

B. Magazines

Akhand Jyoti.

Andrewd Portecus, Applied Science Publisher, London.

Annual Surve of Indian Law, by Chief Justice A.S. Anand, President ILI.

Environmental and People, Society for Environment and Education, (Monthly), Balanagar, Hyderabad.

Environmental Health Perspectives, Journal of the National Institute of the Environment Health Sciences.

Health Hazards of the Human Environment, World Health Organisation, Geneva.

India Today, New Delhi.

Indian Journal of Environment and Ecoplanning, Special Millennium Issues.

J.K. Jain, JAMA, *Journal of the American Medical Association*, Indraprastha Marg, New Delhi.

JIMA, *Journal of the Indian Medical Association*, Indraprastha Marg, New Delhi.

Journal of Medical Sciences (The Journal of Clinical Research and Practice, Kashmir Institute of Medical Sciences, Shrinagar.

Journal of the Indian Law Institutes.

M. Mukunda, *General of Bio Science*, Published by The Indian Academy of Sciences, Bangalore.

M.S. Oommen, *Climate Change and the Quest for Sustainable Development* (Annual), Delhi.

Medicao Legal Journal, Published quarterly for the Medico Legal Society, Mrs Diana Brahams.

Neurosciences Today, The Special Journal of Neurology and Neurosurgery, Sanjay Malik, New Delhi.

Paryavaran Sandesh, Hindi and English, *Quarterly News Letter of WWF* (I), Joldhpur Division.

Pollution Control Acts, Rules and Notifications, issued by Central Pollution Control Board, New Delhi.

Rishi Prasad.

Science Reporter.

TEERI, Information Monitor on Environmental Science, Karnal Road, Delhi.

The Competition Success Review.

V.S. Vyas and V. Ranareddy, *Essessing Environmental Politics and Policy Implementation in India,* Weakly Journal.

Vigyan.

World Medical Journal, Official Journal of the World Medical Association Inc. Printed Deutscher Arzte-Verlag Kolin, Germany.

C. Reports

All High Court Reports.

All India Report.

Ambient Noise Level, A Report prepared by SPCBs: (a) Rajasthan; (b) Meghalaya; (c) Assam; (d) Parivesh Batori, Newletter, SPCB, Assam, January to June, 2001; (e) Delhi.

Citizens Report.

Cochin University Law Review.

Environment and People.

Law Review.

Lioyd's Law Reports Medical, ANGUS MOON, London.

Rajasthan Law Reporteer.

Supreme Court Cases.

Western Law Reports.

D. Dictionary

Americana Dictionary.

Bhargava's Dictionary.

Encyclopedia Americana.

Encyclopedia Britannica.

Encyclopedia of Environmental Science, 1975.

Himayala's Encylopaedic Dictionary of Environmental Pollution.

International Encyclopedia of Ecology and Environment

Vandna Pandey, *Ecyclopaeic Dictionary of Environmental Pollution.*

Webster Dictionary.

E. Media
Aaj Tak.
All India Radio.
Discovery Channel.
Doordarshan, National and Metro.
National Geographic Channel.
Star News.
Zee News.

F. News Papers
Dainik Bhaskar.
Employment News.
Hindustan Times.
Indian Express.
Punjab Kesari.
Rajasthan Patrika.
Rashtriya Sahara.
The Navbharat Times.
The Tribune.
Times of India.

G. Inter Net Web Sites
http://enfor.nic.in/divisions/c polls/c poll.html
http://envfor.nic.in/
http://www.erpenvironment.org/
http://www.globalpolicy.org/visitctr/membersh.htm
http://www.hinduonnet.com/thehindu/2002/03/hdline.htm
http://www.islamicvoice.com/may97/#Top
http://www.islamicvoice.com/may97/#Top
http://www.nrdc.org/wildlife/marine/nlfa.asp
http://www.oneworld.org/slefj/index.htm
http://www.un.org/esa/earthsummit
http://www.un.org/esa/sustdev
http://www.usaep.org/
http://www.worldbank.org/search.htm
www.ashokvc@giasbm01.vsnl.net.in
www.cbs.dk/departments/ikl/cbem
www.cse@cseindia.org
www.dep@worldbank.org
www.dhanush@giasmd01.vsnl.net.in

www.masroor@greenpress.sdnpk.undp.org

www.murcott@mit.edu,AAAS Annual Conference, IIASA "Sustainability Indicators Symposium," Seattle, WA 2/16/ 97

www.sdasgupta@worldbank.org

www.ssl4@cornell.edu

H. Misc

Inaugral Adress by J.N Kaushal, Former Minister of Law at National Seminar on Law "Towards Environmental Protection" held at Chandigarh in 1984.

Stockholm Declaration, 1972.

The State of World Population, 1995, United National Population Fund (UNFPA).

Index